A DISCOURSE ON STATESMANSHIP

A DISCOURSE ON
Statesmanship

?? THE DESIGN AND TRANSFORMATION OF THE AMERICAN POLITY

PAUL EIDELBERG

UNIVERSITY OF ILLINOIS PRESS
URBANA, CHICAGO, LONDON

For Phyllis

LIBRARY OF CONGRESS CATALOGING IN PUBLICATION DATA

Eidelberg, Paul.
  A discourse on statesmanship.

  Bibliography: p.
  1. United States—Constitutional history.
2. Political science—History—United States.
I. Title.
JK31.E39   320.9'73   74–8913
ISBN 0–252–00428–0

ACKNOWLEDGMENTS

WHILE this Discourse was nearing completion, the world lost a great man, Leo Strauss. Many will remember him always as their teacher, will rightly proclaim his profound learning and wisdom. Yet Leo Strauss was also a "warrior spirit." Like Socrates he possessed the courage to stand alone, to challenge the conceits of an epoch. More than this, he restored to life the ruling questions of the noblest minds, ancient as well as modern, and, in the process, recreated the discipline of political philosophy. The future growth of this discipline may very well depend on whether students of Leo Strauss preserve and further explore a distinction which he himself personified, I mean the distinction between the scholar and the philosopher. All the more reason, therefore, to recall Nietzsche's "Three Metamorphoses": "How the spirit becomes a camel; and the camel a lion; and the lion, finally, a child."

Here I especially want to acknowledge the inspiration of my friend Joseph Levinson, now teaching at Bar Ilan University in Israel. He is in truth that "genius of the heart from whose touch everyone walks away richer . . . richer in himself, newer to himself than before, broken open, blown at and sounded by a thawing wind, perhaps more unsure, tenderer, more fragile, more broken, but full of hopes that as yet have no names."

Meanwhile, I wish to thank my colleague Mr. Donald Maletz for our many discussions as well as for his perceptive comments on Book I of the manuscript. I also wish to thank Mr. Frank Williams, Assistant Director of the University of Illinois Press, for his enthusiastic support of my Discourse.

Finally, a word of gratitude to my wife Phyllis for her tireless devotion, and to my daughter Sharen for being one of us.

CONTENTS

vii

BOOK ONE

THE AMERICAN 'POLITY'

Toward a Renaissance of Statesmanship:
The Politics of Magnanimity

"He found any kind of one-sidedness incomprehensible."

in re Goethe

T HIS DISCOURSE has three major aims. Its first and paramount aim is to generate a new school of statesmanship. Its second aim is to prepare the grounds for a synthesis of classical and modern political science. Its third aim is to advance a new interpretation of American political history. These aims will be pursued by means of a philosophical reconstruction of two models of statesmanship. The first model will be constructed primarily from the writings of Alexander Hamilton and James Madison and will be called the "politics of magnanimity." The second model will be constructed from the writings of Woodrow Wilson and will be called the "politics of compassion." By statesmanship I mean the coordination of political theory and political practice. In the statesmanship of Hamilton and Madison, however, the coordination of theory and practice is rendered exceedingly complex and subtle by the fact that their reflections on man, society, and government exhibit many of the tensions which divide classical from modern political philosophy. Nevertheless, the Discourse will attempt to show that these tensions—for ex-

3

ample, between virtue and freedom, or between reason and passion—were tentatively resolved via the political articulation of what the founders chose to call, in seemingly paralogistic language, "a more perfect Union." Accordingly, a philosophical reconstruction of Hamilton's and Madison's statesmanship will require, first, a true understanding of the political character of that union or of the regime whose political form is prescribed in the original Constitution. Second, it will require knowledge of whether the regime in question was the best that could have been established in the United States given the human and material resources available to the founders. Such knowledge presupposes a coherent, logical, and necessary system of political criteria in terms of which every known form of government can be analyzed and ranked according to its respective merit.[1] A system of this order will be developed and will be used to analyze and evaluate the American regime at the time of its formation and during its twentieth-century transformation. As the subtitle of this Discourse suggests, the regime prescribed in the original Constitution has undergone a profound revolution, one whose most fundamental principles were first articulated, politically and systematically, in the statesmanship of Woodrow Wilson; a revolution, moreover, which is being carried to its logical conclusion in our own time.

Precisely the lack of a truly comprehensive system of regime criteria accounts for the great variety of partial and conflicting interpretations of the American Constitution enunciated by political scientists, historians, and statesmen since the very founding of the Republic. I have especially in view those interpretations which may be classified as "democratic" or as "oligarchic." None of these interpretations—the most prominent of which will be discussed in a moment—is entirely false. Each

[1] For an elaboration of the meaning of "coherent, logical, and necessary," see Alfred North Whitehead, *Process and Reality* (New York: Harper Torchbooks, 1960), pp. 4–6 (hereafter abbreviated as PR, followed by page number). See also Friedrich Nietzsche, *Beyond Good and Evil* (New York: Vintage Books, 1966), Walter Kaufmann, trans., Aph. 211 (hereafter abbreviated as BGE).

merely results from incomplete criteria of regime analysis, criteria which, however useful, cannot adequately account for all the factors determinitive of the political character of the regime established by the founders. Of course, in referring to a "coherent, logical, and necessary system of political criteria," I have in mind nothing less than a fully articulated political philosophy. Judged by this standard, it is hardly an exaggeration to say that no scholar has adequately applied to the study of the American regime the criteria of regime analysis developed by any philosopher, ancient or modern.

In undertaking such a task, I shall employ the system of regime criteria developed in Aristotle's *Politics*, a system whose comprehensiveness has yet to be surpassed. This is not to say that Aristotle is the last word in political science, or that the American regime—which is not an ancient *polis*, but a modern, extended republic—can be fully understood according to Aristotelian criteria. Indeed, however modestly, I shall attempt to correct certain Aristotelian principles in the light of my own philosophical reflections, in the development of which I am as much indebted to Whitehead as to Aristotle. Nevertheless, I wish to make it perfectly clear that, even by itself, the *Politics*, when properly understood and properly applied to the American Constitution, can profoundly enrich our understanding of that Constitution, hence the statesmanship of the founders. To this extent, Aristotle can facilitate the task of rediscovering and reconstructing the art of statesmanship itself.

A serious and sustained attempt to rediscover and reconstruct the art of statesmanship is especially necessary. Today, virtually every college and university in the United States has a department of political science, or its equivalent. This is very much a twentieth-century development. But while the twentieth century has witnessed a remarkable growth in the number of departments of political science, it has also witnessed a no less remarkable decline in the caliber of statesmanship. Yet never has this country had so profound and urgent a need for the highest level of statesmanship, a statesmanship capable of inspiring the American people with a sense of national pride and purpose: of pride rooted in strength, tempered by modesty, and so just and generous as to be indistinguishable from magnanimity; of purpose so lofty as to present mankind with the example of a people whose deliberative and educative institutions bring into harmony the range of human values such that freedom dwells with virtue, equality with excellence, wealth with beauty. As already intimated, however, a rebirth of national pride and purpose will require not only a renaissance in the art of statesmanship, but also a veritable revolution in the character and teaching of political science.

It cannot be emphasized too strongly that the quality of American statesmanship is very much dependent on the quality of higher education—the education which statesmen receive in their youth when students at American colleges and universities. If it be true, as few would deny, that contemporary statesmanship is at best mediocre, it may also be true, as few would admit, that this mediocrity is partly attributable to the teachings of the social sciences in general, and of political science in particular. If politics is portrayed as something low or devoid of nobility of purpose, do not expect men of the highest caliber to pursue such a vocation. As will be seen in a moment, however, this is precisely the manner in which politics has been portrayed by American higher education for the better part of the twentieth century. Nor is this all. It is bad enough to degrade ordinary politics; it is infinitely worse to degrade the political thought of those statesmen who gave to this nation its fundamental law, the Constitution. Yet this very degradation has been the prevailing tendency among political scientists and historians during the present century. If a nation is in danger of moral disintegration, if it has lost confidence in its past and is confused about its future, examine well its institutions of learning. Therein may be the principal cause of its malaise—perhaps, too, the hope for its salvation. But the salvation of the American republic, insofar as it depends on politics, depends on redeeming its founders from the degradations of too many of its well-intended educators. In seeking to redeem the founders, however, I seek nothing less than to redeem the art of statesmanship.

The present Discourse will rescue the statesman from two kinds of degradation. These two kinds of degradation will be illustrated here by briefly reviewing twentieth-century studies of the founding fathers and of their work, the Constitution. On the one hand, statesmen of the caliber of Madison may be degraded by reducing the politics of *founding* to the politics of *ordinary* legislation, or by explaining the political thought of the former in terms of the material interests of the latter. This is the tendency of what may be called the quasi-Marxist school of political science, a tendency that has dominated American education for the better part of this century. On the other hand, statesmen like Madison may be degraded by a more or less implicit, but in any event, invidious, comparison of his writings with those of political philosophers of the caliber of Aristotle. Such is the unfortunate tendency of the Straussian school of political science. This two-fold degradation of the founders—one from the "left," the other from the "right"—will now be elaborated as a preface to the formulation of a comprehensive methodology for the study of statesmanship.

As just intimated, the degradation of American statesmanship may be traced to the teaching of Karl Marx. It was a young Marx who wrote in *The German Ideology:*

> [W]e do not set out from what men say, imagine, conceive, nor from men as narrated, thought of, imagined, conceived, in order to arrive at men in the flesh. We set out from real, active men, and on the basis of their real life-process we demonstrate the development of the *ideological reflexes* and echoes of this life-process. The *phantoms* formed in the human brain are also, necessarily, *sublimates* of their material life-process, which is empirically verifiable and bound to material premises. Morality, religion, metaphysics, all the rest of ideology and their corresponding forms of consciousness, thus no longer retain the semblance of independence.[2]

[2] Karl Marx and Frederick Engels, *The German Ideology* (New York: In-

7

This nonreflexive mode of thought reminded Nietzsche of the notice on the sideshow, in Swift: "The largest elephant in the world except himself to be seen here."[3] Whatever the case, the above passage reveals two sides of Marx, one fostering the school of historicism, the other the school of positivism. Though influenced by the former, most political and other social scientists

---

ternational Publishers, 1968), pp. 14, 28–29 (italics added). See also Karl Marx, *Early Writings* (New York: McGraw-Hill Book Co., 1964), pp. 56–57, and the following footnote.

[3] Friedrich Nietzsche, *The Use and Abuse of History* (Indianapolis: Bobbs-Merrill Co., 1957), p. 38. The dilemma may be stated as follows. A theory which claims that "the 'inward nature' of men, as well as their 'consciousness' of it, 'i.e.,' their 'reason,' has at all times been an historical product . . . based 'upon external compulsion'" (*The German Ideology*, p. 113) must exempt itself from its own conclusion, as Marx attempts to do when he says: (1) "communist consciousness . . . may . . . arise among the other classes too through the contemplation of the situation of this class" (p. 69), and (2) "consciousness can sometimes appear further advanced than the contemporary empirical relationships" (p. 72). But this will not do. The possible validity of the statement, "consciousness has at *all times* been an historical product based on external compulsion," depends on the *superhistorical* character of Marx's own consciousness implied in that statement. That statement, to be valid, must not be simply or wholly an "ideological reflex" or sublimate produced by "external compulsion." In other words, to avoid its self-negation, a theory which posits the historicity of all thought productions must also posit at least the partial self-negation of history or the termination of the historical process as determined by material causes. Once it does this, however, such a theory can no longer be regarded as based solely on empirical science. But see Shlomo Avineri, *The Social and Political Thought of Karl Marx* (Cambridge: Cambridge University Press, 1970), chs. 3–4, *passim*. This excellent work, which redeems much of Marx, nevertheless fails to take due account of the powerful tendency of Marx's writings to degrade reason, however much that degradation may have been influenced by polemical intentions (or advanced by the more mechanistic and deterministic language of Engel's writings). Furthermore, if, as Avineri interprets Marx, "every historical occurrence is the sum of its own history" (p. 93), then the degradation of reason manifest in the sociological reductionism of the social sciences must be attributed, in part, to the admittedly more complex epistemology of Marx himself—as Avineri might agree (pp. 52, 181, 187, 258). But the simplification of Marx by the social sciences (referred to above as quasi-Marxism) indicates that every historical occurrence is *not* the *sum* of its own history, being evidence of the selective emphasis and partial independence of reason. See Roger Garaudy, *Marxism in the Twentieth Century* (New York: Charles Scribner's Sons, 1970), René Hague, trans., p. 56, for a similar error, and compare chs. 2–3 with pp. 266–269 below.

lean toward the latter. The reverse might be said of historians. Together, the effect of these two schools on American political thought and practice has been devastating. This will be amply shown in Book II. The Marxian degradation of statesmanship may be illustrated as follows.

Consider, for example, Charles Beard's economic interpretation of the Constitution published in 1913. This interpretation may be regarded as an answer to the question, what motivated the statesmen who designed the Constitution? According to Beard, they were motivated by the economic interests of the propertied class. Needless to say, this is *not* what those statesmen would have had others think of their motives. Thus, in *Federalist* 1, Hamilton writes: "Yes, my countrymen, I own to you that, after having given it [the new Constitution] an attentive consideration, I am clearly of [the] opinion it is *your* interest to adopt it. I am convinced that this is the safest course for *your* liberty, *your* dignity, and *your* happiness."[4] With the help of *The German Ideology*, Beard could reply by saying that "each new class which puts itself in the place of one ruling before it, is compelled, merely in order to carry through its aim, to represent its interest as the common interest of all the members of society."[5] Still, supposing Hamilton was the spokesman for a particular class, why should he feel *compelled* to represent its interest as the common interest of all the members of society? Obviously, to win the support of people from classes other than his own. But he could hardly win their support unless they *believed* that there was such a thing as the "common interest," a belief which presupposes that men ought to act out of motives larger than their own self-interest. Certainly it would be futile and absurd for a statesman to argue that the Constitution would serve the "common good" if the members of his society regarded such

[4] Hamilton, Jay, and Madison, *The Federalist* (New York: Modern Library, 1938), Edward Mead Earle, ed., p. 6 (italics added). Unless otherwise indicated, all page references to *The Federalist* will be to this edition and will appear in the body of the text.

[5] Marx and Engels, *The German Ideology*, pp. 40–41.

notions as the "common good" as a phantom of the brain or a fiction. Suppose, on the other hand, that as a result of an education permeated by Marxian or quasi-Marxian modes of thought, Americans no longer believed in the reality of the "common good." How might this affect the level and character of statesmanship?

To answer this question it would first be necessary to understand how the notion of the "common good" functions in political discourse, and in a community whose members do not regard such notions as fictions. It would be necessary to know (1) the performative use of the notion; (2) its effect upon the statesman; (3) its effect upon his audience or community; and (4) the process through which the meaning of the notion is articulated. A brief analysis must suffice for now.

Clearly, the statesman uses the notion of the "common good" to commend a common course of action or public policy whose *importance*, and not merely its utility, might not otherwise be generally *recognized*, let alone supported, by men of diverse wants and opinions. By commending some policy in the name of the *common* good, the statesman is compelled to show the relevance of that policy for different men or to give reasons showing how it will contribute to their common good despite their differences. He knows that men will not readily agree to any newly proposed course of action unless they see, or are given reasons to believe, that it will serve their particular interests, and (in our hypothetical community) that it conforms to long-established notions of justice or fairness. But to show the relevance or importance of any newly proposed policy, the statesman must relate its novelty to that which is familiar, again, the existing wants and opinions of his audience. By so doing, he evokes the interest of his audience. Or, to put the matter another way: In the process of giving reasons for pursuing some course of action, the statesman brings certain interests into the foreground while retreating others into the background. However imperceptibly, he creates and destroys interests by altering their relative value or the intensity with which they are pursued. The language of his discourse accomplishes this by arousing and modulating desire or aversion for one object or another. The statesman—and I have been speaking of the *genuine* statesman—thus modifies the moral and intellectual horizon of his audience. But this he could not do without first winning their trust, which he could hardly elicit unless they believed he was capable of acting out of a motive larger than his own self-interest—that motive being the common good. Indeed, lacking that belief they could not readily be disposed to consider any novel proposal seriously.

Finally, it should be noted that the statesman's defense of any policy commended in terms of the common good is also an articulation of the meaning of the common good. (The articulation of the means to any end is an articulation of the meaning of that end.) The meaning of the common good thus articulated by the statesman modulates and assimilates diverse thoughts and feelings regarding the particular good embodied in his proposed policy. That good *becomes*—it can never simply reaffirm—a common good (differentially enjoyed by the various members of the community). Its articulation by the statesman becomes the community's standard of judgment. By that standard, embodied in laws or in institutions, the diverse wants and opinions of men may be criticized on the one hand, and moderated on the other. In other words, the common good may be regarded as the statesman's project in virtue of which he constructs or transforms or intensifies a community. Viewed in this light, the common good is the rationale as well as the passion of statesmanship.

Consider, by contrast, a "community" whose members regard the common good as a fiction—again, as a result of having been educated according to quasi-Marxian modes of thought. Since the members of such a society would believe that no individual ever acted out of a motive larger than self-interest, mutual distrust (to say nothing of fear) would prevail, rendering it more difficult for the statesman to synthesize diverse wants and opinions, and impossible to do so by moral suasion. Indeed, he himself could hardly be more than the precarious agent of some tenuous alliance of individuals seeking to secure and advance their interests over others. So long as no group had a monopoly of power (for then tyranny would be the logical result), statesmanship would degenerate into a form of brokerage. "Public" policy would be nothing more than the result of bargaining between ever-shifting coalitions of individuals whose claims would be self-justifying, since there would exist no public standard by which to determine their relative justice. Deceit, together with the power of numbers and wealth, would decide every conflict of interest. Under such circumstances, statesmanship would be reduced to cunning manipulation or to abject servility.

In our hypothetical community, where people believed that the common good was a knowable entity, a more noble politics was possible. The statesman's project, which he pursued in the name of the common good, was constitutive of the character of his people, as was their character constitutive of his project. To his magnanimity, in other words, was joined their deference—two qualities which are inconceivable without belief in the rational accessibility of the common good.

Our hypothetical community is rendered meaningless, however by the economic reduction of politics. The language of the statesman becomes revelatory not of political intentions, but of private motives. In vain does Hamilton say in *Federalist* 1: "I frankly acknowledge to you my convictions [regarding the merits of the new Constitution], and I will freely lay before you the reasons on which they are founded. The consciousness of good intentions disdains ambiguity. I shall not, however, multiply professions on this head. *My motives must remain in the depository of my own breast.*" [6] If Hamilton's motives were brought to the foreground by the economic interpretation of the Constitution, his professed reasons for supporting the Constitution were retreated into the background. Henceforth the meaning of the

[6] *Federalist* 1, p. 6 (italics added). It is no reflection on Hamilton's (or Madison's and Jay's) integrity to say that the language of *The Federalist* is, from time to time, deliberately ambiguous. We ought not expect from the public discourses of statesmen the candor possible in the political treatises of philosophers. As to the latter, however, see Leo Strauss, *Persecution and the Art of Writing* (Glencoe, Ill.: Free Press, 1952). On the topic of candor, more later.

Constitution was to be found not in the intentionality of its language or in the cognitions of its authors. These were but sublimates or "rationalizations" of material premises of which economics was primordial. Not the common good, but the economic interests of the propertied class—this was the material cause of the Constitution. Psychologically translated, the animating principle of the Constitution was "self-interest."

Basically the same conclusion can be found in Richard Hofstadter's historicist interpretation of the Constitution. This interpretation conveys the teaching that the political ideas of the founders merely reflect what the Consitution was intended to foster, namely, the capitalistic spirit of the age. "They thought man was a creature of rapacious self-interest, and yet they wanted him to be free—free, in essence, to contend, to engage in an umpired strife, to use property to get property."[7] Competition and cupidity were to be umpired by the "balanced government" or Newtonian equipoise prescribed in the Constitution. Hofstadter suggests, however, that that Newtonian Constitution has no relevance for our own times, that it was based on the founders' individualistic and static conception of human nature discredited by post-Darwinian science. Indeed, says he, "Any attempt . . . to tear their ideas out of the eighteenth-century context is sure to make them seem starkly reactionary."[8] Influenced by such a teaching, few students would retain any incentive to study the founders seriously. They might even conclude that the statesmanship of the founders was obsolete.

This, in effect, is the teaching fostered by John Roche's democratic interpretation of the Constitution, an interpretation based on the "group" or "group-interest" theory of politics. "The Constitution," according to Roche, "was not . . . a triumph of architectonic genius; it was a patch-work sewn together under the pressure of both time and events"; it was guided by "no over-

[7] Richard Hofstadter, *The American Political Tradition* (New York: Vintage Books, 1956), p. 16 (first published in 1948) (cited hereafter as *Hofstadter*).

[8] *Ibid.*, p. 15, and see pp. 16–17. A critique of Hofstadter will be found in my *Philosophy of the American Constitution* (New York: Free Press, 1968), pp. 5–12.

13

arching principles"; indeed, it "was neither a victory for abstract theory nor a great practical success."[9] In other words, the founders were preoccupied merely with particular interests of immediate and limited importance, not with general and long-range considerations informed by political principles of abiding value. In these particular and immediate interests, couched in terms of such fictions as the "common good" or the "public interest," Roche sees the real foundation of the Constitution.[10] In thus describing the work or statesmanship of the founders, Roche claims that he has more or less escaped from "the solipsistic web of his own environment" and has come "to appreciate the past roughly on its own terms."[11] In truth, however, he has merely superimposed upon the founding a liberalized version of Marxism. Here Roche differs hardly at all from Beard, despite the latter's oligarchic interpretation of the Constitution. In vain does Hamilton say in *Federalist* 1 to readers of Roche's positivistic persuasion:

> [The Constitution] affects too many particular interests . . . not to involve in its discussion a variety of objects foreign to its merits, and of views, passions and prejudices little favorable to the discovery of truth. . . . So numerous indeed and so powerful are the causes which serve to give a false bias to the judgment, that we, upon many occasions, see wise and good men on the wrong as well as on the right side of questions of the first magnitude to society (3–4).

And in *Federalist* 31:

> In disquisitions of every kind, there are certain primary truths, or first principles, upon which all subsequent reasonings must depend. . . . Though it cannot be pretended that the principles of moral and political knowledge have, in general, the

[9] John P. Roche, "The Founding Fathers: A Reform Caucus in Action," *American Political Science Review*, LV (Dec. 1961), 815–816.

[10] *Ibid.*, pp. 800–801, 807. The inverted commas are Roche's, testifying to his positivist orientation.

[11] *Ibid.*, p. 815. Other evidence of Roche's flirtation with historicism may be seen in his essay "Judicial Self-Restraint," *American Political Science Review*, LXIX (Sept. 1955), 762.

same degree of certainty with those of the mathematics, yet they have much better claims in this respect than, to judge from the conduct of men in particular situations, we should be disposed to allow them. The obscurity is much oftener in the passions and prejudices of the reasoner than in the subject (188–189).

Finally, in *Federalist* 71:

It is a just observation, that the people commonly *intend* the PUBLIC GOOD. . . . But their good sense would despise the adulator who should pretend that they always *reason right* about the *means* of promoting it. . . . [When] the interests of the people are at variance with their inclinations, it is the duty of the persons whom they have appointed to be the guardians of those interests, to withstand the temporary delusion . . . [men] who ha[ve] courage and magnanimity enough to serve them at the peril of their displeasure (464–465).

To Roche, these are but the words of an "inspired propagandist" who possessed an "unmatched talent for dirty political infighting."[12] This, of course, is the language of a degraded politics applied to a politics of magnanimity.

Finally, there is Martin Diamond's quasi-Aristotelian interpretation of the Constitution. Based, as will be shown in Book I, on a fallacious application of Aristotle's criteria of regime analysis, this interpretation yields not only a democratic view of the Constitution, but also materialistic conclusions comparable to those of the commentators examined earlier. It should be understood, however, that Diamond does not affirm the primacy of material causality per se. Rather, that causality was deliberately built into the Constitution via its system of countervailing passions and interests. Or to put the matter another way: Inasmuch as Diamond contends that "*The Federalist* . . . seems to speak with contempt" for such traditional ends of government as "the nurturing of a particular religion, education, military courage, civic-spiritedness, moderation, individual excellence in the virtues, etc.," there remains nothing left for government to pursue

[12] Roche, "The Founding Fathers: A Reform Caucus in Action," pp. 804, 808.

than "narrow," "limited," and "immediate" interests which, for the most part, would be economic.[13] Thus, when *Federalist* 51 proclaims that "Justice is the end of government . . . [and] of civil society," Diamond translates "justice" to mean "primarily . . . the protection of economic interests" (62). Here, perhaps unwittingly, Diamond posits an economic interpretation of the Constitution on non-Marxian grounds. On the other hand, since his interpretation virtually denies the relevance of moral ends in the political thought of the founders, it also approaches the "group-interest" theory of the Constitution presented by Roche. To be sure, Diamond rejects the moral relativism implicit in Roche's teaching. Nevertheless, his interpretation of the intended character of the American regime is close to Roche's interpretation regarding the politics of its founders. To his credit, however, Diamond is not limited by the bias of "group-interest" theory which prevents Roche from distinguishing between ordinary politics and the politics of founding. The only distinction Roche can make is that some politicians are more clever or more successful than others. And though he admits that the founders were "superb democratic politicians," he concludes that the Constitution was not a great practical success! For Diamond, the founders succeeded all too well—too well in that they deliberately fostered a society in which men would be engaged in a "ceaseless striving after immediate interest" (67). Unlike Roche, whose relativism disables him from distinguishing a noble politics from a base politics, Diamond, by virtue of his misinterpretation and misapplication of the noble politics of Aristotle, more than insinuates that the founders lowered the goals of political life such that now the ceaseless pursuit of those goals seems to confirm the conclusions of "group-interest" theory, a theory which cannot but cast into contempt the noble ends of which Diamond speaks and affirms.

[13] Martin Diamond, "Democracy and *The Federalist*: A Reconsideration of the Framer's Intent," *American Political Science Review*, LIII (March 1959), 64 (cited hereafter as *Diamond* and, unless otherwise indicated, by page number appearing in the text).

And so, for the better part of this century, one generation of American students after another have been taught that the fundamental law of their country, the Constitution, is rooted in a principle universally regarded with contumely, namely, the principle of self-interest.[14] This is not only a degradation of the Constitution; it is also a degradation of statesmanship. More than scholarship will be required to overcome that degradation. We are beset by all-powerful modes of thought which only time and philosophy can transcend.

To that end this Discourse is dedicated. It continues my earlier study, *The Philosophy of the American Constitution*. But whereas that study centered on the debates of the Federal Convention, the present work centers on *The Federalist*, and from two temporal perspectives. Book I contrasts the politics of *The Federalist* with the *Politics* of Aristotle; Book II contrasts Hamilton's and Madison's statesmanship with the statesmanship of Woodrow Wilson, one of this country's greatest political scientists, and the very President who revolutionized the ruler-ruled relationship embodied in the Constitution. Book I will show, by means of a rigorous and detailed application of Aristotelian criteria, that the Republic established by the founders most closely resembles what Aristotle called a '*polity*,' a regime that synthesizes, at the very least, democratic and oligarchic attributes. It will also be shown that the American 'polity,' as articulated in the writings of the founders, represents a political synthesis of classical, Christian, and modern principles, for which reason it cannot be fully comprehended by Aristotelian criteria. For that very reason, the seventh chapter of Book I will explore a teleological mode of regime analysis oriented away from the notion of *completeness* toward the notion of *comprehensiveness*, signifying a shift from Aristotle's entelechies toward—but only *toward*—

---

[14] Diamond goes so far as to say that, in the political thought or intentions of the founders regarding America's future, "there is not even the suggestion that the pursuit of interest should be an especially enlightened pursuit" (*ibid.*, p. 66). Not only will Book I of this Discourse rescue the founders from such degradation, but, in Chapter VII, the principle of self-interest itself will be redeemed from contumely.

Whitehead's philosophy of creativity.[15] As for Book II, it will confirm the argument of Book I by examining the transformation of the Constitution and the degradation of statesmanship since the first decade of the twentieth century.

Looking over the entire work, its organization is structured by what may be called "quadri-modal regime analysis," which is an adaptation of Aristotle's methodology of the four causes discussed in his *Physics* and underlying his *Politics*.[16] This means that the regime established by the founders will be analyzed in terms of what shall be called its "material," "formal," "final," and "efficient" causes. The material mode of regime analysis emphasizes the economic system of a country, the diverse occupations, habits, and moral dispositions of its citizens, and the factual distribution of power among the various groups composing the community as a whole. In contrast, the formal mode of regime analysis emphasizes the legal structure or institutional arrangements affecting the decision-making processes of government. The final or teleological mode of regime analysis emphasizes the ends or values of a political community as reflected in the data of the two previous modes of analysis. Last, the efficient or dynamic mode of regime analysis emphasizes the various causes which lead to revolutionary change or the transformation of regimes. It should be borne in mind, however, that these four modes of analysis, though distinct in thought, are inseparable in reality.[17]

[15] In this Discourse, "comprehensiveness" is to be understood as involving a unifying synthesis of diverse data, a synthesis, therefore, which is not merely additive. See Whitehead, PR 4–6, and Nietzsche, BGE, Aphs. 205, 211, 257, 262.

[16] See Aristotle, *Physics*, Bk. II, chs. 1–3, and *Politics*, 1288b20–40, where different uses of the term "best" correspond to different modes of regime analysis. Thus: (1) the best regime in theory requires primary emphasis on the teleological mode of analysis; (2) the best regime in practice requires primary emphasis on the formal mode of analysis; (3) the best regime for a particular people requires primary emphasis on the material mode of analysis; and (4) the best method of preserving or changing any existing regime requires primary emphasis on the efficient mode of analysis.

[17] This fact will necessitate occasional repetition of some of the evidence drawn from *The Federalist*; but each instance of repetition will bear the significance of a different mode of regime analysis.

Finally, a word about the political epistemology underlying this inquiry. Apart from philosophical reflection, I look at the world of politics from the perspective of the statesman, especially of philosophic statesmen who not only practiced the art of politics, but whose writings reveal a rhetoric based on a comprehensive understanding of the principles and purposes of government on the one hand, and of the diverse passions of men on the other. Through dialectical analysis of the statesman's writings or recorded speeches, I reconstruct his unstated philosophical assumptions and political intentions. These assumptions and intentions comprise what may be termed his "meaning horizon." The data of his meaning horizon are graded, however, according to my own criteria of relevance in the process of being incorporated into a more comprehensive whole. The construction of this larger whole is necessitated by the very nature and limitations of statesmanship. It cannot be said too often, but the statesman must emphasize not the *desirable* so much as the *feasible*, for which reason the political standards evident in his discourse will be lower than those found in the works of some philosophers. On the other hand, what the statesman publicly defends as feasible is modulated by what he privately regards as desirable, which suggests that his own standards may be higher than those of some philosophers, but in any event higher than those he avows in public. (Hence it would be foolish, if not unjust, to treat the statesman's discourse as if it were a philosophical disquisition.) Furthermore, what the statesman defends as feasible—and many things are feasible—may not only be superior to prevailing practices, but also will tend to assimilate those practices to what he regards as desirable. To be more precise, what limits the moral level of the statesman's discourse (apart from his own character) is the limited power of rhetoric. It belongs to the nature of his art that the statesman must persuade different men to a common course of action. Accordingly, in choosing one course of action rather than another, and in defending his choice of alternatives in the public forum, the statesman must take account of the character of his audience, the potentialities of his people—their conflicting opinions, passions, and interests—all of which will impose limits on what he may say or may accomplish. Yet only by constructing the more comprehensive whole mentioned earlier can those limits be seen as limits.

Clearly, the construction of that more comprehensive whole is beyond the power of any of the prevailing methods of political analysis. Either they are inadequate in epistemology, or they are lacking in moral richness. What is needed is a new politics, a politics that transcends the quarrel between ancients and moderns, that neither degrades the one nor exalts the other. I have called this the politics of magnanimity. This politics employs an epistemology which does not regard the mind as a passive medium reflecting immutable verities or the transient data of the political world. Here, by the way, Straussians join hands with positivists: both look upon themselves as disinterested spectators of the political—one emphasizing universal values, the other particular facts. In contrast, the politics of magnanimity, without succumbing to moral relativism, affirms the creative agency of the mind in its selection and evaluation of political phenomena. This intellectual creativity requires the sternest discipline if it is to bring into coordination and mutual intensification the welter of values and relationships immanent in the present, that is, if it is to fulfill the requirements of comprehensiveness. And so, in constructing a more comprehensive whole which does justice to the statesman, I shall allow his discourse to elicit from me, while I seek to elicit from his discourse, a universe which contains us both. Here I proceed on the assumption that the meaning of *any* discourse (or finite set of facts) is not self-contained. Abstracted from an infinitude, it bears a perspective for every part of that infinitude.[18] Accordingly, the statesman's writings, like the philosopher's and the poet's, may be regarded as a lure for thought and feeling the revelation of which constitutes a species of autobiography. By this I con-

[18] This is not to deny the possibility of finite truths. See Whitehead, *Science and the Modern World* (New York: Free Press, 1967), p. 163 (cited hereafter as SMW followed immediately by page number).

fess only the obvious: What the political scientist knows and chooses to reveal about the political depends no less upon his own character than upon the character of the political. Postulating, however, in the place of what Nietzsche called "soul-atomism," the notion of the individual as a creative center of formative relationships, it may then be said that the "autobiography" of the political scientist is constitutive of the political just as the political is constitutive of his "autobiography." (This is to deny naive realism as well as naive subjectivism or psychologism.)

It follows from the preceding that the political scientist, no less than the statesman, is partly responsible for the character of political life—a point elaborated in Book II of the Discourse. It also follows that there is as much need of a renaissance in the teaching of political science as there is need of a renaissance in the art of statesmanship. Accordingly, I shall propose, after the conclusion of this inquiry, the establishment of a national university including an institute of statesmanship. My object is to foster a politics of magnanimity that will synthesize classical and modern modes of thought. Some of the fundamental principles of that synthesis underlie the following inquiry.

CHAPTER I

Aristotle's Criteria of Regime Analysis:

Preliminary Considerations

IN THIS and in the following two chapters, I shall attempt to peel away the many layers of confusion which have long obscured the true political character of the American Constitution. Only after removing these confusions can Aristotle's criteria of regime analysis be systematically applied and fully appreciated for their explanatory power. Nevertheless, a preliminary consideration of those criteria in this chapter will facilitate their application in those that follow.

Beginning on the surface, it should first be noted that Aristotle's criteria for analyzing and evaluating the political character of regimes have different degrees of generality. Consider, for example, his well-known division of regimes into three genera and six species. The genera are described as the rule of the One, the Few, and the Many. To each of these genera correspond, respectively, two species: kingship and tyranny, aristocracy and oligarchy, the 'polity' and democracy.[1] Clearly, this classification

---

[1] *The Politics of Aristotle* (London: Oxford University Press, 1952), pp. 114–115, Ernest Barker, trans., hereafter cited as *Politics*, with page references appearing in the text unless otherwise indicated. In using Barker's translation, I shall occasionally omit, modify, or substitute my own for his bracketed interpolations. Also, where Barker translates *politeia* as "constitution" (or "state"), I shall substitute "regime" (or "country"). The term "regime" will also be used synonymously with "political community," but will more closely signify a peo-

employs both quantitative and qualitative criteria involving the number and character of those who rule or exercise political power. These criteria may be used to determine not only the generic differences *between* the various regimes, but also the generic tensions *within* a regime whose legislative, executive, and judicial institutions have different gradations of regime bias. In each of these institutions, the following particular criteria are applicable: (1) the number *and* character of those eligible for office; (2) the number *and* character of those eligible to appoint them; (3) the method of appointment; (4) the duration or tenure of appointment; and (5) the particular powers or functions which each institution may exercise. These for the most part formal criteria reveal that a regime may have a greater (or lesser) number of the same generic attributes. One democracy, for example, may be more (or less) democratic than another regime of the same species. Or, these criteria show how a regime may combine, in an incredible variety of ways, the political attributes of regimes generically different from each other—combining, for example, certain attributes of democracy and oligarchy. A profusion of regimes is the result, regimes which shade into each other as in a spectrum, and not always is it easy, even for political scientists, to distinguish one from another.

Indeed, not only is it frequently difficult to distinguish one kind of regime from another, but students of politics differ profoundly in their understanding of what distinguishes a regime or *political* community from other forms of human association. Aristotle's *Politics* begins with this very problem. But whereas *The Politics* proceeds to analyze the qualitative differences between a political community and its constituent elements, the village and the family, this Discourse shall first differentiate a political community from the *organized* groups of which it is

ple's way of life—their culture, including their political institutions. And whereas the latter will be collectively designated by the term "government," "form of government" will signify the generic character of the regime as a whole. Finally, with Barker, I shall use single quotation marks around the word 'polity' to distinguish the name of this regime from the name given to regimes in general.

largely composed. Accordingly, its initial bearing shall be taken not from the Greek *polis*, but from the more familiar pluralistic or "polyarchic" society of our own times. The ensuing discussion will therefore keep in view the prevailing theoretical explanation of such a society, again, the "group" or "group-interest" theory referred to earlier.[2]

1

It goes without saying that no individual is unqualifiedly self-sufficient. Virtually every day we see people associate for the purpose of satisfying a variety of needs and interests which the individual cannot satisfy by himself alone. We are aware of an enormous number of organized groups or associations: civic and cultural, commercial and industrial, scientific and professional. But even these types of association are not wholly self-sufficient. Formed to promote limited or a limited number of ends or values, each is enmeshed in a vast, complex network of interdependency too obvious to require illustration. The mere fact that the same individual may be a member of more than one of these groups is indicative of their limited and dependent character. Furthermore, most groups are ephemeral; relatively few survive the life-span of an individual. Lacking *comprehensiveness*—which is to say variety and breadth of purpose—they also lack *permanence*.[3] None could seriously claim that it was organized or empowered to "establish Justice, insure domestic Tranquility, provide for the common defence, promote the general Welfare, and secure the Blessings of Liberty to ourselves and our Posterity." Such grand and sweeping aims may be proclaimed and perhaps on occasion pursued by political parties;

[2] See Arthur Bentley, *The Process of Government* (Cambridge: Harvard University Press, 1967, first published in 1908) (hereafter cited as *Bentley*); David Truman, *The Governmental Process* (New York: Alfred A. Knopf, 1953); Robert Dahl, *A Preface to Democratic Theory* (Chicago: University of Chicago Press, 1956), which partly traces itself to the Madison of *Federalist* 10—a common error among pluralists.

[3] Here, as elsewhere, the term "permanence" is to be construed in a relative sense.

but even these associations, however abiding their names, lack, and do not really seek, the self-sufficiency at which a political community aims and may be capable of achieving. Therein is one reason why Aristotle does not begin his inquiry into the nature of a political community by examining the "groups" of which it is composed. There are more revealing reasons, however.

Because their interests are not only limited and interdependent, but mutually obstructive, these groups ultimately require for their mutual adjustment the *assimilative and internalized persuasions* of a larger community. Consider only the response of groups to government decisions adversely affecting their interests. That the vast majority should so readily accede or accommodate themselves to such decisions cannot be explained wholly in terms of calculation and potential coercion. Much more profound and effective persuasions are at work, as should be obvious by the mere fact that these groups were formed in an on-going regime that has already shaped the attitudes and expectations of its members. (This is why the same individual can so readily become a member of different groups or, conversely, why different individuals can so readily cooperate despite their diverse group affiliations.) But to be more precise, it should be noted that the groups under discussion are *voluntary* associations. The same cannot be said of a political community, into which the individual is born and from which he inherits, from infancy onward, not only a body of commonly shared habits, beliefs, and values, but the very language with which he thinks and communicates with others—and all this long before he becomes a member of any voluntary association or interest group.[4] Is it any wonder that a sense of nationality endures in the individual even if he becomes an expatriate?

---

[4] "Group" theorists such as Bentley and Truman admit the prior existence of a "habit background" or of "rules of the game" facilitating the peaceful resolution of group conflict. But this admission is fatal to the theory. The theory holds that a society is a mere aggregation of groups. This is contradicted by the admission in question, which tacitly affirms what may be called a "holistic" view of society as opposed to the pluralistic view of "group" theory. In fact, however, the "group" theory of society confusedly compounds sociological determinism

Thus certain *binding and holistic* persuasions exist in a political community that are not to be found, by definition, in voluntary associations or interest groups.[5] These persuasions, inculcated through various forms of education, represent men's collective efforts to overcome self-defeating particularity. At the same time they also represent the discriminating and generalizing powers of individuality, elaborating, modifying, supplanting, and transcending antecedent persuasions.[6] (Think only of the Constitution, especially the words "to form a more perfect Union . . . [for] ourselves and our Posterity.") It may be said,

and atomistic individualism. The former is applied to the mentality of the individuals composing the groups, the latter to the actions of the groups themselves. I reject both types of one-sidedness and, with one qualification, adhere to the general principle that, just as the environment enters into the character of each thing, so each thing extends its character into the environment. See Whitehead, *Modes of Thought* (New York: Capricorn Books, 1958), pp. 188–189 (hereafter abbreviated as MT). The qualification involves the ruler-ruled relationship subsisting between the political whole and its constituent parts. Here is where I am closer to Aristotle than to Whitehead who, it appears, does not have a clear-cut ruler-ruled relationship in his notion of society. Concerning the latter, see Whitehead, PR 136–139, but compare with his *Adventures of Ideas* (New York: Macmillan Co., 1933), on "Laws of Nature," esp. pp. 142–147 (hereafter abbreviated as AI), and *The Function of Reason* (Boston: Beacon Press, 1966), p. 15 (hereafter abbreviated as FR).

[5] To be sure, binding persuasions will be found in certain professions (such as law and medicine); but these derive from, or require the support of, the larger community. (Consider, for example, the Hippocratic Oath, which prohibits abortion, and the liberal abortion laws of contemporary society.) As for the relevance of the notion of binding persuasions for tribal communities and tyrannies, this depends on the degree of rationality and freedom implicit in the notion. But that is a matter I cannot dwell on here, except to point out that countless people have risked their lives to escape from communist regimes to those of a liberal and *seemingly* less binding persuasion.

[6] There is an irreducible and critical individuality empirically evident even in the most tradition-bound societies. This individuality, which has relatively few significant examples of world-historical significance, breaks the shackles of repetition characteristic of inanimate matter; but lest it succumb to self-defeating idiosyncrasy, its extensive endurance requires the assimilation of antecedent persuasions. Here it is to be noted that the tension between individuality and some related system of sociological persuasions, though real, is temporal and misleading, since the former requires the latter for its content, and the latter requires the former for its transcendence, that is, for its being made relevant for future occasions.

therefore, that a political community, by virtue of its holistic and enduring persuasions, is the expression of men's quest for fullness of being and immortality—which may help to explain the gravity and significance of treason.[7]

As just intimated, however, the holistic and binding persuasions of a political community are partly dependent upon coercive and punitive sanctions. This dependency should be neither minimized nor misunderstood. Viewed candidly, the coercive and punitive sanctions of a political community, though seemingly negative and sometimes harsh, really reflect, and, by example sustain, the community's moral standards and sensibilities, hence those positive values which endow human activity with gradations of importance on the one hand, and with different intensities of feeling on the other. Contrast some voluntary association or interest group. Apart from loose analogies, coercive and punitive aspects are virtually absent.[8] Lacking the power required for the government of a political community— the power appropriate to the all-embracing purposes of such a community—interest groups, generally speaking, arouse in their members neither fear nor reverence. But then, men neither fear nor revere what can be made in one day and be dissolved the next.

Of course, the government of a political community may also fail to inspire fear or reverence, especially after it has long been portrayed as nothing more than an arena for group conflict. Any theory which regards a political community as a mere aggregation of groups, or which attempts to explain the founding of a regime solely in terms of contending group interests, is bound to trivialize politics and obscure the art of statesmanship. An alternative approach to the study of what is a regime is necessary.

[7] Consider, in this connection, religious orders and associations on the one hand, and heresy on the other.

[8] In practice, of course, not all voluntary associations are strictly "voluntary." (Consider, for example, various labor unions and professional organizations.) Some can therefore impose sanctions on recalcitrant members, but sanctions which fall short of the denial of civil and political rights—a distinction that makes all the difference.

27

2

The approach to be developed here reconstructs and subsequently modifies the Aristotelian notion of a regime as some sort of whole or compound. To understand such a whole, one may begin by analyzing it into the simplest parts or elements (2). At first glance, this method of "whole-part" analysis seems to be employed by "group" theory. But everything depends on whether the political whole is viewed mechanistically or teleologically. If mechanistically, as is the case with "group" theory, then the whole is nothing more than the sum of its parts. This means, first, that any good ascribed to the whole which is distinct from the good of any of its parts is a mere fiction (such as the "common good"). Second, it means that groups do not participate in a common adventure whose aims are higher than their own particular interests. Finally, it means that whatever any group conceives to be its own interest is self-justifying, which is to say there are no holistic standards by which to determine whether the interest of one group is intrinsically superior or preferable to another's. (It would seem, therefore, that the whole is infinitely less than the sum of its parts.) For Aristotle, however, who is teleologically oriented, the whole which is the political community is more than the sum of its parts. Accordingly, the method of "whole-part" analysis is not sufficient; or rather, it requires the incorporation of the *genetic* method, a method based on the recognition that political communities are products of growth, that they have grown out of the parts of which they are composed. Only now the parts, instead of consisting in so many interest groups, will consist of families and villages—two kinds of association which suggest, in a way interest groups do not, that a political community has a natural origin.[9] From this dis-

[9] There is good reason for starting with the family, for apart from more obvious reasons, the head of a family generally regards its members as extensions of himself, so that in pursuing his own good he is inclined to serve the "common good." If some "group" theorist should reply that those who direct the affairs of an interest group may also be inclined to serve the "common good" of the group, I should be very pleased to assent. Only I would ask of him: How is it

cussion it follows that the genetic and "whole-part" methods of analysis must be employed simultaneously in the study of regimes.

By itself, the family—the smallest association—can provide only the most rudimentary and recurrent of daily needs, such as food, clothing, and shelter. It can afford scant protection against hostile neighbors. Insecurity of provision, intensified by fear of violence, limits the family to necessity and prevents it from cultivating arts which might supply the simplest amenities of life. When, however, families associate with each other to form villages, the division of labor thus made possible engenders various wants and provides, to some extent, for their satisfaction. Greater security liberates the mind from preoccupation with bare necessity. The commingling of people with diverse skills and experiences, and different customs and languages, stimulates thought, imagination, and desire. New and more efficient ways of satisfying basic needs alter the patterns of daily existence, liberating men for less toilsome activity. Still, the village, bound to its agricultural economy, is limited in its human potentialities. The life of the village is largely regulated by the seasons and their fluctuations. It is geared more to production than to anything else. But production has an end beyond itself in the consumption or use of whatever goods are produced. Should the method of their production become an object of interest, the door will have been opened to the domain of free or self-directed activity, which is of the essence of life (10). *Homo faber* is incomplete. His completion requires the fellowship of a *political* community which a union of several villages makes possible.

In the political community, all the latent and diverse powers of men are stimulated and encouraged. A more complex division of labor renders production more efficient, and, at the same time, enlarges the sphere of leisured activity. Arts and sciences may flourish, and, with these, philosophy. The political community thus provides for the greatest variety of goods. Because

that an interest group, which is a complex entity, should have a "common good," while a political community, which is also a complex entity, should not?

its aim is not mere life but the good life, it makes possible self-sufficiency, the completion or perfection of human nature.

This progressive development from the family to the village, and from the village to the political community, is a *natural* one. To be sure, a variety of contingent causes are at work, such as famine and war. But such causes, when not wholly destructive, only serve to arouse natural tendencies. These natural tendencies are evident long after political communities have come into existence. We see them at work when a young man from a small rural town goes to the big city. He is not content to remain within the secure and friendly circle of his fellow townsmen, with their simple and similar ways of thinking and doing things. Something in him, some yearning or dimly felt need, urges him away. For good or ill, the city lures him on, to its many tensions and contradictions. Once there he will dwell among a strange assortment of people joined helter-skelter in a great variety of occupations and vocations: commercial and industrial, artistic and technical, administrative and professional. Soon he will become affected by the city's multifarious inventions and artistic productions. These will provide comforts and occasion discomfort, will amuse and dismay, will elevate and degrade.[10] Now suppose that this young man had become well settled in the city, had eventually worked his way through one of its colleges, and had become especially interested in urban problems. Let him by chance meet and become friends with a well-to-do individual who was in the process of forming a civic or cultural association concerned about the city's environment—perhaps its moral or its aesthetic environment. This individual had grown up

[10] Of course, the *polis* which Aristotle has most in mind is something less and something more than this megalopolis. It lacks, in addition to the vices, the variety of the big city, and, of greater significance, it does not equally provide for the cultivation of the private life. On the other hand, Aristotle's *polis* unites some of the best features of the city with the best features of the village: it combines the urbanity of the one and the conviviality of the other. In his *polis*, city and countryside become friends and contribute to the highest form of friendship, the friendship of men who share the life of self-sufficient activity, which is the life of the mind.

and still resided in a section of the city where people lived in secure comfort and among beautiful things. And yet, like the young man from that small rural town, he too had not been content with his life. Something in him—call it philanthropy or ambition or even boredom—had urged him to look beyond his own well-being and to concern himself with the good of the city. That "something" is what distinguishes man as the social animal *par excellence*. Let me explain.

The distinctive quality of living as opposed to nonliving things is surplus energy, energy above and beyond that required for mere survival. We see this energy exhibited especially in the higher animals, for example, among puppies at play. It is so powerful in man that it sets him apart from all other creatures, to the extent that it may be rightly called "creative" energy. However remote the notion of creativity from conventional interpretations of Aristotle, the phenomenon of creative energy substantiates his observation that the aim of a political community is not mere life, but the good life—an observation extended by Whitehead when he said that the art of life is to live, to live well, and to live better.[11] Clearly, it was this creative energy that made possible the adventure of that young man who left the monotony and security of a small rural town for the many-faceted and tension-ridden life of the big city. And again it was the same kind of energy that underlaid the philanthropy or the ambition, or that overcame the boredom, of the friend who sought to improve the moral or the aesthetic environment of that city. Now, what I see in this creative energy is man's quest for fullness of being. Man seeks to enlarge himself: to extend his self into society and to incorporate society into his self. This reciprocity exemplifies what may be seen in nature as a whole. Just as the character of the environment enters into each thing, so each thing extends its character into the environment. In other words, "nature [*physis*] is a process of expansive

[11] See Whitehead, FR 8. As used in this Discourse, the word "creative" does not signify absolute novelty. Nothing can be made out of nothing. See Whitehead, PR 31–32, 46–47.

development" issuing into increasingly complex "prehensive unifications"[12]—signifying that *nature itself is social.* In man, however, nature is radically social. For man is the only creature endowed with the power of speech, of language, of conceptual means of communication. He alone can communicate to his fellows by sounds and symbols indicative not merely of pleasures and pains, but also of thoughts concerning the common good, indeed, thoughts which enable man to extend his being into the far reaches of space and time. It was the creative power of speech that joined those two men just spoken of, and enabled them to deliberate on ways of improving the environment of their city.

Now, in saying that nature is social, I do not mean that nature is without conflict or discord. And when I say that man's nature is radically social, I do not mean that he is merely a most gregarious animal overflowing with sympathy or concern for his fellow men. Man's capacity for sympathy is more limited than many would like to believe. Not that human aggressiveness ought to be exaggerated. On this topic, however, an old error persists, namely, that man's aggressiveness provides unambiguous evidence for the claim that he is *a*social by nature. To the contrary, it could well be argued that the aggressiveness seen in mankind, like the sympathy by which it is often occasioned, represents, or may represent, an intensification of man's social nature. To be more precise, we frequently see in the aggressiveness of an individual an overflow of energy, creative as well as destructive, by which he seeks to overcome discordance or to eliminate whatever disjoins him from the realization of his own vision of society, a society for which he would as readily sacrifice himself as others. The fact that certain individuals may regard themselves as the center of the universe, or that they may wish to create the world in their own image, only confirms the radically social—more comprehensively, the *political*—nature of man.

It will be noticed that the emphasis I have placed on man's

[12] See Whitehead, SMW 72, 79, 83–84; and see above, p. 25, n. 4, for my qualification of the previous statement.

social nature does not overshadow the theme of individuality. The conspicuous absence of the latter is, perhaps, a shortcoming of Aristotle's political philosophy (but also, incidentally, of "group" theory). Although this theme will be explored in subsequent chapters, it should be pointed out that the modern emphasis on the *individual* (hence, on rights and freedom), and the classical emphasis on the *social* or *political* (hence, on duties and virtue), can be philosophically adjusted to each other in a more comprehensive view. Without going to the roots of the problem, but without digressing any further, the following points may be made. On the one hand, it is the living individual, and not any collectivity (as language may sometimes suggest), that in fact strives for fullness of being. On the other hand, there is not the slightest reason to believe that any individual could possibly achieve such plenitude were he never to live or to have lived in a political community. Only in a political community can he fully develop his moral and intellectual powers, for only in such a community can he enjoy the freedom and the leisure necessary for the cultivation of human excellence. At the same time, however, only in such a community can individuality flourish, an individuality which, when properly understood, is the concrete and emphatic expression of human excellence. Thus, insofar as it makes possible the fullest development of man's nature, the political community would seem to exemplify the natural *par excellence*. This leads me to elaborate upon the notion that a political community is a whole greater than the sum of its parts.

In the union of male and female which results in procreation, a surplus of energy eventuates in the development of a new individual whose powers are obviously more comprehensive than those of its gametic elements. Similarly in the union of families into villages and of villages into a political community may be seen a surplus of energy eventuating in the development of an individual whose powers transcend those of any individual which either of these smaller associations could nurture, whether separately or as a mere aggregate. I have in mind, of course, no

33

ordinary individual, but someone like a theoretical physicist or a philosopher. In saying, therefore, that the political whole is greater than the sum of its parts, I mean that each part participates in a perfection greater than itself. From this it follows that the whole provides a standard which determines the value of each part or of its contribution to the perfection of the whole. (The importance of this principle cannot be exaggerated, for upon its recognition depends the realization of a politics of magnanimity or of an exemplary form of statesmanship.)

One other point, alluded to earlier, requires elaboration. However much chance may play a role in the genesis and development of a political community, chance nevertheless falls within the sphere of moral action.[13] An earthquake may decimate a village. Still, the earthquake itself is not determinative of what the survivors will do to overcome their misfortune. The destruction will occasion lamentation; it will also occasion reflection and purposive action. Rationality remains: means are chosen with a view to ends, limited only by material circumstances and by intellectual and moral resources. Purposive action, however, need not be wholly cognitive, for the mode of final causality also operates through inclinations or the promptings of innate tendencies. It is natural for the infant to learn how to speak; for the child to wonder what lies beyond the heavens; for men to join in common endeavors; for someone to seek beyond the horizon of hearth and home a city wherein the wonder of the child becomes the quest of the sage.

Now, if we were to go back to the political community and study, instead of its teleological development, the character of its various groups, we could then employ the material mode of regime analysis. Farmers and agricultural workers; skilled and unskilled mechanics; merchants and shopkeepers; men of leisure

[13] See Aristotle, *Physics* 196b10–197b14. The most decisive questions of political life hinge on this issue. Here I can only note that whether political society is by nature or by convention, or whether nature provides the norm of human conduct, is intimately connected with the metaphysical status of chance, as may be seen in Rousseau's *Second Discourse*. Also, the entire edifice of the behavioral sciences hangs on this question.

and day laborers; the rich and the poor—these and other groups mentioned earlier would be found in different proportions, varying from one regime to another; and, as the distribution of power among these groups varied, so too would the political character of the regime and the degree in which it manifested human excellence. Here would again be seen—only now from the perspective of the material mode of regime analysis—why it is often difficult to distinguish one regime from another. But to elaborate upon that mode of analysis at this point would be premature. For having distinguished a political community from other forms of human association, the general criteria which distinguish the different kinds of regimes themselves should now be considered.

3

These criteria, again, involve two factors, quantitative and qualitative. The quantitative factor is simply the number or proportion of those members of a community who have some share in political rule, either by electing men to office, or by holding office themselves. The qualitative factor involves the moral and intellectual character of those who share in political rule—the habits and values descriptive of their way of life. As already noted, political rule may be of the One, the Few, or the Many. Of decisive political importance, however, is whether the one is a king in whom human excellence is personified, or a tyrant himself dominated by some domineering passion; or whether the few consists of an aristocracy informed by wisdom and virtue, or an oligarchy motivated by the worship of wealth; or, finally, whether the many compose a 'polity' of moderate citizens, or a democracy of licentious individuals. In each case the qualitative factor is determinative of whether a regime is good or bad, just or unjust. A regime is just if the character of its rulers and the ends which they pursue are such as to result in public policies which give to each part of the community its due. Stated another way, a regime is just if its "establishment"

rules for the good of the whole. A regime is unjust if its "establishment" rules for the good of only a part, or if the character of
the rulers and the ends which they pursue result in policies
which serve only their private or class interests.

According to Aristotle, kingship, aristocracy, and the 'polity'
are just forms of government; the remaining three—democracy,
oligarchy, and tyranny—are unjust, but of these, tyranny is the
worst and democracy is the best.[14]

Turning to a more detailed examination of Aristotle's regime
analysis, consider what he regards as the best regime in theory
and the best in practice.

The best regime in theory is one ruled by "a single man, or a
whole family, or a number of persons, surpassing all others in
goodness, but where ruled as well as rulers are fitted to play
their part in the attainment of the most desirable mode of life"
(152). The qualification—"the most desirable mode of life"—
refers to a philosophically articulated standard of excellence
transcending cultural relativity. A primitive community might
very well be ruled by a single man "surpassing all others in
goodness." But a primitive community is not fully a *whole*; it is
essentially incomplete or lacking perfection. The knowledge
and virtues required of its ruler fall far short of those required
of one who would rule a civilized or political community. It is
one thing to rule men bound by toil, with simple wants, ignorant
of sophisticated arts and sciences. It is another and more noble
thing to rule free men, men who must be persuaded more by
reasoned argument than by fear and superstition, indeed, men
who may themselves be capable of exercising political rule. Now,
given a standard of what constitutes the perfection of human
nature—and Aristotle meticulously develops such a standard in
the *Nicomachean Ethics*—a determination can be made of what
the best regime is in relation to that standard. For the best regime will be one whose paramount end or organizing principle
is the cultivation of human excellence.

To say that the best regime is one ruled by a single person or

14 Aristotle, *Politics*, pp. 123–126, 132–134, 142, 186, 206.

36

a number of persons surpassing all others in goodness is to imply that the wise should rule the less wise. This ruler-ruled relationship, according to Aristotle, is a natural one, however often it may be contradicted in practice. Thus, it is natural that parents should rule children, for the young partake of a lesser degree of perfection, having less knowledge and less command over their appetites or desires. Even between adults, it goes against the grain to see a mediocre or incompetent person exercising authority over men superior to him in knowledge and virtue. This feeling—aptly described by the colloquialism "it goes against the grain"—is a natural one, and testifies to the ruler-ruled relationship implicit in nature.

These every day feelings and observations point beyond themselves to one conclusion: *the best regime in theory is kingship.* "A whole is never intended by nature to be inferior to a part; and a man so greatly superior to others stands to them in the relation of a whole to its parts. The only course which remains is that he should receive obedience, and should have sovereign power without any limit of tenure—not turn by turn with others" (151). This, for Aristotle, is a logical rather than a "practical" conclusion. Yet this conclusion has most important practical implications. To begin with, it points to the second-best regime, an aristocracy ruled in turn by men of good birth and merit. It so happens, however, that the coming into being of the first- and second-best regimes is more reasonably to be wished for than expected. Both require extraordinary human and material resources, to say nothing of extraordinary good luck.

Bearing this in mind, Aristotle examines a variety of kingships: hereditary and elective monarchies, as well as constitutional and absolute monarchies. And he considers what kind of society is appropriate to each, and whether and under what circumstances discretionary rule or the rule of reason is preferable to, or more expedient than, the rule of law. Kingship, or the rule of the "best" man, was more common and more advantageous in remote antiquity, when societies were relatively small and simple. With the growth of large societies and the development of arts and sciences, political power had to be divided except, perhaps, under tyrannies. What this means is that the rule of the "best" man was possible only in *pre-philosophic* times. Like Plato, Aristotle had no illusions about the possibility of philosophers becoming kings. Or as *Publius* writes in *Federalist* 49, "a nation of philosophers is as little to be expected as the philosophical race of kings wished for by Plato" (329). Nor was Aristotle sanguinary about the possibility of a genuine aristocracy. "In no state," he writes, "would you find as many as a hundred men of good birth and merit" (206). The wise and the virtuous are too few in number to rule, or too weak in power to prevail over the many, especially in large, populated countries (114, 143). To be sure, good men may exercise political power, but not as a general rule, and never exclusively. As Madison says, with deliberate understatement in *Federalist* 10: "Enlightened statesmen will not always be at the helm" (57). If true virtue is rare, a regime ruled by virtuous men is rarer still. Hence Madison could suggest that, in designing a constitution which is to govern men, the statesman cannot literally translate into that constitution, or into political practice, the highest standards of human excellence articulated by political theory. To secure justice or the common good when only the very few are wholly motivated by justice or goodness, the wise statesman will dilute or "lower" his standards, rendering them more conformable to the generality of men.[15] Of such men, Madison says, "neither moral nor religious motives can be relied on as an *adequate*" foundation for establishing a just regime.[16] The average man is

[15] Aristotle's thoughts on this issue will be discussed later, especially in Chapter VII.

[16] *Federalist* 10, p. 58 (italics added). This requires some amplification. Contrary to Diamond's interpretation (below, p. 71), Madison does not unqualifiedly deprecate the efficacy of moral and religious motives. As the context makes clear, he merely contends that, given a situation in which the many have the same impulse of passion or of interest opposed to the rights of the few, then, "If th[at] impulse and the opportunity [to act on it] be suffered to coincide, we well know that neither moral nor religious motives can be relied on as an adequate control." This suggests that moral and religious motives may very well be efficacious when the average man acts in the capacity of an individual, rather

simply not good enough to be governed *solely* by moral or religious motives. He is not good enough to be governed *solely* by reason, by the "enlightened reason" of the philosophers spoken of in *Federalist* 49. Instead, he is more apt to be governed by opinions long-established and widely shared—and precisely *because* they are long-established and widely shared. This prejudice, according to *Publius*, can be a salutary one, provided that the received opinions about the most important political things have been formed as a result of a wise and relatively permanent body of laws. Should such laws be lacking in a society, the average man will be thrust upon himself, will be swayed more by the impulse of passion, by immediate and self-regarding interests, than by reason or a concern for the common good. The society of which he is a member will be torn asunder by the inescapable distinctions and inequalities among men. In a letter to Jefferson dated a month before *Federalist* 10 was published, Madison wrote:

> In all civilized societies, distinctions are various and unavoidable. A distinction of property results from the very protection which a free Government gives to unequal faculties of acquiring it. There will be rich and poor; creditors and debtors; a landed interest, a monied interest, a mercantile interest, a manufacturing interest. . . . However erroneous or ridiculous these grounds of dissention and faction may appear to the *enlightened* Statesman or the *benevolent* philosopher, the bulk of mankind who are neither Statesmen nor Philosophers, will continue to view them in a different light.[17]

Here, as elsewhere, Madison's opinion of the many—be they rich or poor—bears the mark of Aristotle's realism. Not that

than as a member of a group, especially of a group consisting of a class-conscious majority. (This may remind the reader of Reinhold Niebuhr's *Moral Man and Immoral Society*.) See p. 89 below, and compare James Madison, *The Writings of James Madison* (9 vols.; New York: G. P. Putnam's Sons, 1900–10), Gaillard Hunt, ed., II, 367–369 (hereafter cited as Madison, *Writings*).

17 *Ibid.*, V, 29 (italics added). That Madison should speak of "benevolent" philosophers suggests that he may have had philosophers of another description in mind, perhaps Machiavelli and Hobbes.

either of these men regarded the bulk of mankind as base or wicked. But such were their intellectual and moral standards on the one hand, and their experience of men on the other, that both concluded mankind, as a rule, was neither wise nor virtuous. A regime cannot be based on exceptions.

Having disposed of kingship and aristocracy as "practical" forms of government, Aristotle is left with but one worthy of being called just—the 'polity.' Not for any reason, therefore, does he regard the 'polity' as the best practical regime, one he recommends wherever a country possesses moderately good human and material resources. What is remarkable, however, is that for Aristotle, the best practical regime combines the attributes of two bad regimes—democracy and oligarchy! This is a paradox of crucial significance for understanding and evaluating the regime established by the founders, hence the caliber of their statesmanship. Its explanation requires, to begin with, an examination of the fundamental difference between democracy and oligarchy, one which will prove to be of decisive importance for political life in general.

4

As already indicated, Aristotle regards democracy and oligarchy as unjust regimes. Stated very simply, democracy is an unjust regime because the many, who comprise the poor, rule in their own interests and at the expense of the few, who comprise the rich. Conversely, oligarchy is an unjust regime because the few, who are rich, rule in their own interests and at the expense of the many, who are poor. But according to Aristotle, "The real ground of the difference between oligarchy and democracy is (not numbers, but) poverty and riches. It is inevitable that any regime should be an oligarchy if the rulers under it are rulers in virtue of riches, whether they are few or many; and it is equally inevitable that a regime under which the poor rule should be a democracy. It happens, however . . . that the rich are few and the poor are numerous" (116). The factor of number is thus an accidental as opposed to an essential attribute of both regimes. Poverty and riches, however, will be found in virtually every regime, so that virtually every regime harbors within itself democratic and oligarchic tendencies or tensions implicating the fundamental question of political life, the question of who should rule. Partisans of democracy and of oligarchy divide over this question for two related reasons: first, because they have different conceptions of justice or of what constitutes a just distribution of political power; and second, because they have conflicting interests which bias their understanding of the requirements of justice. The partisan of democracy claims that justice requires *equality* in the distribution of office—and so it does, but only for those who are in fact equal. Meanwhile, the partisan of oligarchy claims that justice requires *inequality* in the distribution of office—and so it does, but now only for those who are in fact *unequal* (117). This is a controversy over *who* should get *what*, a controversy involving *persons* and *things*. Now justice is relative to persons. We give to the young certain things, to adults other things, discriminating between what is appropriate for the one and what is appropriate for the other. Similarly, we distinguish among the young themselves, and to each we try to give what is appropriate to his particular needs and capacities. The same may be said of adults. We agree that it goes against the grain to see an incompetent person exercising authority over persons superior to him in merit. We feel that such an arrangement is contrary to the dictates of justice. It fails to relate justly persons and things. A just relationship requires that, among *different* persons, each receive a share in political things, such as office, according to his capacities or merit.

That partisans of democracy and of oligarchy overlook or slight this factor of merit does not mean, however, that their respective opinions regarding justice are wholly erroneous. Nor can their opinions be explained away as "rationalizations" of economic or other material motives. Such motives are present in virtually everyone to a greater or lesser extent; and they are *causes* of our opinions. But they are not the *only* causes. Non-cognitive or so-called subrational causes are appetitive. They impel us to seek that which we opine to be good. But that man is impelled to seek what he *opines* to be good suggests, as Madison points out in *Federalist* 10, that "his opinions and his passions will have a reciprocal influence on each other" (55). This may be illustrated in the following way. Reflecting on a conversation with an acquaintance the previous day, we suddenly realize that some remark we made had insulting implications. No sooner did the thought occur than we felt pained, if not ashamed.[18] Here a passion is evoked by an act of the intellect, indicating that reason, contrary to Hume, has some independent agency.[19] This does not mean that reason can move us in the absence of desire (or when in conflict with desire). Nevertheless, because we have many competing desires articulated as well as opposed, respectively, by corresponding and conflicting opinions, *critical reflection* may occur and alter the gradation of importance we attached to our original opinions and their related desires. Viewed in this light, the bias of an opinion concerning justice may be explained as its failure to synthesize or comprehensively and logically articulate a multiplicity of competing desires. But to illustrate quite simply the one-sided and unempirical character of any political psychology that reduces political opinions to economic motives, consider these embarrassingly obvious facts: (1) Not *all* poor people hold democratic views of justice—a fact not to be attributed to ignorance or deception, unless one prefers to forget that Socrates was a poor man. (2) Not *all* rich people hold oligarchic views of justice—

[18] See William James, *Varieties of Religious Experience* (New York: Modern Library, n.d.), p. 53, and Aristotle, *de Anima* 427b21.

[19] See David Hume, *Treatise of Human Nature* (London: Oxford University Press, 1955), L. A. Selby-Bigge, ed., and compare pp. 415, 458–459, and 462, where Hume is not wholly consistent in his analysis of the relation between reason and passion. For a critique of Hume on related points, see Aron Gurwitsch, *Studies in Phenomenology and Psychology* (Evanston: Northwestern University Press, 1966), ch. 7, "On the Intentionality of Consciousness." See also Aristotle, *de Anima* 433a1–25.

unless one prefers to forget the benefactor of Karl Marx. Clearly, economic factors cannot adequately account for the every day experiences of political life. Recognizing this, politicians, seeking to influence the opinions of the rich and the poor, ignore the lessons of behavioral political scientists to the extent of appealing not only to men's economic interests (and passions) but to their intellects as well. If only because behaviorists deny the agency of our intellects in the formation of our own political opinions, there is good reason to consider seriously a nonbehavioral approach to the study of politics.[20]

Returning, therefore, to the quarrel between democrats and oligarchs, it was suggested earlier that their respective opinions regarding the requirements of justice are partial or incomplete. The partisan of democracy claims that because all men are equal in one respect, namely, that they are men, born free and not slaves, they should be equal in other respects, especially in political power. That is, each individual has a right to an effectively equal voice in the determination of public policy. Clearly, this opinion favors the interest of the poor. In contrast, the partisan of oligarchy claims that because men are superior in one respect —in their case wealth—they should be superior in other respects, again, especially in political power (118). Clearly, this opinion favors the interest of the rich. While both claims are partially just, they are based not only on different conceptions of justice, but also on different conceptions of the purpose of a political community. Thus, if property were the end for which men come together and form a community, it would then seem that those with the larger share of property (as in the case of a business partnership) should have a proportionately larger share of political power. Against this the partisan of democracy might argue that men form political societies to secure their lives and liberty, or that self-preservation is the end of the community. And

---

[20] See also James, *Varieties of Religious Experience*, pp. 15–16, 19–20; Whitehead, FR ch. 1; Hans Jonas, *The Phenomenon of Life* (New York: Harper & Row, 1966), especially his critique of cybernetics, pp. 108–134, and the sequel on "The Nobility of Sight."

since its preservation may depend as much on the arms (to say nothing of the labor) of the many as on the wealth of the few, any political discrimination based on wealth is unjust.

Now, if the arguments of these oligarchs and democrats are synthesized, the result would be something like this: The purpose of the political community is nothing more than "comfortable preservation"—a basis on which the two partisans may tacitly agree. According to certain scholars, this is the very basis on which the founders established the American Constitution.[21] To be sure, property and safety are prominent themes in *The Federalist* (which is perfectly consistent with the character of a 'polity'). But one looks in vain in *The Federalist* for the oligarchic and democratic arguments corresponding to those themes. This is not surprising. *Publius* is neither a partisan of oligarchy nor of democracy.[22] He is skeptical of the wealthy as well as of the poor. Madison, it is clear, regards the bulk of mankind—rich and poor alike—as more foolish than wise, and as no less prone to vice than to virtue. The opinions of both classes regarding justice are biased in their own interests; and were either class to have a monopoly of political power, it would oppress the other. Furthermore, *Publius* would have been most imprudent to articulate publicly the quarrel between the partisans of oligarchy and democracy. That quarrel underlies, but is obscured by, the language of ordinary political controversy. To be sure, the times were not ordinary; but to expose the true grounds of ordinary political controversy is more likely to inflame men's passions than to inspire their intellects. Precisely in this light are we to understand why the debates of the Federal Convention were held in secret, and why they were more candid and more revealing of fundamental issues than were the published papers of *The Federalist*. Finally, given the character of the generality of men, *Publius* had good reason to place considerable, but by no means exclusive, emphasis on property and self-preservation. By no means, however, does this give war-

[21] See *Diamond*, p. 62.
[22] See p. 95, n. 63, below.

rant for the oligarchic or the democratic interpretations of the Constitution.

Indeed, the skeptical attitude toward the rich and the poor manifested throughout *The Federalist* may even be regarded as an implicit critique of the oligarchic and democratic conceptions of justice philosophically articulated in Aristotle's *Politics*. Thus, when Madison proclaims, however ambiguously, that justice is the end of government and of civil society, there is good reason to believe that this statesman would take the side of that philosopher who, in responding to the partisans of oligarchy and democracy, declares that a political community is not merely a business partnership entered into for the purpose of promoting wealth and commerce, nor simply a defense alliance formed to secure men's lives and liberty (118). Nevertheless, and leaving their differences aside for the present, both Aristotle and Madison would admit that rich and poor, by contributing to the prosperity and safety of the community, do contribute to the common good, in consequence of which the political claims of their respective partisans do partake of justice.[23] One begins to see, therefore, why combining the principles of democracy and oligarchy to form a 'polity' may result in the establishment of a just regime.

But to probe a little deeper, recall that a 'polity,' like a democracy, is a specific form of the rule of the Many. To qualify as a just regime, the character and composition of the many who rule in a 'polity' must differ substantially from the character and

[23] This discussion suggests to Mr. James Ceaser a fundamental difference between the claims of certain present-day partisans of democracy and those portrayed by Aristotle. The former, it appears, do not feel obliged to justify their claim to political power on the basis of any contribution to the common good. They deem the bare fact of being human sufficient to justify an individual's claim to share in political rule. I attribute this modern form of egalitarianism to the cooperation of two forces: (1) atomistic individualism, which may be traced to Hobbes and Locke, and (2) nineteenth-century humanism, which Nietzsche aptly characterized as "Christianity without God," a humanism which today asserts the unqualified dignity of the individual. Both of these forces engender moral relativism which, as has been seen, denies a common good transcending any private good.

composition of the many who rule in a democracy. (The same obviously applies to the few who rule in an aristocracy vis-à-vis the few who rule in an oligarchy.) Leaving the detailed exploration of this problem for subsequent chapters, here only the following point is emphasized: Insofar as its citizens share in a common way of life, a 'polity' cannot consist of, or be divided between, unmitigated democrats on one side and unmitigated oligarchs on the other. This means that a 'polity,' contrary to what was suggested above, cannot be established by the unqualified combination of democratic and oligarchic principles, hence by doctrinaire partisans of democracy joined by doctrinaire partisans of oligarchy. The founding of such a regime requires statesmen who stand above those narrow partisans, statesmen capable of persuading the rich and the poor to moderate their competing claims to political power. Now, given a political situation in which those claims are advanced simultaneously, the statesman will have to employ two rhetorical strategies, one directed at the rich, the other at the poor.

To persuade the rich to moderate their claims, one may turn their opinions against their interests. Thus, suppose the few who are rich argue that justice requires the rule of those who are superior in wealth. Paraphrasing Aristotle, to them it can be logically replied that if there be one person among the few who is richer than all the rest—or if the collective wealth of the many exceeds that of the few—then either that one person or the many must rule instead of the few, and on the very same ground which the few claim for *their* right to rule.[24] As already intimated, how-

---

[24] See Aristotle, *Politics*, pp. 133–134, 261. Aristotle proceeds to turn the opinion of the many against themselves, saying: "If the reason why they should be sovereign is their being stronger than the Few, we are logically driven to conclude that where one man is stronger than all the rest—or a group of more than one, but fewer than the Many, is stronger—that one man or group must be sovereign instead of the Many" (133–134). This rebuttal lacks any practical relevance for the founding if only because no public figure claimed the right of the many to rule on the ground of their superior strength. Such a claim may even have appeared frivolous in democratic Athens, despite its navy being in the hands of the demos. To be sure, Plato can have the impetuous Thrasymachus say that justice is the interest of the stronger. But in addition to being a non-

ever, the enunciation of this counterargument in public, at least in the language just presented, would be necessary only in a political situation marked by the overt clashing of powerful oligarchic and democratic passions, in the absence of which such an argument might serve only to arouse those passions. In any event, that counterargument was not manifestly required in the political situation which confronted the founders, and precisely because the political claims of the rich were not as extreme as those urged by the partisans of oligarchy portrayed in Aristotle's *Politics*. Whatever oligarchic claims were in evidence at the time of the founding, their *political* articulation lacked the clarity to be expected from a *philosophical* exploration of the grounds underlying such claims (129). In other words, during the founding period, the claims or opinions of the rich regarding justice or the question of who should rule were relatively moderate, or they were publicly advanced in a somewhat obscure or indirect manner. This conclusion is confirmed in *Federalist* 54, significantly, a paper dealing with the issue of whether slaves should be represented as persons or as property.

Writing to a predominantly New York audience, Madison, in superb rhetorical fashion, conjures up a southern slaveholder and has him say the following in support of the three-fifths rule:

> "We subscribe to the doctrine," might one of our Southern brethren observe, "that representation relates more immediately to persons, and taxation more immediately to property, and we join in the application of this distinction to the case of our slaves. But we must deny the fact, that slaves are considered merely as property, and in no respect whatever as persons. . . . In being compelled to labor, not for himself, but for a master; in being vendible by one master to another . . . in being subject at all times to be restrained in his liberty . . . the slave may . . . fall under the legal denomination of property. In being protected, on the other hand, in his life and in his limbs, against

Athenian, Thrasymachus is presented as a partisan of tyranny. In contrast, Plato has Glaucon insinuate the notion that justice is the interest of the weaker (*Republic* 358e–359b)! (But perhaps the word "stronger" is ambiguous? In the Greek it could mean superior in other than a physical sense.)

the violence of all others, even the master of his labor and his liberty; and in being punishable himself for all violence committed against others,—the slave is no less evidently regarded by the law as a . . . moral person, not as a mere article of property. The federal Constitution, therefore, decides with great propriety on the case of our slaves, when it views them in the mixed character of persons and of property" (354–355).

In the very next paragraph, however, Madison's clever slaveholder goes on to say:

"This question may be placed in another light. It is agreed on all sides, that numbers are the best scale of wealth and taxation, as they are the only proper scale of representation. Would the convention have been impartial or consistent, if they had rejected the slaves from the list of inhabitants, when the shares of representation [of the states in the lower House] were to be calculated, and inserted them on the lists when the tariff of contributions was to be adjusted?"

Here a democratic assertion (that numbers are the *only* proper scale of representation) is used to further oligarchic and perhaps aristocratic interests! This rhetorical device is frequently employed in *The Federalist*. Note, too, the contention that numbers are the best scale of wealth, suggestive of Aristotle's logical *tour de force* against the partisans of the rich. (Incidentally, if that contention was then plausible, its utterance suggests the absence of extreme poverty and riches during the founding period, meaning that the distribution of wealth among the American people at that time was such as to favor the establishment of a moderate form of government.)[25] Finally, and in further illustration of the opinions of the rich regarding justice and the manner in which some may have sought to advance their interests, the same southern slaveholder is made to say:

"We have hitherto proceeded on the idea that representation related to persons only, and not at all to property. But is it a just idea? Government is instituted no less for protection of the property, than of the persons, of individuals. The one as well as

[25] See *Federalist* 35, p. 214, and *Federalist* 60, pp. 390–394.

the other therefore, may be considered as represented by those who are charged with the government" (357).[26]

To these and other statements Madison responds: "Such is the reasoning which an advocate for the Southern interests might employ on this subject; and although it may appear to be a little strained in some points, yet, on the whole, I must confess that it fully reconciles me to the scale of representation which the convention have established" (358). Notwithstanding Madison's anti-slavery sentiments expressed during that convention,[27] there is no doubt that he believed "Government is instituted no less for protection of the property, than of the persons, of individuals." But if "The one as well as the other . . . may be considered as represented by those who are charged with the government," then the political principles or character of those charged with the government may *not* be considered as simply democratic or as simply oligarchic. Perhaps they should be regarded as a mean between the two?

Turning to the problem of moderating the political claims of the many, this may be accomplished by reversing one of the rhetorical devices employed by Madison in *Federalist* 54, or by his imaginary slaveholder. Thus, instead of using seemingly democratic principles on behalf of aristocratic values, one may use aristocratic values on behalf of seemingly democratic principles. This requires the translation of quantity into quality, of numbers into merit, or the association of large numbers of people with wisdom and virtue. Aristotle elaborates upon this problem with great candor and philosophical clarity in the *Politics*, arguing both for and against the proposition that the collective wisdom and virtue of the many exceeds that of the few (123–126, 132–134). Of course, such clarity should not be expected from *The Federalist*, whose authors were necessarily constrained

[26] Note well the sequel, especially its rhetoric regarding the federal Constitution.

[27] See Max Farrand, ed., *The Records of the Federal Convention of 1787* (4 vols.; New Haven: Yale University Press, 1937), I, 135, II, 415 (hereafter cited as *Farrand*).

by practical and rhetorical considerations.[28] Indeed, it would have been most imprudent to contrast the many and the few in these terms. Nevertheless, two things are to be noted: first, the relationship between quantity and quality is a prominent theme in *The Federalist*, and second, related to that theme is the frequent association of wisdom and virtue (or their equivalent) and the modes of electing men to the various departments of government. As for the first, in *Federalist* 10 Madison contends that representatives elected by the people in a large republic are likely to be superior in merit to those elected in a small republic. (This is his tactful way of telling the people of New York, including the politicians, that the quality of men elected to the newly proposed House of Representatives will usually be superior to their counterparts in the state legislatures—where the word superior may be construed to mean, primarily, less democratic.) Unlike Aristotle, however, Madison does not *explicitly* formulate a positive argument to the effect that, within limits, greater collective wisdom and virtue may be expected to govern a larger than a smaller number of men involved in the election of representatives.[29] Instead, he applies Aristotle's point—that "a numerous body is less likely to be corrupted" (142)—to the election of representatives. In his own words: "as each representative will be chosen by a greater number of citizens . . . it will be more difficult for unworthy candidates to practice with success the vicious arts by which elections are too often carried [in small electoral districts swayed by the promises of demagogues or manipulated by the bribes of the rich, I infer from *Federalist* 57]; and the suffrages of the people being more free [of such influences], will be more likely to centre in men who possess the most attractive merit and the most diffusive and

---

[28] Yet even Aristotle may have been deliberately ambiguous in certain places in the *Politics*, especially in Books IV and VI where he presents guidelines for constructing democracies. Indeed, we shall see that Aristotle may have employed rhetorical devices comparable to that of the founders! See below, pp. 124–130.

[29] It should be noted, however, that, unlike Madison, Aristotle had in mind a deliberative assembly wherein the many were engaged in the choosing of magistrates (*Politics*, pp. 125–126).

established characters" (60, 374). This defense of the House of Representatives, an institution seemingly representing only numbers, hence the "many," in terms characteristic of the few, insinuates into public discourse a salutary teaching. It may dispose the partisans of democracy to justify the political claims of the many in terms of merit, and not solely in terms of the numerical and doctrinaire principle of "one man, one vote." Furthermore, by justifying their claims in terms of merit, the statesman may engender among the many the incentive to become more worthy of the respect thus accorded them. Contrast, however, the teaching of *Federalist* 58, where Madison seems to reverse the relationship between quantity and quality.

Unlike *Federalist* 10 and 57, which relate the number of electors to the quality of those elected to the House of Representatives, *Federalist* 58 relates the number of representatives to the quality of their deliberations and to the quality of government as a whole. Says Madison:

> [T]he more numerous an assembly may be, of whatever characters composed, the greater is known to be the ascendancy of passion over reason. In [addition], the larger the number, the greater will be the proportion of members of limited information and of weak capacities. [This follows from the argument of *Federalist* 10, insofar as a more numerous assembly would consist of men representing smaller electoral districts. The interests of such districts would tend to be narrow, and their citizens would be more susceptible to those "vicious arts" which result in the election of petty politicians.] Now, it is precisely on characters of this description that the eloquence and address of the few are known to act with all their force. . . . Ignorance will be the dupe of cunning, and passion the slave of sophistry and declamation. The people can never err more than in supposing that by multiplying their representatives beyond a certain limit, they strengthen the barrier against the government of the few. . . . The countenance of the government may become more democratic, but the soul that animates it will be more oligarchic (381–382).[30]

[30] See *Federalist* 54, p. 355, *Federalist* 55, p. 361, *Federalist* 62, p. 403, *Fed-*

Here Madison has the uneasy task of defending a House of Representatives originally composed of a mere sixty-five members. But notice the subtle use of democratic language to justify what, in terms of its "countenance" or size alone, could reasonably be regarded as an oligarchic institution. On the other hand, even though the "soul" of this institution seems intended to be democratic, that soul, contrary to democratic tendencies—and I have elided Madison's pejorative reference to democratic Athens— is evidently intended to be governed more by reason than by passion.[31] Thus are compounded (if not confounded) arguments adapted to an audience consisting of diverse kinds of men— say arguments suggestive of different kinds of regimes—where the language appropriate to one regime is used, sometimes only in appearance, to advance the interests and values of another. This conclusion may be elaborated as follows.

Bear in mind that *The Federalist* consists of eighty-five papers, and that these papers defend different institutions and electoral processes, each of which affects the interests and values of diverse classes of citizens in unequal ways. Now, assuming the rhetorical skill of the authors, the following tentative conclusions may be drawn: (1) the rhetorical subtlety of *The Federalist*, elicited from its substantive arguments, is indicative of the composition and character of its audience; (2) that audience consisted, for the most part, of more or less moderate partisans of democracy and oligarchy; (3) these partisans, though fairly sophisticated—judging from the intellectual quality of *The Federalist*—were nevertheless susceptible to its rhetorical modulations, that is, to the "countenance" of its arguments; (4) the

---

eralist 63, p. 408, and below, p. 101. Hamilton seems to take a different position in *Federalist* 70; but the reader should not be misled by his rhetoric, inasmuch as the purpose of that paper is to justify a unitary executive in terms of "energy," rather than in terms of "deliberation and wisdom" (*ibid.*, p. 455).

[31] *Federalist* 58 may be distinguished from *Federalist* 10 as follows: Whereas the latter argues that it is relatively difficult to corrupt large numbers of *electors*, the former argues that it is relatively easy to corrupt large numbers of the *elected* (when joined in a single assembly). These are not logically contradictory positions, and for the reasons bracketed in the above passage.

countenance of those arguments conceals as well as reveals the "soul" which animated them; and (5) as a general rule, the papers of *The Federalist* are addressed more to the many than to the few, in appearance, and more to the few than to the many, in reality.

Concerning those few, most are not to be confused with the few *par excellence*. Nevertheless, by frequently relating quantity and quality in public discourse, the statesman may teach the "many"—democrats as well as oligarchs—that the institutions of government must be designed not only to secure liberty and property, but also to enlarge the role of reason and virtue in political life. Such a teaching would tend to moderate the political pretensions of rich and poor alike, would tend to make partisans of democracy less democratic and partisans of oligarchy less oligarchic. But this is to render both more just— precisely what is required for establishing that just regime called a 'polity.'[32]

Having shown why the combination of democratic and oligarchic principles, properly qualified, results in a just regime— again, the 'polity'—it must now be noted that such a 'polity' is only a paradigm. Political reality is more complicated. In no political community is the entire populace likely to be wholly preoccupied with comfortable preservation. The wise and the virtuous may be rare, but between the wise and the unwise on the one hand, and between the virtuous and the unvirtuous on the other, there are infinite gradations. Madison does not say in *Federalist* 10 that enlightened statesmen will *never* or even *seldom* be at the helm. He expects at least some representatives to be of such caliber as "to refine and enlarge the public views," representatives "whose wisdom may best discern the true interest of their country, and whose patriotism and love of justice will be least likely to sacrifice it to temporary or partial consid-

[32] Of course, I have oversimplified the statesman's problem, in part by exaggerating the efficacy of rhetoric. In fact, to persuade the rich and the poor to moderate their claims to political power, the statesman will require a class of citizens distinct from and perhaps larger than both. But this is a topic reserved especially for Chapter V.

erations" (59). And here Madison is referring only to the *popularly* elected branch of the national legislature, the House of Representatives. As for the Senate, inasmuch as the "State legislatures who appoint the senators, will in general be composed of the most enlightened and respectable citizens, there is reason to presume," says Jay in *Federalist* 64, "that their attention and their votes will be directed to those men only who have become the most distinguished by their abilities and virtue, and in whom the people perceive just grounds for confidence" (417). Finally, in *Federalist* 68, after analyzing the advantages of the electoral college method of choosing a President, Hamilton concludes with these words: "It will not be too strong to say, that there will be a constant probability of seeing the station filled by characters preeminent for ability and virtue" (444).

Admittedly, the qualities of representatives, senators, and presidents may fall considerably short of the standard of excellence elucidated by Aristotle in the *Nicomachean Ethics*. But it is not contended here that the Constitution exemplifies an aristocratic form of government. Nothing in the Constitution explicitly indicates that the new government will have, as one of its ends, the cultivation of virtue (although, justice, the cardinal virtue of political life, is the first moral end proclaimed in the Preamble). As Aristotle points out, however, "even in countries which do not make the encouragement of goodness a matter of public policy, there may still be found individuals of good repute and esteemed to be of high quality." And he concludes by saying that "a constitution [by which he means a *regime*, and *not a written document*,] which pays regard to all the three factors—wealth, goodness, and numbers—as the Carthaginian does, may be called an aristocratic regime" (173). Here the term "aristocratic" is not to be construed in its highest or paradigmatic sense—else the factors of wealth and numbers would have been excluded. Indeed, in his analysis of the Carthaginian regime in Book II of the *Politics*, Aristotle identifies it as a 'polity,' but one inclined toward oligarchy (84–87). This confusion of terms is clarified in Book IV:

The form of regime called 'polity' is embellished, in most countries, by a higher title. The mixture attempted in it seeks only to blend the rich and the poor . . . but the rich are regarded by common opinion as holding the position of gentlemen [and a 'polity' in which they are included thus comes to be embellished by the higher title of aristocracy]. In reality there are *three* elements which may claim an equal share in the mixed form of regime—free birth, wealth, and merit. . . . Obviously, therefore, we ought always to use the term 'polity' for a mixture of only two elements, where these elements are the rich and the poor; and we ought to confine the name 'aristocracy' to a mixture of three, which is really more of an aristocracy than any other form so-called—except the first and true form [of which we spoke earlier] (176).

As Aristotle later explains, the only difference between "aristocracies" and 'polities' consists in their different ways of combining the rich and the poor, or the elements of oligarchy and democracy (222). It is to be presumed that the rich are better educated than the poor, that many are men of leisure, so that if the abilities and virtues of a sufficient number of the rich are rewarded with the honors of office, the regime may be classified as an "aristocracy"—though not of paradigmatic quality (175). The likelihood of such an "aristocracy" presupposes a 'polity' whose mixture of elements inclines the regime more toward oligarchy than toward democracy (for reasons too obvious to require elaboration). Given, however, the ambiguities inherent in the factors of numbers, wealth, and merit, as well as the variety of ways by which these factors may be combined, Aristotle uses the terms 'polity' and "aristocracy" interchangeably. For the purpose of this study, the regime established by the founders of the American Constitution will be referred to solely as a 'polity,' but with the understanding that that regime does not exclude "aristocratic" elements. Not only did Hamilton, Madison, and Jay present arguments showing how the design of the new government would facilitate the advancement of men of ability and virtue to positions of political leadership, but such men were in fact subsequently elected or appointed to high office, including the authors of *The Federalist*.[33]

It should now be clearer why a 'polity' is a just regime, and why it may be the best practical regime. But before the latter claim can be fully established, the differences between a 'polity' and the regime with which it is most easily confused, democracy, will have to be analyzed.[34] Only by dispelling that confusion can we possibly understand and evaluate the statesmanship of the founding fathers.

---

[33] No less than sixteen of the thirty-nine signatories of the Constitution became members of the First Congress: Abraham Baldwin, Richard Bassett, Pierce Butler, Daniel Carroll, George Clymer, William Few, Thomas Fitzsimmons, Nicholas Gilman. William S. Johnson, Rufus King, John Langdon, James Madison, Robert Morris, William Patterson, George Read, and Roger Sherman. In addition, Washington was elected President, Hamilton was appointed Secretary of the Treasury, James Wilson was appointed to the Supreme Court, while Gouverneur Morris received the post of Ambassador to France. (Morris returned to the United States in 1800 to be appointed to the Senate.)

[34] See Aristotle, *Politics*, pp. 161, 175, 206, 222.

CHAPTER II

Radical Democracy and the American 'Polity'

THE QUESTION before us is whether the regime established by the founding fathers exemplifies a democracy or a 'polity.' This is not a mere academic inquiry. For if Aristotle's criteria of regime analysis are largely applicable to eighteenth-century America, then those commentators who claim that the regime in question is a democracy are in fact claiming (no doubt without intending to) that the founders established what amounts to an unjust form of government! Now, of the two democratic interpretations referred to in the Introduction, only Diamond's can be said to employ, at least tacitly, what appear to be Aristotelian criteria. If he has properly applied those criteria so as to necessitate the conclusion that the regime established under the Constitution *is* a democracy, grave doubt will have been cast on the caliber of the founders' statesmanship, to say the very least. Of course, if no better form of government could have been established given the human resources available to the founders, this would reflect favorably on their statesmanship, but not on the character of the American people. Be this as it may, precisely because Diamond's apparent use of Aristotelian criteria leads him to conclusions very different from my own, a consideration of his argument from time to time will help to clarify what is at stake in the following inquiry. I wish to make it perfectly clear, however, that my principal object is not to refute his interpretation of the founding—I have more constructive aims in view—

but again to peel away the layers of confusion which have so long obscured the true political character of the original Constitution as well as the very art of statesmanship.[1] Bearing this in mind, a more concrete application of Aristotle's quantitative criteria of regime analysis may now be undertaken.

1

With those criteria the laws of a particular country may be analyzed with a view to ascertaining the proportion of adults who share in political rule. Two factors, already mentioned, must be considered at the outset of the investigation: (1) the number of people eligible to vote in political elections, and (2) the number of citizens eligible for political office. Both may be limited by means of a property (or other) qualification, and the qualification affecting the number of those eligible to vote may differ from that affecting the number of those eligible for office. This difference complicates matters, and should it manifest itself in a particular regime, it renders more difficult the problem of evaluating the regime's political character. Consider its manifestation in the United States at the time of the founding.

Using quantitative criteria for the purpose of determining the political character of the regime described in *The Federalist*, the question, to repeat, is whether their application will provide, in this instance, unambiguous results, results pointing to the conclusion that the founders established a democratic form of government. Consider, first, the suffrage. According to Diamond (who relies on a study by Robert E. Brown), "the property qualifications in *nearly* all the original states were *probably* so small as to exclude never more than twenty-five per cent, and in *most* cases as little as only five to ten per cent, of the adult white male

[1] It should also be noted that Diamond's essay, "Democracy and *The Federalist*: A Reconsideration of the Framers' Intent," seems to have had considerable influence, especially among those associated with the Straussian school of scholarship. It will be found unrevised in Willmoore Kendall and George Carey, eds., *Liberalism Versus Conservatism* (Princeton, N.J.: D. Van Nostrand Co., Inc., 1966), pp. 10–24, and in Morton Frisch and Richard Stevens, eds., *American Political Thought* (New York: Charles Scribner's Sons, 1971), pp. 52–70.

population."[2] To construe the words I have italicized in a manner most favorable to a democratic interpretation, it will be assumed that the states implicitly excluded by the term "nearly" had no property qualifications at all (which is not borne out, however, by the constitutions in force in *all* the states at the time of the founding). And it will further be assumed that the property qualifications prescribed by the state constitutions were in fact, and not "probably," so small as to exclude from the suffrage little more than 5 percent of the "adult white male population." Now, inasmuch as the House of Representatives, under the new Constitution, was to be elected by voters who "shall have the qualifications requisite for electors of the most numerous branch of the State legislatures," two conclusions would seem to follow: (1) that the state constitutions were generically democratic, and (2) that the federal Constitution, at least as regards the House, remained within the democratic spectrum. Leaving the second conclusion aside for the present, we ought to weigh against the first conclusion the fact that a majority of the state constitutions prescribed much higher qualifications for office than for voting.[3] Consider only those qualifications affecting the legislative

[2] *Diamond*, p. 58. But see Edward Dumbauld, ed., *The Political Writings of Thomas Jefferson* (New York: The Liberal Arts Press, 1955), p. 114, Jefferson to Kerchival, July 12, 1816, where Jefferson says that "the House of Representatives [i.e., the Virginia House of Delegates] is chosen by less than half the people and not at all in proportion to those who do choose." Does Jefferson mean, in this obscure statement, that less than half the adult white males were eligible to vote?—for he certainly could not have meant half the population. Here we may consult *Federalist 57*. According to Madison, "each representative . . . will be elected by five or six thousand citizens" (p. 374). Since the first Congress consisted of sixty-five representatives, it would then follow that 325,000 to 390,000 men were eligible to vote. Given a population estimated at three million, it follows that roughly 11 to 13 percent of the population were eligible to vote for representatives. Today it is much closer to 75 percent.

[3] Diamond's essay is curiously silent about this point. He seems to think that the suffrage requirements for the House, the mode of electing the President, and the amending process support his contention that the Constitution did not depart from the "democratic standards" of the period (*Diamond*, pp. 58–59). Of course, this begs the issue, since the question is whether the standards of that period were *in fact* democratic. (On this question, see my *Philosophy of the American Constitution*, Appendix 2.) On the other hand, had Diamond men-

branches of the state governments in the table "Property Qualifications for Voting and for Office."

Property Qualifications for Voting and for Office

STATE	VOTING	LOWER HOUSE	UPPER HOUSE
Ga.	10 £ property	250 acres or 250 £ property	(unicameral)
Md.	50 acres or 30 £ in money	500 £ real or personal property	1000 £ real or personal property
Mass.	3 £ annual rental income or 60 £ estate	100 £ freehold or 200 £ estate	300 £ freehold or 600 £ estate
N.H.	50 £ in money	100 £ estate, one-half in freehold	200 £ freehold
N.J.	50 £ in money	500 £ real or personal property	1000 £ real or personal property
N.C.	Taxpayer (House); 50 acres (Senate)	100 acres	300 acres
S.C.	50 acres of town lot; or tax equal to tax on 50 acres	500 acres or 150 £	200 £ freehold

Source: *The Federal and State Constitutions, Colonial Charters, and Other
Organic Laws of the United States* (2 vols.; Washington, D.C.: Government
Printing Office, 1878).

Notice that the average property qualification for office in
these states was roughly ten times higher than the average property qualification for voting. It should also be borne in mind that

tioned the property qualifications required for office in the state governments,
he would have had a stronger case against those who claim that the Constitution
represent a "conservative reaction" against the democratic principles of the
Revolution.

the original Constitution did not alter these qualifications.[4] If, therefore, some 5 percent of the adult white male population were excluded from the suffrage, it seems reasonable to infer that a considerably higher percentage must have been excluded from office in the state legislatures in question.[5] Nor is this all. It must also be remembered that, under the original Constitution, the state legislatures appointed the members of the United States Senate. To be sure, apart from age, citizenship, and residence requirements, virtually anyone was legally eligible to become a senator. But given the property qualifications required for most electors of the Senate, what proportion of the adult population could in fact be appointed to this office? Furthermore, there are other ways of excluding men from office besides that of a property qualification. Also to be considered is the monetary compensation provided for the officeholder. This topic will be discussed at greater length later. Here, suffice it to say that the compensation provided by law for members of the state legislatures was then so low as to exclude, and by design, all but men of considerable means. And what is more, the rationale behind this practice—to be discussed in a moment—was

[4] Diamond slights this fact, although the states were integral parts of a political whole. Or, he explains it away by referring to the professed view of some of the founders that the states were "hotbeds" of democracy. (Of this, more later.) The length of his essay can hardly justify (given the serious implications of its interpretation of the Constitution) his ignoring all but the suffrage provisions of the state constitutions. If he should maintain, however, that the founders expected the gradual elimination of all the state property qualifications for office—and it is true that the Constitution does not preclude such an eventuality—it would not be *philosophically* determinative of the political character of the Constitution itself. As shall be seen later, it is philosophically incorrect to superimpose upon the *form* of the original Constitution the subsequent developments of the United States, for the latter are to be understood under the mode of *efficient* causality, that is, under the category of change.

[5] Diamond might have argued that the factor of who is eligible to vote is, in the long run, politically more decisive than the factor of who is eligible for office. (See Aristotle, *Politics*, pp. 218, 126.) But here again we are dealing with the mode of efficient causality referred to in the previous footnote. Virtually all commentators on the founding fail to distinguish between the various modes of regime analysis, including among these commentators political scientists influenced by the *Politics* of Aristotle.

determinative of the small monetary compensation provided by law for no less than the first thirteen congresses of the United States.

Leaving this aside, however, what must be the percentage of those eligible for voting and for office to qualify a regime as democratic? Clearly, the factor of number admits of infinite degrees and so precludes the possibility of defining the line where democracy ends and oligarchy—I should say a 'polity'—begins. Political science lacks the precision of mathematical physics. Along the political spectrum, democracies shade into 'polities,' 'polities' into oligarchies. The American regime may have been democratic from its very outset; but such a conclusion gains no unequivocal support from Aristotle's quantitative criteria. Indeed, at one point, Aristotle goes so far as to say: "We may lay it down generally that a system which does not allow every citizen to share [in political rule] is oligarchical, and that one which does so is democratic" (171). But this is not Aristotle's last word on the subject (of which more later).

The preceding was intended to show that quantitative criteria are not sufficient to determine the political typology of a regime when at issue is whether a particular regime is a democracy or a 'polity,' or even an oligarchy. As Aristotle cautions, "it is not sufficient to distinguish democracy and oligarchy merely by the criterion of poverty and wealth, any more than it is to do so merely by that of number" (163). Nevertheless, there is a powerful tendency among contemporary political scientists to rely excessively on quantitative criteria. This tendency coincides with the predilection of people in general to classify all regimes as either democratic or "authoritarian." Aristotle observed a similar tendency among his own contemporaries—only they classified regimes as democratic or as oligarchic (161). Although this tendency points to an important political truth, namely, that most political controversies involve a conflict between the poor and the rich, it greatly oversimplifies the character of the two classes and the variety of regimes that fall under and between the two paradigms in question (156, 166–167). Hence it obscures crucial differences which, if ignored by statesmen, can lead to grave errors in the construction, reform, or preservation of a regime, especially of a 'polity.' But this, only in passing.

Inasmuch as quantitative criteria do not yield unambiguous results regarding the generic character of most of the state constitutions, they do not permit us to conclude, without further evidence, that the *federal* government established under the Constitution exemplifies a democracy. A consideration of Aristotle's qualitative criteria of regime analysis is in order.

2

Concerning the democratic paradigm alone, Aristotle distinguishes no less than four varieties. Of these varieties it will only be necessary for the purpose of this inquiry to consider the best and the worst, beginning with the latter.

In the worst variety of democracy, there are no qualifications for voting or for holding office (apart from age, citizenship, and perhaps residence requirements). Accordingly, each individual has a right to an equal voice in public affairs. This fact alone has profound moral and intellectual consequences. First of all, it fosters the notion that one individual is as good as any other, that his opinions, or his likes and dislikes, are as valid as another's.[6] Such a notion is utterly destructive of morality and even of rationality. The problem of morality—the question of how men should live—becomes a matter of personal taste, from which it would follow that there is no more rationality in choosing to live like a Socrates than a de Sade. Rationality, hence truth itself, requires an aesthetic awareness of limits, moral as well as logical. In the absence of limits, the bare statement that each individual should have an equal voice in public affairs is palpably absurd. This absurdity is acknowledged by the fact that a person is required to reach a certain age before he is deemed qualified to participate in the *deliberative* or elective process called "voting,"

[6] See John Stuart Mill, *Representative Government* in *Utilitarianism, Liberty, and Representative Government* (New York: E. P. Dutton & Co., 1951), p. 388. The three essays contained in this collection will henceforth be cited individually.

an activity which presupposes some experience with different types of human character on the one hand, and some understanding of public issues on the other. Notice that the mere specification of an age requirement for voting confirms a principle of nature, that adults ought not be governed by children, a principle, we have seen, which bears the implication that the wise should not be ruled by the unwise. It can be argued, therefore, that the age requirement for voting is in tension with the notion that each individual has a right to an equal voice in public affairs, for it goes without saying that age is not absolutely determinative of the line to be drawn between maturity and immaturity. But from this it follows that the question of how men should live is not reducible to mere opinion or personal taste. Required is knowledge, which is not equally accessible to all and is not to be achieved without experience and the proper cultivation of the mind over a considerable period of time. All this applies with greater force to the different age qualifications for holding various public offices: think of the progressively increasing age requirements for being a Representative or a Senator or a President of the United States. These differences—related to the increasing complexity of each office—suggest that politics has or necessitates what may be termed a "wisdom principle," one which makes moral and intellectual distinctions among citizens and which thereby imposes some limits on what men may or may not do. The tendency of radical democracy is to level these distinctions, hence to break down the distinction between wisdom and unwisdom, between maturity and immaturity, between adulthood and adolescence. But this is to undermine all limits; it is to give men an unbounded liberty.

Liberty is indeed the first aim of democracy. It is to be noted, however, that Aristotle distinguishes between two forms of liberty. One form may be termed "political," and consists in ruling and being ruled in turn. This form of liberty, of course, is not peculiar to democracies alone. What distinguishes democratic liberty is that it is based on an egalitarian conception of justice. As Aristotle puts it: "The democratic conception of justice is the enjoyment of arithmetical equality, and not the enjoyment of proportionate equality on the basis of desert" (258). As a consequence, in the worst variety of democracy, where this conception of justice is most pronounced, all citizens, whether rich or poor, wise or unwise, may have an equal voice in public affairs. Or as modest men now teach, the egalitarian conception of justice requires dogmatic adherence to the principle of "one man, one vote." From this it follows that, in a democracy, especially of the radical type, the wise who are few will be ruled by the unwise who are many—and as a matter of principle as well as of policy.[7]

The other form of liberty prevalent in radical democracy may be called "personal" liberty. It consists in "living as you like," free from the restraints of government, law, or custom. This is an individualistic as well as an egalitarian conception of liberty. In democratic societies where this view of liberty prevails, the individual is virtually autonomous, a law unto himself. He need defer to no one, for his opinion as to how men should live, and, therefore, as to how *he* should live, is as valid as anyone else's. Why, indeed, should he defer to any established standards of personal conduct when, in the political domain, not qualitative, but quantitative criteria are decisive? Or if the vote of one person is to count neither more nor less than the vote of another on public matters affecting the way of life of an entire community, on what grounds, other than the force of mere numbers, should the individual feel constrained as to the manner in which he governs his personal life? Stated another way: If there are no rational and objective political truths regarding how men should live, then there are no theoretical limits as to how any individual should live. From this it would follow that politics, as an intellectual discipline, can be nothing more than a descriptive as opposed to a normative science. Neither the political scientist nor the statesman can provide the ordinary citizen any rational grounds for preferring one way of life over another. Indeed, it

[7] The rule of the unwise will more or less prevail in *all* actual regimes. But only radical democracy fosters a public teaching that "justifies" the rule of the unwise, since it implicitly denies the possibility of wisdom.

would be absurd for the ordinary citizen to defer to their judgment, since his likes and dislikes are as valid as theirs.

The denial of politics as preeminently the science of the best regime logically points to what Aristotle regards as the worst regime, insofar as the worst variety of democracy is a form of tyranny or its immediate precursor. As a form of tyranny, radical democracy involves two factors corresponding to its two-fold conception of liberty. On the one hand, its egalitarian conception of liberty—which is to say, its egalitarian conception of justice—eventuates in majoritarian tyranny, or what Madison called majority faction. On the other hand, and in tension with the preceding, its conception of liberty as "living as you like" or "doing as you please" eventuates in the tyranny of the individual. It is precisely for this reason that Aristotle denies that radical democracy is even a *regime* (169).[8] For a regime is nothing less than a commonly shared way of life governed by law; and by law Aristotle means not only written but moral law —habitual ways of doing things or well-established modes of conduct. Where, however, the individual is autonomous, a law unto himself, he ceases to be a citizen with duties and obligations. He becomes, instead, a consumer of "rights," and his "rights" multiply with his wants and appetites. Dignified by the term "rights," his wants and appetites become demands made against society. And since there are no public standards regarding what *is* right—not even a *common sense* as to what is *reasonable*—the most extravagant demands made by individuals against society may be taken seriously or may become objects of negotiation. This is what is meant by saying that the egalitarian conception of personal liberty culminates in the tyranny of the individual. Conceptually, however, this "justifies" tyranny pure and simple. For if it cannot be rationally and objectively determined as to who should rule, it does not only follow that *no one* should rule. Equally logical is the conclusion that *anyone may*

[8] I am now blurring the distinction between radical democracy—which may still be under the rule of law—and anarchy. See Aristotle's distinction between the fourth and "fifth" variety of democracy, *Politics*, p. 168.

rule. No longer may we speak of the *right* of the individual to do as he pleases: he may very well please to tyrannize over others. To be sure, this seems to contradict the notion of liberty. But this only means that liberty has become a paralogism, a self-contradiction; it only means that liberty has become irrational. This is the inevitable consequence of denying the power of human reason to discover objective political truths. For truth, as noted earlier, is a limit without which there can be no conceptual constraints, not even the constraints afforded by the law of contradiction. Without such limits the individual is thrust wholly upon himself, cast upon the sea of impulse and desire. In the process, society becomes a vast Bedlam and Bridewell.

Before insanity and criminality reign supreme, or before the tyranny of the one erases the political arithmetic of "one man, one vote," the individual enjoys considerable freedom. He is more or less able to gratify, with little delay, his appetites and desires. Indeed, quick and successful self-indulgence becomes a matter for praise—almost a virtue. Meanwhile, moderation becomes an object of scorn, a sign of cowardice. Moderation, of course, imposes limits on the individual's freedom to live as he likes, and he lives to enjoy his freedom. He does so, however, only to the extent that he is protected by law or lawfully constituted authority. Without these the individual is defenseless, a prey to the appetites of others. But the law imposes restraints upon him no less than upon others. It stands in irksome contradiction to the notion of liberty as "living as you like"; and in a radically permissive society, the individual has been indoctrinated from childhood to believe in, and to act upon, this notion of freedom. Accordingly, he will look upon the mildest of externally imposed restraints with impatience and with outright hostility. Any attempt by government to place some limits on his freedom to say and do as he pleases will be denounced as tyrannical (or as "authoritarian"). Even the rule of lawfully constituted majorities will appear to him as a form of tyranny. Such is the extent of his self-righteousness or self-serving conceit that he will seek to overturn any law or institution or moral code—indeed, all "establishments"—that hinder him from saying or doing whatever he pleases. Self-expression is the only law he will recognize. Any other would be condemned by this opinionated and nondeferential individual as placing him in a position of inequality or as engendering within him oppressive feelings of inferiority. Such individuals, animated against all privilege, preeminence, and authority, are ripe for the demagogue, who will know how to intensify and direct their negative passions, in particular, the passion of *ressentiment* (136). With their support, the demagogue will seek to maximize liberty and equality by leveling all legal and moral restraints on desires on the one hand, and all vestiges of inequality based on wealth and merit on the other. Laws will now be overturned with every breeze of popular passion; or they will be ignored, flaunted, unenforced. Political instability, along with ceaseless change in society at large, will nurture a profound insecurity in the private and solipsistic world of the individual. The lawless rule of men will replace the humane rule of law. No one will quite know who he is or where he is going. He will need someone to tell him. Someone will.

Such, then, is the life and death of radical democracy: unbounded liberty its beginning, tyranny its end. Now all men are indeed equal—equal as slaves.[9] That slavery commenced with the subordination of reason to the consuming passions, with the sacrifice of the intellect to a welter of desires. Among these desires there exists no rational order. All being equal in principle, each desire makes imperious claims, none deferring to another, until some passion arises to lord it over the rest. Radical democracy thus witnesses a curious inversion of nature. It is natural enough to resist, inwardly or outwardly, externally imposed authority. We thereby testify to the principle of life as self-directed activity. But self-directed activity presupposes a *self*—an organized unity, not a random multiplicity. It is the case, however, that we begin life and pass through childhood as creatures governed primarily by bodily desires. Unless these desires of youth

[9] See Plato, *Republic* 557e–564a.

are moderated or endowed with some kind of order, the powers of the critical intellect are not likely to reach maturity. Imagine an undisciplined youth come of age in a radical democracy. There he will learn from various educators that the question of how men should live is a matter of opinion and not of knowledge, that on this question, each individual is, in effect, the source of truth. The quest of the philosopher having thus been denied, each individual becomes a "philosopher" or may freely express and pursue his own "philosophy" of life. Each may claim an equal voice in public affairs. But now each voice is not the voice of reason, but of one or another passion. We have been taught, however, that all passions are equal, that there is no hierarchical order among them. If so, how can we become *self*-directed individuals? The self will have been fragmented. We shall have become not self-directed individuals so much as *random* individuals. The random individual is governed by the random impulses of passion or by the random stimuli of public fads, fancies, and opinions. In the midst of all this randomness, life, understood as self-directed activity, is more apt to become other-directed activity. For the only self-directed activity is activity consistent with knowledge. Stated another way: Freedom is action consistent with insight. To be genuinely free requires the due subordination of passion to reason. But in radical democracy, reason is but the slave of the passions, and, eventually, of whatever passion dominates the emergent tyrant. Thus, what began as a quest for freedom or self-directed activity ends in utter servitude. Life is reduced to matter.[10]

3

Bearing in mind the major characteristics of radical democracy, compare the regime established by the founding fathers. Surely the two are very different things. Nevertheless, one of the most serious students of *The Federalist*, again, Martin Diamond,

[10] The dichotomy of reason and passion emphasized in the preceding discussion is taken from a classical perspective, rather than from the perspective of the synthesis adumbrated in Chapter VII.

characterizes the government described therein as "profoundly democratic," or as designed for a profoundly democratic society.[11] To be sure, Diamond would admit that this society, unlike that of radical democracy, was to be governed by the rule of law. Furthermore, he would admit that the regime envisioned by the founders is a "decent" one, or one that was designed to remedy the worst vices of democracy.[12] These vices are peculiar to the principle of popular government, namely, that all political authority resides in the people rather than in any privileged class. The inherent consequence of this principle is that political power falls into the hands of the many who are apt to be as tyrannical as the few. The founders, particularly James Madison, regarded that principle as posing the fundamental problem of statesmanship, a problem never solved hitherto. Madison attempted to solve this problem while remaining "perfectly faithful to the *principle* of popular government" itself.[13] This said, Diamond's interpretation of Madison's solution may now be examined.

To solve the problem of popular government the statesman must design a system that can prevent the many from becoming a majority faction, a majority united and activated by some common impulse of passions or of interest dangerous to the rights of the few. The Madisonian solution requires the fragmentation of economic power on the one hand, and of political power on the other. The former necessitates the development of a large commercial society: call this the "material" or socioeconomic aspect of the Madisonian solution. The latter requires, among other things, the extended application of the representative principle: call this the "formal" or institutional aspect of the Madisonian solution. Reserving the latter for treatment in the next chapter, here is how Diamond describes the socioeconomic aspect of Madison's solution to the problem of majority faction: "In a large

[11] *Diamond*, p. 66. Diamond does not alter this opinion in the first edition of Diamond, Fisk, and Garfinkel, *The Democratic Republic* (Chicago: Rand McNally & Co., 1966), p. 79, nor in the 1970 revised edition, p. 96.

[12] *Ibid.*, 2nd ed., p. 100, n. 23.

[13] *Diamond*, p. 54.

commercial society the interest of the many can be fragmented into many narrower, more limited interests. The mass will not unite as a mass to make extreme demands upon the few, the struggle over which will destroy society; the mass will fragment into relatively small groups, seeking small immediate advantages for their narrow and particular interests" (66). At this point the following question arises: What kind of regime is required for the successful operation of the Madisonian solution? That is, what kind of regime or country would encourage all citizens to engage in the pursuit of "narrow," "limited," and "immediate" interests? Says Diamond:

> First, the country in which this is to take place will have to be profoundly democratic. That is, all men must be free—and even encouraged—to seek their immediate profit and to associate with others in the process. There must be no rigid class barriers which bar men from the pursuit of immediate interest. Indeed, it is especially the lowly, from whom the most is to be feared, who must feel most sanguine about the prospects of achieving limited and immediate benefits. Second, the gains must be real; that is, the fragmented interests must from time to time achieve real gains, else the scheme would cease to beguile or mollify. But I do not want to develop these themes here. Rather, I want to emphasize only one crucial aspect of Madison's design: that is, the question of the apparently *narrow ends of society* envisaged by the Founding Fathers. Madison's plan, as I have described it, most assuredly does not rest on the "moral and religious motives" whose efficacy he deprecated. Indeed there is not even the suggestion that the pursuit of interest should be an especially enlightened pursuit. Rather, the problem posed by the dangerous passions and interests of the many is solved primarily by a reliance upon passion and interest themselves.[14]

If this interpretation is substantially correct, then one of two conclusions follow: Either the founding fathers regarded the

[14] *Ibid.*, p. 66 (italics added). Notice that Diamond here refers to the narrow ends of *society*, whereas in the first passage cited on p. 80 he refers to the narrow ends of *government*, thus obscuring the differences which these two "realms" signified for the founders (and for moderns in general). Of this, more later.

American people with contempt, or the ends which they encouraged the American people to pursue are contemptible. I shall show that neither conclusion is warranted by a more systematic study of the evidence.[15]

The radical democracy described earlier was well understood by the classically educated members of the Federal Convention. The licentiousness and leveling propensities of democracy, its libertarian and egalitarian excesses, were precisely what the founders sought to prevent. Their task, it is true, was not to pre-

[15] Diamond admits the necessity of a more "systematic study" near the outset of his essay, where he says: "For the reflections on the Fathers which follow, I employ chiefly *The Federalist* as the clue to the political theory upon which rested the founding of the American Republic. That this would be inadequate for a systematic study of the Founding Fathers goes without saying" (*Diamond*, p. 53). It must be assumed, however, in view of the gravity of the issue, that Diamond made such a study prior to the publication of his essay. In this connection it should be noted that Diamond attempts to support his evaluation of the Madisonian solution by certain references to Tocqueville's *Democracy in America*. Of course, Tocqueville was projecting into the future various sociological signs or symptoms evident to him some fifty years *after* the founding. But here is one of Diamond's references to Tocqueville (p. 67): "The Madisonian solution involved a fundamental reliance on ceaseless striving after immediate interest (perhaps now immediate gratification). Tocqueville appreciated that this 'permanent agitation . . . is characteristic of a peaceful democracy. . . . In the midst of this universal tumult, this incessant conflict of jarring interests, this continual striving of men after fortune, where is that calm to be found which is necessary for the deeper combinations of the intellect?' " Note that Diamond is projecting or imposing upon the Madisonian solution what seems to be characteristic of twentieth-century American society. On the other hand, the low level of ends which he attributes to the founders appears to be descriptive not of American society as a whole, so much as of that part of society comprising the poor, or in Diamond's own terms, "the lowly, from whom the most is to be feared." For the pursuit of immediate gratification describes what Edward Banfield calls "present-oriented" people, under which category he includes the "working class," but more emphatically, the "lower class" whose members have no steady employment. Of the typical lower-class person, Banfield says: "Impulse governs his behavior, either because he cannot discipline himself to sacrifice a present for a future satisfaction or because he has no sense of a future." See his *The Unheavenly City* (Boston: Little, Brown & Co., 1970), p. 53. It goes without saying, however, that American society is predominantly middle class, as it was in the late eighteenth century. Whether the middle class of today, which Banfield regards as "future-oriented," is as provident as was the middle class of former times need not now concern us.

vent the rule of the majority, so much as to prevent the majority from oppressing the few. Accordingly, it was not the aim of the Constitution to maximize liberty. Liberty must be balanced by stability, which in turn requires an energetic or powerful government. The problem is formulated by Madison in *Federalist* 37:

> Among the difficulties encountered by the convention, a very important one must have lain in combining the requisite stability and energy in government, with the inviolable attention due to liberty and to the republican form. . . . Energy in government is essential to that security against external and internal danger, and to that prompt and salutary execution of the laws which enter into the very definition of good government. Stability in government is essential to national character and to the advantages annexed to it, as well as to that repose and confidence in the minds of the people, which are among the chief blessings of civil society. An irregular and mutable legislation is not more an evil in itself than it is odious to the people. . . . On comparing, however, these valuable ingredients [of stability and energy] with the vital principles of liberty, we must perceive at once the difficulty of mingling them together in their due proportions (226–227).

That difficulty was not resolved by giving liberty a "preferred position" in the Constitution such that it would take precedence over competing values regardless of circumstances. As Madison writes in *Federalist* 53, "liberty . . . lies within extremes, which afford sufficient latitude for all the variations which may be required by the various situations and circumstances of civil society" (347).[16] So far were the founders from giving liberty a "preferred position" in the Constitution that it was placed *last* among the ends of government enumerated in the Preamble. Furthermore, in *Federalist* 51 Madison boldly proclaims: "In framing a government which is to be administered by men over men, the great difficulty lies in this: you must *first* enable the

---

[16] The context involves the duration of the tenure of the House of Representatives. Note, also, that Madison speaks of "rational liberty" (*Federalist* 53, p. 348).

government to control the governed . . ."(337).[17] To accomplish this objective a powerful government is necessary, one capable of enacting and enforcing a stable body of laws. But there is no more effective way of attaining that objective than by cultivating among the people a reverence for law itself. Mutable legislation is to be avoided because it undermines "that veneration which time bestows on everything, and without which perhaps the wisest and freest governments would not possess the requisite stability."[18]

Similarly, it was not the aim of the Constitution to maximize equality. Among the ends enumerated in the Preamble, equality is conspicuous by its absence. To maximize equality is to level all moral and intellectual standards or distinctions among men, and to produce thereby a stultifying uniformity, itself destructive of liberty. According to *Federalist* 10, however, "the first object of government" is the protection of the "diversity in the faculties of man, from which the rights of property originate" (55).[19] Of paramount importance here is the term "faculties." From the diverse and unequal faculties of men results the diverse and unequal distribution of property. This distribution of property is *right* insofar as it conforms to the principle of distributive justice which prescribes to each according to his merit. And one person is superior to another in merit precisely because the faculties of his mind—such as "judgment, desire, volition, memory, [and] imagination"—are superior.[20] This is not meant to deny the importance of the principle of equality underlying the Constitution and exemplified in the popular election of the House of Representatives. But that principle is to be construed to mean, primarily, *equality of opportunity* on the one hand, and the exclusion of hereditary ranks or privileges on the other.[21] In this

[17] Italics added. Madison goes on to say: "and in the next place oblige it to control itself. A dependence on the people is, no doubt, the primary control on the government. . . ."

[18] *Federalist* 49, pp. 328–329, and see *Federalist* 62, p. 407.

[19] See Aristotle, *Politics*, pp. 63, 298, 302.

[20] These faculties are enumerated in *Federalist* 37, p. 228.

[21] See *The Federalist*, pp. 81, 243, 412–413, 466, 479, and Madison, VI, 112

connection, consider the following passage from *Federalist* 36, in which Hamilton writes: "There are strong minds in every walk of life that will rise superior to the disadvantages of situation, and will command the tribute due to their merit, not only from the classes to which they particularly belong, but from the society in general. The door ought to be equally open to all . . ." (217).[22]

To the principle of arithmetical equality is thus opposed the principle of proportionate equality, which is itself related to the unequal faculties among men. Leaving aside, however, the primacy of the faculties, that *Federalist* 10 should also emphasize property when speaking of the first object of government is of fundamental importance. Oddly enough, some commentators seem to think that this emphasis on property supports a democratic interpretation of the Constitution.[23] In truth it is neutral if not opposed to such an interpretation.

In his *de Officiis*, Cicero writes: "The man in an administrative office . . . must make it his first care that everyone shall have what belongs to him and that private citizens suffer no invasion of their property rights by act of the state."[24] In his *Rhetoric*, Aristotle defines "justice" as "the virtue through which everybody enjoys his own possessions in accordance with the law."[25] This is not the last word of Aristotle on the meaning of justice (if only because it appears in the *Rhetoric*). But, as Cicero suggests, it is the proper beginning for the statesman. Still, why is the protection of property so important a function of government?

The most obvious answer is this: If widespread insecurity of property exists, government, whatever its form, will lose the support necessary for its continued existence, and for many good reasons. In the first place, it goes without saying that property, in one form or another, is a necessary means for sustaining life.

ff. The topic of equality of opportunity will be treated in Chapter IX.

[22] Note well the sequel.

[23] See *Diamond*, p. 62.

[24] Cicero, *de Officiis*, Bk. II, 73.

[25] *Aristotle's Rhetoric and Poetics* (New York: Modern Library, 1954), W. R. Roberts, trans., 1366b8–10.

Second, property is an important element of political power. Third, and as Aristotle points out, property is necessary for the cultivation of certain virtues, such as liberality (50). Or as James Wilson, a prominent member of the Federal Convention, has written: "On property some of the virtues depend for their more free and enlarged exercise. Would the same room be left for the benign indulgence of generosity and beneficence—would the same room be left for the becoming returns of esteem and gratitude . . . ?"[26] Fourth, property facilitates self-sufficiency or the enjoyment of leisure, hence the cultivation of human excellence. All these reasons are well enough understood. But there are other and more subtle reasons why the protection of property is of fundamental political importance.

Justice obviously requires that men enjoy the fruits of honest labor. As already indicated, however, justice is also a virtue, a habitude or disposition which energizes men to act justly toward each other, rendering to each his due. By securing each person in his property, government cannot but foster the virtue of justice, and, with this, a more perfect union. For a more perfect union requires mutual trust and confidence, civic peace or domestic tranquility, all of which would be lacking were justice lacking in the relations between men. Nor can there be civic peace where justice means nothing more than arithmetical equality. So long as men are unequal in their faculties, that is, in their intellectual and moral endowments, civic strife will prevail unless arithmetical equality is supplemented by proportionate equality, which again requires that each receive his due or be rewarded on the basis of merit. Of course, there are different things involved in giving to each his due. There is property, but there is also honor or deference. Yet the two are subtly related.

From the early years of childhood onward, the possession and the giving and receiving of property teaches us some of the first lessons in justice. According to Hamilton, the rights of property

[26] *The Works of James Wilson*, Robert G. McCloskey, ed. (2 vols.; Cambridge: Harvard University Press, 1967), II, 719 hereafter cited as *Works of James Wilson*.

cannot be severed from *the rules of morality and justice* which underlie those rights. Through these rules—rules involving good faith, fulfillment of promises and contracts—men are schooled in some of the most distinct ideas of right and wrong, of justice and injustice, of honor and dishonor.[27] Consistent therewith, the Constitution prohibits the states from enacting any "law impairing the obligation of contracts." This legal protection of property promotes the virtue of justice and secures men's honor. Nor is this all.

The protection of property is indispensable for the construction and preservation of a 'polity.' Recall Aristotle's remark that in a 'polity' "the rich are regarded by common opinion as holding the position of gentlemen" (176). Or as Madison says in *Federalist* 54: "If the law allows an opulent citizen but a single vote in the choice of his representative, the respect and consequence which he derives from his fortunate situation very frequently guide the votes of others to the objects of his choice; and through this imperceptible channel the rights of property are conveyed into the public representation" (357).[28] Unless common opinion has been debased by a corrosive cynicism, the average man will tend to defer to men of wealth on the not unreasonable supposition that wealth is an accompaniment of certain intellectual and moral qualities, or that it affords its possessors the means of acquiring the education and variety of experience necessary for public office. It should be understood, however, that by protecting the faculties from which the rights of property originate, government secures not only the interests of the rich, but of the learned as well. It is not the poor, and not even the middle class, who are the great patrons of the liberal arts. Uncorrupted, the average man will admire intellectual excellence; but do not expect him to contribute to its support.

[27] See my *Philosophy of the American Constitution*, p. 126.

[28] Compare *Federalist* 60, p. 394, and *Federalist* 45, p. 301. Although these words are uttered by Madison's imaginary slaveholder, there can be no doubt that Madison himself held the position in question. See Madison, *Writings*, II, 172.

True, he will defer not to wealth, so much as to the intellect; but if he cultivates the latter, it will be for the sake of the former. Thus, if property has no secure status, neither, in the long run, will any intellectual and moral distinctions among men. In a non-deferential society, statesmanship is a mere pretention, government an object of ridicule.

Perhaps because we live in an age whose mentality has been shaped by Marxian modes of thought, the theme of deference, which runs throughout *The Federalist*, has largely been over-looked by students of the founding. Yet the entire work pre-supposes that it was addressed to a deferential audience, one amenable to reasoned argument. Every statement referring to the kinds of men likely to be appointed to the various branches of government implies this theme of deference and clearly suggests a deferential people with virtue and modesty enough to recog-nize and honor their "betters." "Who are to be the objects of popular choice?"—asks Madison in *Federalist* 57, and he an-swers: "'Every citizen whose merit may recommend him to the esteem and confidence of his country" (371).[29] And in *Federalist* 35 Hamilton writes:

> Mechanics and manufacturers will always be inclined, with few exceptions, to give their votes to merchants, in preference to per-sons of their own professions or trades. . . . They are sensible that their habits in life have not been such as to give them those acquired endowments, without which, in a deliberative assem-bly, the greatest natural abilities are for the most part useless.
> . . .
> With regard to the learned professions, little need be ob-served; they truly form no distinct interest in society, and ac-cording to their situation and talents, will be indiscriminately the objects of the confidence and choice of each other, and of other parts of the community (213–214).[30]

[29] See references to *Federalist* 10, 64, and 69 cited above, pp. 53–54, for further evidence bearing on the theme of deference.

[30] To be sure, the Constitution prohibits titles of nobility, and it does not exhort the people, as did some of the state constitutions, to choose for their rulers men of wisdom and virtue. But again, no claim is being made here that

If mechanics in New York were deferential, no less so were farmers in Virginia. During the debates over the ratification of the Constitution, Madison informed Jefferson (then in Paris) about the state of public opinion in Virginia and in other parts of the Union:

> It is worthy of remark that whilst in Virginia and some of the other States in the middle and Southern Districts of the Union, the men of intelligence, patriotism, property, and independent circumstances, are thus divided [over ratification], all this description, with a few exceptions, in the Eastern States, and most of the Middle States, are zealously attached to the proposed Constitution. In New England, the men of letters, the principal officers of Government, the Judges and lawyers, the Clergy, and men of property, furnish only here and there an adversary. It is not less worthy of remark that in Virginia where *the mass of the people have been so much accustomed to be guided by their rulers on all new and intricate questions*, they should on the present which certainly surpasses the judgment of the greater part of them, not only go before, but contrary to their most popular leaders. And the phenomenon is the more wonderful, as a popular ground is taken by all the adversaries to the new Constitution [such as Patrick Henry].[31]

Not that Madison expected such deference to persist indefinitely into the future. Apart from other considerations, did he not say that "Enlightened statesmen will not always be at the helm"? For this very reason it was of the first importance to provide something more certain and enduring than deference for men, namely, reverence for law. The reasonable prejudice that inclines the average man to associate wealth with merit must be reinforced by the yet more reasonable prejudice that a body

the government established under the Constitution is, or was intended to be, an "aristocracy." What needs to be emphasized, however, is the relationship between property and deference as well as the reasons why the protection of the former is indispensable to the latter, especially if a regime is to be and remain a 'polity.'

[31] *Writings*, V, 66 (italics added). Of course, it was well known that General Washington supported the Constitution.

of fundamental laws which has long governed a nation must be wise in theory and salutary in practice. Should this be done, the average man will revere that body of laws and, at the same time, its founders. Only by this two-fold reverence can *any* regime endure, including the very best.

It may be argued, however, that the reverence for law promoted by the founders is nothing more than the necessary precondition for the peaceful but otherwise ceaseless and universal pursuit of immediate economic interests; that the government itself would have no higher or nobler ends in view; indeed, that it *need* have no higher or nobler ends in view, since it was designed for a "profoundly democratic" society in which such ends are not pursued. This, in effect, is the argument urged by Diamond. He writes:

> What is striking [about *The Federalist*] is the apparent exclusion from the functions of government of a wide range of non-economic tasks traditionally considered the decisive business of government. It is tempting to speculate that this reduction in the tasks of government has something to do with *The Federalist*'s defense of popular government. The traditional criticism of popular government was that it gave over the art of government into the hands of the many, which is to say the unwise. It would be a formidable reply to reduce the complexity of the governmental art to dimensions more commensurate with the capacity of the many (63).

In support of this "speculation," Diamond cites "two statements by Madison, years apart, to illustrate the possibility that he may have had something like [the preceding] in mind." These two statements are cited as follows: " 'There can be no doubt that there are subjects to which the capacities of the bulk of mankind are unequal.' But on the other hand, 'the confidence of the [Republican party] in the capacity of mankind for self-government' is what distinguished it from the Federalist party which distrusted that capacity" (63–64). From these two statements Diamond draws this remarkable conclusion: "The confidence [*sic*] in mankind's capacities would seem to require having removed from government the subjects to which those capacities are unequal."[32]

Now, it should be noted at the very outset that the first of the two statements just cited was made by Madison in a letter to Edmund Randolph written during the debates over the *ratification of the Constitution*. Here is the passage from which it is abstracted: "Whatever respect may be due to the rights of private judgment, and no man feels more of it than I do, there can be no doubt that there are subjects to which the capacities of the bulk of mankind are unequal, and on which they must and will be governed by those with whom they happen to have acquaintance and confidence. The proposed Constitution is of this description."[33] Clearly, Madison is simply saying, what almost no one would deny, that most men are intellectually unequal to the task of deliberating wisely on so profound and so complex a matter as the *founding* of a new form of government. (Surely many university educated men today would have modesty enough to admit this of themselves.) But while most people lack the political wisdom required for the founding of a regime, they may well have the good sense and moderation to recognize and defer to men who do possess such wisdom. The capacity of a people for self-government requires nothing more than this good sense and moderation.[34]

As for the second of the two statements in question, let us assume the truth of Madison's contention that what distinguished

[32] *Diamond*, p. 64. Presumably Diamond means "The [lack of] confidence in mankind's capacities. . . ."

[33] *Writings*, V, 81. The sequel of this passage, which bears more directly on the problem of founding regimes, will be considered.

[34] Notice that the passage from Madison's letter to Randolph is perfectly consistent with his letter to Jefferson (cited earlier), where he speaks of the deferential character of the people of Virginia. Those people may not have had the intellectual capacity to deliberate wisely on so fundamental a problem as the establishment of a new Constitution. Nor might they have been good enough to be governed solely by "moral and religious motives" had they engaged in such deliberations. Nevertheless, in Madison's opinion, they seem to have possessed enough moderation or modesty to have deferred to the superior wisdom of others. Indeed, they apparently possessed enough good sense to have rejected popular leaders who opposed the Constitution on popular grounds!

Federalists from Republicans is that the former did not possess the latter's confidence in the capacity of mankind for self-government. If so, then, arguing from Diamond's own grounds, the Federalists would have gone further than Republicans in "remov[ing] from government the subjects to which those capacities are unequal." That is to say, the Federalists would have reduced the tasks or lowered the ends of government to a level below that desired by the Republicans. From this it would have to be concluded—on the basis of Diamond's method of exegesis—that a constitution designed wholly by Federalists would have been more democratic than one designed wholly by Republicans![35]

Whatever the case, recall the subjects or "noneconomic" ends which Diamond claims the founders removed from the concerns of government, namely, "the nurturing of a particular religion, education, military courage, civic-spiritedness, moderation, individual excellence in the virtues, etc." No argument is required to show, however, that if this entire catalog of "noneconomic" ends were excluded from the concerns of government the consequence would be sheer anarchy! Indeed, the annihilation of the entire body of criminal and civil law, so intimately related to morality, would have to have been contemplated by the founders if Diamond's interpretation of their *intentions* is correct—an interpretation that renders the Constitution an absurdity or a self-contradiction. That Constitution, to repeat, preserved the constitutions of the several states. Most of those constitutions made provision for the fostering of religion (in some, a particular religion), as well as for education and the cultivation of such virtues as moderation and civic-mindedness.[36] This is more than

[35] See above, pp. 75–76, and below, pp. 254–255.

[36] Again, see my *Philosophy of the American Constitution*, Appendix 2. If it be argued that the founders looked toward the separation of church and state—which is true enough—it does not necessarily follow that the consequences of separation would remove from government the other subjects of which Diamond speaks. It should be borne in mind that the criminal and civil law is based very much on the Christian tradition. Also to be borne in mind—and this cannot be said too often—is the error of superimposing upon the original Constitution the

can be said of many of the contemporaneous monarchic and "aristocratic" governments of Europe and England! In those days, both here and abroad, education was under the control of the clergy and was generally regarded as a private matter removed from the functions of government.[37] Nevertheless, during the debates of the Federal Convention, Madison proposed to invest Congress explicitly with the power to establish a national university, a proposal that was almost adopted, and probably would have been had not some delegates felt that Congress possessed that power by implication.[38] Furthermore, while the convention was sitting, the Continental Congress, proceeding on with its regular business, unanimously passed the *Northwest Ordinance*, the third article of which declared that: "Religion, Morality *and knowledge being necessary to good government and the happiness of mankind,* Schools and means of education shall forever be encouraged."[39] Hence it is not surprising that Washington, in his first state of the union message, proposed the establishment of a national university, as did Madison when he became President. (Of this, more under the teleological mode of regime analysis.)

Still, some may speculate that because the Constitution did not make explicit provision for the cultivation of human excellence, the virtues fostered by the state constitutions would sooner or later give way to a ceaseless and universal pursuit of narrow, limited, and immediate interests, so that American society would be held together merely by some sort of self-

subsequent developments in the United States. As noted earlier, those developments must be considered under the mode of efficient causality.

[37] See Ellwood P. Cubberley, *Public Education in the United States* (Boston: Houghton Mifflin Co., 1934), p. 85.

[38] See my *Philosophy of the American Constitution*, p. 27.

[39] *Journals of the Continental Congress 1774–1789* (New York: Johnson Reprint Corp., 1968), XXXII, 340 (italicizing in the original). It is to be noted that only eight states were represented at the time, and that only Yates of New York voted in the negative, although the state itself was carried. It should also be noted that the Northwest Ordinance of 1787 remained in force *after* the Constitution was ratified, and that the establishment clause of the First Amendment did not affect the article cited above.

regulating system of countervailing passions. Supposing this to be true, the serious student may wonder how the founders thought of themselves, or of their act of founding, in relation to future generations of Americans who would live under that system, for most assuredly they did not regard the motives of such a system as descriptive of their own. Here is how Diamond speculates upon this question:

> There is . . . in *The Federalist* a profound distinction made between the qualities necessary for Founders and the qualities necessary for the men who come after. It is a distinction that bears on the question of the Founding Fathers' view of what is required for the good life and on their defense of popular government. Founding . . . requires that "reason" and not the "passions," "sit in judgment." But . . . the society once founded will subsequently depend precisely upon the passions, only moderated in their consequences by having been guided into proper channels. The reason of the Founders constructs the system within which the passions of the men who come after may be relied upon (67).

Examine, however, the context out of which the words quoted in the above passage were extracted.

The context is *Federalist* 49. The argument is explicitly directed against a proposal advanced by Jefferson in his "Notes on the State of Virginia." That proposal would have required that constitutional disputes among the various branches of government be referred to and resolved by popular conventions. *Publius* rejects this proposal on the basis of two subtly related arguments. The first argument is this. Referring constitutional disputes to popular conventions would result in frequent alterations in the fundamental law and thus "deprive the government of that veneration which time bestows on every thing, and without which perhaps the wisest and freest governments would not possess the requisite stability." Note well *Publius*'s explanation:

> If it be true that all governments rest on opinion, it is no less true that the strength of opinion in each individual, and its practical influence on his conduct, depend much on the number

which he supposes to have entertained the same opinion. The reason of man, like man himself, is timid and cautious when left alone, and acquires firmness and confidence in proportion to the number with which it is associated. When the examples which fortify opinion are *ancient* as well as *numerous*, they are known to have a double effect. In a nation of philosophers, this consideration ought to be disregarded. A reverence for the laws would be sufficiently inculcated by the voice of an enlightened reason. But a nation of philosophers is as little to be expected as the philosophical race of kings wished for by Plato. And in every other nation, the most rational government will not find it a superfluous advantage to have the prejudices of the community on its side (329).[40]

The second argument against referring constitutional disputes to popular conventions is this. Such disputes inevitably involve the very fundamental principles of government; they affect the vital interests of the community; they intensify class and party divisions; they become opportunities for vaunting ambition.

The *passions*, therefore, not the *reason*, of the public would sit in judgment. But it is the reason, alone, of the public, that ought to control and regulate the government. The passions ought to be controlled and regulated by the government (331).

The first sentence contains the words cited by Diamond in the passage referred to earlier. The second sentence reveals that *reason* is essential not only for the founding of a regime, but for its subsequent existence. The third sentence reveals that government, insofar as it *controls* and *regulates* the passions, is the truly rational agency of the whole. Yet, this must be qualified, for reason alone is not sufficient for the government of men. Reason will not be effective without reverence for law. Therein is to be understood why *Publius* felt that the most "rational government" requires veneration of the laws, and why neither reason nor reverence would be forthcoming if the Constitution were subject to frequent change.

[40] See Aristotle, *Politics*, p. 73, and Edmund Burke, *Reflections on the Revolution in France* (Indianapolis: Bobbs-Merrill Co., 1955), p. 99.

85

"A reverence for the laws would be sufficiently inculcated by the voice of an enlightened reason"—the reason of the philosopher. It goes without saying, however, that the average man is not a philosopher; he is not governed by "enlightened reason." The philosopher would revere the laws insofar as they were consistent with reason. The average man reveres the laws because they are old and revered by the rest of the community. Now, if the laws are frequently changed, they cannot become old and venerable; and the general run of men will not respect laws made yesterday and which they are free to change today. This applies *a fortiori* to the Constitution. Frequent disputes about the Constitution necessarily encourage divergent and conflicting opinions about its principles and purposes, shattering the community consensus about this fundamental and paramount law. The average man will not respect a Constitution about which there is a welter of conflicting interpretations. Reverence for the Constitution is based on general agreement about its meaning; but such agreement requires a stable body of opinion about the Constitution which is not disturbed too often. Only if there prevails that salutary prejudice of the average man, who reveres things because they are old and revered by the community—who identifies the good with what is ancient, and the true with what is commonly believed—only then can "rational government" exist or be effective. *Publius* understood Plato well enough.

Reverence, of course, is not characteristic of libertarian and egalitarian democracy, nor is reason. Yet reason is one of the most prominent themes of *The Federalist*. Despite its emphasis on passions and interests—which so preoccupies commentators —*The Federalist* itself affirms that reason is the highest principle of political life. At the very outset of *The Federalist*, Hamilton declares: "It has been frequently remarked that it seems to have been reserved to the people of this country, by their conduct and example, to decide the important question, whether societies of men are really capable or not of establishing good government from *reflection and choice*, or whether they are forever

86

destined to depend for their political constitutions on accident and force" (3) (italics added). As already noted, however, Hamilton was well aware that the proposed Constitution "affects too many particular interests, innovates upon too many local institutions, not to involve in its discussion a variety of objects foreign to its merits, and of views, passions and prejudices little favorable to the discovery of truth."[41] But the quest for truth, or the rational discussion of public issues, was not to cease with the adoption of the Constitution. Madison expects representatives, or many of them, to educate public opinion. This they could hardly do unless their constituents were moderate people amenable to reason. But whether they will be amenable to reason depends very much on the stability of government and the consistency and continuity of its laws. In view of its size and tenure, the House of Representatives was not organized with these ends in view. Hence the need for a Senate so designed as to enable it to deliberate, as Madison has written, "with more coolness, with more system, and with more wisdom."[42] That Senate, according to *Federalist* 63, is to represent the "cool and deliberate sense of the community." It is to uphold the authority of "reason, justice, and truth" (409–410).[43] To say, therefore, that *The Federalist* conveys the teaching that reason is necessary only for the founding of a regime, but not for its subsequent existence, is simply false.

It is certainly true, however, that there is "in *The Federalist* a profound distinction made between the qualities necessary for Founders and the qualities necessary for the men who come after." But I know of no political philosopher who would not

[41] *Federalist* 1, pp. 3–4ff. Compare *Federalist* 31, pp. 188–189.

[42] Farrand, I, 151.

[43] If we were to superimpose upon these ends the political philosophy of Locke mediated by Diamond's understanding of Aristotle, we might then translate "reason" to mean "calculation"; "justice" to mean primarily the "protection of economic interests"; and "truth" to mean the "correct calculation of means by which to gratify those interests." But reason, justice, and truth do not require us to succumb to the almost universal practice of reading Locke into the Constitution.

say the same of founders in general. As Montesquieu has written: "At the birth of societies, the rulers of republics establish institutions; and afterwards the institutions mould the rulers."[44] When Madison says that "Enlightened statesmen will not always be at the helm," he is merely uttering a truism. But from this it does not follow that the founders thought "they had created a system of institutions and an arrangement of the passions and interests, that would be durable and self-perpetuating . . . [and that afterwards] men of their own kind . . . would not be needed."[45] To the contrary, one of the very purposes of the national university proposed by Washington and Madison was to train future statesmen. Nor was there anything novel in this; for in those days the training of statesmen was one of the two principal purposes of the various colleges and universities in the United States.[46]

That Madison did not have a very high opinion of the bulk of mankind only prompted him to urge and to undertake, in his own way, their enlightenment. But there is nothing exceptional in his opinion of mankind so long as a distinction is maintained between the intellectual capacities required for deliberating on the institutions and policies necessary for good government and those required for deliberating on the qualities required for good rulers.[47] Although no absolute distinction is in order, experience nevertheless reveals that most men are better judges of the latter than of the former. The reason is simple enough. The ordinary man may know little of the complexities of politics, which requires considerable education and experience in public affairs; but he learns much about human character from his various dealings with men in every day life. Nor should we think it especially demeaning to mankind in general when Madison cautions against relying on moral and religious motives as an adequate safeguard against majority faction. This is little more

[44] *Considerations sur les Causes de la Grandeur des Romains et de leur Decadence* (Paris, 1899), p. 4 (my translation).

[45] *Diamond*, p. 68.

[46] The other purpose was training for the ministry.

[47] But see Aristotle, *Politics*, pp. 125–126.

than a warning against a naive trust in the goodness of human nature. Thus, in *Federalist* 55, Madison writes: "As there is a degree of depravity in mankind which requires a certain degree of circumspection and distrust, so there are other qualities in human nature which justify a certain portion of esteem and confidence. Republican government presupposes the existence of these qualities in a higher degree than any other form" (365).[48] Finally, in the Virginia ratifying convention, Madison said: "I go on this great republican principle, that the people will have virtue and intelligence to select men of virtue and wisdom. Is there no virtue among us? If there be not, we are in a wretched situation. No theoretical checks—no form of government can render us secure. To suppose that any form of government will secure liberty or happiness without any virtue in the people, is a chimerical idea."[49]

Despite these estimations of the character of the American people, students of the original Constitution, especially those who claim it is inclined toward oligarchy, attempt to bolster their position by emphasizing other statements of the founders, statements referring to the "follies" and "licentiousness" of the people or to the "turbulence" of democracies in general. Are we to conclude from such statements that the American people, by and large, were indeed foolish and wicked, or rather, that the founders really believed they were? If so, then the many passages previously cited from *The Federalist* and other sources, which portray the American people as sensible and modest enough to recognize their "betters" and to honor them with office, are not merely deceptive, but absurd. I think they are neither. Again it must be remembered that *The Federalist*, though remarkable for its degree of candor, is not as candid as the debates of the Federal Convention in which the more disparaging remarks in question will be found.[50] Even in *The Fed-*

[48] Compare Madison, *Writings*, II, 366–369.

[49] *Ibid.*, V, 223. The entire paragraph from which this is taken conforms to the passage in *Federalist* 55 quoted above.

[50] See *Farrand*, I, 26–27, 215, 218.

eralist, however, there is an abundance of passages emphasizing the dangers of popular passions and fluctuations and to the sullied history of popular governments in general. Yet these very deprecations may themselves constitute the best testimony of the founders' *good* opinion of the American people! For to no other than a deferential people could they speak with such candor and with the apparent confidence that such candor would be efficacious. Hence, so far as concerns those disparaging remarks, it is reasonable to believe they are the result of deliberate exaggeration.

The same may be said of references to the state governments as "hotbeds" of democracy. Some students may be content with a literal interpretation.[51] Another one is possible, however. Thus, let us assume that the founders were prudent statesmen; that many were skilled in the art of rhetoric; and that one in particular, namely, James Madison, had learned well the canons of this art which he studied so assiduously at the College of New Jersey (now Princeton) under president John Witherspoon, a classical scholar, and the only clergyman to sign the Declaration of Independence.[52] This assumed, consider the statesman's problem or objective. Stated very simply (and therefore inadequately), it was to establish a form of government that would guard against the danger of majority faction. Symptoms of that danger had appeared. How should the prudent statesman address himself to this problem? The following passage from Aristotle's *Politics* is most pertinent:

> The preservation of a regime [but this will also apply to its reform] may not only be due to the fact that a nation is far removed from the menace of any danger: it may also, on occasion, be due to the very opposite. When danger is imminent, men are alarmed, and they therefore keep a firmer grip on their regime. All who are concerned for the country should therefore

[51] See *Diamond*, p. 58.
[52] See *The Works of the Reverend John Witherspoon* (4 vols.; Philadelphia: W. W. Woodward, Publisher, 1802), 2nd ed., "Lectures on Eloquence," III, 475–592, hereafter cited as *Works*.

foster alarms, which will put men on their guard, and will make them keep an unwearied watch like sentinels on night-duty. They must, in a word, *make the remote come near.* . . . Ordinary men cannot see the beginning of troubles ahead; it requires the genuine statesman (226) [italics added].

The genuine statesman will detect the seed of danger before it springs full-blown upon his people. He will know the kinds of soil—the "hotbeds"—which nurture that seed. He will not be guided by any "clear and present danger" doctrine, a doctrine appropriate for ordinary men. No, he will *deliberately exaggerate* the degree of any danger to his regime, precisely because of those ordinary men.

4

But what enables the genuine statesman to see what the ordinary man does not see? Consider some questionable act or tendency of a legislature. How is it that the genuine statesman may see in it something pernicious and fraught with grave but distant danger, whereas the ordinary decent man will not see that danger, and may not even see the act or tendency as pernicious despite his decency? A good man, precisely because he is good, is concerned about the consequences of his actions, and for others as well as for himself. His very goodness motivates inquiry and reflection and thus facilitates the development and maturity of his intellect. Now, give this good man the power and responsibility of the statesman, say the founder of a regime. What he now does or fails to do will affect the destiny of a people. He will weigh alternative courses of action. He will consider immediate and long-range consequences. Always he will bear in mind the different kinds of men who comprise the community, their diverse opinions, passions, and interests, their virtues and their vices. And, with a knowledge of the past and a vision of the future, he will balance competing yet interdependent values, adjusting one to another that the whole of which they are parts— the common good—may thus become the richer and more magnificent. How can the intellectual and moral refinement of such a statesman fail to discern what cannot be discerned by the ordinary man, indeed, by the ordinary legislator? Let him be motivated by the love of fame. This very passion will enlarge his intellectual horizons, while his sense of honor will direct it toward a good transcending the praises of his contemporaries.

May not true realism, rising above preoccupation with mediocrity, require us to see in some of the founding fathers statesmen of such caliber? There is, of course, that anti-heroic realism of an age profoundly influenced by reductionist modes of thought, a "realism" which attempts to explain the higher in terms of the lower, and which thereby casts into obscurity the meaning of that love of fame and sense of honor which animate great statesmen. Given, however, the pervasiveness of that anti-heroic mentality, perhaps the political standards and the very language of such statesmen are incomprehensible to contemporary men? Whatever the case, how are we to explain the fact that Hamilton and Madison, respectively, described the British House of Commons as "democratic" and as "popular."[53] What can these terms mean when used to designate the political character of an institution whose members received no pay and required the possession of "real estate of the clear value of [three to] six hundred pounds sterling per year"?[54] Perhaps the education of these founders imbued them with classical and aristocratic sensibilities such that they might well have looked upon mankind with contempt were it not for the influence of Christianity?[55] Mingling with modernity, these two traditions may be seen in the Declaration of Independence. Notice the aristocratic sense of honor pervading the language of the Declaration. Indeed, underlying this

[53] *Farrand*, I, 362; *Federalist* 63, p. 415, and compare Mill, *Representative Government*, p. 307. See also *Federalist* 71, pp. 467–468, *Federalist* 76, pp. 495–496, and *Farrand*, I, 450, 457. As will be seen in the next chapter, the terms "democratic" and "popular" are *not* equivalent.

[54] *Federalist* 57, p. 375. The higher qualification applied to representatives from counties, the lower to those of cities and boroughs. See also *Annals of Congress*, 1st Cong., 1st Sess., 680 (hereafter cited as *Annals*).

[55] See James Walsh, *The Education of the Founders of the Republic* (New York: Fordham University Press, 1935), *passim*.

Declaration, as will be shown later, is an aristocratic conception of human nature—even though it proclaims that "all men are created equal."[56]

Given Hamilton's evaluation of the British House of Commons, we can better understand why he might have regarded the state governments as "hotbeds" of democracy. Clearly, he was using oligarchic if not aristocratic criteria of regime analysis far more exclusive than those employed by contemporary political scientists. What is truly remarkable, however, is that Hamilton's estimate of the House of Commons as democratic presupposes political criteria even *higher* than those Aristotle would have employed to characterize such an institution! Of course, all this is indecisive for determining what in fact was the actual political character of the state governments in 1787. It only suggests the heights from which Hamilton looked down upon them—which is borne out in the following passage from *Federalist* 17: "The regulation of the mere domestic police of a State appears to me to hold out slender allurements to ambition. Commerce, finance, negotiation, and war seem to comprehend all the objects which have charms for minds governed by that passion; and all the powers necessary to those objects ought, in the first instance, to be lodged in the national depository" (101). But even Hamilton's apparent disdain for the state governments is misleading, for here he was trying to reassure those who feared that the national government would gradually encroach upon the powers of the states. The possession of those powers, he says, "would contribute nothing to the dignity, to the importance, or to the splendor of the national government."[57] Whatever the case, here I touch upon the most important theme that distinguishes Hamilton's from Madison's contributions to *The Federalist*.[58]

We have been told, in effect, that the ends or objects which

[56] See Appendix I, and compare the Virginia Declaration of Rights, Articles 1, 2, 17, 18, as well as the property qualifications for office prescribed in Articles 3 and 4 of the Plan of Government, Madison, *Writings*, I, 35–43.

[57] *Federalist* 17, p. 102, and compare *Federalist* 34, p. 204.

[58] Of the twenty-six references to *The Federalist* in Diamond's essay, only two of Hamilton's papers are cited (assuming that contemporary scholarship

the new government was intended to foster are of a mediocre character; that they are "narrow" and "limited" as befitting a profoundly democratic society. Can this rightly be said of the second principal author of *The Federalist*, Alexander Hamilton? One of the persistent themes of Hamilton's papers in *The Federalist* is the theme of *greatness*. This theme has been brilliantly developed by Gerald Stourzh in his *Alexander Hamilton and the Idea of Republican Government*.[59] In the headnote of his book, Stourzh cites the following passage from a paper Hamilton wrote in 1778 criticizing the weakness of the Continental Congress:

> The station of a member of C——ss, is the most illustrious and important of any I am able to conceive. He is to be regarded not only as a legislator, but as the founder of an empire. A man of virtue and ability, dignified with so precious a trust, would rejoice that fortune had given him birth at a time, and placed him in circumstances so favourable for promoting human happiness. He would esteem it not more the duty, than the privilege and ornament of his office, to do good to mankind; from this commanding eminence, he would look down with contempt upon every mean or interested pursuit.

In his exposition of Hamilton's vision of empire, Stourzh refers to Francis Bacon's *Essay* 55, "Of Honor and Reputation," in which Bacon set forth "a scale of political honor and greatness that evokes images almost beyond our comprehension."[60] Wrote Bacon:

> In the first place are *conditores imperiorum*, founders of states and commonwealths; such as were Romulus, Cyrus, [and] Ceasar. . . . In the second place are *legislatores*, lawgivers; which are also called *second founders*, or *perpetui principes*, because they govern by their ordinances after they are gone; such were Lycurgus, Solon [and] Justinian. . . . In the third place

---

has correctly identified the ambiguous ones). Also to be noted is that Diamond cites none of Hamilton's papers on the presidency and the Supreme Court.

[59] Gerald Stourzh, *Alexander Hamilton and the Idea of Republican Government* (Stanford: Stanford University Press, 1970) (hereafter cited as *Stourzh*).

[60] *Ibid.*, p. 174.

are *liberatores*, or *salvatores*, such as compound the long miseries of civil wars, or deliver their countries from servitude of strangers or tyrants; as Augustus Ceasar . . . King Henry the Seventh of England, [and] King Henry the Fourth of France. In the fourth place are *propagatores* or *propugnatores imperii* . . . such as in honourable wars enlarge their territories, or make noble defence against invaders. And in the last place are *patres patriae* . . . which reign justly, and make the times good wherein they live. Both which last kinds need no examples, they are in such number.[61]

As Stourzh notes, "Bacon's scale of political honor and greatness is only the most elaborate exposition of an idea that linked classical antiquity with early modern thought."[62] In Hamilton, that idea is preserved, and it is visible in *The Federalist*, as the following passages reveal:

From the disorders that disfigure the annals of those republics [of classical antiquity] the advocates of despotism have drawn arguments, not only against the forms of republican government, but against the very principles of civil liberty. They have decried all free government as inconsistent with the order of society. . . . Happily for mankind, stupendous fabrics reared on the basis of liberty, which have flourished for ages, have, in a few glorious instances, refuted their gloomy sophisms. And, I trust, America will be the broad and solid foundation of other edifices, not less magnificent. . . .[63]

As anticipated earlier, Hamilton envisioned a rich and powerful empire, extending its influence throughout the world:

That unequaled spirit of enterprise, which signalizes the genius of the American merchants and navigators, and which is in itself an inexhaustible mine of national wealth, would be stifled and lost, and poverty and disgrace would overspread a country

[61] Francis Bacon, *Essays* (New York: Modern Library, 1955), H. D. Dick, trans, pp. 137–138.

[62] *Stourzh*, p. 174.

[63] *Federalist* 9, p. 48. In this passage, Hamilton refers to, and thus distinguishes between, the "friends and partisans" of free government, thus permitting us to appreciate his detachment. Compare Madison in *Federalist* 10, p. 53.

which, with wisdom, might make herself the admiration and envy of the world. . . . Let Americans disdain to be the instruments of European greatness! Let the thirteen States, bound together in a strict and indissoluable Union, concur in erecting one great American system, superior to the control of all transatlantic force or influence, and able to dictate the terms of the connection between the old and the new world![64]

Pervading Hamilton's papers in *The Federalist* is an appeal to national "pride," "honor," "dignity," "reputation," "splendor," "glory," as opposed to national "insignificance," "humiliation," and "disgrace."[65] To attain the one and to avoid the other, the new government would have to encourage foreign and domestic commerce. To protect the former, a powerful navy would be required; to extend the latter to the Mississippi, a powerful army. Contrary to modern liberalism, Hamilton did not harbor a pessimistic fear of power. No less skeptical of human nature than Jefferson, Hamilton nevertheless possessed a firm confidence in human greatness: "Th[e] supposition of universal venality in human nature is little less an error in political reasoning, than the supposition of universal rectitude. The institution of delegated power implies, that there is a portion of virtue and honor among mankind, which may be a reasonable foundation of confidence; and experience justifies the theory."[66] "There are men," wrote Hamilton, "who, under any circumstances, will have the courage to do their duty at every hazard."[67] Such men "could neither be distressed nor won into a sacrifice of their duty"; and although "this stern virtue is the growth of few soils," government should nonetheless be designed to attract those rare individuals and should invest them with sufficient power to advance the cause of national greatness.[68] Jealousy of power bespeaks the fear of petty minds. We are told, said Hamilton to the New York legislature early in 1787, that

[64] *Federalist* 11, pp. 66, 69.
[65] See *Federalist* 6, 15, 22, 30, and 34, and *Farrand*, I, 466–467.
[66] *Federalist* 76, p. 495.
[67] *Federalist* 73, p. 479.
[68] *Ibid.*, p. 475.

it is dangerous to trust power any where; that *power* is liable to *abuse*, with a variety of trite maxims of the same kind. General propositions of this nature are easily framed, the truth of which cannot be denied, but they rarely convey any precise idea. To these we might oppose other propositions equally true and equally indefinite. It might be said that too little power is as dangerous as too much, that it leads to anarchy, and from anarchy to despotism. But the question still recurs, what is this *too much or too little?* Where is the measure or standard to ascertain the happy mean?

Powers must be granted, or civil Society cannot exist; the possibility of abuse is no argument against the *thing*.[69]

Hamilton was, of course, the patron of a powerful executive. The unity of the office, its tenure and indefinite reeligibility, are among the major ingredients of executive power. With unity came responsibility—for Hamilton, an elevating responsibility. With a four-year tenure came independence. Here is the way Hamilton defends the tenure in *Federalist* 71:

[A] man acting in the capacity of chief magistrate, under a consciousness that in a very short time he *must* lay down his office, will be apt to feel himself too little interested in it to hazard any material censure or perplexity, from the independent exertion of his powers, or from encountering the ill-humors, however transient, which may happen to prevail, either in a considerable part of the society itself, or even in a predominant faction in the legislative body. . . .

When occasions present themselves, in which the interests of the people are at variance with their inclinations, it is the duty of the persons whom they have appointed to be the guardians of those interests, to withstand the temporary delusion, in order to give them time and opportunity for more cool and sedate reflection. Instances might be cited in which a conduct of this kind has saved the people from very fatal consequences of their own mistakes, and has procured lasting monuments of their

[69] Cited in *Stourzh*, p. 182. Madison expressed similar sentiments in the Virginia ratifying convention: "If powers be necessary, apparent danger is not a sufficient reason against conceding them." Madison, *Writings*, V, 125.

gratitude to the men who had courage and magnanimity enough to serve them at the peril of their displeasure (464–465).

Nevertheless, a presidential tenure of four years is not sufficient for the attainment of national greatness. To do great and lasting good, to fulfill the great purposes of the Constitution—as Hamilton conceived it—a President must look forward to a continuance of his office beyond the period of four years:

> Even the love of fame, the ruling passion of the noblest minds, which would prompt a man to plan and undertake extensive and arduous enterprises for the public benefit, requiring considerable time to mature and perfect them, if he could flatter himself with the prospect of being allowed to finish what he had begun, would, on the contrary, deter him from the undertaking, when he foresaw that he must quit the scene before he could accomplish the work, and must commit that, together with his own reputation, to hands which might be unequal or unfriendly to the task. The most to be expected from the generality of men, in such a situation, is the negative merit of not doing harm, instead of the positive merit of doing good.[70]

The Constitution invests the presidency with great power if only to attract to this office men motivated by the love of fame, but whose love of fame is identified with the public good. Only such men will possess the courage and the magnanimity to risk the censure or displeasure of their contemporaries. Only such men will undertake comprehensive and long-range plans aimed at the achievement of national glory. With contempt for mere popularity, such men look beyond the praises of the living, for their love of fame is a passion for immortality, the immortality of greatness.

Taking up the love of fame in connection with the topic of rebellion, Aristotle writes:

[70] *Federalist* 72, p. 470. See *Stourzh*, pp. 94–106, and contrast Madison, *Writings*, VI, 174: "The strongest passions and most dangerous weaknesses of the human breast; ambition, avarice, vanity, the honourable or venal love of fame, are all in conspiracy against the desire and duty of peace." This is one of Madison's most Lockean statements. It is not, however, his only word on the subject. See pp. 209–210, 256 below.

A man who resolves to risk rebellion out of a desire for fame behaves in a different way from men who attempt the lives of tyrants with an eye to gain great gain or high honours. Men of that sort are merely moved by greed or ambition; the man who desires true fame will attack a ruler in the same high spirit as if he were offered the chance of some other great adventure likely to win a man name and fame among his fellows—he will want to get glory, and not a kingdom. It is true that those who are moved by such reasons are only a handful. Their action supposes an utter disregard for their own safety in the event of failure (239).

Several years after Hamilton's death, Gouverneur Morris wrote: "General Hamilton was of that kind of men, who may most safely be trusted, for he was more covetous of glory than of wealth or power."[71] Hamilton indeed had a contempt for wealth—though he knew how to use the wealthy for his cause. And, too, he had a contempt for popularity—even while he served the cause of popular government. In serving that cause Hamilton displayed the classical virtue of magnanimity, the very virtue he saw essential to the presidency.

We conclude this chapter by means of a summary of its most salient points. From an elaboration of two fundamental principles discussed by Aristotle, there emerged the soul of radical democracy. By means of a critique of Diamond's democratic interpretation of *The Federalist*, it was shown that the egalitarianism and libertarianism of radical democracy were deliberately guarded against by the architects of the American Constitution. These two related evils were to be prevented by protecting the unequal human faculties on the one hand, and the unequal distribution of property on the other. In the process of analyzing the significance of property, the theme of *deference* was developed, a quality singularly lacking in democracies of the extreme type. Also developed was the theme of *reverence for law*, on which depends the rule of reason over the divisive and consuming passions of men. The rule of reason requires, of course, the rule of

[71] Cited in *Stourzh*, p. 202.

99

enlightened men. Accordingly, I touched upon the theme of *education*, a most important concern of the founders (as will be shown at greater length in another chapter). Finally, certain aspects of statesmanship were considered to elucidate the theme of *greatness*. From the discussion of the above themes certain conclusions may be drawn: first, the character of the American people was basically sound and conducive to the establishment of a good form of government; second, the founders, *in their own ways* (to be further elaborated), sought to preserve and even to elevate the character of the American people; third, the Constitution does not make explicit *all* the intentions of those statesmen, hence all the ends which the government established under that Constitution was intended to foster; fourth, the Constitution nevertheless embodies a broad range of humane values, but the weight to be given to each of these values is not easily determined, if only in view of the ambiguities of language; fifth, and last, whatever be its political character, the Constitution was designed to endure yet transcend mediocrity.

CHAPTER III

The "New" Science of Politics

I T WAS NOT very difficult to distinguish Aristotle's worst variety of democracy from the republic described in *The Federalist*; but what about his *best* variety of democracy? This question will be taken up at the end of the chapter. Here, two facts are to be borne in mind: first, that *any* democracy, according to Aristotle, is an unjust regime, and, second, that *The Federalist* never refers to the proposed Constitution as democratic. Furthermore, it is only the good reputation which democracy enjoys in our time that enables men to say, without embarrassment, that the American people have been living under such a regime for almost two hundred years. Of course, words should not be mistaken for things. What we call a "democracy" may in fact be quite different from what Aristotle called by that name. Indeed, even if it were discovered that some of the founders spoke of the government established under the Constitution as some form of democracy, it is perfectly possible that what they *meant* by the term, *or* what that government *actually* exemplified, is roughly equivalent to what Aristotle called a 'polity'! Thus, in his notes to a speech before the New York ratifying convention, Hamilton refers to the proposed government as a "representative democracy."[1] But then we have also seen him refer to the British House of Commons as a democratic institution, an institution that Aristotle would almost certainly have classified as oligarchic.

[1] See my *Philosophy of the American Constitution*, p. 304, n. 29.

These terminological differences have the profoundest implications, involving nothing less than the quarrel between classical
and modern political science. For if, in our time, men commonly
regard as just a regime which Aristotle regards as unjust, then
unless Aristotle's criteria of regime analysis are erronious or
no longer relevant, the possibility arises that modern political
science, beginning with Machiavelli, Hobbes, and Locke, may
have lowered the standards or the goals of political life. This is
precisely the conclusion meticulously developed by the Straussian school of thought, a school whose members are among the
most serious students of politics. To be sure, that conclusion is
based on classical standards, indeed, on Aristotelian criteria of
regime analysis. Whether such criteria are adequate for evaluating modernity may, for the time being, be left open. One thing,
however, is certain: A proper understanding of Aristotle's criteria precludes the pejorative extension of the "Straussian"
conclusion to the political thought and statesmanship of the
founding fathers. (Here, justice requires me to point out that, according to Strauss himself, "The United States . . . may be said to
be the only country in the world which was founded in explicit
opposition to Machiavellian principles."[2] But if the doctrines of
Hobbes and Locke are rooted in these principles, it follows that
Professor Strauss would not wholly accept the "Straussian" conclusion applied to the founders.)[3] In any event, beginning with
the next chapter, that conclusion will be refuted by the systematic and detailed application of Aristotle's criteria of regime anal-

[2] Leo Strauss, *Thoughts on Machiavelli* (Glencoe, Ill.: Free Press, 1958), p.
13. See also Leo Strauss, *Liberalism Ancient and Modern* (New York: Basic
Books, Inc., 1968), p. 15, where Strauss writes that "There is a direct connection between the [classical] notion of the mixed regime and modern republi-
canism."

[3] After clarifying the statement cited in the previous footnote, Strauss turns
to Locke's *Some Thoughts Concerning Education*, of which he says: "Locke
takes his models from the ancient Romans and Greeks. . . ." And he continues:
"Not a few points which Locke meant [regarding the education and political
role of gentlemen] are brought out clearly in the *Federalist Papers*"—especially
in *Federalist* 35, with respect to which Strauss mentions Hamilton's expectations regarding the leading role of the "learned professions" (*ibid.*, p. 16).

ysis to the Constitution itself. Meantime, it will be necessary to remove the terminological confusions regarding the political character of the Constitution, as well as the related confusions regarding the political orientation of its founders—this, to establish whether their orientation was modern or classical or something else.

1

In studying the political character of any regime, a distinction must be made between its formal or legal character and its material or sociological character. As Aristotle explains: "It should be noted . . . that in actual life it is often the case that regimes which are not legally democratic are made to work democratically by the habits and training of the people. Conversely, there are other cases where the legal regime inclines towards democracy, but is made by training and habits to work in a way which inclines more towards oligarchy" (170). Much the same distinction may be found in a speech delivered by Edmund Randolph at the Federal Convention; in fact, it was the very speech introducing the Virginia Plan. Here is the relevant passage: "Our chief danger arises from the democratic parts of our [state] constitutions. It is a maxim which I hold incontrovertible, that the powers of government exercised by the people swallows up the other branches. None of the constitutions have provided sufficient checks against the democracy."[4] When Randolph declares that the "chief danger arises from the democratic parts of our constitutions," this implies that there were other parts of those constitutions, which, in his opinion, were *not* democratic. And when he says that "the powers of government exercised by the people swallows up the other branches," this implies that the powers of these other branches were not exercised by the people *de jure*, hence, that the political practices of those states did not wholly conform to their respective constitutions. From this it appears that the "hotbeds" of democracy referred to earlier were

[4] *Farrand*, I, 26–27.

centered in the democratic parts of the state governments, and as the sequel to the above passage clearly indicates, the parts in question were the *lower* branches of the state legislatures. It happens to be the case, however, that most of these legislatures appointed, by *joint* ballot, the delegates to the Federal Convention, and further, that the members of those very legislatures dominated the state conventions which ratified the Constitution.[5] If the caliber of the founders is an indicator of the character of those legislatures, and if the latter, in turn, are indicators of the character of American society in the eighteenth century, then, if that society was profoundly democratic, we shall need a definition of democracy significantly different from anything found in Aristotle's *Politics*.[6]

According to Aristotle, "when the masses govern the country with a view to the common interest, the name used for this species is the generic name common to all regimes (or polities)—the name of 'Polity'" (114). The perversion of a 'polity' is a democracy wherein the many rule solely with a view to their own interests (115). At this point, recall Diamond's interpretation of the Madisonian solution to the problem of popular government. That solution was said to have required a "profoundly democratic" regime, which is to say a regime Aristotle classifies as a perverted form of government! Obviously Diamond's interpretation, which is supposed to explicate the "framers' intent," should not itself be interpreted as to require so incredible a conclusion. In fact, when describing the profoundly democratic regime envisioned by the founders, he does not say it involved the rule of the many at the expense of the few—which would

---

[5] In this connection, see *Federalist* 49, pp. 330–331.

[6] Against this it may be argued that the Constitution was designed for the *future*, for a society that was *expected* to become profoundly democratic, and that the Constitution was *intended* to prevent only the worst defects of such a society. We have already cast doubt on this interpretation by means of textual analysis. There remains, however, two problems: first, to evaluate, on *philosophical* grounds, the formal character of each part of the Constitution; and second, to examine the Constitution under the category of change (by the method of efficient causality). This shall be done in subsequent chapters.

hardly be a solution to the problem of popular government. Of course, Madison himself declared in *The Federalist* that the solution to that problem requires the establishment, not of a democracy, but of a *republic* of a certain kind. Here Diamond seems to agree with his own interpretation of Madison's distinction between a democracy and a republic, namely, that these two regimes are two species of the genus "popular government." He explains the difference between the two species as follows—on which note we arrive at the formal aspect of Diamond's interpretation of the Madisonian solution:

> Democracy means in *The Federalist* that form of popular government where the citizens "assemble and administer the government in person." Republics differ in that the people rule through representatives and, of course, in the consequences of that difference. The crucial point is that republics and democracies are equally forms of popular government, but that the one form is vastly preferable to the other because of the substantive consequences of the difference in form.[7]

From this it is reasonable to infer that a republic is "vastly preferable" to a democracy because the "substantive consequences of the difference in form" between the two is the difference between a just and unjust regime. This is borne out in the very passage from *The Federalist* which Diamond refers to above. The passage appears in *Federalist* 10, where Madison says:

> [A] pure democracy, by which I mean a society consisting of a small number of citizens, who assemble and administer the government in person, can admit of no cure for the mischiefs of faction. A common passion or interest will, in most every case, be felt by a majority of the whole; a communication and concert result from the form of government itself; and there is nothing to check the inducements to sacrifice the weaker party or an ab-

---

[7] *Diamond*, p. 54. See my critique of Diamond's classification in *The Philosophy of the American Constitution*, pp. 21–22. In the discussion that follows, I shall adopt Diamond's classification for the sake of elucidating related and other issues.

noxious individual. [Did Madison have Socrates in mind here?] Hence it is that such democracies have ever been spectacles of turbulence and contention; have ever been found incompatible with *personal security or the rights of property*; and have in general been as short in their lives as they have been violent in their deaths [italics added].[8]

The point to be emphasized is that a pure democracy, by virtue of its very form, almost invariably results in the oppression of the weaker party (here, the rich), by the majority (namely, the poor). But the form is only the *formal* cause of this injustice. Its material cause resides in the character of the majority, who simply are not good enough to be governed by moral or religious motives alone, that is, without some other "checks" or restraints. What the form does is to facilitate the "communication and concert" of a "common passion or interest" directed toward unjust ends. That being the case, the form is unjust, and not only on practical grounds, but on theoretical ones as well. It does indeed seem, therefore, that a republic and a democracy, the two species of popular government, stand to each other as just and unjust regimes. Yet Diamond insists that the republic established by the founders is "profoundly democratic," which is to say, in effect, that it is a "democratic republic."[9] From this it follows that a republic can have many of the attributes of a democracy without its form—which might be expected if both are species of the same genus. But lacking the form of a democracy, a democratic republic is *less* democratic than a democracy, and to the

[8] *Federalist* 10, p. 58. My interpolation receives support from *Federalist* 63, p. 410, where Madison says: "What bitter anguish would not the people of Athens have often escaped if their government had contained so provident a safeguard against the tyranny of their own passions? Popular liberty might then have escaped the indelible reproach of decreeing to the same citizens the hemlock on one day and statues on the next." The "provident safeguard" of which Madison speaks is the Senate he is defending in this number, a Senate that is to uphold the authority of "reason, justice, and truth." These are the very words we find in Socrates's speech in the *Apology*, 34–35.

[9] The title of his textbook on American government cited earlier, a title which suggests, however, that republic may be of generic rank. See also *Diamond*, p. 59, where he refers to the "*democratic* republic."

extent of being a just regime. What the democratic republic has in place of the democratic form is of course the *representative* principle. This principle may be consistent with the genus called "popular government"; it may be "wholly popular"; but it cannot be *wholly* democratic. If, by virtue of this principle, an unjust form of government is transformed into a just form of government, it must be due to the cooperation of material causes— again, the character of the many. Somehow this principle of representation must provide, or help to provide, that "check" or restraint lacking in a pure democracy, and without which neither moral nor religious motives are sufficient to prevent the many from endangering "personal security or the rights of property." But if a political principle serves to protect, in addition to personal security, the rights of property—which involve the interests of the rich—then that principle must, at least to some extent, partake of oligarchic attributes.

Contrast, now, Aristotle's method of classifying regimes. Of regimes ruled by the Many, we saw two species, one just, the other unjust—so that the character of the "many" in one must differ from the character of the many in the other. In one regime, the many are moderate; they rule with a view to the common good; that regime is just. Aristotle names such a regime a 'polity.' Meanwhile, in that other regime, the many are licentious; they rule with a view to their own interests; they sacrifice the interests of the rich; this is an unjust regime. Aristotle gives this second regime a name which differs from that of the first: he names it a "democracy." Bearing this in mind, notice that the rule of the many corresponds to the genus which Diamond called "popular government." Each genus has one just and one unjust species. The two unjust species bear the *same* name of "democracy." The two just species bear *different* names, one being a 'polity,' the other being a "republic." It would seem, however, that the two different names designate *the same political things*. Both involve the rule of the many with a view to the common good, which in turn presupposes that the character of the many in both cases is such as to result in political conduct consistent with the common good. Still, there remains the difference in names: the one a 'polity,' the other a "republic."

We have seen that a 'polity,' according to Aristotle, combines democratic and oligarchic attributes. According to Diamond a republic is devoid of oligarchic attributes (58). There seem to be but two ways of resolving this dilemma: (1) either Diamond or Aristotle is in error, or (2) the founding fathers discovered or constructed a *new kind of regime*, one that is "profoundly democratic" yet "just." If the latter is the case, then the American regime cannot be adequately understood in terms of Aristotelian criteria.[10]

Before continuing, it should be made clear that I have been employing the genus-species distinction as understood by Diamond, and, apparently, by Aristotle. The truth is that this distinction, though indispensable for practical purposes, is misleading and philosophically fallacious. No species is wholly derivable from any single genus (no more than is any individual derivable from a single species). In the political domain, no less than in the biological, a species includes a mixture of genera.[11]

Any classification schema represents a selection, from amidst a welter of data, of some set or pattern of characteristics vividly delineating one group of individuals from another. The difficulty resides in the vividness separating the two groups. The vividness results from criteria of relevance underlying the selection of data for emphasis. There can be no emphasis without some exaggeration, which exaggeration, though indispensable, obscures the continuity between the groups (or species) in question. For example, consider two regimes, one called a "democracy," the

[10] Even if this were true, however, it would still indicate that Diamond has not properly applied those criteria.

[11] See Aristotle, *The History of Animals*, 588a18–588b10, and *On the Parts of Animals*, Bk. I, ch. 4; Plato, *Sophist* 253; Whitehead, AI 302, and MT 21. The principle being denied here concerns the classical as well as modern notions of universals and particulars. As Whitehead points out, "every so-called 'universal' is particular in the sense of being just what it is, diverse from everything else; and every so-called 'particular' is universal in the sense of entering into the constitutions of other actual entities" (PR 76).

other an "oligarchy." In one the poor rule, in the other the rich. But what do we mean by the "poor?" Obviously there is continuity between the poor and the rich, and any line drawn between them will rest on criteria of relevance other than arithmetic ones. Suppose, then, we define the poor as those who must work for a living. Leaving aside the ambiguity of the term "work," is it not evident that between those who do and who do not work for a living there is again continuity? Nevertheless, suppose the factor of "working for a living" were selected because it was thought to be determinative of the moral and intellectual character of the poor. Needless to say, however, not only manual laborers, but most businessmen and virtually all college professors work for a living. What is more, within *each* of these groups we find differences in character relevant to different kinds of regimes, indicating that a species includes a mixture of genera. Indeed, were this not the case, a democracy, for example, could not be made *less* democratic.

Whatever the extent of Aristotle's theoretical commitment to the genus-species distinction, whose practical value, to repeat, is undeniable, he was too great a political scientist to allow that distinction to obscure the rich variety of regimes or their multifarious mixtures of generic attributes. Interestingly enough, Madison too seems to have rejected any simplistic application of the genus-species distinction to the multiform character of political life. Thus, in his article "The Spirit of Governments," which was published in *The National Gazette*, Madison declares that "No Government is perhaps reducible to a sole principle of operation. Where the theory approaches nearest to this character, different and often heterogeneous principles mingle their influence in the administration. It is useful, nevertheless, to analyze the several kinds of government, and to characterize them by the spirit which predominates in each."[12] Compare,

---

[12] *Writings*, VI, 93 (Feb. 20, 1792), and note the sequel where Madison is critical of Montesquieu, and where he takes a position independent of that of Locke. See also *Federalist* 37, p. 228, where Madison implicitly rejects the genus-species distinction.

however, the following from *Federalist* 14, where Madison writes: "[I]n modern Europe, to which we owe the great principle of representation, no example is seen of a government wholly popular, and founded, at the same time, wholly on that principle. ... America [alone] can claim the merit of making the discovery [of that principle] the basis of unmixed and extensive republics" (81). Suggested here are at least *two* species of the *genus* republic: one called an "unmixed" republic, the other, by implication, a "mixed" republic. Unlike the mixed republic, the unmixed republic is "wholly popular," meaning free from *hereditary* institutions.[13] On the other hand, in *Federalist* 39, Madison denies—and inconsistently with the implication just drawn from *Federalist* 14—that a genuine republic can have hereditary institutions. He writes: "The government of England, which has one republican branch only, combined with an hereditary aristocracy and monarchy, has, with ... impropriety, been frequently placed on the list of republics" (243). Notice that the House of Commons, to which Madison alludes, is described as "republican" despite the high property qualifications which, we saw, were attached to that office. Accordingly, if the implicit inconsistency between *Federalist* 14 and 39 be ignored, it follows from the two passages cited that an "unmixed" republic, one that is "wholly popular," could nevertheless be classified as some form of *mixed* republic so long as one or another of its offices required some qualification other than hereditary descent, for example property, as was the case with the House of Commons. Such a classification would be consistent with Madison's contention that "different and often heterogeneous principles mingle their influence in the administration of government."[14]

Of course, for Madison to have said in *The Federalist* that the proposed Constitution exemplified a mixed republic would not

[13] That Madison means free of hereditary institutions is confirmed in his *Writings*, VI, 112, as well as in *Federalist* 63, pp. 412–413.

[14] The reader should not interpret these words to suggest the legislative, executive, and judicial principles of government. See Hamilton, *Federalist* 72, p. 468, for the broad meaning of the term "administration."

have been very informative, unless he went on to offer the rhetorically imprudent explanation that such a republic combined
democratic and oligarchic principles. As a matter of fact, however, there was a great deal of controversy during (and after) the
ratification period as to how the Constitution ought to be classified. Madison himself regarded the Constitution as having prescribed "a system of Government emphatically *sui generis* for
designating which there consequently was no appropriate term
or denomination preexisting."[15] This is a bold assertion. It clearly
implies that the principles of the Constitution are not adequately
comprehended by the doctrines of *any* political philosopher,
classical or modern. Madison may be right, but his assertion is
not accompanied by critical analysis of classical and modern political science. This is merely to say that Madison, who was a
scholar in his own right, was not a philosopher, which brings me
to a related distinction.

If, contrary to Madison's contention, the regime he helped to
establish is not *sui generis*, then a distinction would have to be
made between what that regime was *intended* to be, and what it
is in fact. This distinction has been obscured by virtually all
studies of the founding. Yet this very distinction points to that
which differentiates the statesman from the philosopher. The
political thought of the statesman is largely shaped by the philosopher. His fundamental ideas are more or less derivative;
they have been abstracted from various sources or traditions; and
because they have not been subjected to sustained philosophical
analysis and synthesis, there is a tendency—appropriate enough
—toward eclecticism. This is not to say that statesmen are not
thinkers. To the contrary, this Discourse is partly intended to
show that the great statesman, men like Madison and Hamilton,
can teach us more about statesmanship than can the vast majority

[15] *Writings*, IX, 177, letter to Robert S. Garnett, February 11, 1824 (italics
added). In this letter, Madison was referring to the controversy as to whether
the Constitution prescribed a "national" or a "federal" government, a controversy discussed in *Federalist* 39. See also *Federalist* 14, p. 84, where he refers
to the new government as a "novelty in the political world."

of political thinkers. Curiously enough, Diamond comes very close to crediting the founders with having constructed a new kind of government, or what is more accurate, with having established the first government in history to be based on what he calls the "new" science of politics. This is the political science inaugurated by Machiavelli, elaborated by Hobbes, and made respectable by Locke. I shall enlarge upon this new science of politics in a moment. Suffice to say that it differed from the old political science in that it excluded from the ends of government the cultivation of human excellence. But consider Diamond's own interpretation in a passage, part of which has already been cited:

> So far as concerns those ends of government on which *The Federalist* is almost wholly silent, it is reasonable to infer that what the Founders made no provision for they did not rank highly among the legitimate objects of government. *Other political theories* had ranked highly, as objects of government, the nurturing of a particular religion, education, military courage, civic-spiritedness, moderation, individual excellence in the virtues, etc. On all of these *The Federalist* is either silent, or has in mind only pallid versions of the originals, *or even seems to speak with contempt.* The Founders apparently did not consider it necessary to make special provision for excellence. Did they assume these virtues would flourish without governmental or other explicit provision? . . . Or were these virtues less necessary to a country when it had been properly founded on the basis of the *new* "science of politics"?[16]

Notice, first, that *The Federalist* is virtually identified as a work of political theory, thus obscuring the fact that it is governed by rhetorical principles which of course make use of antecedent political theories, but theories which had to be adjusted to the practical purposes of the statesman on the one hand, and to the character of his audience on the other. Now the prudent statesman, like the prudent philosopher, will indeed be silent about certain things—not because he deems them unimportant,

---

[16] *Diamond,* p. 64 (italics added). The closing question is clearly rhetorical.

but because if such things were publicized, they might cause unnecessary division or distract men from the statesman's *first* objective, which is to establish a safe and stable government. Once established, however, he may then go on to advance other ends, such as Washington did when he proposed the establishment of a national university. But leaving this aside, is it credible that the authors of *The Federalist*, that men of their education, courage, civic-spiritedness, moderation, and intellectual capacities, would hold these virtues in contempt? Did they, in other words *despise themselves!*

2

But Diamond's errors are not accidental. As already intimated, they have their origin in the Straussian school of thought, a school which has brilliantly illuminated the quarrel between ancients and moderns.[17] Its major thesis, we have seen, is that modern political science has lowered the goals of political life. The new science of politics of which Diamond speaks and erroneously imputes to the founding fathers has been characterized as political hedonism. Its theoretical basis, as more or less portrayed by the school in question, may be summarized as follows. (1) Contrary to the classical view, man is not by nature a social or political animal. He has no natural inclination toward virtue, no natural concern for the good of others. In other words, prior to civil society—or in the so-called state of nature—each individual lives in a solipsistic world containing no value transcending his own preservation or existence. Because his preservation (or comfortable preservation) is the highest value, or because his destruction (or violent death) is the greatest evil, the individual not only prefers his own good to the good of others, but he would also sacrifice their good whenever his own life is endangered. Self-preservation is therefore the most fundamental law of na-

[17] See Leo Strauss, *The Political Philosophy of Hobbes* (Chicago: University of Chicago Press, 1952), and *Natural Right and History* (Chicago: University of Chicago Press, 1953), and *History of Political Philosophy* (Chicago: Rand McNally & Co., 1972), 2nd ed. (Joseph Cropsey, co-editor).

ture. (2) What makes self-preservation an acute problem, however, is that nature is penurious on the one hand, while man's
desires are insatiable on the other. Furthermore, each individual
is the ultimate judge of what is necessary for his preservation.
With respect to self-preservation, therefore, all men are equal
and perfectly free: (a) equal in that, regardless of differences of
mind and body, one individual's life has no greater or lesser value
than another's; (b) free in that, apart from external impediments,
each individual may do as he pleases without any moral restraints whatsoever. Of course, under these conditions, the state
of nature is a state of war wherein the life of man is "solitary, poor,
nasty, brutish, and short." Yet, nature's poverty, cooperating
with the fear of violent death, impels men out of the state of
nature and into the state of civil society. (3) The laws of civil
society are but conventions or contractual agreements (tacitly
or otherwise) entered into by men for the purpose of securing
their rights to life, liberty, and property. Meanwhile, government is ultimately based on the consent of the governed, since
all men are equal with respect to the right of self-preservation.
As for the purpose of government, it consists not in making men
good—"good" is merely a name men give to their likes or appetites—but rather in facilitating the pursuit and enjoyment of
commodious living. Accordingly, institutions must be designed
to foster yet regulate the acquisitive instincts. This points to the
establishment of a commercial society held in equipoise by a
system of countervailing passions and interests.

The new science of politics thus bases political life on the
passions. It encourages their liberation rather than their restraint. Reason emerges as nothing more than an instrument of
the passions, designing institutional and other techniques for
their gratification. With this emphasis on the passions comes a
new emphasis on freedom. But now freedom means the right to
do anything not prohibited by the civil law. The civil law alone
defines one's duties, which are restricted to the minimum necessary for securing civic peace and prosperity. (Again, the modern
emphasis is on rights, not duties.) Henceforth, instead of foster-

ing human excellence, government will facilitate the enjoyment of commodious self-preservation: the gentleman of Aristotle's *Nicomachean Ethics* has been replaced by the bourgeois of Locke's *Second Treatise of Civil Government*. This, in brief, is the Straussian view of modern political science, a view which Diamond—*not* Strauss—has superimposed on the political thought of the founders and on their work, the Constitution.[18]

Without denying the influence of Locke on the founding, it is a colossal error to transform the founders into his disciples, especially into disciples of his *Second Treatise*.[19] Nor is it correct to make them disciples of Montesquieu whose *Spirit of the Laws* is tendentiously cited by Hamilton in *Federalist* 9.[20] Recall, however, Madison's article on "The Spirit of Governments." In the sequel to the passage cited earlier, Madison wrote:

> Montesquieu has resolved the great operative principles of government into fear, honor, and virtue, applying the first to pure despotisms, the second to regular monarchies, and the third to republics. The portion of truth blended with the ingenuity of this system sufficiently justifies the admiration bestowed on its author. Its accuracy however can never be defended against the criticisms which it has encountered. Montesquieu

[18] Of course, other commentators have regarded the Constitution as Lockean, but none with greater seriousness. See, for example, Louis Hartz, *The Liberal Tradition in America* (New York: Harcourt, Brace & World, 1955).

[19] But see above, p. 102, n. 3. It could be argued that while Locke lowered the goals of *political* life, or of *government*, his *Some Thoughts Concerning Education* more or less preserved the traditional goals of *society*. Even admitting that Locke provides the theoretical foundation for capitalism, hence the encouragement of avarice, the Straussians have by no means proven that the agrarian society preferred by the classics is in truth superior to the commercial society preferred by the moderns. What may be the case, however, is that the moderns have yet to formulate a political philosophy that will reveal the superiority of a commercial society.

[20] See *Spirit of the Laws*, Bk. II, ch. 2, for Montesquieu's definition of aristocracy, Bk. XI, ch. 6, on the legislative, executive, and judicial powers, and contrast Bk. IX, ch. 2 (and Bk. XX, chs. 2, 4) on the peace and moderation peculiar to republics with *Federalist* 6, pp. 29–33. See also *Stourzh*, pp. 64–65, 71, contrasting the differences between Hamilton and Montesquieu on the question of republican virtue, which in turn should be examined in the light of *Federalist* 21, p. 129.

was in politics not a Newton or a Locke, who established immortal systems, the one in matter, the other in mind.[21]

I cannot pause to show that Madison is more indebted to Montesquieu than the above passage would indicate. But notice his
reference to Locke. He does not say that Locke established an
immortal system of politics, but rather of mind, alluding, therefore, to Locke's *Essay Concerning the Human Understanding*.
Yet Madison's "psychology," so to speak, can hardly be identified
with Locke's. Neither he nor Hamilton had the one-sided view
of human nature which Locke inherited from Hobbes. Recall
Federalist 55 where Madison said that just "As there is a degree
of depravity in mankind which requires a certain degree of circumspection and distrust, so there are other qualities in human
nature which justify a certain portion of esteem and confidence"
(365). Or to repeat what Hamilton said in *Federalist* 76: "Th[e]
supposition of universal venality in human nature is little less an
error in political reasoning, than the supposition of universal
rectitude" (495). Neither of these statesmen had a merely bourgeois ethic or a utilitarian understanding of virtue. Both repeatedly denigrate the passions, suggesting thereby the influence of
Puritan Christianity. True, Hamilton and Madison are modern
insofar as they would place less restraints on the passions; yet it
remains a fact that both still looked upon avarice and ambition as
vices. Finally, if not their Christian scruples, then their classical
sense of honor, prevented the founders from regarding the civil
law as man's highest authority, and forbade them to subordinate
all human values to self-preservation.

These influences were still powerful in the college and university curriculums of eighteenth-century America. Of course, there
is no clear way of determining the effect of these colleges and
universities on the founders, or the relative influence of the
various traditions in question. One thing, however, is fairly certain: Men like Madison did *not* understand Locke as Locke is
understood by Diamond. The science of politics imputed to the

[21] *Writings*, VI, 93.

founders was not understood by them to be "new," let alone one involving a contempt for human excellence. *Federalist* 9 does indeed speak of a "great improvement" in the "science of politics"; but what did this great improvement consist in according to its author? Precisely this:

> The efficacy of various principles is now well understood, which were either not known at all, or imperfectly known to the ancients. The regular distribution of power into distinct departments; the introduction of legislative balances and checks; the institution of courts composed of judges holding their offices during good behavior; the representation of the people in the legislature by deputies of their own election . . . [and] the ENLARGMENT of the ORBIT within which such systems are to resolve. . . .[22]

It will be shown in due course that there is nothing in this catalog of "improvements" which was not well understood by Aristotle. But there is one other possible "improvement" that might be attributed to the founders. Thus, according to *Federalist* 51,

> the great security against a gradual concentration of the several powers in the same department, consists in giving to those who administer each department the necessary constitutional means and personal motives to resist encroachments of the others. . . . Ambition must be made to counteract ambition. The interest of the man must be connected with the constitutional rights of the place. It may be a reflection on human nature, that such devices should be necessary to control the abuses of government. But what is government itself, but the greatest of all reflections on human nature? (337)

There is nothing exceptional in this passage, not when balanced by others cited earlier, where both Madison and Hamilton re-

---

[22] *Federalist* 9, pp. 48–49. See *Federalist* 63, pp. 412–413, where Madison suggests a somewhat different view of ancient political practice. Note also that he regards Carthage as a form of *popular government!*—thus placing in question Diamond's interpretative classification referred to above, pp. 104–105. Finally, compare Madison's account of the Cosmi of Crete with Aristotle's *Politics*, p. 82.

veal the brighter side of human nature. Certainly Hamilton did not regard government as a necessary evil. Indeed, we have seen that he regarded the office of a legislator as a "precious trust," one that enables "a man of virtue and ability" to promote human happiness. Such a man—recall Hamilton's words—"would look down with contempt upon every mean or interested pursuit." To be sure, men of this caliber are exceptional, and government, to repeat, cannot be based on the exceptions. Instead, it must be so designed as to supply "by opposite and rival interests, the defect of better motives" (337). But this does not mean that the government established under the Constitution was designed to operate indefinitely *without* such "better motives." Rather, it was designed to avoid the worst of political evils at those inevitable times when enlightened statesmen would not be at the helm. Finally, if *Federalist* 51 may be attributed to Madison, as I believe it may, the "reflection on human nature" of which he speaks may very well have been emphasized to counteract a doctrine which had then gained currency, a doctrine that may be traced to Rousseau, namely, the natural goodness of man. Whatever the case, the indubitable emphasis in *The Federalist* on the passions is but the other side of a work which, by means of an enlightened rhetoric—but rhetoric nonetheless—seeks to *persuade* men to support a Constitution which, in the opinion of its authors, will favor the rule of reason, and partly by balancing one passion against another.

If the founders' science of politics may be traced to Machiavelli through Hobbes and Locke *as understood by Diamond*, James Wilson would have been surprised, not to say shocked, by the revelation. Wilson was a signer of the Declaration of Independence, a member of the Continental Congress, and, in addition to having been a most prominent delegate at the Federal Convention, an associate justice of the United States Supreme Court. An eclectic with considerable erudition, Wilson had a favorable opinion of Locke and a most contrary one of Hobbes (as well as of Hume and Descartes). "Mr. Locke," said Wilson in his law lectures of 1790–91 at the College of Philadelphia, "[was] one of the most able, most sincere, and most amiable assertors of Christianity and true philosophy. . . ." Nevertheless, Wilson admitted that "the writings of Mr. Locke have facilitated the progress, and have given strength to the effects of scepticism . . . [which Mr. Locke] would have deprecated and prevented, had he discovered or foreseen them."[23] Unlike Locke, however, Wilson regarded man as social by nature, and as having duties and obligations whose ultimate sanction is divine law or the will of God.[24] Accepting Cicero's definition of law as right reason, eternal and immutable, Wilson rejected the moral or cultural relativism foreshadowed by Hobbes. In his law lectures he remarked:

[I]t is . . . said, that moral sentiment is different in different countries, in different ages, and under different forms of government and religion; in a word, that it is as much the effect of custom, fashion, and artifice, as our taste in dress, furniture, and the modes of conversation. Facts and narratives have been assembled and accumulated, to evince the great diversity and even contrariety that subsists concerning moral opinions. . . . It may, however, be proper to observe, that it is but candid to consider human nature in her improved, and not in her most rude or depraved forms. "The good experienced man," says Aristotle, "is the last measure of all things." To ascertain moral principles, we appeal not to the common sense of savages, but of men in their most perfect state.

And Wilson went on to say:

Epicurus, as well as some modern advocates of the same philosophy [such as Hobbes], seem to have taken their estimates of human nature from its meanest and most degrading exhibitions; but the noblest and most respectable philosophers of antiquity have chosen, for a much wiser and better purpose, to

[23] Works of James Wilson, I, 104. See ibid., pp. 214–218, 223–224, for Wilson's critique of Hume and Descartes. See also Kathleen Cobwen, ed., The Philosophical Lectures of Samuel Taylor Coleridge (London: Pilot Press, Ltd., 1948), p. 379, where Coleridge says: "Locke is no materialist. He teaches no doctrine of infidelity, whatever may be deduced from them."

[24] Ibid., I, 126–147, 225–242. Wilson also rejected Locke's utilitarian and contractual view of the relationship between parents and children.

view it on the brightest and most advantageous side. "It is impossible," says the incomparable Addison, "to read a passage in Plato or Tully, and a thousand other ancient moralists, without being a greater and a better man for it."[25]

Wilson rejected as simplistic a political philosophy based on egotism or self-interest on the one hand, and utility on the other.[26] Indeed, he regarded a government based on such principles as ignoble. "The cultivation and improvement of the human mind," he said at the Federal Convention, "[i]s the most noble object [of government]."[27] Despite these classical notions, however, Wilson's proposals at the Federal Convention were perhaps more inclined toward democracy than those of any other delegate.[28] Strange indeed was the meaning of "democracy" or of "republic" or of "popular government" in the minds of many of the founders.

Still, what was "new" about the political science of these men? Was it the fragmentation of society into a multiplicity of diverse interests? Plutarch, well studied by Madison and Hamilton, tells us that Numa resorted to the same method in order to overcome factionalism in Rome. What is to be seen here is the method of *divide et impera*. These are in fact the very terms which Madison used to describe his pluralistic solution to the problem of majority faction in that letter he wrote to Jefferson one month before the publication of *Federalist* 10.[29] This principle (which of course Madison did not publicize) illuminates the following statement in *Federalist* 10, namely, that "In the extent and proper structure of the Union . . . we behold a republican remedy for the diseases most incident to republican government" (62). This statement was anticipated by Madison during the Federal Convention, when he declared that "an election of one branch at least of the Legislature by the people immediately . . . was the

[25] *Ibid.*, I, 139, and see Hobbes, *Leviathan*, p. 104. As regards the question as to who should rule, however, Wilson, of course, differed from Aristotle, as is indicated in *Works of James Wilson*, I, 106–107.

[26] *Ibid.*, I, 134, 200, 228–229.

[27] *Farrand*, I, 605; and see *Works of James Wilson*, I, 239.

[28] But see *ibid.*, I, 240, for Wilson's anti-egalitarianism.

[20] *Writings*, V, 31, and see above, p. 39.

only defence against the inconveniences of democracy consistent with the democratic form of Government."[30] According to Aristotle, however, only an amateur politician would seek to remedy the vices of democracy by democratic means (232). What many commentators fail to note is that the major object of *Federalist* 10 is to justify the representative principle as applied to the *lower* branch of the national legislature. Here, recall the previous analysis of *Federalist* 10. The republican remedy for republican vices consisted, partly, in multiplying the number of citizens involved in the election of representatives, thus making it more difficult for demagogues to bribe the people with their promises. To extend the analysis: only if the *lower* branch is directly elected by the people can the loyalties of the people be *divided* between the national and state governments, a division which must necessarily reduce the power of the states. At the same time, the representative principle—the same principle employed in *all* the state governments—makes possible the fragmentation of society into a multiplicity of diverse interests which will now be channeled into the House of Representatives, but an institution which, by virtue of that very fragmentation, will be rendered relatively impotent. Impotent relative to what, however? Can it be a Senate having a different political complexion and purpose? Consider the subtlety of this passage from *Federalist* 53, where Madison is speaking of the tenure of the House of Representatives:

> No argument can be drawn on this subject, from the case of the delegates to the existing Congress. They are elected annually, it is true; but their reelection is considered by the legislative assemblies almost as a matter of course. The election of the representatives of the people would not be governed by the same principle [because the people's preferences in such matters are more fluctuating].
>
> A few of the members, as happens in all such assemblies, will possess superior talents; will, by frequent reelections, become members of long standing; will be thoroughly masters of the

[30] *Farrand*, I, 134–135; and compare the citation in *Diamond*, p. 54, n. 3.

public business, and perhaps not unwilling to avail themselves of those advantages. The greater the proportion of new members, and the less the information of the bulk of the members, the more apt will they be to fall into the snares that may be laid for them. *This remark is no less applicable to the relation which will subsist between the House of Representatives and the Senate* (352).[31]

So, one may indeed behold "a republican remedy for the diseases most incident to republican government." The representative principle, conforming to the principle of *divide et impera*, will accomplish the following objectives: First, it will cool those "hotbeds" of democracy, the state governments, by diverting the loyalties of the people toward the national government. That is, the democratic parts of those state governments will now be less likely to usurp the powers of the nondemocratic parts, for not only the loyalties, but some of the interests, of the people will be diverted toward the national government. Second, because of the fluctuating preferences of the people, their House of Representatives will be a rather mutable body whose very mutability will render it relatively weak in comparison to a more stable Senate. In short, a seemingly big dose of democracy may serve to cure the diseases of democracy, provided, of course, that certain branches of government are constituted by different principles. Divide and *then* rule.[32]

If the regime established by the founders is *sui generis*, it could only be such insofar as it represents a political synthesis of classical, Christian, and modern values. It cannot be called democratic yet just without violating Aristotelian criteria. If this

[31] Italics added. Here the reader will recall my analysis of Madison's rhetorical strategy (pp. 46–53 above), a strategy which uses seemingly democratic arguments on behalf of nondemocratic ends. Hamilton employs the same rhetorical device, the best example of which appears in *Federalist* 84, where he argues against a Bill of Rights on popular grounds! See also *Federalist* 68, pp. 441–442, *Federalist* 71, pp. 464–465, and *Federalist* 78, pp. 505–506, for other examples of this device.

[32] The validity of this statement does not depend on the subsequent career of the House of Representatives, no more than does the validity of any political theory depend on a particular set of historical practices.

perhaps unique regime resembles any of Aristotle's six paradigmatic types, it must be the 'polity' and only the 'polity.' The remaining chapters of Book I will remove any lingering doubt on this matter. But the present chapter cannot be drawn to a close without examining Aristotle's best variety of democracy.

First, certain aspects of the previous argument should be brought into proximity with what follows. Recall the problem of distinguishing a democracy from a 'polity,' a problem resulting from the fact that the two regimes shade into each other. To distinguish clearly between the two, it was necessary to go to the extreme end of the democratic spectrum, there to describe the character of radical democracy: (1) its libertarianism—"living as you like," free from all legal and moral restraints; its lack of moderation or the ceaseless striving after immediate gratification; (2) its egalitarianism—or the leveling of all distinctions based on merit, a leveling corresponding to the decline of deference; (3) its disregard for the rights of property, a consequence of the democratic notion of justice; and (4) its political instability and personal insecurity resulting from the constant overturning of law or the widespread contempt for all forms of authority. Only after elaborating upon these features of radical democracy was it possible to appreciate how profoundly different was the regime envisioned by the founding fathers: (1) where liberty would be restrained and moderation promoted by a government that controlled and regulated the passions; (2) where, consistent with a deferential society, equality would be understood to mean equality of opportunity, with the consequence that men would be rewarded on the basis of merit; (3) where the first but not last object of government would be to protect the rights of property on which justice and the very existence of that deferential society would depend; and (4) where political stability and personal security would be achieved by the operation of countervailing interests and passions, but also by fostering a reverence for law, itself conducive to the rule of reason in public affairs. All this would require (a) the division of society into a multiplicity of diverse interests, to be represented in the House of Representatives, and (b) the restraints and guidance of institutions based on other principles. The question is: Do these other principles conform to those of a 'polity,' or may they still fall within the democratic spectrum? Before this question can be fully resolved, it will be necessary to examine Aristotle's best variety of democracy.

3

Aristotle's discussion of the best variety of democracy is not free from ambiguity, if not contradiction. That he preferred a democracy whose citizens consisted mainly of farmers is clear enough. This means that the best democracy requires a landed property qualification, albeit a small one, for attending the assembly (264, 167). We should not be misled by that qualification. Even the best variety of democracy involves the rule of the poor. Aristotle's farmers would have to work for the necessities of life; they would enjoy little leisure—so little that they would have to "confine the meetings of the assembly to a minimum" (171). Most citizens of Aristotle's best democracy would not have much opportunity to develop the political virtues. They would consist of more or less crude rustics living in isolation from one another. And, within limits, the further they lived from the city, hence the less frequently they held meetings in the assembly, so much the better for the quality of this democracy!— according to Aristotle. He writes: "When [in addition to a populace of farmers] there is also the further advantage of a countryside which lies at a considerable distance from the city, it is easy to construct a good democracy or a good 'polity'" (265). This remarkable passage, which appears in Book VI, renders more challenging the question of how to distinguish a "good" democracy from a good 'polity'?

Before that question can be answered it will be necessary to examine an earlier passage in Book VI where Aristotle first discusses why the best variety of democracy requires a farming populace:

Such people, not having any great amount of property, are busily occupied; and they have thus no time for attending the assembly. Not possessing the necessities of life, they stick to their work, and do not covet what does not belong to them; indeed they find more pleasure in work than they do in politics and government—unless there are large pickings to be got from having a finger in government. The masses covet profits more than they covet honours; witness the patience with which they bore the old-time tyrannies [and still tolerate, I might interject, such modern tyrannies as the Soviet Union] . . . if only they are allowed to get on with their work and are not robbed of their earnings. . . . Any craving which the masses may feel for position and power will be satisfied if they are given the right of electing magistrates and calling them to account (263).

Applying this passage to the one in question, it might be tempting to conclude: "If the farmers attend the assembly, you will have a good democracy; whereas, if, instead of attending the assembly themselves, they elect magistrates, you will have a good 'polity.' " This distinction could then be compared to *The Federalist*'s distinction between a pure democracy and a republic, the latter characterized by the representative principle. There is, however, a difficulty with this interpretation. For even should our rustics elect magistrates, Aristotle might still want readers to regard the arrangement as consistent with democracy. Indeed, in the sequel to the above passage, he constructs a model of what he calls the best variety of democracy, which he describes as follows:

On the one hand all the citizens will enjoy the three rights of electing magistrates, calling them to account, and sitting in the law courts; on the other hand the most important offices will be filled by election, and confined to those who can satisfy a property qualification. The greater the importance of an office, the greater might be the property qualification required. Alternatively, no property qualification might be required for any office, but only men of capacity would actually be appointed. A regime which is governed in this way will be sure to be well governed (its offices will always be in the hands of the best of its members, with the people giving its consent and bearing no grudge against persons of quality); and the men of quality and the notables will be sure to be satisfied, under a system which at once preserves them from being governed by other and inferior persons and ensures (by giving others the right to call them to account) that they will themselves govern justly (264).

Clearly, this description of the "best" variety of democracy is the description of what appears to be a *just* regime—Aristotle's classification of regimes in Book III to the contrary notwithstanding! But to compound his apparent inconsistency, it may be asked how Aristotle can properly speak of a *good* or *best* democracy in the first place, especially when he has also cautioned us that "It cannot properly be said that one form of oligarchy is better than another; it can only be said that one is not so bad as another" (158). Although this caution may appear as a verbal quibble—but is it correct to refer to *good* cheats and cut-throats? —why does Aristotle not apply its logic to a democracy which, like oligarchy, was said to have been a bad regime?[33] It would be easy to dismiss the problem as a contradiction or to explain it away by saying that the *Politics* is a collection of different essays assembled by Aristotle (or by some subsequent editor) under a single title, but not organized into a single treatise.[34] Can it be, however, that Aristotle did not want to disparage democracy beyond what was required in his philosophical analysis of regimes in Book III?—this, in view of his admission that hardly any better regime was possible in his time (143).[35] Furthermore, given the emphatically practical purposes of Book VI (which, together with Books IV and V, provides guidelines for the construction, reform, and preservation of regimes), perhaps Aristotle, seeking to *elevate* democracy, deliberately and with rhetorical intent, described the "best" variety of democracy in terms more appropriate to a 'polity'? Whatever the case, virtually the same confusion of regimes will be found in Book IV

[33] See Diamond *et al.*, *The Democratic Republic*, 2nd ed., p. 100, n. 23.
[34] See Barker's introduction to the *Politics*, xxxvii.
[35] See p. 246, n. 3 below.

where, in two passages separated by only one paragraph, Aristotle identifies a democratic and an aristocratic method of distributing the various powers or functions of a deliberative assembly. Before examining these passages, however, it will be necessary to set forth Aristotle's account of those functions.

> The deliberative element [of government] is sovereign (1) on the issues of war and peace, and the making and breaking of alliances; (2) in the enacting of laws; (3) in cases where the penalty of death, exile, and confiscation is involved; and (4) in the appointment of magistrates and the calling them to account on the expiration of their office (189).

Aristotle goes on to explain that the decision-making power over these issues may be organized in three basic ways: first, the democratic system where *all* the citizens decide on *all* issues; second, the oligarchic system where *all* issues are decided by only *some* of the citizens; and third, the aristocratic system where *some* of the citizens decide on *some* issues, while *all* the citizens decide on others. Each of these basic systems may be constructed in a variety of ways, some better, some worse.

Here is what appears to be the best method of organizing the democratic system:

> [All] the citizens should meet for the two purposes of appointing and examining magistrates, and deliberating on issues of war and foreign policy, but other matters [i.e., the enactment of laws, and the infliction of major penalties] should be left to the control of boards of magistrates which, as far as possible, are kept elective—boards to which men of experience and knowledge ought to be appointed (190).

Bearing in mind that Aristotle expressly designates such a system as democratic (191), compare the following:

> [Another] system of arrangement is that *some* of the citizens should deliberate on *some* matters—but not on all. [The effect will be that on other matters, *all* the citizens will deliberate.] For instance, all the citizens may exercise the deliberative power in regard to war and peace and the examination of magistrates;

but the magistrates only may exercise that power on issues other than these [i.e., the enactment of laws, and the infliction of major penalties], and these magistrates may be appointed by election.[36] When this is the case, the regime is an aristocracy (191).

Notice there are no generic differences between the above "two" modes of organizing the deliberative assembly or its distribution of powers. To be sure, Aristotle may have different kinds of citizens in mind; but this would not alter the *formal* identity of the "two" systems. This being the case, how are we to account for the fact that he calls one "democratic" and the other "aristocratic"?

It must first be recalled that the term "aristocratic" has a relative as well as an absolute signification for Aristotle. Again, "The only regime which can with strict justice be called an aristocracy is one where the members are not merely 'good' in relation to some standard or other, but are absolutely 'the best' (*aristoi*) in point of moral quality" (173). But as Barker notes, Aristotle, "sometimes uses the term aristocracy to denote a mixed constitution—apparently on the ground that the principle of recognition of merit (which is the essential element of aristocracy) is also essential in a good 'polity.' "[37] It would be correct to conclude, therefore, that the method of distributing the deliberative powers, which Aristotle ascribes to an "aristocracy," may equally be ascribed to a 'polity' wherein some regard is given to merit, in addition to wealth and numbers.[38] The question remains, however: How can Aristotle ascribe the same method to a democracy (albeit, of the best variety)?

[36] Barker notes that in the Greek manuscripts the words "or by lot" follow, but he excludes them on grounds it would render the regime democratic. Meanwhile, H. Rackham (Loeb Library, at 1298b8), inserts "not by lot." In my opinion, both translators are in error, and the original should be retained for the reasons about to be discussed. But see also p. 177 below.

[37] *Politics*, Note M, p. 87, and compare pp. 84–85, 176. This could be a 'polity' inclined toward aristocracy—of which Aristotle speaks in the sequel to the passage in question. The reader should bear in mind that just as 'polities' shade into democracies, so do they shade into oligarchies and "aristocracies."

[38] Confirmed below, pp. 134, n. 1, 176, n. 41, referring to relevant passages in the text.

If a good democracy and a 'polity' employ the same method of distributing the deliberative powers, the two regimes must differ in virtue of some other causal factor. As noted earlier, Aristotle's regime analysis distinguishes between formal and material causality: a regime may be one thing *de jure* and a very different thing *de facto*. For example, the laws of two regimes may prescribe an "aristocratic" method of constituting a senate; but whereas one senate may in fact serve the interests of rich and poor alike, the other may in fact serve primarily the interests of the poor. All depends on the character of the men who compose the senate, as well as on the character of their electors. It is one thing if the senators are elected by people who live in the countryside, another if their election is dominated by the heavily concentrated population of the city. The first senate will be more stable, more heedful of the rights of property, more attached to religious and national traditions. The second will be given to frequent change, responding to the fluctuating wants or desires of the many, coveting the multifarious goods of the shopping center (67, 265).

Now, all other things being equal, an arrangement which enables the many to choose magistrates is not as democratic as one providing for the appointment of magistrates by lot. For choosing involves, at least in principle, an act of deliberation. But every act or activity aims at some real or apparent good. We choose one person for office over another because we believe he is superior in merit or better qualified to advance some end or purpose which we judge to be salutary. Hence there is an "aristocratic" attribute in a system that enables the many to choose magistrates, especially if those eligible for office are not limited to the rich. The formal arrangement involves two factors, that of number and that of quality. But the many tend to associate quality with wealth. Thus, for practical purposes, the arrangement in question will include an oligarchic attribute, inclining the regime toward a 'polity.' On the other hand, if we turn from the formal or legal arrangement and look at the actual character of things, we may find not a 'polity,' but a democracy, for the many may choose magistrates who in fact serve democratic ends.

This said, let us go back to the "two" methods of distributing the deliberative powers. Notice that for the so-called democratic method, Aristotle says the enactment of laws "*should* be left to the control of boards of magistrates which, *as far as possible*, are kept elective" (190) (italics added). Here Aristotle is *prescribing* a system which a statesman might employ in constructing the best variety of democracy. What he is prescribing, however, is the very system he subsequently *describes* or designates as "aristocratic." As anticipated, this may be construed as a rhetorical device intended by Aristotle to elevate the character of democracy beyond the definitional limits of that species enunciated in Book III of the *Politics*. But disregarding the rhetoric suggested in that work—which nonetheless was addressed to Greek statesmen—Aristotle is saying, in effect, that it is possible as well as desirable for the best variety of democracy to employ an "aristocratic" method of distributing the various deliberative powers. Should this be done, the *formal* character of the regime would be "aristocratic," while its *material* character would be democratic. The existence of the form, however, would tend to incline the regime somewhat toward "aristocracy," which again may be identified as a 'polity.' (This fact, bear in mind, is of crucial significance for the regime established by the founders.)

Now recall Aristotle's remark that a farming populace removed some distance from the city provides the best material for constructing a "good" democracy or a good 'polity.' From this it should not be inferred that the moral and intellectual character of farmers living under one regime would be equal to that of farmers living under the other. The rustics predominating in Aristotle's democracy are very industrious; they live very simple lives; and *if* they elect gentlemen to office, they may even be regarded as deferential. Nevertheless, they are still poor, and the poor, it should be apparent, do not predominate in Aristotle's 'polity.' This means that the farmers living in the best variety of democracy would enjoy less leisure and would therefore attain a lesser degree of human excellence than would farmers living in a 'polity.' Furthermore, nothing Aristotle says about those rustics suggests a quality of life comparable to that envisioned for the citizens of Madison's republic.[39] This is not the place to enlarge upon Madison's intentions and expectations regarding the way of life of the American people. Nevertheless, while he too preferred a republic consisting mainly of cultivators of the soil, he also anticipated the relative decline of their number in the United States with the growth of commerce. At the time of the founding, however, Madison beheld a rare opportunity. There before him was a population of farmers, a people "so much accustomed to be guided by their rulers on all new and intricate questions." *Now* was the moment to endow *that* people with a form of government appropriate to *their* moral character *and* material conditions, a government superior to any that would be acceptable to the people who would come after them—to people less likely to be guided by their rulers on all new and intricate questions. Only establish a high-toned government now, and one or another of its institutions would serve to mitigate whatever corruption the future held in store.

If it be a reflection on human nature (or on the human condition), that the best regime in theory has never come into being and never will short of a miracle, how much sadder the condition of man if Aristotle was right when he said that the best regime in practice, the 'polity,' is a very rare political phenomenon (183). And yet, if this be so, would it not be to the glory of the founding fathers if the republic they established does indeed exemplify this rare phenomenon? To answer this question, I shall henceforth employ philosophical as well as historical modes of analysis.

[39] See pp. 204–205 below. In this connection (and in light of the remainder of the present paragraph), it may be noted that Mill, who accepted the inevitable ascendancy of democracy, proceeded to prescribe aristocratic checks against its attendant evils, but couched in democratic language. See Mill, *Representative Government*, chs. 5–8.

CHAPTER IV

The 'Polity' under the Formal Mode of Regime Analysis:
The Psychology of Political Forms

BY ITS VERY NATURE, a well-designed 'polity' is difficult to distinguish from a democracy on one side, and from an oligarchy on the other. One reason is that the formal attributes of which a 'polity' is composed do not stand wholly separated from each other; rather they are blended as in a mixture. Says Aristotle: "We may add that it is a good criterion of a proper mixture of democracy and oligarchy that a mixed regime should be able to be described indifferently as either. When this can be said, it must obviously be due to the excellence of the mixture. It is a thing which can generally be said of the mean between two extremes: both of the extremes can be traced in the mean [and it can thus be described by the name of either]" (177–178). A well-designed 'polity' has a variety of democratic and oligarchic attributes which blend into each other. The statesman who would construct such a regime must know what these attributes are and the different methods by which they may be combined. Here he could hardly do better than consult Aristotle's *Politics*, for under the formal mode of regime analysis, it provides the most comprehensive methodology for constructing a 'polity.'

Aristotle's analysis begins by distinguishing three general methods of constructing a 'polity,' each of which requires a mixture of quantitative and qualitative factors. These general methods are subsequently refined and employed for the purpose of designing each of the three ruling parts of the regime, namely, the deliberative assembly, the magisterial offices, and the law courts, which roughly correspond to what we term the legislative, executive, and judicial branches of government. Since each of these branches has a variety of powers or functions which may be exercised by different persons appointed in different ways, there results an incredible number of arrangements by which the quantitative and qualitative factors may be combined. Finally, by judiciously combining both factors in each function as well as in each branch of government, a 'polity' may be constructed which is indeed difficult to distinguish either from a democracy or from an oligarchy.

1

To facilitate this discussion, I shall set forth Aristotle's brief treatment of the three general methods of constructing a 'polity' and then proceed to analyze them individually.

There are three different principles on which men may act in making such a combination or mixture [as to constitute a 'polity']. The first is to take and use simultaneously both democratic and oligarchic rules. . . . In oligarchies the rich are fined if they do not sit in the courts, and the poor receive no pay for sitting. In democracies, on the other hand, the poor are given pay for sitting, and the rich are not fined if they fail to sit. To combine both of these rules is to adopt a common or middle term between either; and for that reason such a method is characteristic of a 'polity.' . . . A second is to strike an average, or take a mean, between the two different rules. One regime, for example, requires no property qualification at all, or only a very low qualification, for the right to attend the assembly: the other requires a high qualification. Here both of the rules cannot be used to provide a common term; and we have to take the mean between the two. The third way of combination is [neither to take the whole of both rules, nor to strike an average between them, but] to combine elements from both, and to mix part of the oligarchical rule with a part of the democratic. In the appointment of magistrates, for example, the use of the lot is regarded as democratic, and the use of the vote as oligarchical. Again, it is considered to be democratic that a property qualification should not be required, and oligarchical that it should be. Here, accordingly, the mode appropriate to an aristocracy [of the mixed type] or a 'polity' is to . . . take from oligarchy the rule that magistrates should be appointed by vote, and from democracy the rule that no property qualification should be required (177).[1]

Clearly the third method of constituting a 'polity' conforms to the mode of constituting every single branch of government prescribed by the American Constitution—and this, quite apart from the property qualifications required for several of the state legislatures and the indirect modes of electing United States Senators, the President, and the Justices of the Supreme Court. But consider only the House of Representatives.

Article I, Section 2, of the Constitution provides that:

> The House of Representatives shall be composed of members chosen every second year by the people of the several states, and the electors in each state shall have the qualifications requisite for electors of the most numerous branch of the state legislature.
>
> No person shall be a Representative who shall not have attained to the age of twenty-five years, and been seven years a citizen of the United States, and who shall not, when elected, be an inhabitant of that state in which he shall be chosen.

To make virtually all citizens eligible for office in the House of Representatives is democratic. But this being a *representative* assembly, very few citizens, needless to say, can, at any one time, or over the course of time, become members of this assembly, for the Constitution also provides that "the number of Representatives shall not exceed one for every thirty-thousand. . . ." Here

---

[1] This last sentence supports my interpretation of those ambiguous passages discussed above, pp. 125–128. For further confirmation, see p. 176, n. 41 below, referring to the relevant passages in the text.

the question arises: Although virtually any adult may be a representative, is the representative principle itself democratic? It would be a grave error to ignore the opinion that an elective office is or may be partly oligarchic. To slight this opinion may well be to trivialize the significance of the representative principle—a dangerous thing to do in democratic times. It would not be inappropriate, therefore, to refer again to *Federalist* 10, where Madison discusses the advantages of a republic, in which the people act through representatives, over a pure democracy, in which the people act directly.

As noted earlier, one salutary effect of the representative principle, according to Madison, is that it serves "to refine and enlarge the public views, by passing them through the medium of a chosen body of citizens, whose wisdom may best discern the true interest of their country, and whose patriotism and love of justice will be least likely to sacrifice it to temporary or partial considerations" (59).[2] In a pure democracy, however, the individual citizen is his own political agent. Accountable to no one, his wants and opinions tend to assume an imperious character. But the logic of pure democracy requires the equality of all wants and opinions, with the result that each individual is thrust upon himself and rendered relatively powerless. To achieve any object, he must combine with others having similar interests, the political consequence of which is the rule of the one opinion shared by the majority. The majority tend to be governed by immediate wants or desires. Linked to the body on the one hand, and mediated by imagination on the other, these wants are especially susceptible to proliferation and fluctuation. Hence arises a proliferation and fluctuation of laws aimed at gratifying the desires of the majority.[3] Now let me complicate the character of

[2] In this connection, see Harry M. Clor, "American Democracy and the Challenge of Radical Democracy," in Robert A. Goldwin, ed., *How Democratic Is America?* (Chicago: Rand McNally & Co., 1971), pp. 87–88, which suggests that *The Federalist* may not be democratic (or merely so), but fails to take an explicit position on the issue.

[3] I assume that the economy is something more than one of scarcity. See Aristotle, *Politics*, p. 171.

these individuals, but under a regime that employs the representative principle.

It is the case that no two individuals hold and retain the same gradation of wants; nor do they hold and retain with equal intensity the same opinions as to how these wants may be satisfied. Instead, each individual has a distinct bias consisting in the importance he attaches, say, to one among a number of diverse interests. This means that, within each individual, there are competing and mutually obstructing wants and, corresponding to these, a variety of possible opinions on public matters philosophically in tension with one another.[4] Suppose, now, that a large number of these individuals periodically choose a person to represent them in a deliberative assembly. For obvious reasons the views of the representative on public matters will be more comprehensive than those of most of his constituents taken individually (which is not to say they will be unbiased). Here, comprehensiveness should be construed to mean understanding the connectedness of diverse things, such as various opinions and interests. Insofar as the representative possesses such comprehensiveness, he will excel most of his constituents in practical wisdom and justice—which, after all, are among the very qualities people seek in a representative. Madison himself argues in *Federalist* 10 that popular elections held in fairly large districts are likely to result in the election of representatives "whose enlightened views and virtuous sentiments [would] render them superior to local prejudices and to schemes of injustice" (61); and earlier, that such representatives would pursue "great and national objects" in contradistinction to merely "local and particular" interests (60). From this, certain consequences follow. First, a representative is in the position to "refine and enlarge" the inevitable bias of his constituents' opinions regarding public matters. Second, he is in the position to promote distributive justice and, in the process, to make his constituents more just than they

---

[4] It follows that an individual is not a unity but a multiplicity, and that the notion of a single interest constituency is, *a fortiori*, a misleading abstraction. See Plato, *Republic* 423a, d.

would be in a democracy. These consequences, it must be emphasized, depend on the discriminating and assimilative powers of reason wherein reside the principle of self-directed or independent activity. To be sure, the representative is not wholly independent. Still, even though he depends for his office on the suffrages of others, this dependency is only in tension, and not simply inconsistent, with the principle of reason. For the fact that he is accountable to his constituents imposes upon him the restraints of other opinions which partake of rationality and which compel him to reflect upon the requirements of distributive justice (264). It goes without saying, however, that everything ultimately depends on the character of those who comprise his constituency. But here I am speaking not of the material but of the formal mode of regime analysis. The representative may in fact lack the intellectual and moral qualities necessary for actualizing the potentialities of the representative principle. Nevertheless, Aristotle is correct in attributing to the elective method of choosing magistrates a synthesis of oligarchic and democratic attributes appropriate to a 'polity.' But there is a more subtle reason for doing so.

That a representative is chosen by a large number of citizens augments the factor of *honor*. Like the representative principle itself, honor involves a dependency-independency relationship. While the representative wants the good opinion of others— which he obviously needs to achieve any political good—he wants to be honored for possessing that which he himself deems honorable or praiseworthy, namely, his own virtues or skill as a statesman. Furthermore, he especially wishes to be honored by men of practical wisdom, men whose character he respects and who are capable of intelligent judgment regarding the very excellence which he possesses and wishes to be recognized.[5] Now, one of the things for which men are honored is their independence (which is one reason why the average man tends to defer to men of independent wealth). But as already noted, indepen-

[5] See Aristotle, *Nicomachean Ethics* 1095b22–30, 1159a21–24, cited and discussed below, p. 259 (hereafter cited as *Nic. Eth.*).

dence, at its deepest level, involves the self-directed activity of reason. The desire for honor thus points beyond itself to that which is intrinsically honorable because intrinsically human— or to that which most dignifies and perfects human nature, namely, the contemplative intellect. It may be said, therefore, that insofar as the representative principle augments the factor of honor, it doubly affirms the principle of rationality and, with this, the theme of independence so prominent in *The Federalist*. That theme, within the context of the representative principle, exemplifies the synthesis of democratic and oligarchic attributes peculiar to a 'polity.'[6] More will be said about the representative principle later when discussing the nature of deliberation. Here I must interrupt the analysis of the third general method of constructing a 'polity' to consider the first.

Recall that this method requires the combination of democratic and oligarchic rules, each taken as a whole. Using Aristotle's example of law courts (which, in Athens, were composed of ordinary citizens rather than professional judges), two combinations are possible. One is to pay the poor for attending the courts while fining the rich for not attending, thus insuring the attendance of both classes (187). The only other alternative is neither to pay the poor nor fine the rich. Aristotle does not mention this alternative, presumably because its practical effect would be to exclude the poor and thus incline the regime toward oligarchy. Be this as it may, perhaps an analogy may be drawn between Aristotle's example and the Constitutional provision that "Senators and Representatives shall receive a compensation for their services, to be ascertained by law, and payed out of the treasury of the United States." Confining the discussion to representatives, it goes without saying that none are fined for failing to attend the House, so that the analogy with Aristotle's example of the law courts seems to break down. Besides, the very provision for paying all representatives is itself democratic. Still, this is not the last word on the subject.

[6] The reader should bear in mind that Aristotle also regards this synthesis as appropriate in an aristocracy of the mixed type.

The principle reason for compensating representatives out of the national treasury was to render them more independent of the state governments. (The same may be said of the Constitutional prohibition against their holding any state office.) But as regards the compensation itself, it will have been observed that no fixed amount is specified in the Constitution—as had been proposed by Madison in opposition to Hamilton. Instead, the sum is to be determined by law, meaning, by the members of Congress themselves. Madison opposed this arrangement on two grounds. First, he thought it was an "indecent thing" to leave members of Congress to regulate their own wages. Second, he thought it "might in time prove a most dangerous one."[7] Why dangerous? If the compensation established by Congress were very high, it would encourage men to seek public office for private gain, or it would attract the poor or their demagogues. On the other hand, if the compensation were very low, not only would the poor be excluded, but so too would many of the middle class, including men of virtue and ability. But such is the complex interdependence of the various attributes which make up political institutions that, over against these considerations, it is necessary to take into account the electoral laws. Given a low property qualification for voting and none at all for holding office in the House of Representatives, were Congress to enact a compensation law effectively excluding all but the rich, sooner or later the voters would elect representatives of less oligarchic inclinations. Of course, these representatives would have to contend with members of the Senate, many of whose electors in the state legislatures hold office on the basis of a considerable property qualification.

Be all this as it may, the political character of the constitutional provision for compensation cannot be accurately determined apart from contemporaneous opinion about this matter. This may be ascertained by examining the compensation law enacted by

[7] *Farrand*, I, 216, 373, and compare his argument at the Virginia ratifying convention in favor of the Constitutional provision in question, *ibid.*, III, 312–316.

the first Congress of the United States. Here we learn that both representatives and senators were to receive, as a compensation for their services, the sum of $6.00 per day for each day Congress was in session. Madison and others complained it was too high, at least for representatives. From the debates over the compensation law, it appears that (1) the states paid their delegates to the Continental Congress an average of approximately $5.50 per day; (2) many states paid their own legislators $2.00 per day; (3) $2.00 a day was deemed the minimum required for room and board (for a single person); and (4) $5.00 was deemed sufficient to defray ordinary daily expenses.[8] Now, in the 1790s, Congress convened on an average of 120 days a year, so that a representative would annually receive, as a compensation for his services, approximately $720. So far as I have been able to determine, $720 in 1800 would be equivalent to $1,716 in 1971— well below the so-called poverty line.[9] The political significance of this data can hardly be exaggerated.

Such data indicates that public office in those days was regarded not as a means of earning a livelihood, but as a public duty to be undertaken by respectable men, that is, by *gentlemen.* Those gentlemen, of course, had private sources of income, either from land or business or the practice of law. The compensation provided for public services was nothing more than that.

[8] *Annals,* 1st Cong., 1st Sess., pp. 651–658, 676–688, *passim.* See also *The Writings of George Washington* (39 vols.; Washington, D.C.: Government Printing Office, 1931–44), XXXI, 50n (cited hereafter as *Writings*); *The Papers of James Madison* (6 vols. to date; Chicago: University of Chicago Press, 1962–69), II, 98, n. 5, 8, III, 263, n. 3, IV, 87–88, 377, n. 12, V, 19, n. 4 (hereafter cited as *Papers*); James Madison, *Letters and Other Writings* (4 vols.; New York: J. B. Lippincott & Co., 1884), I, 489–490. It should be noted that members of Congress received an allowance of six dollars for every twenty miles of travel.

[9] Based on data provided by the Bureau of Labor Statistics in a letter to the author dated November 5, 1971, citing U.S. Consumer Price Index for all items from 1800 to September, 1971. See also U.S. Bureau of the Census, *Historical Statistics of the United States, Colonial Times to 1957* (Washington, D.C.: 1960), p. 116, which shows that the Wholesale Price Index (1910–14 = 100) rose from 86 in 1789 to 129 in 1800. Since Congress did not alter the compensation of its members until 1816, this inflation represents a considerable decline in purchasing power.

The $6.00 per diem for congressmen was calculated to exclude the indigent and the avaricious on the one hand, and, on the other hand, to make it possible for virtuous and talented men of moderate means to hold office without too great a sacrifice of personal interest.[10] At the same time, the compensation was designed to prevent government from falling into the hands of the opulent. Whatever the influence of Locke on the founding—and it was not insignificant—there were strong competitors in the classical and Christian traditions, and those traditions were taught in the colleges of eighteenth-century America primarily with a view to shaping character and preparing men for public service. The utilitarian ethic had to contend with *noblesse oblige*.

It may be said, therefore, that the constitutional provision for compensating representatives, though democratic per se, does not violate the requirements of a 'polity' when juxtaposed by the compensation law itself (and the then prevailing sentiments about this matter). Indeed, if a regime that neither pays the poor for attending the assembly, nor fines the rich for not attending, inclines toward oligarchy, then the $6.00 compensation law compensates for that very tendency. On the other hand, if it be objected that the *principle* of compensation is the politically decisive thing, and not the prevailing attitudes concerning what constitutes an appropriate compensation for legislators, then one is simply arguing that the *de jure* (or the formal cause) is more decisive than the *de facto* (or the material cause), which is contrary to Aristotelian political science. Or if it be said, "Given the constitutional recognition of compensation, the actual compensation for legislators will steadily be increased such that the democratic implications of the principle will *eventually* prevail over political practice"—this is not saying anything different from the preceding objection. Besides, the objection is superimposing on the formal mode of analysis the mode of efficient causality, which is appropriate only when studying a regime under the category of change. Furthermore, nothing in the provision for compensation, nor in the compensation law itself, is

[10] But see Hamilton's view of the matter in *Farrand*, I, 287 (bot.), 299 (top).

intrinsically escalating, so to speak. (Perhaps it should be noted that the reason why Congress was given the power to regulate the pay of its members was simply to facilitate its adjustment should there be significant changes in monetary values.) Indeed, according to Madison—and here he was speaking in the Virginia ratifying convention: "In America, legislative bodies have reduced their own wages lower, rather than augmented them."[11] And as regards the $6.00 compensation law enacted by the first Congress, the fact is that, despite inflation, this law remained in force for the first twenty-six years of the republic.[12] But this fact notwithstanding, the only conclusion to be drawn here is that, *philosophically*, the constitutional provision for compensation, taken in conjunction with the actual compensation law and the contemporaneous opinions about this matter—including the intentions of the lawmakers—conforms to the requirements of a 'polity.'

Returning to the third general method of constructing a 'polity,' other examples may now be considered. Instead of combining democratic and oligarchic rules in a single institution, each may be taken separately and be employed in different institutions. Thus, consistent, respectively, with moderate forms of democracy and oligarchy, low property qualifications may be prescribed for electors of the House and appreciably higher ones for electors of the Senate. Or, direct popular election may be prescribed for one branch and indirect election for the other. (It should be noted, however, that for Aristotle, the extent to which the direct mode of election is democratic—for it may be partly oligarchic—depends on the machinery of election, of which more in a moment. As for the indirect mode of election— which further refines the electoral process—this Aristotle regarded as unambiguously oligarchic (61).) Finally, democratic and oligarchic rules may be employed separately by prescribing a short term of office for the House and a long term of office for

[11] *Writings*, V, 187.

[12] It was changed in 1816, when a fixed salary of $1,500 per year was provided. See above, p. 140, n. 9.

the Senate. This leads us to Aristotle's second method of constructing a 'polity.'

The second method, it will be recalled, required the striking of a mean between democratic and oligarchic principles. Here again is the quantitative domain of ambiguity, as is evident in the case of the duration of the tenure. Nevertheless, the extremes are clear enough. Thus, it is characteristic of democracies, says Aristotle, to eliminate all offices having a life tenure (259). The reason is obvious: it offends the two cardinal principles of democracy, namely, liberty and equality. The very notion of a life tenure implies that there are relatively permanent principles of political rule which should guide and restrain human activity, or impose certain limitations on what men may or may not do; that these principles should control the rate and direction of change; and that certain men are qualified to apply these principles and should apply them even when to do so is contrary to some temporary wave of popular opinion or passion. Furthermore, a long tenure of office does not set well in a nondeferential society. Its members are disinclined to bestow such honors, especially in view of the fact that a long tenure enables a legislator to exercise a degree of independence incompatible with responsiveness to the fluctuating wants of the many. Here it may be noted in passing that Jefferson, our greatest partisan of democracy, wished to reduce to six years what is, for practical purposes, the life tenure of justices of the Supreme Court.[13] Going to the other extreme, however, a tenure of six months was deemed appropriate by Aristotle for democratic offices in general (225–226). But given the size and population of the United States, it may reasonably be assumed that he would have regarded the two-year term of representatives as democratic (195). As for the six-year term of senators (which the founders thought relatively permanent in view of the likelihood of reelection), there is no reason to believe that Aristotle would have considered such a tenure as anything but oligarchic. Perhaps, therefore, he would have regarded the

[13] It should be noted, however, that Jefferson was also a partisan of virtue, but not of legislation having virtue as its end.

four-year term of the President as conformable to the mean between a democratic and oligarchic tenure.

Still another attribute which enables us to strike a mean in the
same branch of government is its *size* or the number of its members.[14] Aristotle, no less than Madison, well understood that the
larger an assembly the more democratic its formal character
(which appears evident if we simply allow it to encompass the
entire adult population of a country).[15] Conversely, the smaller
an assembly the more oligarchic its formal character. This attribute of size is intimately related to various themes discussed
earlier. Consider the related themes of honor and property (and
office is, or was once regarded as, a form of property). Accordingly, the smaller the number of men composing a political assembly, the greater the honor will each receive individually, thus
increasing his influence and independence. In addition, men look
with more concern over things which are their own than when
held in common with others (44). The members of a small assembly will thus tend to be more responsible than the members
of a large one. Besides, each member will be under greater public
scrutiny, and a regard for reputation will impose a salutary restraint on his conduct. Finally, the rationality of a political assembly tends to vary inversely with the size of its membership.
The larger an assembly, the more difficult it is to resolve its
greater diversity of opinions and interests.[16]

It should be evident, therefore, that the various attributes
which go into the making of a political institution involve various moral and psychological distinctions on the one hand, and
partake of different degrees of rationality on the other. The synthesis of democratic and oligarchic attributes in a 'polity' renders
this regime incredibly complex. For example, if the attribute of
size be considered, the presidency is obviously more oligarchic

---

[14] Property qualifications is another attribute which lends itself to the striking of a mean between democracy and oligarchy, but we have already touched
upon this attribute.

[15] See p. 165 below *in re* the *probouloi*.

[16] See *Federalist* 58, pp. 380–382, *Federalist* 63, p. 408, *Federalist* 70, pp.
459–461, and *Federalist* 71, pp. 463–464.

than the Senate and Supreme Court; whereas, if the attribute of the tenure be considered, the presidency is the least oligarchic of these institutions. The problem is further complicated by the different modes of election for these three branches, as well as by their different constitutional powers. All these formal or institutional attributes affect or implicate, in diverse and contrary ways, the generic character of the regime as a whole. Complexity, however, is not necessarily in conflict with rationality. Much depends upon whether there is a coordinating principle. By deliberate design, that coordinating principle is difficult to define in a 'polity.'[17]

Summing up this discussion of Aristotle's general methods of constructing a 'polity,' the first point to be reiterated is that a political institution has a multiplicity of attributes, democratic or oligarchic, or various combinations of both. We shall fail to grasp the complexity and subtlety of political things if this fact is slighted or regarded as mere formalism. What I have tried to set forth may be thought of as a "psychology of political forms" which, like any other, is necessarily an abstraction from a more comprehensive whole. This psychology, however, is a rational one: it gives due agency to reason and shows how reason may be enhanced or attenuated by formal causes. I recognize, and have given evidence of the fact, that a form may be empty of substance. Ultimately, not the forms of institutions but the character of the men composing them is politically decisive for the way of life of a regime. But the forms are not without political effect. They may influence opinions, expectations, and conduct. If well conceived, they may thwart the designs of wicked men; and they may facilitate the efforts of good men to pursue noble objectives by securing their independence and affording them sufficient time to realize those objectives. Nor is this all. For these forms bear witness to the aims or intentions of their architects. They point beyond the deeds of later and lesser men whom the vicissitudes of time may place in position to vitiate these forms or to obscure their true meaning. A comprehensive political science—

[17] But see my *Philosophy of the American Constitution*, pp. 167–168, 190–191.

and to foster such a science is the primary purpose of this Discourse—must include a psychology of political forms showing the reciprocal relationship between reason and passion, or how diverse passions may enlarge or contract the scope of reason, and how reason may energize or de-energize diverse passions. This said, the Discourse turns to Aristotle's analysis of the three ruling elements of government: the deliberative assembly or the legislature, the magisterial offices or the executive, and the law courts or the judiciary. I shall first reconstruct the nature of their respective functions and then proceed to consider how these institutions may be designed in accordance with the general methods of constructing a 'polity.'

2

To begin with, it may appear that Aristotle's conception of the "deliberative" function is more comprehensive than that which men ordinarily attribute to the "legislative" function of government. Yet, contrary to appearances and to the views of political scientists, I shall show that the two are fundamentally equivalent.[18]

As noted in another context, the deliberative element of government, according to Aristotle, is sovereign

1. on the issues of war and peace, and the making and breaking of alliances;

2. in the enacting of laws;

3. in cases where the penalty of death, exile, and confiscation is involved; and

4. in the appointment of magistrates and the calling of them to account on the expiration of their office (189).

Consider, first, the appointment of magistrates, which Aristotle regards as the most important deliberative function (126). This may be explained as follows. Legislators do not deliberate about ends, but about the means by which particular ends may be

---

[18] See Aristotle, *Politics*, p. 193, Barker's note NN.

realized. They do not deliberate about liberty and justice, but about the most expedient or convenient means of securing liberty and justice.[19] As already suggested, however, the most important means are not legal forms or institutional arrangements, so much as the human agents who are to act through these forms or arrangements. But if the moral and intellectual qualities of men are ultimately determinative of a regime's character, or the extent to which it partakes of justice, then the question of *who* should be a magistrate is surely the most important deliberative function. Stated another way: To deliberate on the question of who should exercise political rule is, in effect, to determine what ends or values are to govern the way of life of a regime. In this light one can appreciate the importance which men like James Wilson attributed to the suffrage. In his law lectures he said:

> Under our constitutions, a number of important appointments must be made at every election. To make them is, indeed, the business only of a day. But it ought to be the business of much more than a day, to be prepared for making them well. When a citizen elects to office . . . he performs an act of the first political consequence. He should be employed, on every convenient occasion, in making researches after proper persons for filling the different departments of power; in discussing, with his neighbours and fellow citizens, the qualities, which ought to be possessed by those, who enjoy places of public trust; and in acquiring information, with the spirit of manly candour, concerning the manners and characters of those, who are likely to be candidates for the public choice.[20]

Of course, those who are elected to public office are in the position to educate their electors. The value they place on things, or what they deem right or praiseworthy, sets an example which is

[19] Aristotle, *Rhetoric* 1362a15–20, 1358b21–28, 1359b19–24, and *Nic. Eth.* 1112a30–b20, 1142b27–34. Of course, in deliberating about means, they cannot but elaborate, at least by implication, the *meaning* of the edicts they are seeking to achieve.

[20] *Works*, I, 404. See the sequel and Wilson's hoped for effect of the suffrage on the character of citizens themselves.

bound to influence public opinion (86). Thus, when the electors of the President engage in deliberation, or when the members of the Senate deliberate on whether or not to confirm the President's nomination of a justice to the Supreme Court, they are deliberating upon what kinds of men and, by implication, which ends or values should rule or shape the way of life of their country. And the President thus chosen, or the justice whose nomination is confirmed, may go on to educate the public by the example of their manners and public pronouncements. It was for good reason, therefore, that Aristotle regarded the appointment of magistrates as the most important function of deliberation.

From this it follows, as already intimated, that Aristotle would have regarded, as a deliberative function, the electoral college method of choosing a President. (Note Hamilton's defense of this method in *Federalist* 68: "It was . . . desirable, that the immediate election should be made by men most capable of analyzing the qualities adapted to the station, and acting under circumstances favorable to deliberation. . . .") The same may be said of the President's power to nominate, and the Senate's power to confirm, justices of the Supreme Court. This deliberative activity may be regarded as legislative in the deeper meaning of the term. For to legislate is not only to enact written laws, but to establish public standards relevant to the question of how men should live, involving, therefore, the values which ought to govern men's lives. The appointment of a magistrate, such as a justice of the Supreme Court, is an affirmation of what kinds of men ought to be rewarded with public office, hence, which values ought to receive the public's esteem. Furthermore, *who* is appointed to the Court is an indication of *how* the Constitution will be interpreted or which of its diverse values will receive greater emphasis. One justice will interpret the words "Congress shall make no law . . . abridging freedom of speech" to mean that any utterance or image, including pornography, is a form of speech protected by the First Amendment from government interference; that freedom of speech has a "preferred position" in the Constitution, and takes precedence over all competing values as, for example, public morality.[21] Such an interpretation insinuates the teaching that it is perfectly legitimate to imitate in public things portrayed in pornography. The inevitable consequence is the erosion of all distinctions between what is noble and what is base. In contrast, another justice might argue that (1) the speech protected by the First Amendment is that form of communication which distinguishes the human from the subhuman, namely, that which involves *logos* or reason; (2) the essence of speech is ideational, hence addressed primarily to the intellect (whereas the essence of pornography is visiotactile, hence addressed primarily to the erotic passions); (3) the principal objects of speech include the advancement of truth and of intellectual discernment, as well as the promotion of justice and humane feelings; (4) men will cease to take ideas seriously and will eventually become morally insensitive if any and all utterances, or the portrayal of any or all forms of conduct, are dignified by the term speech and by the protection of law; and finally (5) respect for law itself requires the recognition that law is the product of deliberation in which certain forms of speech are discountenanced as contrary to rational and civilized inquiry. Clearly, deliberation on the issue of who should be a magistrate, such as a justice of the Supreme Court, is of fundamental importance for the way of life of a regime.

Concerning the degree of rationality which enters into the appointment of magistrates, obviously this depends on the intellectual capacity and situation of their electors. Consider, for example, the heads of the various executive departments or the Cabinet. Although the Constitution does not refer to a Cabinet, it does provide that the President "may require the opinion, in writing, of the principal officer in each of the executive departments, upon any subject relating to the duties of their respective offices"; and later, that "he shall nominate, and by and with the advice and consent of the Senate, shall appoint . . . all other offi-

---

[21] It should be understood that, for the purpose of this inquiry, the First Amendment, indeed, the Bill of Rights as a whole, forms no part of the original Constitution. But see Chapters XI and XII below on the subject.

cers of the United States whose appointments are not herein otherwise provided for, and which shall be established by law." Contrary to contemporary usage, Aristotle would have regarded a Cabinet office as *elective*, and precisely because the nomination and confirmation of a Cabinet officer involves a process of *deliberation* and *choice* as opposed to appointment by *lot*. The mere fact that a Secretary of State does not campaign for office, in the sense of seeking the votes of the people, does not affect the issue. Indeed, it may well be argued that, as a matter of principle, an appointment to head the Department of State is more *elective* —more subject to rational considerations—than is the election of a member of the House of Representatives. Consider only the extensive Senate inquiries into the character and political opinions of various presidential nominations. No ordinary citizen engages in such inquiry prior to giving his vote to a candidate for the House of Representatives. Unlike an ordinary body of citizens, the Senate will see, first hand, the credentials of a nominee. It will have the opportunity to question him about his past experience, his political principles, his views on public policies. Nor is this all. If we compare the moral and psychological situation of a citizen choosing between two candidates for office in the House of Representatives with that of a senator deliberating upon whether or not to confirm the nomination of a Secretary of State, it becomes immediately apparent that the decision of the senator implicates his public reputation, whereas no such constraint affects the citizen in the polling booth. (There are disadvantages as well as advantages to the secret ballot.) No one, of course, wants to be known for having given his vote to a person of questionable character or ability. But such is the size of the Senate that its individual members are more subject to public scrutiny. The latter serves to reinforce individual responsibility. In other words, a concern for reputation or honor coincides with a sense of public duty or compensates for a lack thereof. This coincidence of personal motives and public duty is but another exemplification of the psychology of political forms. (It applies, the more so, to the choosing of nominees by the President himself.) It serves to infuse a degree of rationality into politics which would be lacking under purely democratic arrangements. The mode of appointment in question compels a senator to join with others in extensive inquiry and deliberation before deciding upon whether to confirm presidential nominations to the Cabinet or to the Supreme Court. Hence, consistently with Aristotle, there are very good reasons for regarding this mode of appointing magistrates as characteristic of a 'polity' if not of an "aristocracy" of the mixed type.

Related to the deliberative function of appointing magistrates is that of calling them to account. The importance of this function derives from the fact that magistrates are charged with the administration of the laws. Since the laws are general and need to be applied or adapted to a variety of particular and unforeseen cases and circumstances, administrators require some discretionary power. They must themselves deliberate on the most appropriate means of accomplishing the general purposes of the law. They must be "examined," however, to see whether their decisions are consistent with the lawmaking body, and if not consistent, whether they are to be charged with incompetence or, more seriously, with an abuse of authority. This conforms perfectly to Congress's investigatory powers, its exercise of "legislative oversight" vis-à-vis administrative agencies, and finally, to the Senate's power to try all impeachments.

Consider, now, the deliberative function concerning the issues of war and peace and the making of alliances. Clearly, the power of Congress to declare war and the Senate's role in the making of treaties are embraced by Aristotle's criteria. On these issues a country may decide whether it wishes to devote itself to external glory or to internal perfection; whether it wishes to direct its energies toward the acquisition of empire or toward the attainment of those intellectual and moral qualities which dignify peace, leisure, and human nature itself. This does not mean, however, that a vote for war is a vote against human excellence. The contrary may sometimes be the case. Justice does not require a nation to commit suicide. Indeed, it requires a nation to transmit whatever blessings it enjoys to posterity. National self-preservation thus becomes a dictate of morality, for what is to be preserved is a nation's way of life: its traditions, its virtues, its skills and knowledge, as well as those institutions which secure its liberty and promote its happiness. But always the question is, *how* shall a nation preserve its way of life? What portion of its resources should be used for defense, for education, for the care of the needy? What foreign policy will, in the long run, be most conducive to the common good? This is a crucial and complex problem requiring profound and comprehensive deliberation.

Finally, there is the deliberative function of lawmaking itself. To be sure, Congress, at least in theory, is the principal lawmaking body. But the word "principal" already suggests that other parts of American government are involved in the lawmaking or legislative process. Thus, the Constitution provides that the President "shall from time to time give to the Congress information of the state of the union, and recommend to their consideration such measures as he shall judge necessary and expedient." This means that the President can initiate legislation. And quite apart from this, he can influence the character of legislation by the mere threat of his veto power. In addition, the President is charged with the duty to "take care that the laws be faithfully executed." As a consequence, the President may not only *initiate* legislation, but he can bring legislation to a *conclusion* by virtue of his power to administer the laws. Now, it is the case that no law, certainly no body of laws, has a univocal tendency. In any law will be found various interests or values graded in relevance. Some laws are weighty with history, aligned with habit and expectation; others are recent, uncertain in consequence. If long established, their meanings have been elaborated by precedent; if recent, they are laden with ambiguity but pregnant with possibility.[22] In either event, the law is general and must be applied to particular cases. Analogical reasoning is necessary, in the process of which some values are advanced to

[22] See *Federalist* 37, p. 229.

the foreground, others retreated into the background, resulting in a different gradation of relevance among them. The administrator of the laws is thus a lawmaker, admittedly, without the latitude of the principal lawmakers.

What holds for the administration of the laws by the executive holds for the interpretation of the laws by the judiciary (of which, more later). "Experience has instructed us," says Madison in *Federalist* 37, "that no skill in the science of government has yet been able to discriminate and define, with sufficient certainty, its three great provinces—the legislative, executive, and judiciary" (229). Still, distinctions are possible and proper. Congress, it was said, is the principal lawmaking body, at least in theory. It can disregard the recommendations of the President and override the executive veto. Should an executive agency attempt to thwart its will, Congress has numerous ways of asserting its supremacy, for example, by withholding appropriations. As for the Supreme Court, Congress can control its appellate jurisdiction; it can initiate constitutional amendments to overturn Supreme Court decisions; indeed, it can nullify or circumvent decisions of the Court by rewriting affected legislation, and it has frequently done so.[23] Finally, given the Senate's exclusive power to try all impeachments—which, of course, is a judicial function—a united Congress can make its will supreme, at least within no limits imposed by its so-called coequal branches. Not by accident, therefore, is the first and by far longest article of the Constitution devoted to the organization and powers of Congress—although the significance of this fact for the political character of the regime as a whole ought not be exaggerated. Be this as it may, it should be evident that the various powers assigned to the legislature by the Constitution are coextensive with those ascribed by Aristotle to a deliberative assembly. This said, it will now be appropriate to consider, at greater length, the nature of deliberation, but in relation to the representative principle.

[23] See Stephen L. Wasby, *The Impact of the United States Supreme Court* (Homewood, Ill.: Dorsey Press, 1970), pp. 6–7.

When a legislator engages in debate, the arguments he advances are necessarily biased in favor of his own interests (which bear some relationship, of course, to those of his constituents). In principle, there is nothing reprehensible about this. The common good itself requires the emphatic articulation of particular interests which, to be sure, must be mutually adjusted in the process of deliberation. If a legislator were not biased, he would cease to be an individual, for as suggested earlier, to be an individual is to have a center of purposes or a gradation of values peculiarly one's own. This gradation of values is related, by reciprocal causality, to an indeterminate political whole—call it the common good—whose determination is the purpose of deliberation. Deliberation—and I shall be speaking of deliberation at its best—reveals the mutual obstructiveness yet interdependence of emphatically articulated interests. Again, a particular interest necessarily bears a different degree of importance for each individual. The bias of one legislator in favor of that interest assures its more thorough articulation, and thereby facilitates its appreciation by his colleagues. This appreciation requires that his colleagues see, and therefore be given to see, the partial dependence of their own interests upon the particular interest in question. By emphasizing his own interest, each legislator may contribute to the good of another, provided only that a common course of action can be agreed upon, even though the agreement is entered into for different reasons. (Of this, more later.)

Now, it is the case that one legislator will have a set of interests such that his judgment, though biased in their favor, is more comprehensive than that of another. Say that he harbors within him a greater range of interests (or values) which are so graded in importance as to be mutually supportive, and that his judgment (or the public policy he may be proposing) is commensurate with his interests. In other words, dialectical analysis of his judgment would reveal little tension among his interests. Such a legislator is more capable of adjusting the interests of others to his own, provided he is skilled in the art of deliberation. What this means is that such a legislator is more capable of promoting distributive justice or the common good. For the common good is roughly equivalent to the range of his own interests, so that either may equally be regarded as the *motive* of his actions. It also means that the subjectivity of *this* legislator's judgment approximates objective knowledge of the common good. Objectivity thus turns on a mind whose subjectivity embraces a whole more comprehensive in its values than that perceived by others. This is a cardinal principle of the politics of magnanimity.

To see how the foregoing analysis of deliberation illuminates the representative principle, recall how the principle of reason is augmented by the psychology of political forms. As an integral element of these forms, the representative principle is intended to "refine and enlarge" relatively narrow interests. Nevertheless, any representative will be biased by those very interests, however more comprehensive may be his own view of things. For present purposes, assume that the interests of his constituents are wholly and simply his own. The relevance of those interests for the good of the whole is explored in Congress when the representative articulates them in the form of claims. These claims, which he makes on behalf of his constituents, have to be justified by reasoned argument. He will be confronted, however, by competing claims and competing arguments. Here, it is not simply a question of which claim or argument is right and which is wrong. In all likelihood, neither is entirely one or the other. What the representative learns, if he is not a blockhead, is that good things compete with and often obstruct each other. You cannot devote *all* your resources to education without undermining national defense and, in the process, education. Conversely, you cannot devote all your resources to national defense without undermining education and, in the long run, the very things you want to defend. This means that you cannot have all good things undiluted. Absolutize any value (such as freedom of speech), and you will destroy all other values including the one you have absolutized. This is why the common good requires the mutual adjustment of a variety of goods, or why the public interest requires the mutual adjustment of many particular interests—which is the meaning of compromise. Compromise, properly understood, is the widest satisfaction of good things. But the widest satisfaction of good things necessitates a rational principle, precisely because some good things are more important than others. Given, however, the contingencies of political life—such as war, famine, and pestilence—the pursuit of the most important things must sometimes be postponed or suspended so that lesser things can be cared for. The higher is never self-sufficient; it is dependent on the lower. To enjoy the goods of the mind, the goods of the body must be attended to; to live well one must live.

Fortunately, the representative, contrary to what was assumed a moment ago, is not a mere carbon copy of his constituents. His constituents, though decent enough, have many competing needs and are not very familiar with the needs of others. They do not see how all these needs are caught up in a vast complex of interdependency. Their claims are somewhat narrow, somewhat short-sighted. In contrast, their representative must, as a matter of practical necessity, take a broader and more long-range view of things—which the psychology of political forms will or may facilitate. Within himself he will have adjusted the various claims of his constituents, hence, will have compromised in the proper sense of the term. To be sure, a particular compromise may involve a sacrifice of principle. But there are many principles, and it is impossible to avoid subordinating one principle to another. The problem or the aim of compromise is to give each principle or each value its due, which is the equivalent of distributive justice. This requires conjoint deliberation and comprehensive inquiry into that large complex of interdependent needs or interests which comprise the common good. Engaging in such deliberation, the representative's own views are refined and enlarged. This is what distinguishes deliberation from bargaining. The model for bargaining is the buying and selling that occurs in the marketplace. There, material goods are exchanged, not *opinions* defended by arguments. Not to say that bargaining is a negligible factor in the actual deliberation among representatives. But the essence of deliberation lies elsewhere. When legislators engage in debate about the expediency and justice of their respective claims, their opinions are not merely *exchanged* but *changed* or modified in the process. Deliberation about alternative courses of action and about their immediate and long-range consequences is a learning process which places in question the adequacy or soundness of previously held opinions. Agreement on a common course of action involves commitment which may alter attitudes and expectations. True, each party to the agreement will see in it the satisfaction of his own interests—which he might not have seen, however, prior to deliberation or to the presentation of competing claims or arguments. Successful deliberation reveals that competing claims can be mutually adjusted by a course of action on which participants may agree for different reasons or with different interests in view.[24] Adjustment is also made possible by showing how the proponent of a particular interest has himself competing ones of which he is not fully aware. The fact that every legislator has a multiplicity of interests, and that many do not clearly see how by advancing one interest they may be undermining another which lies in the background of their concerns, makes deliberation a constructive and educational process. But this is only to say that men are fallible. Fortunately, some neglected interest in the background of our concerns may be in the foreground of another's; and its very importance for another may lead him to reveal its relevance for some interest deemed important by us. The representative principle may thus facilitate the acquisition of the art of deliberation, to which extent it partakes of and fosters rationality itself. It was this very art that produced the Constitution.

Turning from the deliberative to the magisterial offices of government, it is perfectly proper to regard the latter as executive. "Among all these offices," says Aristotle, "the title of magistracy should, on the whole, be reserved for those which are charged with the duty, in some given field, of deliberating, deciding, and giving instructions—and more especially with the duty of giving

[24] See my *Philosophy of the American Constitution*, pp. 60–62.

instructions, which is the special mark of the magistrate" (195). Magistrates necessarily deliberate. Their deliberations, however, involve the application of laws in concrete and particular cases. These deliberations issue forth in decisions and instructions having the effect of commands which enforce the laws. It would not be inappropriate, therefore, to regard the justices of the Supreme Court as magistrates. For it is only under exceptional circumstances that the Court requires the assistance of the Executive to effectuate its decisions. Here again the tripartite division of legislative, executive, and judicial functions oversimplifies political realities. Still, it is a useful conceptual framework whose utility is made possible by the specialization of function proper to a large regime. This specialization of function means, of course, that distinct powers are exercised by different men composing separate branches or agencies of government. Apparently such specialization was not developed to any great extent in classical antiquity. In Athens, for example, the same citizen might be a magistrate, a member of the deliberative assembly, as well as a member of one of the law courts. Aristotle was fully aware of the limitations of such a system, and he explicitly recommends specialization of function—which is but to say division or separation of powers—wherever the size or population of a regime permits. Thus:

> In large countries it is both possible and proper that a separate magistracy should be allotted to each separate function. The number of the citizens makes it convenient for a number of persons to enter on office: it permits some of the offices to be held only once in a lifetime, and others (though held more than once) to be held again only after a long interval; and, apart from convenience, each function gets better attention when it is the only one undertaken, and not one among a number of others (195).

Specialization of function or separation of powers facilitates lengthier tenures of office, enabling magistrates to acquire expertise in public affairs. Meanwhile, the legislative and judicial functions of government may become more specialized, and those who perform these functions may become more competent within their respective domains.

Returning to the functions of executive offices, Aristotle enumerates a variety of magistracies analogous to such executive departments of American government as the Departments of Commerce, Agriculture, Justice, Defense, and the Treasury (273–274). In addition to these offices, says Aristotle, "there is another which controls, more than any other office, the whole range of public affairs. The office in question is one which . . . possesses the double power of introducing matters [to the assembly] and of bringing them to completion. . . . The holders of this office are in some regimes called *Probouloi*, or the preliminary council, because they initiate deliberation . . ." (276). As will be seen in a moment, Aristotle regarded the *probouloi* as an oligarchic institution (197). Here suffice to say that its two major functions correspond to those of the presidency whose powers are elaborated by Hamilton in *Federalist* 72:

> The administration of government, in its largest sense, comprehends all the operations of the body politic, whether legislative, executive, or judiciary; but in its most usual and perhaps in its most precise signification, it is limited to executive details, and falls peculiarly within the province of the executive department. The actual conduct of foreign negotiations, the preparatory plans of finance, the application and disbursement of the public moneys in conformity to the general appropriations of the legislature, the arrangement of the army and navy, the direction of the operations of war,—these, and other matters of a like nature, constitute what seems to be most properly understood by the administration of government (468–469).

The "other matters" include, of course, the initiation of legislation generally and the execution or "completion" of the laws.

Given Hamilton's definition of "administration" and his conception of the executive power, it may be necessary to qualify an earlier statement describing Congress as the principal lawmaking body in theory. Certainly the President is in the practical, if not the constitutional, position to perform that role—and not only in times of crises. To begin with, the President has the only national constituency. To some extent he can consolidate his position among that constituency by means of his appointment power (itself of fundamental significance in Aristotle's view of politics). Of greater importance, however, is the power to initiate legislation. Indeed, an analogy may be drawn between the way in which a President may stand in relation to legislation which he has initiated and the way in which a founder stands in relation to the regime he has established.

Assume that the President is a person skilled in the science of legislation, which is the art of politics. He is authorized (and expected) to initiate a legislative program. This he does. The program is introduced by a preamble, setting forth its major aims or objectives. These objectives are related to recognized public problems on the one hand, and to established principles of government on the other. The means for achieving the stated objectives are elaborated in a clear, coherent, and comprehensive manner. At the same time, however, the means are judiciously couched in language of sufficient generality to enable diverse men to agree on a common course of action for different reasons. Accordingly, the program will not be *manifestly* inconsistent with the opinions of a majority of those who must approve it. Indeed, it need only be more or less consistent with the opinions of a large plurality, for some of its anticipated opponents will themselves be divided, and will prefer the President's program—perhaps with some amendments—to any others that might be advanced. If so designed, that program will insinuate, as it were, an intellectual framework which subsequent deliberation and decision are not likely to alter in any fundamental way. The process of deliberation will commence with the linguistic— but therefore substantive—"bias" of the proposed legislative program. Ensuing debate will thus be conceptually structured or constrained. Students of language might call this the phenomenon of "psycholinguistic preemption," a phenomenon which follows contingently upon the power to initiate legislation. (This phenomenon is beautifully exemplified by the Virginia Plan—

between which and the Constitution there exists no generic difference.) Given this power of the President, together with his suspensive veto on the one hand, and his power to determine how the laws are applied in particular cases on the other, there are some grounds for the following conclusion: Of the three articles of the Constitution which organize the three branches of government, the *central* article contains the key to the American 'polity.'[25]

Turning to the "completion" or administration of the laws, it may be said that legislation stands to administration as generality to particularity. Again, the application of laws to concrete cases presupposes deliberation. From deliberation issues detailed instructions having the effect of commands, behind which, of course, are sanctions.[26] But how are the laws to be administered? Aristotle analyzes the problem in terms of three basic factors. First, there is the formal structure of administration. Descriptively, administration is either centralized or decentralized. Prescriptively, the choice depends partly on the size of the regime. Generally speaking, decentralization of administrative (as opposed to legislative) power is more appropriate in a large regime. This is implicit in the very distinction or relationship between the generality of law and the particularity of its application. The law, as law, has as its object the common good. But the common good consists in a proper distribution of goods among numerous persons or groups having different interests and living under diverse circumstances. If the general object of law is to be achieved, and if its detailed administration is to be effective, two related conditions are necessary: (1) knowledge of local needs and circumstances, and (2) some proximity and familiarity between those who administer and those who are affected by the laws. Both conditions will best be achieved by decentraliza-

[25] *Ibid.*, p. 166 (headnote).

[26] See *Federalist* 15, p. 91, where Hamilton says: "It is essential to the idea of law, that it be attended with a sanction; or, in other words, a penalty or punishment for disobedience. If there be no penalty annexed to disobedience, the resolutions or commands which pretend to be laws will, in fact, amount to nothing more than advice or recommendation."

tion of administration. On the one hand, decentralization facilitates the acquisition of specialized knowledge of local needs and, to that extent, offers the greater promise of their being properly satisfied. On the other hand, decentralization allows for a wider distribution of power which, in conjunction with the wider satisfaction of needs, strengthens loyalty to the regime and secures the regime's stability. In short, Aristotle would recommend something like the principle of *federalism* for the American 'polity.'

The second factor of administration, and one affecting its formal structure, consists of two interrelated elements. First there is the subject matter itself. Certain problems are better controlled by a central department, such as defense against external aggression. Other problems are better administered by local officials, for example, the maintenance of order. Thus, whereas the administration of certain subjects should be centralized, others may be decentralized. To complicate matters further, administration may be organized not only by subject matter, but in terms of the persons concerned, or "clientele" (196). One administrative agency may be responsible for the education of the young, another for the care of the aged. Or the "clientele" of one agency may be engaged in agriculture, that of another in commerce.

Finally, and of most importance, is the effect of the different magistracies or administrative agencies on the political character of the regime itself. Here Aristotle anticipates the modern but now discredited notion of a politically neutral administration:

> Are we to say that in all regimes alike (democracy, oligarchy, aristocracy, and monarchy) the same magistracies form the government—with the one difference that the magistrates personally do not come from the same, or a similar, social class, but are drawn from a different class in each different regime (in aristocracies, for example, from the cultured class; in oligarchies from the wealthy; and in democracies from the free-born)? Or shall we say that the magistracies too, as well as the magistrates, differ in some respects from one regime to another; and shall we

then add, as a qualification, that in some cases the same magistracies are suitable, but in other cases they are bound to differ?[27]

The key distinction is between "magistrates" and "magistracies." A magistrate is necessarily a citizen of a particular regime, and he has been more or less shaped by its prevailing beliefs and values (94). In other words, the character of the citizen is relative to that of the regime, so that there are as many types of citizens as there are different types of regimes (101). The citizen of a democracy will be a lover of freedom and equality, whereas the citizen of an aristocracy will be a lover of virtue and honor. The former will have a marked propensity for change or novelty; the latter will be more attached to well-established forms and traditions. As a consequence, the magistracies or offices in these two regimes, being composed of men of different moral character, will pursue different ends or values corresponding to the differences between the two regimes. For example, the kind of administrator who will be placed in charge of public education in a democracy will differ from his counterpart in an aristocracy precisely because the content of education in the two regimes will differ. In a democracy, youth will be encouraged, even at a very early age, to question established principles and practices, consistent with the notion of freedom on the one hand, and the equality of each generation on the other. (Perhaps the only thing that will not be questioned is the value of such questioning —which will be taken for granted. Or to put the matter another way, education in a democracy dogmatically accepts the paramount value of freedom and equality, hence seeks to maximize these values above all others.) In an aristocracy, however, the education of youth will include the inculcation of customs, habits, and manners handed down from generation to generation. (If these customs, habits, and manners are questioned, it will only be *after* they have been duly inculcated. In other words, critical reflection will not be encouraged until moral virtues have

[27] *Politics*, p. 196. The topic of a politically neutral administration will be taken up in connection with Woodrow Wilson, below, pp. 296–304.

become habitudes.) So here we see that the functions of certain magistracies will differ with the character of the magistrates who will in turn differ with the political character of the regime.

On the other hand, there may be certain magistracies whose functions seem to be politically indifferent to the social class from which the magistrates are drawn, hence indifferent to the political character of the regime. Such functions as national defense, public health, and control over the production and distribution of various commodities seem to be of this sort. Notice, however, that these functions involve the goods of the body (231). Perhaps this explains why magistracies or administrative agencies concerned with such goods may be virtually the same despite generic differences in the regime of which they are a part. This is not meant to suggest a "convergence" theory of regimes.[28] For two regimes may have similar economies and yet retain significantly different political and cultural institutions. Nor do I wish to suggest that the functions in question, or the administrative agencies having control over them, are politically neutral. Nothing in the public domain, and nothing of significance in the private domain, is politically neutral. All offices of a regime are intended to preserve that regime's way of life. This is as true of a department of education as it is of a department of defense. The notion of a politically neutral education is nothing more than a superficial myth, one which is peculiar to a liberal democracy.[29] (Unbeknownst to its proponents, that notion logically undermines any *rational* preference for liberal democracy, hence liberal democracy itself.) To see the absurdity of this notion, we need only ask, *Who* is to have control over education? To ask this question is to ask, in effect, *Who* should rule, and for the sake of which ends or values? Or consider the subject of pub-

[28] See John S. Resheter, Jr., *The Soviet Polity* (New York: Dodd, Mead & Co., 1971), pp. 351–362, for a discussion and critique of the "convergence" theory. It should be noted that this theory is a liberalized version of Marxism whose effect on American foreign policy is probably not insignificant.

[29] An exemplification of this myth will be found in Justice Jackson's opinion in *West Virginia Board of Education* v. *Barnette*, 319 U.S. 624, 637 (1943), discussed below, p. 421.

lic health. The resources which a regime devotes to public health depend, in part, on the hierarchy of values characteristic of the regime. Indeed, the relative value of life itself will vary from one regime to another. It is probably safe to say that monarchies tend to place greater value on military glory than on public health; that democracies place greater value on public health than on moral education.[30] Furthermore, the variation, from one regime to another, in the relative importance of a particular office, has consequences for the character of the officeholder. For example, a military officer is likely to receive more honor in a monarchy than in a democracy in view of the greater value attributed to the martial virtues in the former than in the latter. Consequently, the military officer in a monarchy will probably have greater *social* influence than will his democratic counterpart. Will not this affect their moral character? On all these points, therefore, we may conclude that no public administrative office is or can be politically neutral.

One other point remains to be considered. We have seen that the political character of an institution depends partly on its size. We have also seen that an institution such as the *probouloi*, which, like the presidency, has the power to initiate and enforce the laws, is of the first political importance for the character of a regime. According to Aristotle, "if such a body is small, it becomes an oligarchical institution; and a body of *probouloi* will always be small, and therefore will always be oligarchical" (197).[31] It must be remembered, however, that Aristotle is here speaking of the *probouloi* from the perspective of the formal mode of regime analysis. Whether such an institution—be it the *probouloi* or the presidency or some committee of Congress— will in fact pursue oligarchic ends is another matter.

[30] Health was the most prominent theme of President Nixon's state of the union message of 1971, despite his reported admission, shortly thereafter, that the country is suffering from moral decadence. On the preoccupation of democracies with health, see Plato, *Republic* 405a–406b.

[31] See Aristotle's *Athenian Constitution* XXIX; C. Hignett, *A History of the Athenian Constitution to the End of the Fifth Century B.C.* (Oxford: Clarendon Press, 1967), p. 269.

Turning to the third and last department of power, the judiciary, Aristotle distinguishes no less than eight types of law courts:

> There is one for the review of the conduct of magistrates; a second for dealing with any offense against any point of public interest; a third for cases which bear on the constitution [i.e., the regime]; a fourth . . . for cases of disputes about the amount of fines; a fifth for contracts between private persons, where a considerable amount is involved; a sixth for cases of homicide; and a seventh for cases of aliens. . . . Finally, there is an eighth court for contracts between private persons which only involve a small sum. . . (200–201).

Of the first five types of law courts, Aristotle says: "These have all a political character, as they deal with issues which, unless properly handled, create dissension and constitutional disturbance" (201). This statement need hardly be elaborated. Suffice only to emphasize the point that Aristotle would certainly have regarded the American Supreme Court as a political institution, since its decisions affect the fundamental principles and purposes of the regime.

Now, in trying to draw an analogy between the law courts enumerated by Aristotle and the American judicial system (which embraces many functions of the former), the actual organization and composition of the law courts of ancient Greece may rightly be disregarded. For Aristotle offers us not merely a *descriptive* political science but, above all, a *normative* one, a political science that takes its bearing on *the* best regime, the regime which serious reflection reveals to be most conducive to the perfection or completion of human nature. Accordingly, while Aristotle will say that a law court composed of five hundred citizens was the practice of Athens and is appropriate for a democracy, it does not follow that he would recommend such a practice for other kinds of regimes, let alone the best regime in theory. He certainly did not think that the ordinary citizen was best qualified to pass judgment on matters involving the fundamental principles of the regime, or that appointment by lot was the best method of insti-

166

tuting a law court dealing with such matters (202). Nor did he believe it was the best arrangement, especially for large countries, to have the same person serve as a judge, a legislator, and as a magistrate. We have seen that he fully approved of specialization of function. Accordingly, there is every reason to believe that he would have approved of a system of professionally trained judges comparable to that which prevails in the United States. This said, I shall attempt to illuminate the nature of the judicial function by employing certain principles of Aristotle's *Rhetoric.*

Aristotle would agree with behavioral political scientists that the judicial function is a political one, and that judges make law. But Aristotle would make a distinction, obscured by behaviorists, between the grounds on which judges make law and the grounds on which laws are made in a legislative assembly. This distinction may best be seen by analyzing the difference between deliberative and forensic rhetoric.

The legislator, whose activity involves the principles of deliberative rhetoric, "aims at establishing *the expediency or the harmfulness* of a proposed course of action; if he urges its acceptance, he does so on the ground that it will do good; if he urges its rejection, he does so on the ground that it will do harm; and all other points, such as whether the proposal is *just or unjust*, honourable or dishonourable, he brings in as subsidiary and relative to this main consideration."[32] In contrast, judges, whose activity involves the principles of forensic rhetoric, "aim at establishing the *justice or injustice* of some action, and they too bring in all other points as subsidiary and relative to this one."[33] In other words, whereas the legislator emphasizes the expediency of some course of action, but not to the exclusion of considerations of justice, the judge emphasizes the justice of some course of action, but not to the exclusion (at least tacitly) of expedential considerations. Now, by substituting "constitutionality" for "justice," one may readily grasp the major difference between

[32] Aristotle, *Rhetoric* 1358b21–25 (italics added).
[33] *Ibid.*, 1358b25–28 (italics added).

the legislative and judicial functions as comprehended by the American Constitution. Just as legislators are concerned about the constitutionality of their acts, so too are judges concerned about the expediency of their decisions. Their divergent emphases stem from two main factors.

First, the legislator's emphasis on the expedient corresponds to the fact that his mode of activity is oriented more emphatically toward the future. He does not deliberate about things past, "things that could not have been, and cannot now or in the future be, other than they are"; rather, he deliberates on things contingent, and which can be other than they are by human agency.[34] The primary focus of the legislator is on *change*—be it to make things better, or to prevent them from becoming worse. (Although preventing things from becoming worse involves the preservation of things past, such preservation requires the modification or elimination of things obstructing the continued existence of things past.) In any event, the legislative function is fundamentally prospective. Conversely, the judicial function is, for the most part, retrospective. Its primary inquiry is into things past, such as whether a particular act was done in conformity with, or in violation of, preestablished law. Of course, a decision in one case is a precedent for similar cases in the future, for which reason a judge will also inquire into the immediate and long-range consequences of his decision. But the vast majority of decisions go little beyond the individuals involved in litigation. Very few cases are of such nature and magnitude as to affect the regime as a whole. And even in those cases, which invariably and necessarily involve lawmaking, certain distinctions are in order. For the mere fact that the Court must justify its decisions on constitutional grounds, rather than on grounds of expediency, cannot but impose limitations on judicial discretion to an extent far greater than is the case of a legislator. This points to the second factor which distinguishes the judicial from the legislative function.

[34] *Ibid.*, 1357a4–7, 22–27.

Unlike a legislature, a court cannot act until cases are brought before it. Generally speaking, the Supreme Court deals with cases involving the rights of individuals. In rendering decisions, the members of the Court are obliged, by their oath of office, to exercise dispassionate and disinterested judgment. That is, neither personal feelings regarding litigants, nor motives of self-interest, are to obscure their inquiry into the truth and justice of competing claims. As Hamilton says in *Federalist* 78: "The courts must declare the sense of the law; and if they should be disposed to exercise WILL instead of JUDGMENT, the consequence would equally be the substitution of their pleasure to that of the legislative body"(507–508). Obviously much depends on the self-restraint or moral character of the judges.[35] Nevertheless, restraints are also imposed by custom, public expectation, and the ethics of the legal profession itself. That instances of personal feeling or preference have in fact influenced a judge's opinions or decisions in particular cases may preoccupy the tendentious inquiries of legal realists; they do not refute the real as well as legal differences between the judicial and legislative functions. We rightly condemn a judge who acts from purely personal motives, but no one but a self-deluding purist would condemn a legislator for advancing some proposal with a view to his own interests or to those of his constituents. We ought to expect the personal predilections of legislators to influence their deliberations. (Indeed, if they did not, legislators could hardly "refine and enlarge" the views of their constituents.) The only question is whether a particular proposal is, or can be made, consistent with the common good and with the "great outlines" and "objects" of the Constitution. Nevertheless, the question of expediency is central, and not the question of constitutionality. Indeed,

[35] See *ibid.*, 1354b5–11. A remarkable example of judicial self-restraint was that exercised by Justice Felix Frankfurter in his concurring opinion in the "electric chair case" of *Louisiana ex rel. Francis* v. *Resweber*, 329 U.S. 459 (1947). Justice Frankfurter, an opponent of capital punishment, upheld the decision of the court below which resulted in the execution of Francis, after a first attempt had failed because of some electrical or mechanical malfunction.

oftentimes it is the expedient or the "necessary," *as determined by legislation,* that enlarges the meaning of what is constitutional (with and without the cooperation of the Court).[36]

There can be no question, however, but that the judicial function is a political one, if only because interpretation of the law is never politically neutral. Even if it were wholly true that the Supreme Court is governed by precedent—and it is true to a larger extent than is suggested by legal realists who exaggerate, or rather, who misconstrue the sociological and psychological determinants of judicial decisions—still, there are different lines of precedent which may be analogically related to the facts of a particular case, and the Court is free to *choose* which line it wishes to follow. Of course, the persuasiveness of the Court's opinion depends not merely on logic, but also on the moral and political environment. In principle, the judicial opinions of the Court conform no less to the canons of rhetoric than do the arguments of legislators. A capacity for analogical and dialectical reasoning, an understanding of human character, combined with a knowledge of politics in general, and of American legal thought and institutions in particular—all these are required for the rhetoric of Supreme Court pronouncements. Properly speaking, the function of rhetoric "is not simply to succeed in persuading, but rather to discover the means of coming as near such success as the circumstances of each particular case allow."[37] Since no law provides for its own interpretation, and since the set of facts in no two cases are identical, the Court will select means, namely, lines of analogical reasoning, adapted to the ends it has in view, which reasoning will be couched in terms adapted to the character of its "audience" or in terms of the anticipated reaction to the Court's decision. There is nothing questionable about such proceedings. What may render it questionable is a naive legal-

[36] See Chief Justice Marshall's opinion in *McCulloch v. Maryland,* 4 Wheaton 316, 413–418 (1819). Although Marshall, in this case, enlarged the scope of judicial review, he also enlarged the powers of Congress. See also *Federalist* 44, pp. 292–295.

[37] Aristotle, *Rhetoric* 1355b10–12, 1356a21–27. See also my *Philosophy of the American Constitution,* p. 316, n. 30.

istic view of judicial judgment on the one hand, or, on the other hand, a naive realist view which attempts to de rationalize or psychologize judicial judgment. So long as the latter view prevails among political scientists, the public understanding of law will be debased and the *raison d'être* of the Supreme Court will be undermined.

It was said above that the interpretation of law and its application to concrete cases requires analogical reasoning. Such reasoning may result in enlarging the scope of a particular law and therefore its meaning. Frequently this is inevitable given the ambiguity of language and the intentions of the lawmakers. Indeed, the very act or action to which a law is applied is itself subject to ambiguity. Every act which implicates a law impinges upon the whole of which the law is a part. An act is not an isolated event. It has a background of antecedent causes as well as an infinitude of determinate and indeterminate consequences. While it brings into focus two or three competing values, it implicates a multiplicity of others. Consider, for example, unfettered and sensationalist publicizing of a murder trial by the mass communications media. Here, the right of freedom of speech and press competes with the right of the accused to a fair trial. A fair trial requires orderly and rational inquiry into the truth of a particular event in the past. But such an inquiry also requires that all participants in the trial feel the restraints of established legal principles and practices. These restraints may not be felt as strongly, however, if the public—which includes the bulk of the legal profession—is effectively barred from the trial by the absence of all publicity. On the other hand, unfettered and sensationalist publicity by the mass media could result not only in a miscarriage of justice, but also in: (1) a brutalization of the moral sensibilities of the public; (2) a corresponding decline in respect for truth and rational inquiry; (3) a contempt for the mass media, at least by decent people; (4) a widespread cynicism toward law and the legal profession; and (5) a growing disenchantment with the entire political system, at least by enlightened men. Related consequences and values could be mentioned. For example, can the media enlighten the public about political affairs if the public loses confidence in the media's veracity and integrity? As regards the legal profession, will it attract men of the highest caliber if its dignity has been undermined? And given its pervasive power, will the public defer to the legal profession if its standards of conduct are no higher than those of the generality of men?[38]

Be this as it may, in weighing the right of freedom of speech and press against the right of an accused to a fair trial, the Court looks not only to the consequences of alternative decisions, but also to antecedent lines of precedent involving those two rights. A line of precedent may be regarded as the definition or elaboration of the meaning of some general principle. But insofar as everything is related to everything else, the meaning of a principle cannot be fully comprehended abstracted from its implications for the whole of which it is a part. In relation to the infinitude of data discarded by selective emphasis, the meaning of a principle is inexhaustible. Furthermore, by no chain of deductive logic can one move from a general principle, say, as embodied in a law, to a particular decision involving a novel set of facts. Language, and therefore law, cannot avoid indeterminateness. This does not mean that judicial interpretation of law is arbitrary. What is indeterminate in law is rendered determinate by analogical reasoning, which deals with similarities, not identities. Involved is an act of judgment not wholly based on syllogistic logic.[39] Here is a case seemingly unprecedented in law or unforeseen by the lawmaker. Yet the judge applies a law to the case. How is this possible? The truth is that nothing is wholly unprecedented or novel. The apprehension of novelty is made possible by contrast and analogy with an environment of contemporary and antecedent events. Novelty is a matter of emphasis. As soon as novelty is articulated by language, it is assimilated or brought into relationship with the whole. By virtue of its

[38] In this connection, see Justice Douglas's opinion in *Spevak* v. *Klein*, 17L. Ed. 2d 574 (1967).

[39] See Aristotle, *Rhetoric* 1355a5–10.

application to novel occasions, the interpretation of law involves relative creation and destruction. While certain values are emphatically affirmed, others are de-emphasized to the point of negation. Interpretation—and I am speaking of judicial judgment—should minimize destructiveness, should preserve, so far as possible, all antecedent values. But in view of present and pressing needs, antecedent values must be reordered or given a new gradation of importance. This is only to say that a judge should have a tender regard for the past qualified by sensitivity to the needs of the present and future. He should comprehend a broad range of values and bring them into mutual adjustment. The same was suggested in connection with legislators. But the legislator's future orientation besets him with a greater sense of urgency which, in itself, is not conducive to a comprehensive and long-range view of things. Again, because a judge takes his primary (but not exclusive) bearing on constitutional rather than on expediential considerations, the old or long established weighs more in the judicial than in the legislative function. A judge who understands his task—which he cannot without appreciating the fact that the bias inherent in his activity is but the necessary complement of the bias inherent in the legislative activity— will seek to assimilate the new to the old, or the old to the new. If the judge performs his task with wisdom, old and new will enrich and sustain each other. If he lacks tenderness toward the past, the old will be destroyed and the new will be left rootless. Or, should his tenderness for the past be unqualified by wisdom, the new will be destroyed and the old will be left branchless. Here, emphatically, is the politics of magnanimity.

Having analyzed the nature of the judicial function, the question remains, what is the political character of the Supreme Court? By long and well-established custom, the membership of the Court is drawn from the legal profession, a small part of the regime. From the perspective of the formal mode of regime analysis, this attribute of the Court is unquestionably oligarchic. But inasmuch as the Court cannot act until a case is brought before it for decision, and since its appellate jurisdiction is under the control of Congress, and finally, because it has no direct and significant power over such issues as war and peace, foreign policy, and national revenue, the Court inclines more in the direction of a 'polity.'[40] Add, however, the attributes of size and tenure, and the political character of the Court shifts back toward the oligarchic end of the spectrum. Indeed, it is very probable that Aristotle would have regarded the Supreme Court of the United States as an "aristocratic" institution, but again, only from the perspective of the formal mode of regime analysis (202).

This concludes the discussion of the nature of the legislative, executive, and judicial functions or institutions. It remains to examine in detail how the general methods of construcing a 'polity' may be applied to the construction of each of these institutions. For this purpose it will be sufficient to concentrate on the different methods of appointing magistrates, since the same methods apply to all offices of government.

3

To appreciate the subtlety and comprehensivenes of Aristotle's political science in general, and of his formal mode of regime analysis in particular, it will be necessary to cite at length his account of the different modes by which magistrates may be appointed.

> The differences here are connected with three factors, which produce, in combination, all the possible modes. The three factors are (1) the persons appointing, (2) the persons eligible for appointment, and (3) the machinery of appointment. Each

[40] This is consistent with Aristotle's *Politics*, p. 202. It should be noted, however, that there are various ways in which the Court can influence the distribution of national revenues. Apart from its decisions affecting corporations, labor legislation, and social welfare, its decisions on reapportionment and racial discrimination can affect the distribution of power among the various groups composing the community, hence the political composition and policies of Congress and the presidency. But to affect the political composition and policies of Congress and the presidency is to influence, to some extent, such issues as war and peace and foreign policy!

of these three factors admits of a choice of alternatives, and there are thus three choices of alternatives corresponding to the three factors. (1) The persons appointing may be all the citizens, or only a section. (2) The persons eligible for appointment may be all the citizens, or only a section—a section determined by a property qualification, or birth, or merit, or some similar quality. ... (3) The machinery of appointment may be election, or it may be lot. In addition we may also have a conjunction of both alternatives, with the result that (1) for some offices the persons appointing may be all the ciitzens, and for others only a section; (2) for some offices the persons eligible may be all the citizens, and for others only a section; and (3) for some offices the machinery of appointment may be election, and for others it may be lot.

Four modes are possible in handling each of the choices of alternatives. The alternative which consists in all the citizens appointing may mean (1) that all appoint from all by election; (2) that all appoint from all by lot (the appointment from all, in both these cases, being *either* made successively from sections—such as . . . wards and clans—until all have eventually been included, *or* continuously from all) [*the preceding may be compared to a choice between district and at-large elections*]; (3) that all appoint from a section by election; or (4) that all appoint from a section by lot. (But it is also possible that all the citizens, as the appointing body, may appoint to some offices in one of these ways, and to others in another.) Similarly, the alternative which consists in a section of the citizens appointing may mean (1) that the section appoints from all by election; (2) that it appoints from all by lot; (3) that it appoints from a section by election; or (4) that it appoints from a section by lot. (But here, again, it is also possible that a section, as the appointing body, may appoint to some offices in one of these ways and to others in another. . .) (197 198).

Now the question arises as to which of these different electoral arrangements correspond to the different kinds of regimes? Here is Aristotle's answer:

First, there are two which are democratic—(a) that by which all appoint from all *either* by election *or* lot, and (b) that by which all appoint from all *both* by election *and* lot, using the one method in some and the other in other cases [N.B.]. Secondly, *there are various arrangements which fit a 'polity.'* (a) *One is when all appoint from all* (either by election or lot or both by election and lot), *but do so in sections taken successively and not as a continuously active body* [N.B.]. (b) Another is when all appoint from all to some of the offices, but appoint from a section to others (either by election or lot or both by election and lot). (c) Still another arrangement which fits a 'polity'—but a 'polity' inclining more towards oligarchy—is when a section appoints from all, and does so by election for some of the offices and by lot for the others. (d) A last arrangement which fits a 'polity'—but a 'polity' verging on aristocracy—is when a section appoints simultaneously both from all and from a section (i.e. from all to some offices and from a section to others), whether it does so wholly by election, or wholly by lot, or by election for some offices and by lot for others. Thirdly, an arrangement which fits an oligarchy is when a section appoints from a section—by election, by lot, or by a mixture of both. Finally, an arrangement which fits an aristocracy is one under which a section appoints from all, or all appoint from a section, by the method of election (198–199).[41]

Beginning with the first electoral arrangement ascribed by Aristotle to a 'polity,' notice that *all* the citizens are eligible, not only to vote, but to hold office—and this, *without any property qualification!* That Aristotle is not guilty of an oversight is indicated by his having included, among the various electoral arrangements, one which provides that "the persons eligible for appointment may be all the citizens, or only a section—a section determined by a property qualification, or birth, or merit, or some similar quality." To be sure, Aristotle is here referring to the appointment of magistrates. But since their electors—whether members of the deliberative assembly or the citizen-body as a whole—need not have a property qualification, we are left

[41] Italics added after first N.B. See Aristotle's *Politics*, p. 199, n. 1, Barker's note. Notice that the second electoral arrangement ascribed to the 'polity' and the arrangement ascribed to an aristocracy confirms my interpretation of those ambiguous passages referred to above, pp. 125–128.

to wonder how a regime can be a 'polity' when all its citizens are eligible to vote *and* hold office without such a qualification? This may help to explain why a 'polity' leans toward, and is often confused with, a democracy; it does not explain wherein these two regimes significantly differ. But perhaps the problem can be clarified by way of examining the "regime bias" of various electoral arrangements.

Notice that Aristotle does *not* regard appointment by election as necessarily oligarchic. If "all appoint from all *either* by election *or* lot," or use "one method in some and the other in other cases," the arrangement is democratic. Appointment by election is oligarchic *only* if the election is conducted by *districts* and not *at-large*. In fact, the appointment may even be by lot and not be democratic, provided the district method is employed. The reason is this. At-large elections are more susceptible to the control of a majority faction than would be the case if the electorate were fragmented into a multiplicity of electoral districts (216–217). Where the district method prevails, the people in each district determine who will be their own representative, thus insuring the representation of a greater variety of groups than would prevail under at-large elections. For example, at-large elections in the state of New York for United States Representatives would favor urban as opposed to rural interests, with the result that the state's representation in Congress would be more "liberal" or democratic. (The same result would follow if United States Senators were elected on a national ticket.)[42] The district method of elections is but a means of fragmenting the electorate—but therefore the *many*—and of representing the resulting parts. At the same time, however, it is a means of promoting distributive justice. Furthermore, so long as the various parts of the community are represented, they will have an interest in preserving the regime, the effect of which is to promote po-

---

[42] Notice that the contemporary Senate tends to be more "liberal" than the House of Representatives. This is the consequence of popular election of the Senate, on the one hand, *and* the greater concentration of the electorate in cities, on the other.

litical stability. Here may be seen another aspect of Madison's pluralistic solution to the problem of majority faction.

But this also helps to explain why Aristotle attributes to a 'polity' an arrangement whereby "all appoint from all (either by election or lot or both by election and lot), but do so in sections taken successively and not as a continuously active body"—and this, without requiring any property qualification for the electors or for the elected. Incidentally, the constitutional method of electing the President is a perfect example of the political principle which Aristotle has in mind. It was this very principle which led the founding fathers, after deliberating upon various electoral methods, to institute a system whereby the electors of the President would meet in their respective states, rather than convene in one place or constitute a single and continuously active body.[43] Precisely because the electors of one state would not be in communication with those of another, there would be less likelihood of some sudden breeze of popular passion determining the outcome of their separate deliberations. As with the case of district elections, a system of multiple electoral colleges is less subject to control by a single group, and so is more conducive to distributive justice.

From the preceding discussion it follows that the representative principle conforms to the electoral method which Aristotle ascribes to a 'polity,' and doubly so. On the one hand, the states may be regarded as large electoral districts assigned a specific number of representatives; on the other hand, these very states are, generally speaking, divided into smaller electoral districts for the purpose of electing representatives. For the purpose of illustration, I shall digress for a moment to consider the related and contemporary controversy over the reform of American political parties.

It is generally well known that single-member electoral districts, operating in conjunction with the federal system, frustrate attempts to institute rigorous party discipline or to organize

[43] See my *Philosophy of the American Constitution*, pp. 169–186, and *Federalist* 68.

so-called ideologically or programmatically oriented parties. Accordingly, "liberals," who lean more toward the democratic end of the political spectrum, seek to circumvent the constitutional system by advocating centralized as opposed to decentralized party organization. They well know that the constitutional system, in principle, tends to thwart the "will of the majority." In contrast, "conservatives," who lean more toward the oligarchic end of the political spectrum, seek to preserve what they understand to be the constitutional system on grounds that it serves to protect "states rights" or the interests of the minority. Clearly these "conservatives" are not of the class with Hamilton, who had no high regard for "states rights," but who was nevertheless concerned about the interests of the few. Unlike contemporary "conservatives," Hamilton, we have seen, wanted a *powerful executive*, one designed to foster national greatness. (It would be truer to say that contemporary "conservatives" are closer to Madison. And yet, while Madison favored, in large measure, the pluralism advocated by "conservatives," his pluralism was intended not only to prevent majority faction, but, consistent with the principle of *divide et impera*, it was also intended to facilitate political rule on the part of the national government.) Oddly enough, contemporary "liberals" share Hamilton's desire for a powerful executive, but do so primarily with a view to democratic ends or values. Accordingly, they favor a centralized party system under presidential leadership, one that would compel representatives and senators to follow the party line.[44] What these "liberals" have to contend with, however, is the *psychology of political forms* underlying the Constitution. For neither a representative nor a senator derives his honor from being a member of a particular party. Instead, he derives his honor *as a Representative or as a Senator*, that is, from the office itself. It is this

---

[44] This would be accomplished ultimately by centralized party control over campaign funds or a large portion thereof. It should be noted that "liberals" and "conservatives" are biased, respectively, in favor of urban and rural interests, more precisely—in view of suburbia—the interest of the poor and interests of the rich. (But this must be qualified by consideration of the middle class.)

179

office which secures not only his honor, but his independence as well. Both his honor and his independence would be undermined by efforts to circumvent the intended purposes of the representative principle and its analogue, the principle of federalism. Indeed, insofar as "liberals" are animated by democratic majoritarianism, they favor, *theoretically*, the "pure democracy" which Madison condemned in *Federalist* 10 (a regime whose tendencies *every* branch of government prescribed by the original Constitution was intended to prevent). But this is not to say that those tendencies can be avoided or overcome by simple adherence to the principles by contemporary "conservatives."[45]

But to return from our digression, it will be noted that the district method of electing representatives tends to prevent or obstruct the political domination of what may be termed a "homogeneous" majority, which is to say it hinders the rule of the poor. Instead, district elections eventuate in "heterogeneous" majorities consisting of diverse groups whose respective interests or claims are moderated in the deliberative process. The rule of heterogeneous majorities is consistent with distributive justice, which, for practical purposes, can be achieved only in a regime that combines democratic and oligarchic attributes.[46]

Before taking up the other electoral arrangements which conform to a 'polity,' it may be helpful to summarize, in schematic form, those already discussed. For this purpose, it will only be necessary to recall that the arrangement for a democracy and the *first* arrangement for a 'polity' are identical insofar as (1) *all* citizens are eligible to vote; (2) *all* are eligible for office; ap-

[45] See Paul Eidelberg, "Between a Silent and a Tyrannical Majority," *Midway*, 11:1 (Summer 1970), 23–38.

[46] Some analogy may be drawn between what I have termed a *"heterogeneous* majority" and the *"nationally* distributed majority" referred to in *Diamond*, p. 57. The latter is elaborated in *Diamond, et al., The Democratic Republic*, 2nd ed., pp. 95–96. It should be noted, however, that Diamond erroneously imputes to Madison the contemporary notion of "coalition" politics. Bearing in mind the leadership role which Madison envisioned for the Senate (to say nothing of Hamilton's view of the presidency), compare Diamond's tendentious use of the term "coalition" in *ibid.*, p. 96, and the use of that term in *Federalist* 51, p. 341 (top).

pointment in *both* regimes may be either by (3) lot and/or (4) election; *but* that whereas democracies have (5) *at-large* elections, the 'polity' employs (6) *district* elections. By assigning numerical weights or coefficients to each of these six electoral attributes, but only in rough proportion to their regime bias or the extent to which they are democratic or oligarchic, PRELIMINARY SCHEMA I (p. 182) may be constructed.

With the various explanatory notes in view, the different modes of appointment contained in PRELIMINARY SCHEMA I may be applied to different combinations of offices $(x+y+z)$, as in SCHEMA I (p. 183).

This is, of course, a highly simplified schematic of the formal mode of regime analysis. For one thing, it arbitrarily assigns to each office equals weights. Furthermore, the schema ignores, besides the political powers of those offices, such attributes as size and tenure. Nevertheless, it does serve to illustrate graphically why 'polities,' such as indicated in SCHEMA I, incline toward, and are easily mistaken for, democracies. It also suggests why Aristotle would probably regard the 'polities' designated as I_a and I_c as not very well constituted.[47] 'Polities' I_b and I_d, especially the former, are superior, but only in virtue of the presence of district as opposed to at-large elections. Again, district elections insure the representation of a greater variety of groups, which in turn is conducive to distributive justice and political stability. Still, none of these models contains an *explicit* oligarchic attribute. None gives *de jure* recognition to property as a qualification either for voting or for holding office; and for this very reason, even the best of these 'polities' would have a very strong tendency to drift toward the left. Unless there is some such *de jure* or constitutional recognition of property, it will be difficult to justify and sustain the influence of any propertied class.[48] It will be noted, however, that Aristotle's second electoral arrange-

[47] Indeed, none of these models bears much resemblance to Sparta and Carthage, which Aristotle seems to have regarded as 'polities' inclined, respectively, toward oligarchy and aristocracy.

[48] See *Federalist* 60, p. 394.

Preliminary Schema I

Democracy and 'Polity' I

ELIGIBLE TO VOTE	REGIME BIAS (a)	ELIGIBLE FOR OFFICE	REGIME BIAS (b)	OFFICES	DISTRIBUTED REGIME BIAS 3(a+b)	MODE OF APPOINT-MENT	REGIME BIAS (c)	REGIME
All	5D	All	3D	$x+y+z$	24D	L_l	$D+2D$	Democracy
All	5D	All	3D	$x+y+z$	24D	E_l	$G+2D$	Democracy
All	5D	All	3D	$x+y+z$	24D	L_d	$D+2G$	'Polity' I
All	5D	All	3D	$x+y+z$	24D	E_d	$G+2G$	'Polity' I

A. *Explanation of Symbols:*
1. D = Democratic; G = Oligarchic
2. $x+y+z$ = offices of the regime
3. L = Lot: (D); E = Election: (G)
4. l = at-large: (2D); d = district: (2G)

B. *Explanation of Coefficients of Regime Bias:*
1. As already noted, the factor of who is eligible to vote is politically more decisive than the factor of who is eligible for office. Given a *restricted* franchise, those who have the vote are less likely to favor a candidate who wishes to extend the franchise and thereby diminish the power of the existing electorate. Conversely, given an *unrestricted* franchise, the voters are less likely to favor a candidate who wishes to limit the number of persons eligible for office. Accordingly, the factor of who is eligible to vote is assigned a coefficient of (5), whereas the factor for office is assigned a coefficient of (3). Both factors, however, are more important than the mode of appointment, since the latter is dependent on the former.

2. Inasmuch as Aristotle regards the *district* method of appointment as more important than the factor of appointment by *election*, the former is assigned two oligarchic units (2G), whereas the latter is assigned only one (G). On the other hand, since Aristotle regards *at-large* appointments as more important than appointment by *lot*, the former is assigned two democratic units (2D), whereas the latter is assigned only one (D). (Admittedly, appointment by election, which is oligarchic when by district, should perhaps be assigned less oligarchic weight when the election is held at-large. But again recall the paramount importance of the factor concerning the electors, a factor which renders insignificant the distinction just made.)

3. The numerical weights or coefficients of regime bias are in no case to be construed in an absolute sense. They are intended only to suggest relative degrees of regime bias.

Schema I

Democracy and 'Polity' I

MODE OF APPOINTMENT PER OFFICE	REGIME BIAS (c)	DISTRIBUTED REGIME BIAS $3(a+b)$	CUMULATIVE REGIME BIAS $3(a+b)+c$	REGIME
1 $L_1(x+y+z)$	$(D+2D)+(D+2D)+(D+2D)$	24D	33D	Democracy
2 $E_1(x+y+z)$	$(G+2D)+(G+2D)+(G+2D)$	24D	30D+3G	Democracy
3 $L_d(x+y+z)$	$(D+2G)+(D+2G)+(D+2G)$	24D	27D+6G	'Polity' I_a
4 $E_d(x+y+z)$	$(G+2G)+(G+2G)+(G+2G)$	24D	24D+9G	'Polity' I_b
5 $L_1(x+y)+E_1(z)$	$(D+2D)+(D+2D)+(G+2D)$	24D	32D+G	Democracy
6 $E_1(x+y)+L_1(z)$	$(G+2D)+(G+2D)+(D+2D)$	24D	31D+2G	Democracy
7 $L_d(x+y)+E_d(z)$	$(D+2G)+(D+2G)+(G+2G)$	24D	26D+7G	'Polity' I_c
8 $E_d(x+y)+L_d(z)$	$(G+2G)+(G+2G)+(D+2G)$	24D	25D+8G	'Polity' I_d

'POLITY' II

ELIGIBLE TO VOTE	REGIME BIAS (a)	ELIGIBLE FOR OFFICE	REGIME BIAS (b)	OFFICE ARRANGEMENT II_a	DISTRIBUTED REGIME BIAS I (a+b)	OFFICE ARRANGEMENT II_b	DISTRIBUTED REGIME BIAS II (a+b)
All	5D	All	3D	$x+y$	$2(5D+3D)$	x	8D
All	5D	Some	3G	z_q	$5D+3G$	y_q+z_q	$2(5D+3G)$
TOTAL					$21D+3G$		$18D+6G$

SCHEMA II

'POLITY' II

MODE OF APPOINTMENT PER OFFICE (DISTRICT ONLY)	REGIME BIAS (c)	DISTRIBUTED REGIME BIAS (a+b)	CUMULATIVE REGIME BIAS (a+b+c)
OFFICE ARRANGEMENT II_a			
1 $L(x+y)+L(z_q)$	$(D+2G)+(D+2G)+(D+2G)$	$21D+3G$	$24D+9G$
2 $L(x+y)+E(z_q)$	$(D+2G)+(D+2G)+(G+2G)$	$21D+3G$	$23D+10G$
3 $E(x+y)+L(z_q)$	$(G+2G)+(G+2G)+(D+2G)$	$21D+3G$	$22D+11G$
4 $E(x+y)+E(z_q)$	$(G+2G)+(G+2G)+(G+2G)$	$21D+3G$	$21D+12G$
OFFICE ARRANGEMENT II_b			
5 $L(x)+L(y_q+z_q)$	$(D+2G)+(D+2G)+(D+2G)$	$18D+6G$	$21D+12G$
6 $E(x)+L(y_q+z_q)$	$(G+2G)+(D+2G)+(D+2G)$	$18D+6G$	$20D+13G$
7 $L(x)+E(y_q+z_q)$	$(D+2G)+(G+2G)+(G+2G)$	$18D+6G$	$19D+14G$
8 $E(x)+E(y_q+z_q)$	$(G+2G)+(G+2G)+(G+2G)$	$18D+6G$	$18D+15G$

ment for a 'polity' does indeed make provision for a property qualification, but only for *office*, and not for *voting* (and this, too, explains why a 'polity' inclines more toward democracy). That arrangement, it will be recalled, is one in which "all appoint from all to some of the offices, but appoint from a section to others (either by election or lot or both by election and lot)." A "section" here means a group of citizens distinguished by a property qualification. Designating this factor (q), and assigning to it three oligarchic units (3G), PRELIMINARY SCHEMA II and SCHEMA II (p. 184) may be constructed.

Notice that the first electoral arrangement in SCHEMA II has the same regime bias as the fourth electoral arrangement in SCHEMA I, despite the fact that all offices in the former are appointed by lot, whereas all offices in the latter are appointed by election. The anomaly is accounted for by the presence or absence of a property qualification. Notice also that the fourth and fifth electoral arrangements of SCHEMA II have the same regime bias—despite the fact that a property qualification is required for two offices in the latter and for only one office in the former. Here the anomaly is accounted for by the different modes of appointment. Of course, it is wholly problematic, even indeterminate, as to how these attributes should be weighed *numerically* against each other, or even whether each attribute should retain the same weights under different electoral arrangements. Nevertheless, if these schemas accomplish no more than to indicate how different formal attributes not only reinforce but obstruct each other, they will have served their primary purpose. But perhaps they may do more? Perhaps they may even help to illuminate certain aspects of the original Constitution.

Beginning with the House of Representatives, and ignoring the low property qualifications for its electors and the intrastate district method of election, SCHEMA III (p. 186) may be constructed.

To construct a schema for the Senate is more complicated, since the mode of appointing senators does not conform to Aristotle's second electoral arrangement for a 'polity.' What arrange-

SCHEMA III

THE HOUSE OF REPRESENTATIVES

ELIGIBLE TO VOTE	REGIME BIAS (a)	ELIGIBLE FOR OFFICE	REGIME BIAS (b)	MODE OF APPOINTMENT	REGIME BIAS (c)	CUMULATIVE REGIME BIAS $(a+b+c)$
All	5D	All	3D	E_d	G+2G	8D+3G

SCHEMA IV

THE SENATE

ELIGIBLE TO VOTE	REGIME BIAS (a)	ELIGIBLE FOR OFFICE	REGIME BIAS (b)	MODE OF APPOINTMENT	REGIME BIAS (c)	CUMULATIVE REGIME BIAS $(a+b+c)$
Some	5G	All	3D	E_d	G+2G	8G+3D

ment does it most closely resemble? Recall that when "a section appoints from all . . . by the method of election," the arrangement is aristocratic (199). But here Aristotle must mean by a "section" a group of citizens distinguished not by some property qualification so much as by merit. Hence, to ascribe this arrangement to the election of senators by the state legislatures requires an assumption. That is, inasmuch as the electors of the Senate are state *legislators* and not ordinary citizens, it would have to be assumed that the former are men of merit. This is perfectly consistent with the view prevailing among the founders, namely, that an indirect mode of election, which is to say an election by a "select" body of men, will generally result in the appointment of men possessing ability and virtue.[49] All this is further complicated, however, by the existence of thirteen of these select bodies, again, the state legislatures, seven of which, we have seen, had a property qualification for office. So, if the states are taken collectively, the mode of electing the Senate appears less aristocratic and more oligarchic. For this reason, it would seem that the mode in question most closely resembles a 'polity' verging on "aristocracy" in which "a section appoints simultaneously both from all and from a section" (199). Still, to construct a schema comparable to the previous ones, it will be necessary to: (1) ignore the aristocratic implications involved in the election of senators; (2) distribute among *all* the electors of the Senate the property qualifications required for office in seven of the state legislatures; (3) regard the Senate as chosen *from* all, but *by* a section thus qualified. With this simplified version of the Senate, SCHEMA IV (p. 188) may be constructed.

Inasmuch as the number of those eligible to vote is determined by a reduced property qualification, it may be thought that this factor should be assigned a regime bias of something less than five oligarchic units (5G). But it must be borne in mind that the oligarchic bias of that factor cannot but reduce the democratic regime bias assigned to the factor of who is eligible

[49] Again, see *Federalist* 64, p. 417, *Federalist* 63, pp. 408–410, *Federalist* 68, p. 444, and Madison in *Farrand*, I, 50, 152, 423.

Schema IV$_a$

The State Legislatures

ELIGIBLE TO VOTE	ELIGIBLE FOR OFFICE	REGIME BIAS (a)	MODE OF APPOINTMENT	REGIME BIAS (b)	REGIME BIAS (c)	CUMULATIVE REGIME BIAS (a+b+c)
All	Section	5D	E$_d$	3G	G+2G	5D+6G
All	All	5D	E$_d$	3D	G+2G	8D+3G
TOTALS		10D		3D+3G	6G	13D+9G

Schema V

The House of Representatives and the Senate

OFFICE	ELIGIBLE TO VOTE	REGIME BIAS (a)	ELIGIBLE FOR OFFICE	REGIME BIAS (b)	MODE OF APPOINTMENT	REGIME BIAS (c)	CUMULATIVE REGIME BIAS (a+b+c)
House	All	5D	All	3D	E$_d$	3G	8D+3G
Senate	Section	5G	All	3D	E$_d$	3G	3D+8G
TOTALS		5D+5G		6D		6G	11D+11G

for office, leaving the relative weights of the two factors more or less unchanged. Nevertheless, because the electors of the Senate (the members of the state legislatures) were themselves chosen, not by a section (5G), but by all the citizens (5D), it may be argued that I have exaggerated the oligarchic regime bias in question. But let us examine this more closely. Let us divide the thirteen states into two groups and regard each group as a single office, but one with, and the other without, a property qualification.[50] SCHEMA IV$_a$ (p. 188) may then be constructed.

Taking the states collectively, the mode of appointing their legislatures conforms precisely to Aristotle's second electoral arrangement for a 'polity,' where "all appoint from all to some of the offices, but appoint from a section to others." But when the state legislatures are *individually* constituted as electors of the Senate, the total *cumulative* regime bias indicated in SCHEMA IV$_a$ is misleading, in view of the fact that each state, regardless of population, elects an equal number of senators. This fact reduces the proportion of those eligible for the senatorial office, thus reducing the democratic bias of factor (b) relative to the oligarchic bias of factor (a) in SCHEMA IV. So again it appears reasonable to assign five oligarchic units to the latter, so long as three democratic units are assigned to the former. Indeed, all things considered, I believe that SCHEMA IV, relatively speaking, should be more oligarchic than indicated.[51]

Be this as it may, SCHEMAS III and IV may be combined as in SCHEMA V. Here the democratic bias of the House is exactly counterbalanced by the oligarchic bias of the Senate. No doubt such symmetry may occasion skepticism or be regarded as contrived. But the truth is that such symmetry depends on the weights assigned to factor (a). It could be argued, for example, that the coefficient assigned to factor (a) for the House should

[50] I am assuming that the bicameral state legislatures appointed senators by joint ballot, which was, indeed, the prevailing practice.

[51] Again consider the indirect mode of election, as well as the low compensation provided senators—the latter having the effect of a property qualification which of course applies to their electors *and* to members of the House of Representatives.

be greater (or less) than the coefficient assigned to the same factor for the Senate. To this I can only say "perhaps." But the reader will mistake my intentions if he considers these schemas primarily in a quantitative light. Or to borrow from *Federalist* 55: "Nothing can be more fallacious than to found our political calculations on arithmetical principles" (361). If some feel that the Senate relative to the House should be less oligarchic—and they may be right—I might ask them to consider such oligarchic attributes as the size and tenure of the senatorial office, as well as its role in the appointment and treaty-making powers. Or if some feel that the Senate relative to the House should be more oligarchic—and they too may be right—I could ask them to consider the contingency election of the President which the Constitution assigns to the House and not to the Senate. Finally, if some feel that the Constitution is nothing more than "patchwork," there is little point in asking them anything.

Moving on to the mode of appointing the President, it should be evident that the regime bias would differ little from that associated with the mode of appointing the Senate. True, virtually any citizen may be an elector of the President, so far as the Constitution is concerned. But the manner of choosing electors is determined by the state legislatures, so that the regime bias of the latter affects the regime bias of the former. Also, the fact that the electors in each state do not comprise a "continuously active body" is of oligarchic significance (199). It secures —precisely what the founders saw in this attribute—the independence and integrity of the presidency, hence the rational principle of political forms. On the other hand, the contingency election of the President by the House is of some democratic significance, attenuated, however, by the oligarchic principle of "one *state*, one vote."

If the mode of electing the President is somewhat less oligarchic than that of the Senate, the same may not be said of the mode of appointing justices of the Supreme Court. Not only are the people two or three removes from the nominations of justices, and two removes from their confirmation, but as a matter of deeply rooted customary law, the membership of the Court is limited to the legal profession. From a purely formal mode of regime analysis, the appointment of the Court conforms most closely to the oligarchic arrangement defined by Aristotle, namely, "when a section appoints from a section" (199). But given the qualifications required of the latter "section," the Court inclines toward aristocracy.[52]

Now, in view of the oligarchic inclination of the Senate, the Presidency, and the Supreme Court, it may be thought that the original Constitution as a whole is more oligarchic than democratic. In theory, however, these three institutions, taken collectively, can do nothing without the cooperation of the democratically inclined House of Representatives (or vice versa). This means that the regime bias of an institution depends not only on the attributes presented in the above schemas, but also on its specific *powers*. That the Supreme Court is the most oligarchic institution of American government from the perspective of its mode of appointment does not affect the truth of Hamilton's contention in *Federalist* 78 that "the judiciary is beyond comparison the weakest of the three departments of power"; that it "has no influence over either the sword or the purse; no direction either of the strength or of the wealth of the society . . . and must ultimately depend upon the aid of the executive arm even for the efficacy of its judgments" (504). This does not mean that the Court is powerless, or that it cannot profoundly affect society as a whole. Hamilton envisioned no insignificant role for the Court. But no Court could withstand the concerted opposition of the legislature, and for reasons already indicated. As for the executive, powerful as this branch of government is, it can be paralyzed, as already noted, by the withholding of congressional appropriations.[53] To be sure, if the President has the support of a large plurality in Congress, his

[52] See my *Philosophy of the American Constitution*, pp. 125–126, and *Federalist* 35, pp. 214–215.

[53] See Madison, *Writings*, V, 382, and see *Letters and Other Writings*, I, 478–479.

office may then be regarded as the most powerful of all, and for reasons elaborated earlier. But this is a most important "if" indeed. It brings us back to that Congress, and to its two branches, the House and the Senate. It helps to explain why the founders sought to embody in the Senate as many oligarchic attributes as was politically practicable. "I will barely remark," says Madison in *Federalist* 62, "that as the improbability of sinister combinations will be in proportion to the dissimilarity in the genius of the two bodies, it must be politic to distinguish them from each other by every circumstance which will consist with a due harmony in all proper measures, and with the genuine principles of republican government" (403). These principles preclude hereditary institutions and a high property qualification for voting. Both are also precluded by a 'polity' (and by a genuine aristocracy as well). But the genuine principles of republican government do not preclude the oligarchic attributes discussed in this chapter; indeed, they necessitate them.

To conclude this part of the inquiry, under the formal mode of regime analysis, the original Constitution conforms to Aristotle's well-designed 'polity' or the best practical regime. Whether this conclusion can be sustained by Aristotle's material mode of regime analysis is the problem of the next chapter.

CHAPTER V

The 'Polity' under the Material Mode
of Regime Analysis

Whether a 'polity,' the best regime in practice, can be constructed depends on the degree to which it partakes of three general factors which, in their fullness, would constitute the best regime in theory. Aristotle designates these factors as (1) "natural endowment," (2) "habit," and (3) "rational principle" (322). In this chapter, only the first two factors will be considered, and, to correct certain prevalent misconceptions about a 'polity,' I shall begin with the second. It should be understood, however, that none of these factors can be discussed without implicating the others.

1

At the outset of Chapter IV, where the 'polity' was treated under the formal mode of regime analysis, it was said that such a regime is difficult to distinguish from a democracy and from an oligarchy. One reason for this difficulty is the fact that the formal attributes of a 'polity' do not stand wholly separated from each other, but rather are blended as in a mixture. To show that the same holds true of its material attributes, I shall again cite the relevant passage from Aristotle's *Politics*: "We may add that it is a good criterion of a proper mixture of democracy and oligarchy that a mixed regime should be able to be described indifferently as either. When this can be said, it must obviously be due to the excellence of the mixture. It is a thing which can generally be said of the mean between two extremes: both of the extremes can be traced in the mean, [and it can thus be described as either]" (177–178). This passage helps to explain why historians and political scientists are divided over the political character of the Constitution: some saying it is democratic, others that it is oligarchic. As so often is the case in politics, there is some truth in both schools of thought. Besides, it is easier to explain the whole in terms of a part than to comprehend the whole in all its complexity. But another reason for this confusion is that the parts of which a 'polity' is composed do not stand in simple juxtaposition to each other. Rich and poor need not be separated socially; and so far as its political arrangements are concerned, a 'polity' does not require that one branch of government be elected by the rich, while another be elected by the poor. This is borne out in the sequel to the above passage, where Aristotle refers to Sparta as an example of a well-designed 'polity':

> There are many who would describe it as a democracy, on the ground that its organization has a number of democratic features. In the first place, and so far as concerns the bringing up of the young, the children of the rich have the same fare as the children of the poor, and they are educated on a standard which the children of the poor can also attain. The same policy is followed for adolescence; and it is equally followed in adult years. No difference is made between the rich and the poor: the food at the common mess is the same for all, and the dress of the rich is such as any of the poor could also provide for themselves (178).

In a well-designed 'polity,' rich and poor share in a common way of life, and this very fact gives to a 'polity' a democratic appearance. Consistent with these democratic social features of Sparta, there was also "the right of the people to elect to one of the two great institutions, the Senate, and to be eligible themselves for the other, the Ephorate" (178). Popular election of the Spartan senate is democratic; but this does not mean that that senate was in fact democratic or wholly democratic. In his detailed analysis of the Spartan regime in Book II of the *Politics*, Aristotle refers to "the upper classes" as "content with their access to the Senate (for a seat in the Senate is given as a reward for excellence) . . ." (77). The reasons why Sparta was also regarded as oligarchic need not be examined here.[1] What needs to be emphasized is the mixture—the interfusion—of democratic and oligarchic attributes in the social and political fabric of a 'polity.'[2] Aristotle's *Politics* refutes the contention that a mixed regime *necessitates*

---

[1] It should be noted that Aristotle offers Sparta as an example of a regime about which *opinion* differed as to whether it was a democracy or an oligarchy (Aristotle, *Politics*, 178). Yet he also notes the opinion that Sparta contained a monarchic principle in view of its provision for two kings (*ibid.*, 60). Aristotle's own opinion was highly critical of Sparta, perhaps more of its actual policies than of its legal form; and he seems to have been more critical of its oligarchic tendencies than of its democratic ones. Insofar as he regarded Sparta as a 'polity,' three things may be inferred from his analysis of this regime: (1) that he probably regarded its legal form as inclined toward oligarchy; (2) that it did not conform, in his opinion, to a well-designed 'polity,' at least in practice; and (3) that inasmuch as he approved of the democratic institution of common meals— which was violated in practice—he must also have approved of the system of giving rich and poor the same education (*ibid.*, 75–80). See also, Aristotle's critique of Spartan militarism and education (*ibid.*, 318–320, 338–339).

[2] See, however, *Diamond*, pp. 59–60. See also, Robert Brown, *Charles Beard and the Constitution* (Princeton: Princeton University Press, 1956), and *Virginia 1705–1786: Democracy or Aristocracy?* (East Lansing: Michigan State University Press, 1964) (co-authored with B. Katherine Brown). Brown's democratic interpretation of the Constitution and of eighteenth-century America as a whole is based on simplistic criteria regarding democracy. These consist in (1) the *number* of those who are eligible to vote and hold office; (2) the extent of *economic opportunity*; and (3) the degree of *social mobility*. Brown does not examine different *varieties of democracy*. Nor does he consider the shading of one regime into another or the philosophical and psychological implications of the various attributes of political institutions. While he admits that America was a middle-class society, he fails to consider the possibility that such a society may combine both democratic and oligarchic features. Finally, in the second of the two works cited above, he provides evidence on landholding in Virginia which is susceptible to an interpretation contrary to his own basic thesis (pp. 13–14). In opposition to the Browns' study of Virginia, see Louis B. Wright, *The First Gentlemen of Virginia* (Charlottesville: Dominion Books, University Press of Virginia, 1964).

clearly defined classes, each represented in institutions constituted by *wholly* different political principles. Indeed, a regime
thus constituted would not qualify as a well-designed 'polity,'
if only because there would be little reason to confuse it either
with a democracy or with an oligarchy. In other words, such a
'polity' would be poorly designed precisely because it would be
recognized as a mixed regime by virtually anyone!

What distinguishes a well-designed and difficult to recognize
'polity' from the poorly designed and the easy-to-recognize 'polity' just mentioned is that the former, unlike the latter, is not a
stratified regime with a fixed order of classes. The well-designed
'polity' which Aristotle himself has in mind is not divided between the rich and the poor. Rather, it is a middle-class regime
par excellence.[3] Accordingly, under the material mode of regime
analysis, the character of the middle class must be distinguished
from that of the other classes. Unlike the poor, the middle class
does not covet the goods of others (182). This should not be
taken to mean that the middle class is utterly free from this
vice. But inasmuch as the members of the middle class enjoy a
greater degree of security, they do not covet the possessions of
others as the poor covet those of the rich. When the poor are
envious of the rich, they are more apt to be filled with *ill will* or
resentment. On the one hand, they may regard themselves as
victims of injustice. On the other hand, they may regard the possessions of the rich as undeserved if not ill gotten, and their character as suspect if not vicious. Furthermore, given the feeling
of injustice that accompanies their envy, the poor are more susceptible to factional strife or to the seditious designs of ambitious
demagogues. In contrast, should a middle-class person harbor
envy, it will probably be neutral in disposition or unaccompanied
by ill will or the feeling of injustice. Accordingly, such a person

---

[3] To be sure, a "good" democracy will have a middle class; but its size, in
proportion to the whole society, will usually be smaller. Quite apart from the
factor of size, however, the character of the middle class will depend on the
manner in which its members earn their livelihood, as well as on their customs,
religious beliefs, and their education in general.

will not begrudge the more affluent members of society; indeed, he is more likely to respect their character. This would render him more amiable and just in his relations with others and less prone to engage in factional strife.

Anticipating certain aspects of *Federalist* 10, Aristotle notes that "Large countries are generally more free from faction just because they have a large middle class. In small countries, on the other hand, it is easy for the whole population to be divided into only two classes; nothing is left in the middle, and all—or almost all—are either poor or rich" (182). In a 'polity,' the middle class can hold the balance of power between the rich and the poor and prevent either from becoming dominant. The wise statesman will therefore seek to increase the size of the middle class. This is precisely the view expressed by Madison in another of his articles published in *The National Gazette*. Addressing himself to the problem of preventing the ascendency of the rich or of the poor, Madison said that the solution lay in "the silent operation of laws, which, without violating the rights of property, reduce extreme wealth towards a state of mediocrity, and raise extreme indigence towards a state of comfort."[4] While Aristotle would agree with Madison that the statesman should seek to prevent "an immoderate and especially unmerited accumulation of riches" among the few,[5] Madison would agree with Aristotle that the statesman should take measures "to ensure a permanent level of prosperity" (268). Because domestic tranquillity is characteristic of a middle-class regime, Aristotle deemed it "the greatest of blessings for a community that its members should possess a moderate and adequate property" (182).

Lacking the envy of the poor and the avarice of the rich, the middle class possesses the virtues essential to a 'polity,' namely, *moderation* and *justice*. In addition, the possession of adequate property on the part of middle-class persons is conducive to the

[4] *Writings*, VI, 86 (Jan. 23, 1792). It is not entirely clear what Madison meant by the "silent operation of laws," but very likely he had in mind those laws which had abolished primogeniture and entailed estates. See *ibid.*, IX, 106.
[5] *Ibid.*, VI, 86.

virtue of *liberality*, or as Wilson said, generosity. In contrast to the poor, the middle class is less prone to the crimes engendered by poverty (65). In fact, middle-class people will be especially concerned about the preservation of law and order. Meanwhile, they will be less afflicted by the ambition of the rich, who, according to Aristotle, are prone to crimes more destructive of a regime than those of the poor (186). Finally—and this is of crucial importance—the middle class is neither servile like the poor, nor arrogant like the rich. Here it may be noted that the mean between servility and arrogance is deference, a quality especially prominent among members of the middle class. This quality renders them more amenable to reason and to the restraints of law. It makes possible that manly obedience without which one cannot acquire the virtue of command. Indeed, Aristotle maintains that "the best legislators have come from the middle class" (182).

By enlarging the size of the middle class, the statesman contributes to a regime's *stability*, which is a necessary precondition for the cultivation of human excellence. Statesmen, says Aristotle, "should devote their effort to the construction of stability. They must be on their guard against all the elements of destruction; they must leave their country with a body of laws, customary as well as enacted, which will include, *above everything else*, all the elements of preservation" (267) (italics added). This applies, of course, to the founding of a democracy as well as to the founding of a 'polity.' Nevertheless, Aristotle singles out "stability" as "the aim of every 'polity'" (223). The reason may be inferred. Since a 'polity' combines democratic and oligarchic principles, it is susceptible to change in the direction of either one. At the same time, however, because a 'polity' is more democratic than oligarchic, it naturally inclines toward the former (222). Knowing this, the statesman must institute checks against this tendency if the balance of the constitution is to endure.

It is well known that stability was a fundamental concern of the founders. The Senate, for example, was designed with the object of checking anticipated fluctuations of the House of Representatives. Madison regarded the Senate as the "anchor" of the regime. Some of the elements of stability which the founders built into the Senate were the duration of its tenure and its indirect mode of appointment. These attributes, especially the former, were understood by Madison to be necessary for "the establishment of a body in the Government sufficiently respectable for its wisdom and virtue."[6] Taken in conjunction with its small size, the tenure and "select" appointment of the Senate would enable its members to deliberate "with more coolness, with more system, and with more wisdom,"[7] and thus provide for continuity and consistency in public policy.

There was good reason, then, that some of the founders and many opponents of the Constitution regarded the Senate as the "aristocratic" branch of the national legislature[8]—which is not to say that the Senate was designed exclusively or even primarily for Aristotle's genuine *aristoi*. This helps to explain why Diamond errs in saying: "What pre-modern thought had seen in an aristocratic senate—wisdom, nobility, manners, religion, etc.—the Founding Fathers converted into stability, enlightened self-interest, 'a temperate and respectable body of citizens.' "[9] Quite apart from the inaccuracy or inadequacy of this description, there is nothing incompatible with the Senate thus described and Aristotle's estimate of the kind of legislators required for a 'poli-

[6] *Farrand*, I, 423, and see *Federalist* 62, p. 401, and *Federalist* 64, p. 417.

[7] *Farrand*, I, 151, and see *Federalist* 62, pp. 403–407.

[8] See Cecelia M. Kenyon, *The Antifederalists* (Indianapolis: Bobbs-Merrill Co., 1966), pp. 48, 61–67, 105–106, 220; 5–18, 71, 184, 188, 195, 204–218, 383; Morton Bordon, *The Antifederalist Papers* (Ann Arbor: University of Michigan Press, 1965), pp. 170, 181, 189, 199–200.

[9] *Diamond*, p. 60. Why Diamond should regard such a senate as "radically democratic," that is, "when viewed from a pre-modern perspective," is far from being evident, even if we employ the standards of Aristotle's *Nichomachean Ethics*. Would Diamond contend that the British House of Lords was only *democratic*, rather than "radically" democratic relative to those standards? Goodness knows how many religious and well-mannered incompetents graced that body of hereditary nobles which Diamond compares so favorably with the Senate of the United States (*ibid.*, p. 59).

ty.' A Senate composed of a "temperate and respectable body of citizens" who are motivated by "enlightened self-interest" and who legislate with a view to maintaining political stability is indispensable for the preservation of a 'polity.' And though the founders may have been wise as well as temperate and respectable, they could not wisely construct a regime whose preservation would depend on statesmen of their own caliber standing always at the helm. For as we have seen, Aristotle, no less than Madison, recognized the melancholy fact that such statesmen are rare, so much so that even a 'polity' is of rare occurrence. Hence, should such statesmen appear and be so fortunate as to have the opportunity of constructing a 'polity,' "they must leave their country with a body of laws . . . which will include, above everything else, all the elements of preservation" or stability. This they must do if only because their successors, generally speaking, will be lesser men; and perhaps of greater significance, because the circumstances of society or the temper of a people will not allow even men of the caliber of the founders to impose their stamp on the course and character of things.

How sensitive was Madison to the fortuitous element in the founding of regimes! In a letter referred to earlier, written during the debates on ratification, he well noted that "if a government be ever adopted in America, it must result from a fortunate coincidence of leading opinions, and a general confidence of the people in those who may recommend it."[10] This understanding is elaborated in *Federalist* 49, published a few weeks later:

> The danger of disturbing the public tranquillity by interesting too strongly the public passions, is a . . . serious objection against a frequent reference of constitutional questions to the decision of the whole society. Notwithstanding the success which has attended the revisions of our established forms of government, and which does so much honor to the virtue and intelligence of the people of America, it must be confessed that the experiments are of too *ticklish* a nature to be unnecessarily multiplied. We are to recollect that all the existing constitutions

[10] *Writings*, V, 82, to Edmund Randolph (Jan. 10, 1788).

were formed in the midst of *a danger which repressed the passions most unfriendly to order and concord; of an enthusiastic confidence of the people in their patriotic leaders, which stifled the ordinary diversity of opinions on great national questions;* of a universal ardor for new and opposite forms, produced by a universal resentment and indignation against the ancient government; and whilst no *spirit of party* connected with the changes to be made, or the abuses to be reformed, could mingle its leaven in the operation. *The future situations in which we must expect to be usually placed,* do not present any equivalent security against the danger which is apprehended (329–330).[11]

That the founders should emphasize the theme of stability is perfectly understandable in view of all the changes and innovations in the political forms which American society had undergone since the Revolution. Once again a new constitution of government was being established. Here was a body of laws and institutions which had neither the sanctity of immemorial tradition, nor of a lawgiver who could claim divine inspiration.[12] Here, rather, was the work of men, and what men could make others could unmake. All the more need, therefore, to discourage frequent revisions of the Constitution; to cultivate reverence for that Constitution; to emphasize, again and again, the need for stability on which that reverence would so much depend.

2

From the evidence examined in previous chapters, it would be reasonable to say that the founding generation—so largely agrarian—included a middle class whose character conforms more or less to that which Aristotle prescribes for a 'polity.'[13] To

[11] Italics added. Compare Lincoln's Lyceum Address, in *The Life and Writings of Abraham Lincoln* (New York: Modern Library, 1940), p. 238.

[12] But notice Jay's repeated reference to "Providence" in *Federalist* 2, p. 9.

[13] See *Federalist* 35, p. 214, and *Federalist* 60, p. 392. See also Robert Brown, *Middle-Class Democracy and the Revolution in Massachusetts* (Ithaca: Cornell University Press, 1955). Despite its democratic interpretation, the evidence of this work supports the above conclusion, as does the Browns' work on Virginia cited earlier.

be sure, the fact that nine-tenths of the population were then engaged in agriculture should not obscure the commercial propensities of many Americans. Nevertheless, Charles Pinckney of South Carolina was not merely speaking for southern interests when he declared at the Federal Convention: "If that commercial policy is pursued which I conceive to be the true one, the merchants of this Country will not or ought not for a considerable time to have much weight in the political scale."[14] Though more friendly to commerce, Madison shared Pinckney's preference for an agrarian society, a preference hardly visible in *The Federalist*. Compare, however, an article Madison published in *The National Gazette* entitled "A Republican Distribution of Citizens":

> The best distribution is that which would favor *health, virtue, intelligence,* and *competency* in the *greatest number* of citizens. It is needless to add to those objects, *liberty* and safety. The first is presupposed by them [which means that liberty cannot exist without a virtuous and intelligent citizenry]. The last must result from them.
>
> The life of the husbandman is pre-eminently suited to the comfort and happiness of the individual. *Health,* the first of blessings, is an appurtenance of this property and his employment.[15] *Virtue,* the *health of the soul,* is another part of his patrimony. . . . Intelligence may be cultivated in this as well as in any other walk of life. If the mind be less susceptible of polish in retirement than in a crowd, it is more capable of profound and comprehensive efforts. . . . *Competency* is more universally the lot of those who dwell in the country. . . . The extremes both of want and of waste have other abodes. 'Tis not the coun-

[14] *Farrand,* I, 402. Note the sequel, and see my *Philosophy of the American Constitution,* pp. 138–142. Interestingly enough, Hamilton was not so unfriendly toward agricultural interests. His plan of government provided for a landed property qualification for senatorial electors.

[15] Notice that Madison puts first things first. Contrast *Federalist* 10, where he says that the "first" object of government is to protect the diverse human faculties from which the rights of property originate. It is somewhat remarkable that scholars of the most diverse philosophical propensities should either miss or exaggerate the significance of the word "first."

try that peoples either the Bridewells or the Bedlams. These mansions of wretchedness are tenanted from the distresses and vices of overgrown cities. . . .

It follows, that the greater proportion of [husbandmen] to the whole society, the more free, the more independent, and the more happy must be the society itself.[16]

No less than Jefferson, Madison deplored the tendency of the big city to generate criminality and insanity. He also deplored what he termed the city's "mutability of fashion"; and with what must have been profound insight (unfortunately left to silence, or only barely suggested), he compared such mutability with "mutability of policy"—in still another article published in *The National Gazette*.[17] But here a word of caution is necessary. Not only should we avoid the error of exaggerating Madison's agrarianism, as some exaggerate his commitment to a commercial republic, but we should also avoid the error of reading into the founding the meaning which commerce has for us today. At least in New England, men's understanding of commerce was mediated by the puritan notion that work is noble and that it should be intended not for the conceits of man so much as for the glory of God.

Be this as it may, many of the founders foresaw the time when most Americans would be living in cities and would work for others in factories rather than for themselves on the farm. Madison, who seems to have entertained certain Malthusian notions, projected teeming populations, the exhaustion of vacant lands, and the inevitable ascendency of propertyless men.[18] Perhaps it was partly with a view to forestalling that very development that he supported the Louisiana Purchase. Whatever the case, Madison sought to guard against the principal danger attending such a development, the danger of democratic tyranny. As he warned his fellow delegates at the Federal Convention:

[16] *Writings*, VI, 96–99 (March 5, 1792). I have italicized the words "health of the soul."

[17] *Ibid.*, VI, 99–101 (March 22, 1792).

[18] *Ibid.*, I, 463–465n, IX, 168–170.

In framing a system which we wish to last for ages, we should not lose sight of the changes which ages will produce. An increase of population will of necessity increase the proportion of those who will labour under all the hardships of life, and secretly sigh for a more equal distribution of its blessings. These may in time outnumber those who are placed above the feelings of indigence. According to the laws of equal suffrage, the power will slide into the hands of the former. No agrarian attempts have yet been made in this Country, but symptoms of a leveling spirit, as we have understood, have sufficiently appeared in a certain quarter to give notice of the future danger.[19]

To grasp the deeper significance of this passage, it should first be noted that it occurs in a speech in which Madison supported a proposal to invest the Senate with a nine-year term. A Senate thus constituted, he argued, could more effectively guard against the possible occurrence of the "leveling spirit" in the future, when those with property would be outnumbered by those without. Composed of men respectable for their "wisdom and virtue," such a Senate would "aid on such *emergencies*, the preponderance of justice by throwing its weight into that scale."[20] As earlier portions of Madison's speech make evident, in the other scale would be the House of Representatives. There, a future majority, animated by egalitarian envy, would attempt to despoil men of property. (Again it is evident that Madison never regarded the representative principle and the fragmentation of the majority as sufficient for securing the future of the republic against the dangers of democracy.) Also needed (among still other things) was a powerful and high-toned Senate, one, said Madison, that "ought to come from, and represent, the Wealth of the nation."[21] The problem for the founder-statesman was to establish that Senate *now*, that is, while the American people,

[19] *Farrand*, I, 422–423. This speech, delivered on June 26, includes a critique of Pinckney's unabashedly agrarian speech of the previous day. Precisely because he was thus oriented, Pinckney, unlike Madison, was opposed to a powerful national government.

[20] *Ibid.*, I, 423 (italics added).

[21] *Ibid.*, I, 158 (King's notes).

still agrarian, were "so much accustomed to be guided by their rulers on all new and intricate questions." In view of their deferential character, such a people could be persuaded to accept a Senate which, to say the least, would have the appearance of being aristocratic, but which could nonetheless be shown to be consistent with republican government.[22] Such a promising opportunity was not likely to occur again, given the expected increase in population, the exhaustion of uncultivated land, and the equal laws of suffrage—which factors, *left by themselves*, would spawn a people whose character would be shaped more by industrial than by agrarian callings. Establish, however, a high-toned Senate now and, by its steady moral and political influence on the regime as a whole, the cooperation of those three factors would not, under *ordinary* circumstances, be productive of the evil in question. In other words, the "aristocratic" form of the Senate would modify certain democratic tendencies associated with a commercial society such that the laws of the country and the habits of its people would still very much conform to the laws and habits of a 'polity.'[23]

Without encroaching much further on Book II of the present Discourse, where the American 'polity' will be discussed under the category of change, it might be helpful at this point to anticipate the following question: "In view of their prognostication regarding the growth of commerce in the United States and the greater likelihood of democratic envy resulting therefrom, why

[22] See *Federalist* 63, p. 413, where Madison anticipates the charge that the Senate will eventually become a "tyrannical aristocracy"; and see the references cited on p. 199, n. 8 above.

[23] Here someone may argue: "What Madison calls the 'equal laws of suffrage' could not but eventuate in the election of state legislators who would amend the state constitutions so as to eliminate property qualifications for state office. This done, the electors of the Senate would not themselves 'represent the wealth of the nation.' Indeed, the laws of equal suffrage would sooner or later put an end to a Senate chosen by a 'select' body; for with the ascendancy of the 'leveling spirit,' a constitutional amendment would throw the election of the Senate into the hands of the people, a people now congregated in the cities."

To this I would reply that it took some 125 years for the passage of that amendment. But more will be said about this problem in Book II.

did the founders fail to include in the Constitution any property qualifications for office?" Before answering this question, it should first be understood that, had they done so, the regime might still have been a 'polity,' but one inclined toward oligarchy. Be this as it may, the fact is that of the eleven states represented at the Federal Convention, eight voted in favor of instructing the Committee of Detail to include a clause in the Constitution requiring a property qualification for both senators and representatives.[24]

This followed upon a motion proposing qualifications of *landed* property for members of the national legislature. On a motion of Madison, however, the word "landed" was deleted— this, to avoid alienating monied and commercial interests without whose support the Constitution could hardly have been ratified. But precisely because of such diversity of property (and of property values) among the various states, the Committee of Detail could not agree upon a uniform standard. Accordingly, it dodged the issue and reported out a draft constitution containing the following clause: "The Legislature of the United States shall have authority to establish such uniform qualifications of the members of each House, with regard to property, as to the said Legislature shall seem expedient."[25] But if the Convention could not devise a uniform standard, there was little likelihood of one being established by the national legislature, for which reason, presumably, the preceding clause passed into oblivion.[26] So, the fact that the Constitution does not prescribe property qualifications for senators and representatives is not of itself conclusive of the political thought of most of the founders. Indeed, several delegates who opposed property qualifications for members of the national legislature favored limiting the franchise to freeholders. But again the diversity of property and of property values in the various states prevented the establishment of a uniform standard.[27] Finally, it should be noted that

[24] *Farrand*, II, 124–125, 250–251.

[25] *Ibid.*, II, 179.

[26] *Ibid.*, II, 251 (Wilson).

[27] See *Federalist* 52, p. 342.

some of the reasons advanced either for or against property qualifications do not wholly conform to Aristotelian or to contemporary notions. For example, John Dickenson, who favored a freehold qualification for voters, opposed property qualifications for office, saying: "He doubted the policy of interweaving into a Republican constitution a veneration for wealth. He had always understood that a veneration for poverty and virtue, were the objects of republican government."[28] Here is an excellent example of Christianity assimilating democratic and aristocratic values. To be sure, a "veneration for wealth" would eventually rise triumphant, but only after the American regime had shifted from a 'polity' inclined toward democracy, to a 'polity' inclined toward oligarchy. Once again, however, I am encroaching on Book II of this Discourse. Suffice to say that at the time of the founding the agrarian and middle-class character of the American people compared very favorably with Aristotle's prescriptions for the best practical regime, a regime distinguished by moderation and deference.

3

Having discussed the moral habits required of a 'polity,' the next factor to be considered is material endowment. This includes (1) natural resources, (2) geographical situation, (3) extent of territory, and (4) size of population. Again bear in mind that each of these specific factors has implications for the moral character of a regime or the extent to which it partakes of human excellence. Also to be borne in mind is that a 'polity' does not require that each of these factors conform to the standards of the best regime in theory.

The best regime in theory requires a territory whose soil is

[28] *Farrand*, II, 123. Meanwhile, Gouverneur Morris opposed universal suffrage on the ground that it would eventuate in an "aristocracy"! "The aristocracy," he explained, "will grow out of the House of Representatives. Give the votes to the people who have no property, and they will sell them to the rich. . . ." *Ibid.*, II, 202; I, 511–513. Like Dickenson, Morris wanted to restrict the suffrage to freeholders. As for Madison's views on the suffrage, see *ibid.*, II, 203–204, and III, 450–455.

productive of all kinds of crops, and where natural resources for building and other forms of industry are in abundance. Also required is a "convenient commercial center" to facilitate the shipment and distribution of food supplies, raw materials, and various products of industry. In other words, the best regime must be as self-sufficient as possible, enabling its citizens "to live a life of leisure which combines liberality with temperance" or moderation. At the same time, the frontiers of the country "should be difficult of access to enemies, and easy of egress for its inhabitants" (293). For the heights of human excellence can be achieved only under conditions of peace. Although military courage is one of the virtues, it will be found not only in the best, but also in the worst of regimes—in tyrannies bent on war and conquest (245). Besides, "courage," according to Aristotle, "is useless in all life's ordinary affairs" (75).[29] Furthermore, if a country is too exposed to external danger and is compelled, as a consequence, to prepare for and frequently engage in war, it is likely to become intemperate, reckless, and unjust—to say nothing of the possibility of its being conquered by a more powerful adversary. War arouses the passions of hatred, overweening ambition, arrogance, and avarice. Or as may be seen in Washington's Farewell Address:

> The Nation, prompted by illwill and resentment, sometimes impels to War the Government, contrary to the best calculations of policy. The Government sometimes participates in the national propensity, and adopts through passion what reason would reject; at other times, it makes the animosity of the Nation subservient to projects of hostility instigated by pride, ambition and other sinister and pernicious motives. The peace often, sometimes perhaps the Liberty, of Nations, has been the victim.[30]

Not that all wars are unjust. "It is not the inherent nature of actions," says Aristotle, "but the end or object for which they are done, which makes one action differ from another in the way of honour or dishonour" (316). "War must therefore be regarded

[29] But compare *Politics*, p. 321.
[30] *Writings*, XXXV, 232.

as only a means to peace; action as a means to leisure; and acts which are merely necessary, or merely and simply useful, as means to acts which are good in themselves" (317). Hence "the legislator should make leisure and peace the cardinal aims of all legislation bearing on war—or indeed, for that matter, on anything else" (319). From this it may be inferred that a nation, so far as possible, should take its bearing with a view to its internal perfection rather than to external glory. Stated another way: A nation should pursue a policy of "isolationism," without being unprepared for war should that become necessary.

Although many of Hamilton's papers in *The Federalist* take their bearing on external danger and glory, they must be evaluated from several perspectives. First, consider the geopolitical circumstances. Here was a confederation of mutually jealous states bordered by hostile or potentially hostile European powers experienced in the art of *divide et impera*.[31] Second, we must recall Aristotle's injunction that the wise statesman will foster alarms among his people, persuading them to put aside their rivalries in the face of a common and overriding danger. Third, the quest for glory is not a democratic passion, and, when qualified, as apparently was Hamilton's, by a contempt for popularity and worldly goods on the one hand, and a commitment to laudable deeds on the other—that quest rises above mere ambition and reaches the classical or aristocratic ideal of *magnanimity*. Yet, so diverse and complex are the values which entered into the founding—a veritable myriad of passions and principles— that over against the Hamiltonian emphasis on external glory was the more internal but less influential orientation of the Jeffersonian persuasion, one colored by the modern liberal's pessimistic distrust of power.[32]

Between Hamilton and Jefferson, however, stood Madison— who had no apparent difficulty in saying before the Virginia ratifying convention that "national splendour and glory are not

[31] See *Federalist* 4, *Federalist* 7, p. 40, and *Farrand*, I, 285, 289, 297, 316, 319. See also Madison, *Letters and Other Writings*, I, 253.

[32] See *Stourzh*, pp. 99–106.

our objects,"[33] while urging in *The Federalist* that the American people were capable of becoming "one great, respectable, and flourishing empire,"[34] but that a relatively permanent Senate would be necessary to achieve "national character" and the "esteem of foreign powers."[35] Madison, the most persevering patron of a powerful Senate during the Federal Convention; Jefferson, the partisan of the popular assembly (who regarded the Senate as undemocratic); Hamilton, the intellectual architect of presidential power—these and other countervailing emphases are woven into the fabric of the Constitution, as subtle as life itself. Turn again, however, to Washington's Farewell Address, in which Hamilton had no little hand:

> Observe good faith and justice towards all Nations. Cultivate peace and harmony with all. Religion and morality enjoin this conduct; and can it be that good policy does not equally enjoin it? It will be worthy of a free, enlightened, and, at no distant period, a great Nation, to give to mankind the magnanimous and too novel example of a People always guided by an exalted justice and benevolence. . . . Can it be, that Providence has not connected the permanent felicity of a Nation with its virtue?[36]

Notice the loftiness of this teaching, intended to educate a people, to inspire them with historic purpose. Here Washington exhorts his countrymen to set an example to mankind, the unprecedented example of a great and powerful nation whose highest glory speaks not of war and conquest, but of justice and benevolence. The sense of justice, however, is too often confused with, and undermined by, the feeling of benevolence, or it may be enfeebled by an inordinate desire for peace. Accordingly, Washington goes on to say: "If we remain one People, under an efficient government, the period is not far off, when we may defy material injury from external annoyance; when we may take

[33] *Writings*, V, 146, to be compared with Pinckney's speech of June 25 in *Farrand*, I, 402.

[34] *Federalist* 14, p. 84.

[35] *Federalist* 62, p. 405, and *Federalist* 63, p. 407.

[36] *Writings*, XXXV, 231.

such an attitude as will cause the neutrality we may at any time resolve upon to be scrupulously respected . . . *when we may choose peace or war,* as our interest guided by justice shall counsel."[37] But to minimize the likelihood of war, Washington urges his countrymen to remain aloof from the rivalries which ever embroil the powers of Europe, and, apart from commercial relations, "to have with them as little *political* connection as possible." What should be emphasized, however, is this: Men like Washington envisioned a nation acting on principles morally superior to those which hitherto had governed mankind. What nation, especially if great and powerful, had even been animated by an abiding sense of justice and benevolence in its relations with others? Yet, in the Farewell Address, we are given to contemplate a great and powerful nation guided not only by justice and benevolence, but also by the aristocratic ideal of magnanimity. A nation thus conceived and dedicated would indeed be a novelty in the political world. For given its magnanimity, the interests pursued by such a nation would be compatible with the true interests of mankind.

Be this as it may, embodied in Washington's Farewell Address is a policy of qualified isolationism, which is the policy recommended by Aristotle (319). Admittedly, Aristotle's primary emphasis, when speaking of war and peace, is on internal perfection. But this emphasis occurs in the context of his discussion of *the* best regime, where all legislation and policy are directed toward maximizing the leisure required for cultivating human excellence. Such emphasis ought not be expected in a 'polity.' There the notion of human excellence will be diluted, which is not to say it need be contemptible or unworthy of the respect of intelligent and high-minded men. In this light, consider another passage from the Farewell Address:

> Of all the dispositions and habits which lead to political prosperity, Religion and morality are indispensable supports. In vain would that man claim the tribute of Patriotism, who should

[37] *Ibid.,* XXXV, 234 (italics added). See Aristotle, *Politics,* p. 285, and Machiavelli, *The Prince* (New York: Modern Library, 1950), pp. 13, 55.

labour to subvert these great Pillars of human happiness. . . . Let it simply be asked, where is the security for property, for reputation, for life, if the sense of religious obligation *desert* the oaths, which are the instruments of investigation in Courts of Justice? And let us with caution indulge the supposition, that morality can be maintained without religion. Whatever may be conceded to the influence of refined education on minds of peculiar structure, reason and experience both forbid us to expect that National morality can prevail in exclusion of religious principle.[38]

Note the curious mixture of traditions which fructified the founding. Compounded of Puritan Christianity and classical patriotism on the one hand, and the rationalism and utilitarianism of the Enlightenment on the other, the founding reveals an age in contradiction with itself.[39] But a 'polity' is itself a compound of obscured but contradictory elements, especially when partly motivated by commerce and partly by a quest for glory which holds worldly goods in contempt.

In any event, here in America was a land rich with natural resources and separated from Europe by a vast ocean—a promising beginning for a 'polity.' But this was an extensive territory, far larger than that recommended by Aristotle for *the* best regime. The same may be said of its population, a factor infinitely more important for the character of a regime. Too large or too populous a country makes it difficult to maintain order, or to "secure a general habit of obedience to law" (291). Furthermore,

[38] *Writings*, XXV, 229.

[39] See Harry Jaffa, *Crisis of the House Divided* (New York: Doubleday & Co., 1959), pp. 238–239. Although Jaffa's interpretation of this passage of the Farewell Address is generally correct, it obscures the rhetorical necessities of public oratory and exaggerates the differences between Washington and Lincoln on the matter of religion. It was Lincoln who said in his Lyceum Address: "Reason—cold, calculating, unimpassioned reason—must furnish *all* the materials for our future support and defence." (*The Life and Writings of Abraham Lincoln*, Modern Library ed., p. 241, italics added.) The point is that most people *are* utilitarian, and statesmen must emphasize that bias while pointing to a *slightly* higher morality. Washington's Farewell Address is a superb example of the art of the genuine statesman. Analysis reveals the three major factors of a good political address: appeal to sentiment, to interest, and to principle.

friendship, the bond of a political community (the bond that contributes so much to human happiness), can flourish only among men who know each other, men who are joined in various activities—be it work or learning or recreation—and who thereby share similar experiences and feelings, beliefs, and habits. It is the lack of this kind of friendship that constitutes the real poverty of the Great Society. Accordingly, the Good Society must be large enough for self-sufficiency and self-defence, yet small enough for men to be familiar with, or at least know of, each other. Only in such a society can there be the mutual trust or fellow feeling that endows political life with harmony and beauty itself (291–292).

While Aristotle admits that a regime must consist of diverse and numerous elements if it is to be stable and self-sufficient, he also contends, in apparent opposition to the Madison of *Federalist* 10, that excessive heterogeneity is productive of civil discord or faction (60, 210). A large multifarious population cannot achieve the familiarity and mutual trust necessary for friendship. But we have also seen that Aristotle agrees with the author of *Federalist* 10 that large, populous regimes, if well constituted, are generally more free from faction (182). On the other hand, Madison, whose pluralism is so easily exaggerated, was aware of the disadvantages of a large (and, presumably, populous) country. Again in *The National Gazette* he wrote:

> The larger a country, the less easy for its real opinion to be ascertained, and the less difficult to be counterfeited; when ascertained or presumed, the more respectable it is in the eyes of individuals.—This is favorable to the authority of government. [Recall *Federalist* 49.] For the same reason, the more extensive a country, the more insignificant is each individual in his own eyes.—This may be unfavorable to liberty.
>
> Whatever facilitates a general intercourse of sentiments, as good roads, domestic commerce, a free press, and particularly a *circulation of newspapers through the entire body of the people*, and *Representatives going from, and returning among every part of them*, is equivalent to a contraction of territorial

limits, and is favorable to liberty, where these may be too extensive.[40]

It would be a serious error to think of the newspapers spoken of here as *commercial* enterprises (an error that would also distort the meaning of the First Amendment). Like *The National Gazette* itself, those which Madison had in mind would primarily be organs of political education and information. But note especially the role of a representative. Consistent with the teaching of *Federalist* 10, he was not only to "refine and enlarge the public views" when in Congress, but, upon returning to his constituency, he was to educate the people, imbuing them with a sense of national character and purpose. This same objective, of molding a more perfect union among people of diverse interests and opinions, was never absent from the author of *Federalist* 10, who, as President, advanced and elaborated the proposal he had made during the Federal Convention:

> The present is a favorable season . . . for bringing again into view the establishment of a national seminary of learning within the District of Columbia . . . subject to the authority of the General Government. Such an institution claims the patronage of Congress as a monument of their solicitude for the advancement of knowledge, without which the blessings of liberty cannot be fully enjoyed or long preserved; as a model instructive in the formation of other seminaries; as a nursery of enlightened preceptors, and as a central resort of youth and genius from every part of their country, diffusing on their return examples of those national feelings, those liberal sentiments, and those congenial maners which contribute cement to our Union and strength to the great political fabric of which that is the foundation.[41]

So Madison was well aware of the fact that the extended republic, or rather, the pluralistic solution to the problem of majority

[40] *Writings*, VI, 70, in an article entitled "Public Opinion" (Dec. 19, 1791).
[41] *Writings*, VIII, 342–343, seventh state of the union message (Dec. 5, 1815). Madison's second state of the union message also proposed the establishment of a national university, as did his eighth and last (*ibid.*, VIII, 127, 379).

faction, was only half a solution. The other half required the education of public-spirited men who would in turn cultivate among the people "those national feelings, those liberal sentiments, and those congenial manners"—in short, those ingredients of friendship so difficult to achieve in *any* society, let alone one so large and diverse as that which Madison sought to unify.

Looking back at the four specific factors included under natural endowment, the first two—natural resources and geographical situation—were conducive to self-sufficiency and internal perfection, hence favorable for establishing, if not the best regime in theory, then the best in practice, again, a 'polity.' But as long as the founders were so concerned about internal strife and political instability on the one hand, and external safety and even national glory on the other, then, given their commitment to an extended republic as a means of avoiding the one and achieving the other, the government they established would encompass so vast a territory and so multitudinous a people as to make it exceedingly difficult to unite this people by the strongest bonds of friendship. Yet, men like Washington and Madison were well aware of this problem. They sought to overcome it in various ways, above all, by inculcating among the people a "political creed," one that was to be propagated by the colleges of the United States, colleges having, as their model, a national university. To the elaboration of this theme I now turn.

CHAPTER VI

The 'Polity' under the Teleological Mode
of Regime Analysis:
On the Silence of the Constitution

ARISTOTLE refers to rationality as the third factor determinative of the character of the best regime, having in view the extent to which all aspects of the regime are ordered toward the completion or perfection of human nature. The perfection of human nature requires, of course, cultivation of the moral virtues, such as moderation and justice. But their cultivation must be directed toward what, in the natural order of development, comes last, namely, the attainment of intellectual virtue or wisdom. For again, the paramount purpose of the best regime in theory is to cultivate, so far as possible, complete or perfect men. This is not the paramount purpose of the best regime in practice, the 'polity.' Although a 'polity' is a just regime, it is not wholly or simply just. For justice requires the rule of the highest, and the highest, which is wisdom, is not the ruling principle of a 'polity.' Again, a 'polity' is a moderate regime. Yet, too often the citizens of a 'polity' are moderate (or just) not for its own sake—let alone for the sake of something higher—but for the sake of securing material well-being. In any event, their moderation, hence their education, is not ordered with a view to attaining the highest standard of human excellence. Still the question arises: To what extent did the American 'polity' partake of rationality especially as regards the cultivation of the intellect or the perfection of human nature? Before addressing this question directly it will be helpful to consider the Constitution from a world-historical perspective.

It should first be recalled, what too often is forgotten, that never before in recorded history had so numerous and so diverse a people established for themselves a government whose principles were determined by "reflection and choice." Not only was this unprecedented, but so too was the *form* of that government. Because it was, in Madison's words, "a novelty in the political world," its principles could not be defended merely by an appeal to the experiences of other nations, ancient or modern. Indeed, the very criticism of ancient and modern regimes, which we find in the debates of the Federal Convention and throughout *The Federalist*, is based upon principles or standards themselves in question or in need of rational justification. Some republics in antiquity may have been short-lived; but if they were also magnificent, and if such magnificence is necessarily short-lived, why should we prefer longevity? Again, certain republics of antiquity were noted for civic virtue; but if civic virtue requires a *small* republic whose very smallness is not equally conducive to personal liberty, why should we prefer a large republic which is more conducive to personal liberty than to civic virtue? How shall we weigh these competing values? What standards should guide "reflection and choice"? If we cannot take our bearings solely on the experience of history, shall we then turn to the writings of political philosophers?[1] But given their differences and contradictions, from which philosopher shall we choose our standards, and why from only one? Is it any wonder that commentators on the Constitution have hit upon the notion that it is nothing more than a "bundle of compromises"? But leaving this easy and partial truth aside, it may well be argued that never has the establishment of a government been accompanied by so much "reflection and choice," by such extensive appeals to ex-

[1] See, for example, *Federalist* 70, p. 457, *Federalist* 31, pp. 188–189, and compare *Federalist* 37, pp. 226, 228–231, *Federalist* 10, p. 58.

perience on the one hand, and to reason on the other. To be sure, *The Federalist* also appeals to men's passions and interests. But men want *reasons* for any proposed departure from established principles and practices which favor their passions and interests. Inasmuch as the founders could not find, in the conflicting doctrines of political philosophers, a coherent body of principles ready-made for them, and inasmuch as no actual regime, ancient or modern, could provide a model for simple imitation, then, in view of the inadequacy of antecedent theory and practice, it was necessary to think for themselves, to exercise critical reflection, to defend by rational arguments a Constitution which was bound to be opposed by the very fact of its novelty. Knowing this, Madison declared in *Federalist* 14:

> But why is the experiment of an extended republic to be rejected, merely because it may comprise what is new? Is it not the glory of the people of America, that, whilst they have paid a decent regard to the opinions of former times and other nations, they have not suffered a blind veneration for antiquity, for custom, or for names, to overrule the suggestions of their own good sense, the knowledge of their own situation, and the lessons of their own experience? (85)

Here, for the first time, a government was to be established primarily on *rational* as opposed to *customary* foundations, and according to an explicit and more or less coherent body of principles themselves subject to critical analysis. And so Madison could rightly look upon the Constitution not only as a "novelty in the political world," but also as an experiment whose success would be pregnant for mankind as a whole. The idea of an extended republic whose principles are enunciated in a written constitution adopted by popular conventions he regarded as "a revolution which has no parallel in the annals of human society." But this revolutionary example bore with it profound problems. Because the Constitution was established by men, men who could claim no divine sanction, and because it placed under a single and supreme authority thirteen formerly sovereign states whose citizens differed in their manners, habits, and beliefs, how could the founders unite such a people and endow them with a sense of *national* character? And how could this be accomplished when, by the very example of radically innovating upon the past, diverse and ambitious men might be encouraged to undertake new political experiments whose very novelty could not but thwart the development of a national character? The Constitution was but a piece of parchment. We know that the long tenure of the Senate and the longer tenure of the Supreme Court were intended to promote stability and continuity in the laws. We know that the very unity in the presidency was intended to provide the American people with a sense of national unity and purpose. But these are merely formal prescriptions. *How* was all this to be accomplished? What policies would the new government pursue? *Who* would initiate and formulate them? And what ends or values would take precedence over others?

The first thing that should be admitted is that nothing in the *language* of the Constitution proclaims the cultivation of human excellence as the paramount end of government or even as a legitimate object of government. The same cannot be said of several of the state constitutions. For example, the Constitution of Massachusetts declared:

> Wisdom and knowledge, as well as virtue, diffused generally among the people, being necessary for the preservation of their rights and liberties . . . it shall be the duty of legislators and magistrates, in all future periods of this commonwealth, to cherish the interests of literature and the sciences, and all seminaries of them; especially the university at Cambridge, public schools, and grammar-schools . . . to countenance and inculcate the principles of humanity and general benevolence, public and private charity, industry and frugality, honesty and punctuality in their dealings; sincerity, and good humor, and all social affections and generous sentiments, among the people.[2]

While admitting, however, that the language of the federal Constitution is silent about the "duty of legislatures and magis-

[2] *The Federal and State Constitutions*, III, 1907–8. This provision remained in force well beyond the middle of the nineteenth century.

trates" to promote "wisdom and knowledge, as well as virtue," it would be erroneous to conclude from this, or even from *The Federalist*, that the founders did not regard these ends as legitimate objects of government. It is true that the Constitution does not expressly authorize Congress to establish a national university. But it does not follow from this that the founders, or at least many of them, did not intend Congress to establish one. The evidence of the Federal Convention proves the contrary, as do events subsequent to the founding of the new government.

1

The establishment of a national university was a profound concern of Washington.[3] When we consider the enormous difficulties of establishing a new government, of organizing and staffing its various departments, of formulating a variety of policies concerning domestic and foreign affairs, of responding to a welter of pressing and conflicting wants and needs from the diverse parts of a vast country, it is all the more remarkable that Washington should have urged Congress, in his very first state of the union message, to address itself to the problem of education, saying "there is *nothing* which can better deserve your patronage."[4] After discussing the importance of education for a people living under a republican government, Washington concluded with these words: "Whether this desirable object will be the best promoted by affording aids to seminaries of learning already established, by the institution of a national University, or by any other expedients, will be well worthy of a place in the deliberations of the Legislature."[5] Although neither the Senate nor the House acted on this recommendation, the responses of both seem to have been favorable.[6] Still, Washington found it neces-

[3] See David Calhoun, ed., *The Educating of Americans: A Documentary History* (Boston: Houghton Mifflin Co., 1969), pp. 96–99, which indicates Washington's interest in a national university as early as 1775.

[4] *Writings*, XXX, 493 (Jan. 8, 1790) (italics added).

[5] *Ibid.*, XXX, 494.

[6] *Messages and Papers of the Presidents* (20 vols.; New York: Bureau of National Literature Inc., 1897), I, 60–61.

sary to call Congress's attention to the matter six years later in his last state of the union message:

> I have heretofore proposed to the consideration of Congress, the expediency of establishing a National University. . . .
>
> Among the motives to such an Institution, *the assimilation of principles, opinions and manners of our Country men, by the common education of a portion of our Youth from every quarter,* well deserves attention. The more *homogeneous* our Citizens can be made in these particulars, the greater will be our prospect of permanent Union; and *a primary object of such a National Institution should be the education of our Youth in the science of Government.* . . . [W]hat duty [is] *more pressing* on its Legislature, than to patronize a plan for communicating it to those who are to be the future guardians of the liberties of their Country?[7]

Preliminary to any further discussion of this message, there are three points which should be noted. First, Washington conveys not the slightest doubt that Congress has implicit constitutional authority to establish a national university. Indeed, no constitutional issue was raised during the subsequent House debates over Washington's recommendation, not even by its opponents. The second point to be noted, and which clarifies the first, is that Washington did not specifically recommend that the university be located in the nation's capital, but this was a foregone conclusion. Precisely because Congress has complete jurisdiction over the nation's capital, it has the authority to establish therein a national university. Incidentally, it was by an act of Congress in 1790 that the permanent seat of the federal government was fixed in what soon came to be called the District of Columbia. The act authorized the President to appoint three commissioners to survey the territory and to define the ten-square-mile limits for the nation's capital. Furthermore, it was provided

> That the said commissioners, or any two of them, shall have power to purchase or accept such quantity of land . . . within

[7] *Writings,* XXXV, 316–317 (Dec. 7, 1796) (italics added, except for "Government").

the said district, as the President shall deem proper for the use of the United States, and according to such plans as the President shall approve, the said commissioners, or any two of them, shall, prior to the first Monday in December, in the year one thousand eight hundred, provide suitable buildings for the accommodation of Congress, and of the President, and for the public offices of the Government of the United States.[8]

The third point to be noted is this. In proposing the establishment of a national university, Washington did not specifically request congressional appropriations for this purpose. In fact, however, the President, working in conjunction with the District commissioners, had set aside nineteen acres of land as a site for his cherished university. Indeed, the year before, Washington informed the commissioners that he would personally donate fifty shares of stock valued at five thousand pounds sterling as an endowment for the university; and the commissioners, prompted by the President, sent him a memorial requesting Congress to "take such measures as that they [the commissioners] may be able to receive any donations which may be made to the institution."[9] Washington transmitted the memorial to Madison who introduced it to the House of Representatives. The memorial was then referred to a select committee which had already been appointed for the purpose of deliberating on Washington's recommendations concerning the national university.

Turning to the debates, three major arguments were advanced against Washington's recommendation. First, various representatives claimed that the recommendation implied a request for appropriations to which they were opposed.[10] This was denied

---

[8] *Annals*, 1st Cong., 1st Sess., 2234 (July 16, 1790).

[9] *Annals*, 4th Cong., 2nd Sess., 1600 (Dec. 12, 1796), and *Writings*, XXXIV, 106–108, 146–151. For further information on the stock in question (which apparently was much more valuable than suggested), see Cubberley, *Public Education in the United States*, p. 267, n. 1, and *Annals*, 4th Cong., 2nd Sess., 1705 (Dec. 27, 1796).

[10] Beyond expressing favorable sentiments in their reply to Washington's message, the Senate did not discuss the issue, presumably because it was thought to involve appropriations which, of course, had to be initiated in the House.

by others, who maintained that all Congress need do was grant the commissioners of the District authority or rights of incorporation necessary for receiving donations such as Washington's. The second major argument was that no need existed at this time for such a university; that it would not and could not be attended or taken advantage of by people from the distant parts of the nation. To this it was replied that the contemplated university looked beyond the present and the immediate future, if only because the federal government could not occupy the District of Columbia until 1800. More important, however, it was argued that a republican government is based on wisdom, that it requires an informed and educated people, and that the proposed university would well serve this end, especially when situated in the nation's capital. Finally, and perhaps the most revealing statement against the proposed university, but one neither elaborated nor debated, was made by George Nicholas of Virginia:

> The President had said (and the Commissioners after him) it was to establish *an uniformity of principles and manners throughout the Union.* This, he believed, could not be affected by any institution. If, said he, you incorporate men to build an University, *are you not pledging yourselves to make up any deficiency?* . . . The district of country from whence he came might stand in great need of Seminaries of Learning, as had been hinted . . . but their ignorance must continue until they were sensible of their want of instruction. He believed *there was no federal quality in knowledge,* and no federal aid was necessary to the spread of it. . . . [H]e should not give his countenance to the national plan proposed because . . . he did not think it would be attended with any good effect, but with much evil.[11]

Little comment is necessary, save to say that Nicholas's statement virtually anticipates the political ascendency of Jeffersonianism. Be this as it may, after considerable debate, ending on December 27, 1796, a lame-duck session of the House of Repre-

[11] *Annals,* 4th Cong., 2nd Sess., 1700 (Dec. 26, 1796) (italics added).

sentatives killed the measure by voting for postponement. The vote was 37 to 36.[12]

In his last will and testament Washington again urged Congress to establish a national university, to which end he bequeathed the endowment already mentioned. He wanted the university to be in the nation's capital and to receive support from, and be under the jurisdiction of, the national government. To the nation's capital

> youth of fortune and talents from all parts [of the country] might be sent for the completion of their education in all the branches of polite literature; in arts and sciences, in acquiring knowledge in the principles of politics and good government; and (as a matter of infinite importance, in my judgment) by associating with each other, and forming friendships in juvenile years, be enabled to free themselves in a proper degree from those local prejudices and habitual jealousies . . . which, when carried to excess, are never failing sources of disquietude to the public mind, and pregnant of mischievious consequences to this country. . . .[13]

Washington had conveyed these ideas to Jefferson almost two years before his last state of the union message. By locating the university in the nation's capital, wrote Washington, it would "afford the Students an opportunity of attending the debates in Congress, and thereby becoming more liberally, and better acquainted with the principles of law, and government."[14] In 1800 the government moved to its permanent location. By then Washington was dead. The following year Jefferson ascended to the presidency: Jefferson, the founder of the University of Virginia, who believed that the silence of the Constitution, as regards education, prohibited Congress from establishing a national university.[15]

---

[12] *Ibid.*, 1711 (Dec. 27, 1796). The above discussion is based on *ibid.*, 1595, 1600–1601, 1697–1702, 1704–1711 (Dec. 8–9, 26–27, 1796).

[13] *Writings*, XXXVII, 280.

[14] *Writings*, XXXIV, 147, to Jefferson (March 15, 1795).

[15] Nevertheless, in his sixth state of the union message, Jefferson proposed a

This was not the opinion, we have seen, of Jefferson's successor. Like Washington, Madison envisioned a university located in the nation's capital (and under the jurisdiction of the general government) as a school for future statesmen. Some of its graduates might eventually enter the national government, others various state governments, but all would have been imbued with "national feelings" as well as with "liberal sentiments" and "congenial manners." At the same time, a national university would generate a body of national ideas which would eventually permeate society at large. Its graduates would enter upon various callings, private as well as public, and would influence, by their example, the opinions and attitudes of their fellow citizens. Recall, too, that Madison conceived of a national university as a model for other universities across the country. This is all the more significant in view of his desire to have the state governments establish more schools, academies, and colleges, and to extend education to the poor as well as to the rich. Such institutions, said Madison, not only enlighten the public mind, but they educate teachers for yet other learned institutions, and, at the same time, they educate men for public office. Madison did not regard public schools and colleges as intended merely to facilitate the pursuit of private interests, or to make citizens more efficient consumers. Institutions of learning were certainly to enlighten the people about their individual rights and thus help to secure personal liberty. But they were no less intended to educate men for public duties and public trusts. "The American people," wrote Madison, "owe it to themselves, and to the cause of free Government, to prove by their establishments for the advancement and diffusion of Knowledge, that their political Institutions . . . are as favorable to the intellectual and moral improvement of Man as they are conformable to his individual and social Rights."[16] Still, inasmuch as the schools and colleges envisioned here would be supported by the state governments

constitutional amendment authorizing Congress to support a "national establishment for education." See *Messages and Papers of the Presidents*, I, 397–398.

[16] *Writings*, IX, 107–108, to W. T. Barry (Aug., 4, 1822).

(which, collectively, were then more subject to powerful centrifugal forces), all the greater was the need for a national university, one that would disseminate national principles and national feelings, and thus serve to strengthen the bonds of union.

Of course, Madison understood that the simultaneous advancement of commerce and of the means of communication might also help to assimilate and unify this diverse society. But he was far from leaving the achievement of this end to the free play of private interests. He was ever mindful of sectional rivalries, of political, social, and economic differences which might eventually destroy the Union. If the Union was to become truly a union, the government would indeed have to control and regulate the passions of men. If reason, embodied in law, was to prevail over the public councils, public institutions of learning were indispensable to inculcate a respect for reason and to educate men in the science of law. Law, by the mere fact of its generality, is a unifying force. By the systematic articulation of precedent, law reveals the relevance of the past to the present and thus teaches the living that they themselves do not have a monopoly of wisdom. In this way law promotes moderation. But again there is needed a *national* institution that will train a body of lawyers, some of whom will become state legislators and judges, others who will become legislators and judges for the nation as a whole. Surely the national university Madison had in mind would have had a law school, one whose students would be close to Congress and to the Supreme Court. And surely some of these students, upon returning to their respective states, would convey the principles of national legislation and thus strengthen the bonds of union. Indeed, when the idea of a "central seminary of Jurisprudence" was communicated to Madison, he approved of the idea on the following grounds:

> It is not only desirable . . . that the national code should receive whatever improvements the cultivation of law as a science may impart but that the local codes should be improved in like man-

ner, and a general knowledge of each facilitated by an infusion of every practicable identity through the whole. . . .

This would be a species of consolidation having the happy tendency to diminish local prejudices, to cherish mutual confidence . . . without impairing the constitutional separation and independence of the states themselves, which are deemed essential to the security of individual liberty as well as to the preservation of republican government.[17]

The Madisonian solution to the problem of faction is not sociological fragmentation: it is unity amidst diversity, and the primary emphasis is on the former, not the latter. This ought not appear so strange. The Constitution was established "to form a more perfect *Union*." A more perfect union requires a body of commonly shared beliefs and feelings. If we focus on the pluralism or diversity emphasized in *Federalist* 10, we shall fail to appreciate the contrary motifs emphasized elsewhere in *The Federalist*. At the same time we may fail to grasp the art of statesmanship.

A more perfect union will require diversity as a means of avoiding majoritarian tyranny. The preservation of diversity, however, as well as the control of its anarchic tendencies, requires that it be *institutionalized*. It can be institutionalized by establishing a House of Representatives. But this is not sufficient. By itself, diversity, even when institutionalized, is unstable and purposeless. Hence the need for a Senate to provide stability and continuity in public policy. The Senate thus makes possible the development of a national character. At the same time, the Senate may facilitate the exercise of presidential leadership which in turn may provide direction or purpose to the regime as a whole. Meanwhile, public policies must be kept within the limits of fundamental constitutional principles. This is the duty of a permanent judiciary, an institution relatively insulated from the fluctuating opinions, passions, and interests of society at large.

But these are formal institutional arrangements the efficacy of

[17] *Ibid.*, IX, 63–64, to Peter S. Du Ponceau (May, 1821).

which will depend on the character of men and the ends to which they are dedicated. Other institutions will therefore be necessary to shape men's character with a view to those ends. Government will have to promote education. The republic of the founders, more than other forms of government, requires an enlightened citizen-body precisely because the republic rests on the consent of the governed.[18] On the other hand, higher institutions of learning are required precisely because the governed must also be educated *by their governors*. But inasmuch as this republic encompasses a vast territory populated by a diverse people, all the more need for one university, raised above others in eminence by its location in the nation's capital, a university that educates statesmen, men capable of providing this diverse people with a sense of national unity and purpose. Is it not evident that the education of such men must include education in patriotism as well as in the science of government?

Contrary to the contemporary "liberal" persuasion, Madison was far from believing that education can or should be politically neutral. Indeed, he wished to foster among the American people what he termed a "political creed."[19] So for that matter did Jefferson. As Rector of the University of Virginia, he proposed, with success, that the Board of Visitors give *official* recognition to the political works of Locke and Sidney as embodying the true principles of liberty. Furthermore, under Jefferson's leadership, the board resolved to make mandatory the study of the Declaration of Independence, *The Federalist*, the Virginia Resolutions of 1799, and Washington's Farewell Address.[20] These were to comprise a textbook for the university's law school which was also referred to as the School of Politics. Prior to the action of the board, however, Jefferson had written to Madison (who was then a board member) for his opinion on the intended proposal. Madison's reply is most revealing.

[18] See Madison, *Writings*, IX, 103–108, cited earlier.

[19] *Ibid.*, IX, 220.

[20] *The Writings of Thomas Jefferson* (20 vols.; Washington, D.C.: Memorial Edition, 1902–4), XV, 410–461, March 4, 1825 (cited hereafter as *Writings of Jefferson*).

To begin with, Madison agreed that "It is certainly very material that the true doctrines of liberty, as exemplified in our political system, should be inculcated on those who are to sustain and may administer it. . . . Sidney and Locke are admirably calculated to impress on young minds the right of nations to establish their own governments, and to inspire a love of free ones; but afford no aid in guarding our republican charters against constructive violations."[21] As for the Virginia Resolutions of 1799, here Madison was in a charming dilemma. He had himself authored those resolutions, and, over the ensuing years, he had frequently to defend them against the contention that they justified nullification, hence disunion. Whatever the truth of that contention, Madison, while reaffirming the principles of the Virginia Resolutions, said that their inclusion in Jefferson's proposed textbook would "excite prejudices against the University as under Party Banners . . . [and so] would divide and exclude where meant to unite and fortify."[22] He proposed, instead, that certain portions or standards be selected "without requiring an unqualified conformity to them." He then proceeded to recommend a textbook that included, in addition to the Declaration of Independence, *The Federalist*, the Farewell Address, and Washington's First Inaugural. Said Madison: "Th[is] selection would give them authority with the Students, and might controul or counteract deviations of the Professor. . . . [But] the most effectual safeguard against heretical intrusions into the School of Politics, will be an Able and Orthodox Professor, whose course of instruction will be an example to his successors. . . ."[23] No doubt this will appear very strange to contemporary educators and to men in public office, especially those who know not what it is to found or preserve a regime. In any event, it should be noted that Washington's First Inaugural, even more than his Farewell Address, emphasized religious and moral motifs. Also, it set forth the example of a President publicly declining any personal

---

[21] *Writings*, IX, 218–219.
[22] *Ibid.*, 219–220.
[23] *Ibid.*, 220.

emoluments or salary which Congress might prescribe for his office.[24]

Returning to Madison, however, it may be thought inconsistent of him to want to cultivate a political orthodoxy on the one hand, and "liberal sentiments" on the other. But Madison believed he understood the *true* principles of republican government and that these were embodied in the text he proposed for the University of Virginia's School of Politics. To imbue students with those principles would be to inculcate genuine patriotism, not national chauvinism. Properly understood, patriotism means a concern for the common good, a love of one's own people, their traditions, their institutions, their great men, their noble purposes. True patriotism is rooted in gratitude for the blessings which the past has bestowed upon the present. But the highest form of gratitude is displayed by the great-souled man, the man who incorporates the past into a more perfect union for the future. In Madison, therefore, patriotism is not a facade for the intellectual and moral complacency typical of some "conservatives." Just as the true lover seeks the perfection of his beloved, so the true patriot seeks the perfection of his country. In 1787, however, America was very much a new country composed of diverse people. Patriotism therefore requires liberal sentiments —the capacity of men to be friends despite their differences. But this in turn requires that what men have in common be more important than their differences. Hence the need for a political orthodoxy which includes something more fundamental than an "agreement to disagree" or a toleration of diversity. For if there exists no recognized body of political truths concerning how men should live, tolerance and intolerance become equally justifiable. On the other hand, if there are such truths, then there are certain kinds of behavior which men of liberal sentiments need not and will not tolerate. Here it might be noted that decent "liberals" who reject all public orthodoxies are nevertheless shocked and dismayed by the intolerance of certain youth who reject all "establishments," meaning regimes or all public ortho-

[24] *Messages and Papers of the Presidents*, I, 44–45.

doxies. They do not see that their own intellectual and moral skepticism sanctions this intolerance, indeed, is a cause of it. May not *their* skepticism also be a facade for intellectual and moral complacency? Whatever the case, this skepticism is at war with patriotism. It cannot but undermine reverence for all "establishments." But if a society be lacking such reverence, what will govern most men will not be liberal sentiments so much as fear, distrust, and a concern for personal safety and advantage. The alternative to Madison's patriotism is ingratitude, self-righteousness, and self-indulgence.

Although one cannot say precisely what would have been the curriculum at the proposed national university, very likely it would not have differed significantly from that of the University of Virginia or of Madison's alma mater, the College of New Jersey. A brief sketch of the latter, however, would be more revealing of the education of the founders themselves.[25]

2

As noted earlier, eighteenth-century higher education in America was in a state of tension and transition. Controlled by various religious denominations, the colonial colleges educated men primarily for the ministry, and their curriculums were designed with this end in view. By mid-century, however, secular studies had made great inroads to the extent that the religious purpose of most of these colleges, though still very prominent, could no longer be said to dominate the curriculums. The College of New Jersey was the first college in America to eliminate religious qualifications for admission and for membership on the faculty. Although the classics were studied seriously, that is, with a view to disciplining the mind and shaping character, Plato, Aristotle, Xenophon, Polybius, and Cicero had to compete with Machiavelli, Hobbes, Locke, Montesquieu, and Rousseau. The Old Testament was studied in Greek and in Hebrew, but the revelations of the Bible could now be questioned by the

[25] But see *Writings of Jefferson*, "Manuscripts from the University of Virginia Collection," XIX, 359–499, *passim*.

new science of Bacon and Newton. Students received lectures on Aristotle's *Nicomachean Ethics* and the *Politics;* but the teleological conception of human nature and of the origin of civil society had to contend with the mechanistic psychology of Hobbes and the contract theory of Locke. While the classics emphasized the primacy of reason, the moderns emphasized the primacy of the passions.

These tensions were profound, and not merely because at stake was the question of what is man and how should men live. So much can be said of any college or university today in which the ancients are taught alongside the moderns. True, what dominates the curriculum today are the moderns, and not even the greats such as those mentioned above. No, the tensions here spoken of were profound because, at the time of the founding, the answers of antiquity to the question of what is man and how should men live were still taken seriously, and the answers of modernity had not yet congealed, had yet to hold complete sway over thought, action, and passion.

Meanwhile, at Princeton, Aristotle's *Rhetoric* and Cicero's *Orations* were studied intensively. Considerable emphasis was given to public oratory and political writing, especially under Witherspoon, who was appointed president in 1765. Public debates were organized for upperclassmen and were frequently conducted in Latin. These were modeled after the medieval method of disputation. A student would present an argument on some subject; two other students were assigned for the purpose of critical analysis—one with a view to substance, the other with a view to form. Following rebuttal, the audience would join in discussion and debate. When students engaged in disputations on such topics as "Does man have free will?" or "What is patriotism?" they were not merely engaging in academic exercises to amuse the mind already encrusted with stale habit. These were then matters of profound significance for the life of individuals and societies.

The colleges of eighteenth-century America not only sought to cultivate the intellect. They deliberately fostered virtue and trained men for public duty. Witherspoon's sermons and lectures each combined moral teaching and scholarship. It was then understood that liberal education (in addition to pursuing knowledge for its own sake) was the education of *gentlemen*, more precisely, of Christian gentlemen. Accordingly, while it taught men humility, universality, and fortitude, it imbued them with dignity, patriotism, and boldness. The cultivation of the great-souled man—the magnanimous man—was then the purpose of liberal education. It was taken for granted, however, that the aim of *all* public institutions was to make men good.

Witherspoon, though definitely inclined toward the classics, was an eclectic who appreciated modern political philosophy.[26] Not only was he a signer of the Declaration of Independence, but for six years he was a member of the Continental Congress. His interest in politics, eloquence, and law was quite evident in the College of New Jersey, which, by the way, was called the "patriot college" even before the Revolution. To judge from the subsequent careers of his students, Witherspoon's influence on the new nation was nothing short of remarkable. Six of his students, including James Madison, were delegates at the Federal Convention. In addition, twenty Senators, twenty-three Representatives, thirteen Governors, three Justices of the Supreme Court, one President, and one Vice-President were Princeton graduates.[27]

Of course, it is impossible to determine Witherspoon's impact on the framers of the American Constitution. A multiplicity of diverse intellectual, social, and economic causes leavened the founding. Hence, as already admitted, the relative influence of classical, Christian, and modern modes of thought on the design of the Constitution cannot be precisely determined. To be sure, numerous statements may be abstracted from the writings of Hobbes, Locke, Hume, Montesquieu, Rousseau, and others, and then be assimilated to statements abstracted from the writings of

[26] See his "Lectures on Moral Philosophy" in *Works*, III, 367–472.
[27] See *The Papers of Woodrow Wilson* (11 vols., to date; Princeton: Princeton University Press, 1966–71), X, 18–19 (hereafter cited as *Papers*).

men like Madison and Hamilton. It would be strange indeed if these statesmen had not been influenced by the teachings of those philosophers. But while similarities may be assembled, so too may many differences.[28] The truly difficult problem is to determine their gradation of relevance in the founding of the American 'polity,' a task requiring more than scholarship. Whatever the case, none of the founders were "Aristotelians" or "Lockeans," which is not to say they did not incline more toward one than toward the other. What can be said with confidence is that they took political philosophy seriously. Some were philosophic statesmen, although their "political philosophy" was fundamentally eclectic. Their upbringing, the training of their youth, their habits, manners, and moral dispositions, can be said to have been largely shaped by the classical and Christian traditions. But their mature thoughts on man, society, and government owe no less to modernity than to antiquity. The actions of men, however, and the ends they pursue, are not wholly determined by the intellect. As Madison said, and contrary to what he learned from Hume, reason and passion have a *reciprocal* influence on each other. Certain moral dispositions not only render men more receptive to one assemblage of ideas than to another, but even shift the meanings of these ideas or their gradation of relevance. Life is ever more subtle and complex than language or literary interpretations will allow. Whatever the case, it can hardly be doubted that the education of many of the founders in philosophy, eloquence, patriotism, and virtue accounts for the high caliber of their statesmanship, hence in large measure for the Constitution itself.

3

It was suggested in this discussion of the College of New Jersey that patriotism was an important theme of college life.

[28] Hobbes *contended* that money is the blood of the commonwealth. Hamilton *professed* (in *Federalist* 30, p. 182), that "Money is . . . the vital principle of the body-politic." But Hamilton—indeed, the founding fathers as a whole—would have looked with contempt upon the man who wrote that "The *value*, or WORTH of a man, is as of all things, his price. . . ."

Similarly, the fostering of "national feelings," we saw, was a principal object of Madison's national university. Perhaps the author of *Federalist* 10 looked upon such a university as necessary for providing the unifying influence unattainable under fragmented Christianity. Some state universities had eliminated professorships in divinity, partly to avoid sectarian rivalry. The opening of the University of Virginia in 1825 followed the example. Nevertheless, Jefferson, on behalf of the Board of Visitors, invited the various religious denominations of the state to establish, *within the confines of the university*, religious schools and places of public worship. Students of the university were "expected" to attend the worship of their choice. At the same time, the university extended the full use of its facilities to any and all religious schools accepting its invitation.[29] The wall of separation between church and state had many passageways at the University of Virginia.

Madison agreed with this policy. Like Washington, he regarded religion as the foundation of morality and as essential to human happiness. But given the multiplicity of religious sects and the power of religious passions on the one hand, and what he understood to be the rights of conscience on the other, it was his conviction that civil and religious discord as well as infringements on those rights of conscience would result if government were to favor one religion over another.[30] Furthermore, it was his opinion that the separation of church and state was conducive to the advancement of religion itself.

As is well known from Supreme Court decisions regarding the "establishment clause" of the First Amendment, authority for Madison's thoughts on the subject is based on the *Memorial and Remonstrance against Religious Assessments* of 1785. What is less well known is that while the assessment bill (on behalf of Christian clergymen) was opposed by Madison, it was supported by no less than George Washington.[31] Of greater sig-

29 *Writings of Jefferson*, XIX, 449, 414–415.
30 Madison, *Writings*, IX, 230, 125–126.
31 *Ibid.*, II, 183, n. 1.

nificance, however, are Madison's reasons for opposing the assessment. In the Virginia House of Delegates he argued (1) that the assessment was unnecessary for the support of religion, indeed, that the suggestion of its necessity dishonors Christianity; (2) that man has a *natural propensity* for religion, but that a union of religious and secular authority generally resulted in religious persecution and war; (3) that separation of church and state is essential to the integrity of both; and (4) that the evils feared by such separation could be avoided (a) by "laws to cherish virtue"; (b) by the steady dispensation of justice; (c) by the personal example of public men; (d) by private associations for religion; and (e) by the education of youth.[32] It should be noted that the *Memorial and Remonstrance* not only distinguishes between true and false religion, but it claims that the "purity and efficacy of religion" would be enhanced if religious and civil authorities were separated.[33] Madison earnestly held this opinion throughout his adult life. Thus, in December, 1773, he posed this question in a letter to his friend William Bradford: "Is an ecclesiastical establishment absolutely necessary to support civil society in a supreme government? and how far is it hurtful to a dependent State?" The following month, in another letter to Bradford, he wrote: "Pride, ignorance and knavery [prevail] among the priesthood and vice and wickedness among the laity. . . . persecution rages among some . . . pray for liberty of conscience." In the first of these letters, Madison admitted that certain publications were "loose in their principles, encourage[r]s of free enquiry even such as destroys the most essential truths, [and] enemies to serious religion. . . ." Yet, a few months later Madison could write to Bradford: "Religious bondage shackles and debilitates the mind. . . ."[34] Here Madison is not saying that religion per se shackles and debilitates the mind, but that religious *bondage* does, meaning imposed religious orthodoxy. As

[32] Madison, *Letters and Other Writings*, I, 116–117, 175, 274.

[33] Madison, *Writings*, II, 187, 189.

[34] *Papers*, I, 101 (Dec. 1, 1773), I, 106 (Jan. 24, 1774), and I, 112 (April 1, 1774).

will be seen in the next chapter, Madison regarded the religious life as the most noble life of man. His public efforts to secure liberty of conscience were intended not to liberate man *from* religion, but *for* religion (at least as he understood it). Accordingly, in 1776, Madison attempted, *without success*, to amend an article in the Virginia Declaration of Rights pertaining to religion, an amendment that would have in effect prohibited government support of any religious establishment.[35] Reflecting on this subject some forty-three years later, Madison expressed the following opinion:

> Religious instruction is now diffused throughout the community by preachers of every sect with almost equal zeal, though with very unequal acquirements; and at private houses . . . occasionally in such as are *appropriated to civil use, as well as buildings appropriated to that use.* The qualifications of the preachers . . . are understood to be improving. On a general comparison of the present and former times, the balance is certainly and vastly on the side of the present, as to the number of religious teachers . . . and the attendance of the people on their instructions. It was the universal opinion of the century preceding the last, that civil government could not stand without the prop of a religious establishment, and that the Christian religion itself, would perish if not supported by a legal provision for its clergy. The experience of Virginia conspicuously corroborates the disproof of both opinions. The civil government, though bereft of everything like an associated hierarchy, possesses the requisite stability and performs its functions with complete success; whilst the number, the industry, and the morality of the priesthood, and the devotion of the people have been manifestly increased by the total separation of the church from the state.[36]

Whether the reflections contained in the above passage are correct or not, certain conclusions may be drawn from the foregoing

[35] *Ibid.,* I, 174.

[36] Madison, *Writings,* VIII, 431–432 (italics added), and compare IX, 484–487. Compare the above discussion with such Supreme Court decisions as *Illinois ex rel. McCollum* v. *Bd. of Education,* 333 U.S. 203 (1948), *School District of Abington* v. *Schempp,* 370 U.S. 203 (1963), and *United States* v. *Seeger,* 380 U.S. 163 (1965).

discussion: (1) that Madison deemed religion as of the greatest importance in the life of man; (2) that religion itself would be undermined if government were to render it any material support; and (3) that no government in the United States could be stable or maintain domestic tranquillity if it alienated the adherents of one religion by favoring those of another—and this it could only avoid by the total separation of church and state. (But, as the words italicized in the above passage indicate, the separation is not as "total" as required by the latitudinarian interpretations of the Supreme Court.)

This goes far toward explaining why *The Federalist* is virtually silent about religion. It may be correct to say that *The Federalist* does not include "the nurturing of a *particular* religion" among the legitimate objects of government (although it is not correct to say this of the founders as a whole).[37] But which *particular* religion might *The Federalist* have sought to promote as an object of government? And had it done so, would New York (to say nothing of other states) have ratified the Constitution? Let the First Amendment answer this question. The very most that might have been incorporated in the Constitution was a clause comparable to Article 16 of the Virginia Declaration of Rights, namely: "That Religion, or the duty we owe to our CREATOR, and the manner of discharging it, can be directed only by reason and conviction, not by force or violence; and therefore all men are equally entitled to the free exercise of religion, according to the dictates of conscience; and that it is the mutual duty of all to practice Christian forbearance, love, and charity towards others."[38] This can hardly be called the nurturing of a particular religion, although such a provision *might* have been favorable to religion in general had it been embodied in the Constitution—especially in our time when the Supreme Court has come close to reducing or relegating religion to the realm of private *feeling*. But it is difficult to believe that the presence or absence of such a provision could have materially affected

[37] *Diamond*, p. 64 (italics added).
[38] Madison, *Writings*, I, 40.

the moral character of American society. Besides, if Madison's reflections were correct—and he thought they were applicable to states other than Virginia—the Constitution did not retard the progress of religion, at least during the first few decades of the republic. But more will be said on this matter when the Constitution is examined under the category of change.

We have seen that men like Washington regarded religion as essential to good government and to human happiness. Suppose, however—and the Farewell Address suggests the possibility— that he valued religion more as a means than as an end in itself. How well then does religion lend itself to Washington's purpose! The paramount theme of his address is patriotism or national unity, and religion emphasizes the brotherhood of men under one God. It restrains the passions which divide; it teaches men their duties toward one another; it fosters respect for authority; hence it conduces to the preservation of a more perfect union. Supposing, therefore, that Washington privately believed little more than this about the importance of religion, or, more cautiously, of *established* religions; still, even then he is not far from the related thoughts of Plato and Aristotle. Plato banishes Cephalus from the ensuing dialogue of the *Republic*—Cephalus who represents the old or established religion. True, religion has an important political function in Plato's second best regime, the *Laws*. Certainly it is not relegated to the realm of private judgment, which is almost to say the realm of chance. Indeed, reverence for the laws depends on the cultivation of piety. Piety, however, is not one of the virtues included in Aristotle's *Nichomachean Ethics*. To be sure, of all the elements necessary for the "existence" of the best regime, Aristotle ranks public worship, or an establishment for the service of the gods, as first in the order of importance (299). But what is of first importance for the existence of the best regime is not the same as the regime's highest end. So here, on the subject of religion, a 'polity' can be expected to fall short of the highest standard. Because it fails to make the cultivation of human excellence a matter of public policy, it does not give due importance to religion as a means to that end. Yet it would be misleading to say this of the 'polity' established by the founders. What can be said is that the founders did not make the cultivation of human excellence the paramount and ordering principle of political rule. They did not establish in practice what no statesmen have ever established, namely, the best regime in theory. Accordingly, they did not institutionalize religion as the most important element for the existence of the best political community. It remains everlastingly true, however, that the founders, generally speaking, regarded the cultivation of human excellence as a legitimate object of government—some, as the most important object of government—and that Washington and Madison *attempted* to promote this end by urging Congress, at various times, to establish a national university, a veritable school for statesmen.

CHAPTER VII

A New Teleological Mode of Regime Analysis:
The Politics of Magnanimity

Honor is the object with which the great-souled man is especially concerned. Great honors accorded by persons of worth will afford him pleasure in a moderate degree; he will feel he is receiving only what belongs
to him, or even less, for no honor can be adequate to the merits of perfect
virtue. Honors rendered by common people and on trivial grounds he will
utterly despise. In fact, he does not care much even about receiving honor,
which is the greatest of external goods. Rather, he is fond of conferring
benefits, but ashamed to receive them. It is also characteristic of the great-
souled man to be haughty toward men of position and fortune. Furthermore, he cares more for truth than for what other people think. Hence he
will speak frankly and openly, since concealment shows timidity. As a consequence, he is bound to make enemies. Nevertheless, he does not bear a
grudge, for it is not the mark of greatness of soul to recall things against
people, especially wrongs they have done you, but rather to overlook them.

Adapted from Aristotle's Nicomachean Ethics

T HE EVIDENCE and argument presented in the previous
chapter should be sufficient to refute the contention that the
founders lowered the ends or goals of political life. That contention, though based on a misapplication of Aristotelian criteria
to the political thought of *The Federalist*, nevertheless derives
persuasive force from the very nobility of classical political
philosophy so brilliantly illuminated by Leo Strauss, among
whose students will be found some of the most profound scholars
developed in this country. I wish once again to make it perfectly

clear that nothing in this book is intended to deny the important influence of modern political philosophy on the founders, much as that influence has been exaggerated. What many scholars fail to recognize, however—and this bears repeating—is that eighteenth-century American political thought contained diverse elements in tension with one another; that democratic and utilitarian values had yet to congeal into rigid dogma or stale habit; that classical and Christian values still retained more than superficial influence over political thought and practice. Admittedly the passions of self-interest, so prominent in modern political philosophy, receive an emphasis in *The Federalist* not to be found in Aristotle's *Politics*. But apart from the fact that *The Federalist* is not primarily a philosophic treatise on government, it would be more just, when focusing on the passions of self-interest, to compare *The Federalist* with Aristotle's *Rhetoric*—and for reasons obvious enough not to require further elaboration. On the other hand, one aim of this Discourse, to be pursued in the present chapter, is to rescue the principle of self-interest from past contumely. This will require a philosophical exposition transcending the traditional dichotomy of self and society. Beginning, therefore, on the level of scholarship, I shall re-examine the Madisonian understanding of justice and self-interest. I shall then proceed to construct a meaning horizon for the principle of enlightened self-interest that transcends its Tocquevillian counterpart. My ultimate objective—approached heuristically in this chapter—is to overcome the quarrel between ancients and moderns such that the good life and the good society will be seen to require a synthesis of the classical emphasis on virtue and the modern emphasis on freedom and individuality. A synthesis of this order would provide a new teleological mode of regime analysis, the possibility of which was foreshadowed in the founding.

1

Recall Madison's remark in *Federalist* 51 that "Justice is the end of government . . . [and] of civil society." To substantiate his contention that the term justice "refers *primarily* to the protection of economic interests," Diamond enlists the support of *Federalist* 10. "There," he notes, "the 'first object of government' is [said to be] the protection of the diverse human faculties from which arise the 'rights of property' and the unequal distribution of property."[1] But let Madison speak for himself: "The diversity in the faculties of men, from which the rights of property originate, is not less an insuperable obstacle to a uniformity of interests. The protection of these faculties is the first object of government" (55). Two things are to be noted: (1) the first object of government is *not* to protect the rights of property, but rather the *diverse human faculties* from which these rights originate; (2) the rights of property do not derive from a discrete set of faculties which have no other function than to make it possible for men to acquire and use property. Hence, to protect the faculties is to protect what is distinctively human—the very powers of the mind. Stated another way, but in justice to *Federalist* 10 as a whole—whose central problem is the danger of majority faction—to protect the diversity in the faculties of men is to prevent the leveling of all moral and intellectual distinctions, which again is the tendency of democracy. Thus, insofar as the meaning of justice spoken of in *Federalist* 51 is informed by *Federalist* 10, it cannot be said to "refer *primarily* to the protection of economic interests." To be sure, Madison admits that "the most common and durable source of factions has been the various and unequal distribution of property." But for this very reason he might just as well have said, had he chosen to do so, that the protection of the rights of property constitutes the most practical means of guarding against the stultification of the mind which would be produced by the leveling spirit of democracy. Even had Madison chosen to say that the first object of government is the protection of property, then, viewing his political thought *as a whole*, this could justly be interpreted to mean the protection of all that is rightfully our own, including the use of

[1] *Diamond*, p. 62 (italics added). See also Leo Strauss, *Natural Right and History*, p. 245.

our faculties. Here I have especially in mind an article Madison wrote for *The National Gazette* entitled "Property," in which he says:

> This term in its particular application means "that dominion which one man claims and exercises over the external things of the world, in exclusion of every other individual." In its larger and juster meaning, it embraces every thing to which a man may attach a value and have a right; and *which leaves to everyone else the like advantage*. In the former sense, a man's land, or merchandize, or money is called his property. In the latter sense, a man has a property in his opinions and the free communication of them. He has property of peculiar value in his religious opinions, and in the profession and practice dictated by them. He has property very dear to him in the safety and liberty of his person. He has an equal property in the free use of his faculties and free choice of the objects on which to employ them. In a word, as a man is said to have a right to his property, he may be equally said to have a property in his rights.
>
> Where an excess of power prevails, property of no sort is duly respected. No man is safe in his opinions, his person, his faculties or his possessions. Where there is an excess of liberty, the effect is the same, though from an opposite cause.
>
> Government is instituted to protect property of every sort; as well that which lies in the various rights of individuals, as that which the term particularly expresses. This being the end of government, that alone is a *just* government, which *impartially* secures to every man, whatever in his *own*.

Madison goes on to say that a just government will "protect [men] in the enjoyment and communication of their opinions, in which they have an equal, and in the estimation of some, a more valuable property"; and that "Conscience is the most sacred of all property; other property depending in part on positive law, the exercise of that [namely, of conscience], being a natural and inalienable right."[2]

From this it should be apparent that the paramount concern

[2] *Writings*, VI, 101–102 (March 29, 1792).

of the author of *Federalist* 10 and of the First Amendment was to secure *intellectual freedom*. Here it is fitting to recall his allusion to Socrates in *Federalist* 63: "What bitter anguish would not the people of Athens have often escaped if their government had contained so provident a safeguard [as the Senate which is here proposed] against the tyranny of their own passions? Popular liberty might then have escaped the indelible reproach of decreeing to the same citizens the hemlock on one day and statues on the next" (410). To secure intellectual freedom it will be necessary to fragment the many, one effect of which might be to encourage the pursuit of "self-interest" rather than the common good. No doubt such pursuits will generally be narrow and limited. When have the pursuits of the many been otherwise? Recall Aristotle's opinion of the many: They are preoccupied with their own interests; they care less for the common good; and what they love most is material well-being rather than honor and knowledge. And yet, in contrast to the teaching of Aristotle, Madison, we have seen, again and again urged the importance of educating the people and of enlightening them about public affairs. But Madison was no less concerned about protecting the few, especially in the domain of the intellect. Besides, only the few could educate the people; could transcend the narrow and limited pursuit of economic interests; could diffuse among the people examples of those national feelings, those liberal sentiments, and those congenial manners which alone can sustain a pluralistic society on the one hand, yet a more perfect union on the other. Far from lowering the goals of "political" life, it can well be argued that the founders—perhaps because they harbored in their souls aspects of the Enlightenment qualified by classical and Christian motifs—sought a *higher* level of life for "society" as a whole than was thought practicable in classical antiquity.

Even if it were true, however, that the founders lowered their sights or standards for the purpose of establishing political institutions, they did so consistently with the teaching of Aristotle. For as Aristotle says, before discussing the character of a 'polity':

We have now to consider what is the best regime and the best way of life for the *majority* of countries and men. In doing so we shall not employ a standard of excellence above the reach of ordinary men, or a standard of education requiring exceptional endowments and equipment, or the standard of a regime which attains an ideal height. We shall only be concerned with the sort of life which most men are able to share and the sort of regime which it is possible for most countries to enjoy. The 'aristocracies,' so called . . . [will not serve us for this purpose: they] either lie, at one extreme, beyond the reach of most countries, or they approach, at the other, so closely to the regime called 'polity' that they need not be considered separately and must be treated as identical with it (180).[3]

Notice that Aristotle "lowers" the standards for constructing a 'polity' to make them comformable to the character of ordinary men. Ordinary men are not primarily motivated by a deep and abiding concern for the common good, let alone by a love of wisdom and virtue. Hence, to employ the highest standards of political life, such as those of a genuine aristocracy, is impracticable. Indeed, to attempt to translate into political practice the highest standards ascertainable by political theory would amount to arrant utopianism. Furthermore, such utopianism would not only undermine the good, or the potentiality for good, that does exist in a particular community, but it might very well eventuate in tyranny.

To construct a 'polity,' however, is *not* to lower the goals attainable by men in general. Rather, it is simply to follow the course of moderation, one which requires the founder to employ, as his standard, "a mean of the kind attainable by every individual" (180). To follow such a course is to enable a majority of

[3] Here the best practical regime is said to be one which it is possible for "most countries to enjoy." Yet, Aristotle also said that the 'polity' "has never been established—or, at the most, has only been established on a few occasions and in a few countries" (*Politics*, p. 183). If the latter is correct, it would follow that virtually all regimes are unjust! This conclusion is confirmed by Aristotle's contention that "Nowadays, when countries have become . . . larger, we may almost say that it is hardly even possible for any other form of regime [namely, a *democracy*] to exist" (*ibid.*, p. 143).

men to achieve a quality of life superior to that of other regimes.

The good life *par excellence* is attainable only by the very few—but attainable nonetheless in a 'polity.' It should also be noted that a 'polity' does not require the participation of the very few in political rule, although it does not preclude such participation. This means that the common good does not ordinarily depend on uncommon virtue. But inasmuch as a 'polity' is the best practical regime, no other *actual* regime is more conducive to the cultivation of virtue. This is not to say that the majority of citizens living in a 'polity' will harbor a concern for the common good that may always be relied upon to transcend their private interests. It will be sufficient if they are governed by something approximating "enlightened self-interest," which seems to involve the coincidence of "self-interest" and the common good.

Before continuing, some preliminary clarification of the principle of "self-interest" is necessary. It has already been suggested that "self-interest" refers to material well-being. But consider the following passage from a letter Madison wrote to James Monroe in 1786:

> There is no maxim, in my opinion, which is more liable to be misapplied, and which, therefore, more needs elucidation, than the current one, that the interest of the majority is the political standard of right and wrong. Taking the word "interest" as synonomous with "ultimate happiness," in which sense it is *qualified with every necessary moral ingredient*, the proposition is no doubt true. But taking it in the popular sense, as referring to immediate augmentation of property and wealth, nothing can be more false. In the latter sense, it would be in the interest of the majority . . . to despoil and enslave the minority. . . .[4]

Notice the two meanings of the term "interest," one as understood by the "many," the other as understood by the "few." The "many" seek "immediate augmentation of property and wealth." According to Diamond, this is precisely what underlies or animates the Madisonian solution to the problem of majority fac-

[4] *Writings*, II, 273 (Oct. 5, 1786) (italics added).

tion—in Diamond's own words, the "ceaseless striving after immediate interest."[5] Yet this is precisely what Madison rejects in the above passage. The truth is that the "ceaseless striving after immediate interest" or after "immediate augmentation of property and wealth" is indistinguishable from the vice of *avarice*. Avarice may well be the vice of the "many" (including many of the rich).[6] But it is a vice which is looked upon with contempt by the "few." We have seen that Madison wanted to eliminate the extremes of riches as well as of poverty; that he regarded virtue as the health of the soul; and that he sought to extend education to the many for the sake of their moral as well as intellectual improvement. Not that he envisioned a society of virtuous citizens all animated by a love of justice. He did not indulge the utopian hope that moral motives alone would ever become a sufficient foundation for securing the common good. "Interest" must continue to check "interest" so long as men were men. But he never entertained the notion that justice could be secured *without* virtuous men. Nor did he even believe that the representative principle would be sufficient "to refine and enlarge the public views, by passing them through the medium of a chosen body of citizens, whose wisdom may best discern the true interest of their country, and whose patriotism and love of justice will be least likely to sacrifice it to temporary or partial considerations." Had he thought this sufficient, Madison would not have urged the establishment of more schools, academies, and colleges. These institutions, more directly than those of government, were to refine and enlarge men's moral and intellectual horizons, hence what people conceive to be their "interest" or "happiness."

Projecting Madison's intention, let us assume that to refine and enlarge the popular notion of "interest" is to transform it into "enlightened self-interest," so that the pursuit of happiness would be qualified by moderation and justice. Under such a dis-

[5] *Diamond*, p. 67.
[6] Presumably, however, the rich are not dominated by the desire for *immediate* gain.

pensation, the many would restrain their desire for *immediate* augmentation of wealth, and, following Madison's teaching, they would respect the rights of property, including the faculties from which those rights originate. Such conduct, they will have learned, would be consistent with their own interests. Having learned this they would have also acquired, with experience, some measure of *prudence*. That is, insofar as they are governed by "enlightened self-interest," they would be able to distinguish between their immediate and long-range interests; they would understand how their interests affect those of others, and how the interests of others affect their own; and finally, they would know how to adjust all these competing interests so as to secure their own "happiness." The moral implications of this state of affairs where the many are motivated by "enlightened self-interest" must now be considered.

To begin with, the many, though moderate and just, may still be largely preoccupied with material well-being. Their moderation and justice may be no more elevated than the utilitarian ethic epitomized by the proverb "honesty is the best policy." It would nonetheless be misleading to say that the "ceaseless striving after immediate interests" is characteristic of the many envisioned by Madison. And it would be even more misleading to attempt to support this characterization, as Diamond does, by citing Tocqueville on the principle of "self-interest rightly understood":

> The principle of self-interest rightly understood is not a lofty one, but it is clear and sure. It does not aim at mighty objects, but attains . . . all those at which it aims. . . . By its admirable conformity to human weaknesses it easily obtains great dominion; nor is that dominion precarious, since the principle checks one personal interest by another, and uses, to direct the passions, the very same instrument that excites them.[7]

[7] *Diamond*, pp. 66–67. I have corrected Diamond's quotation, since it erroneously inserts the word "it" before attains, and fails to indicate the second elision. The original will be found in Alexis de Tocqueville, *Democracy in America* (2 vols.; New York: Vintage Books, 1945), Phillips Bradley, ed., II, 131 (cited hereafter as *Tocqueville*).

Consider, however, the immediate but uncited sequel to the above passage:

> The principle of self-interest rightly understood produces no great acts of self-sacrifice, but it suggests daily small acts of self-denial. By itself it cannot suffice to make a man virtuous; but it disciplines a number of persons in habits of regularity, temperance, moderation, foresight, self-command; and if it does not lead men straight to virtue by the will, it gradually draws them in that direction by their habits.[8]

Before explaining why the principle of "self-interest rightly understood" can lead to virtue, it will be necessary to supply another omission, namely, Tocqueville's definition of the principle:

> I doubt whether men were more virtuous in aristocratic ages than in others, but they were incessantly talking of the beauties of virtue, and its *utility* was only studied in secret. . . .
>
> In the United States hardly anybody talks of the beauty of virtue, but they maintain that virtue is *useful* and prove it every day. . . .
>
> The Americans . . . are fond of explaining almost all the actions of their lives by the principle of self-interest rightly understood; they show . . . how an enlightened regard for themselves . . . prompts them to assist one another and inclines them willingly to sacrifice a portion of their time and property to the welfare of the state. In this respect I think they frequently fail to do themselves justice; for in the United States as well as elsewhere people are sometimes seen to give way to those *disinterested* . . . impulses that are natural to man; but the Americans seldom admit that they yield to emotions of this kind; they are more anxious to do honor to their philosophy than to themselves.[9]

In short, a person governed by the principle of "self-interest rightly understood" acts justly not by the promptings of virtue, but out of long-range calculations aimed at his own private ad-

---

[8] See the sequel which moves Tocqueville to conclude that "the principle of self-interest rightly understood appears to me the best suited of all philosophical theories to the wants of the men of our time. . . ."

[9] *Ibid.*, pp. 129–130 (italics added). Consider, in this connection, the "group-interest" theory of politics.

vantage. This utilitarian ethic is exemplified in *Federalist* 51, where it is said that institutions of government must be designed in such a way that "the private interest of every individual may be a sentinel over the public rights" (337). It should be borne in mind, however, that *habitual* acts of justice may lead men toward virtue itself. This may be explained as follows.

The external actions of men, if sufficiently consistent and repetitive, evoke internal dispositions such that act and motive tend to coincide. Thus, if the laws and institutions of society compel a person toward consistently just actions, and, at the same time, are so designed as to "interest" him in acting justly, then the psychological disjunction between "disinterested" and "self-interested" action will *tend* to diminish such that acting justly may eventually become a habitude. The initial motive or incentive may have been fear of punishment or of social stigma; or it may have been the expectation of material reward or of social esteem. For most, if not all, men, such motives will never be entirely absent. Nevertheless, they may be supplemented by a genuine desire to act justly even at the risk of material loss and social disaffection.[10]

Here it may be noted that the criminal law and most of the civil law are rooted in, and supportive of, morality.[11] Indeed, law and morality are dependent upon each other for their effectiveness. This means, however, that political institutions are morally educative agents. Contrary to the Straussian school, the founders never conceived of "institutional substitutes for virtue."[12] True, *Federalist* 51 declares that there is "great security . . . in giving to those who administer each department [of gov-

[10] See John F. Kennedy, *Profiles in Courage* (New York: Harper & Row, 1964), ch. 1, and compare the "group-interest" theory of Bertram M. Gross, *The Legislative Struggle: A Study in Social Combat* (New York: McGraw-Hill Book Co., 1953), ch. 1.

[11] See Patrick Devlin, *The Enforcement of Morals* (London: Oxford University Press, 1965), ch. 1.

[12] I must confess to having once shared this prejudice, a prejudice that partly accounts for my critique of the founders in the concluding chapter of *The Philosophy of the American Constitution*—a critique which the present Discourse corrects to the vindication of those great men.

ernment] the necessary constitutional means and personal motives to resist encroachments of the others"; that "the interest of
the man must be connected with the constitutional rights of the
place"; and that "This policy of supplying, by opposite and rival
interests, the defect of better motives, might be traced through
the whole system of human affairs, private as well as public"
(337). But all this harks back to *Federalist* 10 where Madison
says that "neither moral nor religious motives can be relied on as
an *adequate* control" against injustice. Again, this does not mean
that such motives can be dispensed with by the system of institutional checks and balances. The very notion of institutional substitutes for virtue is a paralogism. For if men's *overt* conduct is
consistent with virtue as a *result* of institutions, then these institutions lead men toward virtue, however indirectly.

The above discussion is not intended to suggest—as Tocqueville clearly does—that men's actions are ever wholly *disinterested* or selfless. One of the great efforts of modern political
philosophy has been to break down that notion inherited from
Christianity. Although the political consequences of that effort
may thus far have been more destructive than constructive, the
effort itself, in my opinion, is philosophically justifiable. This
leads me back to the concept of "enlightened self-interest."

Insofar as "enlightened self-interest" is equivalent to Tocqueville's principle of "self-interest rightly understood," it remains
the motive of the "many" or of the ordinary man. But now the
ordinary man is decent. His desire for material well-being is
qualified by "habits of regularity, temperance, moderation, fore-
sight, [and] self-command." As *habits*, he is not psychologically
free to dispense with them at any moment should his interest
come into conflict with the interests of others. Still, it must be
admitted that, psychologically, his good and the good of others
stand to each other in a *contingent* as opposed to a *necessary*
relationship. Perhaps this is why Tocqueville would not identify
the principle of enlightened self-interest with virtue per se. Yet
I shall argue that that principle may be said to animate even a
paragon of virtue, once it is liberated from a meaning horizon

dominated by the opposition of Christian and modern motifs.

To prepare the grounds for this argument, I shall first contrast an exchange of letters between Madison and his friend William Bradford in 1773. Seeking Madison's advice as to the profession for which he might best be suited, Bradford wrote:

> Could I think myself properly qualified for the ministry I should be at no loss what choice to make. As I have always borne in mind that *I was born for others as well as for myself* I have always been desirous of being in that station in which I could be of most use to my fellow-creature: And in my opinion a devine may be the most useful as well as the most happy member of society. But as there are some insuprable objections to my entering that state my choice is now divided between law, physic [i.e., medicine] and merchandize. If I am rightly acquainted with my own genius it points rather to the first than to either of the others. . . . The grand objection urged against law is, that it is prejudicial to morals. It must indeed be owned that the conduct of the generality of lawyers is very reproachable, but that ought not to make their profession so as it is not the necessary consequence of it. . . . As gain is the sole pursuit of the merchant he is much more likely to contract an inordinate desire of wealth than the lawyers, whose pursuit is as much after fame as wealth; indeed, *they are both improper pursuits*. . . . [But] why should a lawyer be more dishonest than a merchant? If he is, he certainly mistakes his true interest. Honesty is a surer though perhaps a slower way of rising than dishonesty. It leads to reputation and reputation to wealth. . . . It is then the lawyer's interest to be honest, and next to the divine, can there be a more useful member of a society than an honest lawyer? Can there be a nobler character than his whose business it is to support the laws of his country and to defend the oppressed from the violence of the oppressor: whose whole life is spent in actions which *tend* the public good. . . .?[13]

Notice that Bradford deems the pursuit of wealth and fame "improper," presumably because such pursuits involve self-preference, whereas, Bradford, as a Christian, "was born for

---

[13] Madison, *Papers*, I, 91–92 (Aug. 12, 1773) (italics added).

others *as well as* for [him]self." Nevertheless, his discussion of the profession of law, in contradistinction to the practice of many lawyers, suggests the theme of enlightened self-interest—only *not* in the Tocquevillian sense of "self-interest rightly understood." For in speaking of the honest lawyer, notice how Bradford sings the praises of civic virtue and how exalted he feels by the vision of serving the public. Public service clearly appears as the *primary* reason for his preference for law. That law may also serve his material interests seems to be a *secondary* reason, perhaps a *necessary* but not a *sufficient* one. Certainly Bradford does not feel, if words convey feeling, that promoting the public good is merely a means of promoting his own good. It seems truer to say that promoting the public good constitutes the principal interest of his self. Stated another way: Insofar as the desire to serve the public is an essential part of Bradford's self, the fulfillment of that desire would be the expression of his self or of his self-actualization. If so, the public good *is* Bradford's *private* interest, the two being distinguishable but inseparable. Enlightened self-interest may thus involve, instead of a *means-end* relationship—which it has for Tocqueville—a *whole-part* relationship such that public and private good stand to each other in a mutually dependent and necessary as opposed to contingent relationship. Thus understood, enlightened self-interest is the conceptual equivalent of justice. Reserving the development of this point until later, consider Madison's response to Bradford's letter.

> You forbid any recommendation of divinity by suggesting that you have insuperable objections; therefore I can only condole with the church on the loss of a fine genius and persuasive orator. I cannot however surpress thus much of my advice on that head that you would always keep the ministry obliquely in view whatever your profession be. This will lead you to cultivate an acquaintance occasionally with *the most sublime of all sciences* and will qualify you for a change of public character if you should hereafter desire it. I have sometimes thought there could not be a stronger testimony in favor of religion or

against temporal enjoyments even the most rational and manly than for men who occupy the most honorable and gainful departments and are rising in reputation and wealth, publicly to declare their unsatisfactoriness by becoming fervent advocates in the cause of Christ. . . . If I am to speak my sentiments of merchandize, physic and law, I must say they are all honorable and useful professions and think you ought to have more regard to their suitableness to your genius than to their comparative excellence. As far as I know your endowments I should pronounce law the most eligible. It alone can bring into use many parts of knowledge you have acquired and will still have a taste for, and pay you for cultivating the arts of eloquence. It is a sort of general lover that wooes all the Muses and Graces. This cannot be said so truly of commerce and physic, and therefore less learning and smaller understanding will do for them.[14]

Here we see that theology, or the knowledge of God and of man's relation to God, is "the most sublime of all sciences." Its excellence does not depend on the personal preferences and capacities of men. It is a self-sufficient good, higher in dignity than the wealth acquired by the merchant and the honor achieved by the lawyer. Certain implications may be adduced from these considerations. First, the science of theology is more noble than, say, the science of law, because its subject matter is more noble. That is, the dignity of a science depends on the dignity of its object. Or to put the matter another way: the science of theology is more noble than the science of law because the former requires, to a greater extent than the latter, the perfection of the theoretical intellect, the noblest part of man's nature. On the other hand, insofar as the science of law "wooes all the Muses and Graces," it may be regarded as more noble than, say, the science of medicine. Or, whereas the object of medicine is mere life, the object of law, broadly understood, is the good life. For thus understood, the science of law is none other than the science of politics.[15]

It goes without saying, however, that different individuals

[14] *Ibid.*, I, 96 (Sept. 25, 1793) (italics added). "Theology," of course, is the most sublime science in Aristotle, *Metaphysics* 983a6–10.

[15] See Aristotle, *Nic. Eth.* 1145a7–14; 1094a26–1094b10.

partake of different aspects and degrees of the good life as well as of human happiness. These differences depend on two major factors, the first being the extent to which an individual possesses the powers peculiar to human nature, the second being the extent to which he can exercise those powers well. Notice that Bradford and Madison acknowledge the existence of an objective standard of human excellence. A devine, says Bradford, may be "the most happy member of society," which Madison confirms by saying—in the language of Christian Aristotelianism —not only that divinity is "the most sublime of all sciences," but also that the religious life surpasses all "temporal enjoyments even the most rational and manly." More clearly than Bradford, Madison here suggests that the happiness of the individual depends on the excellence of his intellectual and moral powers. Bradford feels that his "endowments" are well-suited to the profession of law, but he is concerned about the integrity of this profession. He wants to cultivate his own "genius," but only by pursuing an honorable calling. Madison assures his friend that the various professions mentioned in his letter are all honorable, so that rather than choose a profession on the basis of its "comparative excellence," he should consider, instead, its suitability to his own "genius." Finally, the mere fact that both men are discussing *alternative* professions suggests that whether an individual can enjoy a good life depends on the opportunities afforded him by his community. In a subsequent letter to Bradford, Madison wrote:

> You are happy in dwelling in a land where those inestimable privileges are fully enjoyed and [the] public has long felt the good effects of their religious as well as civil liberty. . . . Industry and virtue have been promoted by mutual emulation and mutual inspection. Commerce and the arts have flourished, and I can not help attributing those continual exertions of genius . . . to the inspiration of liberty and that love of fame and knowledge which always accompany it.[16]

[16] *Papers*, I, 112 (March 4, 1774). How lofty, how exhilarating, are these reflections of Madison, then twenty-four years of age.

Notice that Madison, unlike Bradford, does not disparage the love of fame—that exalted passion of revolutionary ages. Instead, he beholds in America a land of rich and unprecedented opportunity. Here liberty (and the absence of rigid class distinctions) make possible a flourishing individuality. Here, virtue, not externally imposed obedience, is encouraged. Here the thrust of one's own "genius" may come forth, affirming the principle of life as self-directed activity. Here the diverse faculties of the mind are free, free to engage in a variety of honorable callings: in commerce, in the arts, in politics, in the advancement of knowledge. Here men may pursue happiness, but happiness "qualified with every necessary moral ingredient."

In the above exchange between Madison and Bradford, three kinds of interests can be distinguished: wealth, honor, and wisdom. These three interests correspond to three paradigmatic individuals: the moneymaker, the statesman, and the philosopher. By a paradigmatic individual I mean a self consciously organized around a single interest. In other words, a paradigmatic self may be regarded as a system of values and relationships graded in relevance to some central interest. If the central interest of the self is wealth, all other values derive their relevance from that interest, and the various mental powers of the individual are energized and developed accordingly. This is why philosophy is of peripheral value for a moneymaker, and why he lacks the power of philosophical reflection. Conversely, if the central interest of the self is wisdom, all other values derive their relevance from that interest, and again the various mental powers of the individual are energized and developed accordingly. This is why moneymaking is of peripheral value for a philosopher who, nevertheless, is quite capable of mastering the art of economics.[17]

With the above in mind, consider the following meaning horizon organized around the self of a moneymaker. For him, the principle of enlightened self-interest may be translated to mean

[17] See Xenophon, *Oeconomicus, passim*. It should be noted that I am not using the term "why" to denote efficient causality.

that "honesty is the best policy," more precisely, that being honest in one's dealings with others is, in the long run, the best method of advancing and securing one's own interests. This meaning of enlightened self-interest places the good of the moneymaker and the good of others in a *contingent* relationship. If the moneymaker possessed the ring of Gyges, nothing in that relationship would prevent him from robbing others blind. (Here I am not speaking of a moneymaker habituated to virtue, but one whose material interest is the center of his self, such that all other values are graded in relation to that interest.) To say, therefore, that the good of others stands only in a contingent relationship to his own good means that his own perceived good may sometimes *necessitate* another's harm. From this it follows that the principle of enlightened self-interest is compatible with *injustice*—but only under a meaning horizon organized around the atomic self of that paradigmatic moneymaker. Under such a meaning horizon, the principle of enlightened self-interest appears to be morally neutral. (It is as morally neutral as money, which can be used for good as well as bad ends.) It remains to be seen, however, whether that principle is morally neutral under other meaning horizons, for example, one organized around the self of a paradigmatic statesman. This topic can be illuminated by examining Aristotle's treatment of honor in the *Nicomachean Ethics*.

It was said above that a paradigmatic individual may be regarded as a system of values and relationships graded in relevance to some central interest. This central interest is what the individual loves most or actually pursues as his highest good. It shapes his character or way of life. Of this Aristotle says:

> To judge from the lives that men lead, most men, and men of the most vulgar type, seem (not without some ground) to identify the good, or happiness, with pleasure; which is the reason why they love the life of enjoyment. For there are, we may say, three prominent types of life—that just mentioned, the political, and thirdly the contemplative life. . . . A consideration of the prominent types of life shows that people of superior refinement and of active disposition identify happiness with honour;

for this is, roughly speaking, the end of the political life. But it seems too superficial to be what we are looking for, since it is thought to depend on those who bestow honour rather than on him who receives it, but the good we divine to be something proper to a man and not easily taken from him. Further, men seem to pursue honour *in order that* they may be assured of their goodness; at least it is by men of practical wisdom that they seek to be honoured, and among those who know them, and on the ground of their virtue; clearly, then, according to them, at any rate, virtue is better. And perhaps one might even suppose this to be, rather than honour, the end of the political life.[18]

Later, in the context of his discussion of love and friendship, Aristotle recurs to the theme of honor by saying: "[T]hose who desire honour from good men, and men who know, are aiming at confirming their own opinion of themselves; they delight in honour, therefore, *because* they believe in their own goodness on the strength of the judgment of those who speak about them."[19]

The words I have italicized in the above two passages indicate that the political man does not pursue honor as an end-in-itself. What he aims at and delights in is the confirmation of his own virtue or excellence, namely, practical wisdom. Furthermore, the political man seeks the esteem of those who can fully appreciate his own excellence, men who themselves possess practical wisdom. Madison suggests as much when he says, in a letter to Edmund Randolph written in 1788, that "Popular favor or disfavor, is no criterion of the character maintained with those whose esteem an honourable ambition must court."[20] No man of refinement (be he a statesman or a political scientist) would feel honored if praised by the vulgar or by the ignorant, or by men to whom he is a complete stranger. And he might even be pained

---

[18] Richard McKeon, ed., *Introduction to Aristotle* (New York: Modern Library, 1947), *Nicomachean Ethics* 1095b14–31, W. D. Ross, trans. (italics added). Contrast the following discussion with Harold Lasswell's contention that the politician seeks *deference* above all other goods.

[19] *Ibid.*, 1159a21–24 (italics added).

[20] *Writings*, V, 297 (Nov. 2, 1788).

or embarrassed if praised by the wicked. This very fact is sufficient to show that a person who delights in honor delights in that which is the object of honor, namely, his particular excellence, especially when esteemed by others whose judgment he respects. To be sure, Aristotle suggests that the political man is not self-sufficient; that his self-esteem depends partly on the esteem of others. Nevertheless, the central concern of the political man is not for honor so much as for the confirmation of his own virtue; and it is for this reason that Aristotle says that virtue may be the end of political life.

If only "because" the political man is dependent on others for the confirmation of his own excellence, he must seek to promote the public good. Indeed, only by promoting the public good can he be known as a man of practical wisdom. Yet, it would be a mistake to infer from this that the political man seeks to promote the public good merely as a means of heightening his self-esteem. For promoting the public good is the actualization as well as the object of his excellence. Or to put the matter another way: promoting the public good is the articulation of his self. This is not a question of selflessness or unselfishness. To the contrary, the process may be described as one of self-enlargement by way of synthesizing a multiplicity of diverse values and relationships. Only a dogmatic skepticism based on atomistic individualism regards as naive this process of growth whereby the public interest may become one's private interest or the focus of one's private concern. The self can be small: it can be concerned primarily with immediate interests or with the good of some narrow interest group. Hence we speak of small-time politicians. The self can be large: it can be concerned with long-range interests or with the good of a nation. Hence we speak of great statesmen. Here, common opinion is sound enough. But contrary to common opinion, it is the small, not the large, self that is the closer to being selfless. And again contrary to common opinion, the small-time politician is not a political so much as an economic man: we call him a broker, and his good stands in a *contingent* relationship with the good of others. Of the political man properly speaking—

the man who seeks honor from men of practical wisdom, the man who delights in the confirmation of his own excellence—his good stands in a *necessary* relationship with the good of others. Accordingly, we may say that within the meaning horizon of the political man, the principle of enlightened self-interest coincides with justice—and not by "coincidence."

Without pausing to elaborate, it follows from the preceding argument that, within the meaning horizon of the philosopher, enlightened self-interest coincides with wisdom. This concludes my *explicit* treatment of that principle. It remains to construct the meaning horizon of the paradigmatic statesman, in whom the love of honor must be distinguished from the love of fame.

To begin with, the love of fame assimilates and transcends the love of honor. Unlike men who seek honor from those who know them, hence the living, those who seek fame wish even more to be honored by posterity. And unlike men who, in seeking honor, do so out of a need to be reassured of their own virtue, those who seek fame do so out of that adornment of the virtues called magnanimity.[21] Of course, the distinction drawn here is too sharp. Nevertheless, recall what Aristotle says in the *Politics* concerning the rare few who, in seeking fame, seek neither a kingdom nor high honors, but "glory," and do so in utter disregard for their own safety in the event of failure. Such men, Aristotle points out, "must have in their hearts the resolve of Dion —a resolve to which only a few can rise—when he sailed on his expedition against Dionysius the Younger with his little band of followers: 'I am of this mind—whatever the point I am able to reach, it is enough for me to have got so far in this undertaking; yes, if I die at once, just after getting ashore, it will be well for me to die like that'" (239). In Dion's quest for glory may be seen what Plato called the "spirited" part of the soul. To that aspect of the soul may be related the sense of honor or of self-

---

[21] But see Whitehead, AI 371–372, where he goes so far as to say that this "egotistic desire for fame . . . is the craving for sympathy." Compare Aristotle, *Nic. Eth.* 1124a1–19. Here I stand closer to Aristotle, but closer still to Nietzsche.

respect. Now, whereas the sense of honor will often exist without the passion for fame, the passion for fame will seldom if ever exist without the sense of honor. Governed by the sense of honor, the statesman will do his duty and act justly, for he will be no less concerned about his own self-respect than with the respect of others. Recall Hamilton's remark: "There are men who, under any circumstances, will have the courage to do their duty at every hazard"—who therefore would hazard the villification of their countrymen. If, however, the statesman's sense of honor is accompanied by the love of fame, he will then attempt to do more than is required by duty or by justice, for he will aspire to the supramoral domain of the *noble*. Here another distinction is in order.

The statesman referred to in Hamilton's remark may be said to be governed by a sense of obligation in contradistinction to, but not to the exclusion of, the sense of honor. But whereas the sense of honor involves self-respect—Aristotle would say self-love—the sense of obligation involves respect for, and subordination to, something that stands over and against the self. Thus understood, the notion of obligation provides a Christian meaning horizon for Hamilton's remark concerning those men who would do their duty at every hazard. This meaning horizon clashes, however, with Hamilton's earlier reference to the love of fame as "the ruling passion of the noblest minds." The value placed on fame is classical; the supremacy ascribed to the passion is modern. For Aristotle, fame (or honor) is the greatest of external goods. He even associates the love of honor with the great-souled man, the magnanimous man. Now the great-souled man is fond of conferring benefits but reluctant to accept any lest he become obligated to others. In such a man the love of fame is necessarily consistent with the public good. And so it is for the Hamiltonian statesman. But the Hamiltonian statesman is partly governed by the sense of obligation, which of course is also consistent with the common good, but which nonetheless involves an element of self-denial missing in the more simple and self-assertive passion for fame. Here classical pride and Christian

selflessness are somehow synthesized in the Hamiltonian statesman whose overflowing soul reminds us of *eros* and *agape*. But
let Hamilton speak for himself, and consider once more these
words he addressed to the Continental Congress:

> The station of a member of C——ss, is the most illustrious and
> important of any I am able to conceive. He is to be regarded not
> only as a legislator, but as the founder of an empire. A man of
> virtue and ability, dignified with so precious a trust, would re-
> joice that fortune had given him birth at a time, and placed him
> in circumstances so favourable for promoting human happiness.
> He would esteem it not more the duty, than the privilege and
> ornament of his office, to do good to mankind; from this com-
> manding eminence, he would look down with contempt upon
> every mean or interested pursuit.

While appreciating Hamilton's classical magnanimity, one ought
not slight his modernity, his exaltation of the love of fame as the
ruling passion of the *noblest* minds—in contrast to which, so
proud is Aristotle's great-souled man that he looks down even
on fame. On the other hand, thanks to the influence of Christianity, the Hamiltonian statesman is doubly prompted to doing
good. For in addition to his magnanimity, his sense of obligation
(which tempers his love of fame) renders him more altruistic
than his classical counterpart. This sense of obligation, I am
suggesting, is not truly integral to classical political philosophy
—I mean to the *philosophical* strata of classical wisdom. Nowhere is this more evident than in Plato's *Republic*.

2

In the seventh book of that dialogue, Socrates tells Glaucon
that the very men they trained as philosophers would have to be
compelled to rule in the best city constructed earlier in speech—
yea, even though these philosophers owed that city the philosophic cultivation of their souls. But here are Socrates' own
words:

> "Well, then, Glaucon," I said, "consider that we won't be
> doing injustice to the philosophers who come to be among us,

but rather that we will say just things to them *while compelling them besides* to care for and guard the others. We'll say that when such men come to be in the other cities it is fitting for them not to participate in the labors of those cities. For they grow up spontaneously against the will of the regime in each; and a nature that grows up by itself and doesn't owe its rearing to anyone has justice on its side when it is not eager to pay off the price of rearing to anyone. 'But you we have begotten for yourselves and for the rest of the city like leaders and kings in hives; you have been better and more perfectly educated and are more able to participate in both lives. So you must go down [into the cave], each in his turn, into the common dwelling of the others and get habituated along with them to seeing the dark things.' "[22]

That the philosopher should have to be compelled to care for the city which educated him as a philosopher clearly indicates that he would not feel obligated to do so. This means, if I may generalize, that for the classics, no less than for the moderns, the individual prefers his own good to the good of others.[23] To be sure, there are profound differences. For unlike the individualism of the moderns, the individualism of the classics does not deny that men are naturally concerned about the good

[22] *The Republic of Plato* (New York: Basic Books, Inc., 1968), 520a–c, Allan Bloom, trans. (italics added). See also 539e–540a.

[23] This is not contradicted by the example of Socrates in the *Crito*. There is every good reason to believe that Socrates' refusal to escape was not motivated by a concern for the welfare of Athens so much as for the sake of preserving the nobility of his own soul. (A younger Socrates might well have chosen to act differently, but for the very same reason.) Thus, in the *Apology*, Socrates makes it clear enough (after being condemned) that the individual's pursuit of wisdom and virtue takes precedence over his concern for the welfare of his city (36, and compare 31). True, Socrates can say in the *Crito* that he is a child and slave of the laws. In the *Apology*, however, he tells the court that he will not obey the laws should they prohibit him from philosophizing. The teachings of the two dialogues contradict each other only because of the different intellectual capacities of their respective audiences. Crito is a simple soul initially governed by *public opinion*, but subsequently persuaded by Socrates to be guided by the *laws*. (Note, too, the different settings of the dialogues: one occurs in a public place and in broad daylight, the other in the privacy of a prison cell before sunrise.)

of others. The virtuous man of Plato's *Republic* will act justly toward his fellows even without the restraint of law and without the expectation of reward or honor. But he will do this not for *their* sake *so much as* for the health and happiness of his own soul or for his own self-perfection. Furthermore, unlike the classics, the moderns, especially Hobbes, broadcast the principle of individual self-preference in the baldest terms, while relegating to political insignificance the category of the *noble* or the classical emphasis on the *magnanimous* man. We live in the full tide of this development: witness the anti-heroic so manifest in the behavioral sciences, to say nothing of the literature of recent decades. Countless are the disciples of Hobbes (ignorant of their genealogy) who now explain the behavior of statesmen as so many attempts to win the approval of others or to gratify some deep-seated need, but in any event as motivated by private or self-serving interests so-called. This herd psychology is well calculated to emasculate the statesman, a topic I shall enlarge upon in Chapter X, where Hamilton will be pitted against the political science of Harold Lasswell. Here it is only necessary to point out that when "the ruling passion of the noblest minds" is reduced to the mind's privation, fewer men will be animated by the love of fame, which is to say that fewer will be the number of genuine statesmen. Meanwhile, the notion of obligation, which requires the recognition of something standing over against us, something that transcends the merely human—this Christian notion of obligation will be retreated into obscurity no less than the classical notion of honor. If not replaced by a mundane and monotonous humanism, it will give way to hedonic individualism. But this only in passing.

Returning to classical individualism, I have yet to show its presence in Aristotle. Although there is much in Aristotelian philosophy that seems to depreciate individuality,[24] his *Nico-*

---

[24] The classics seem to regard forms alone as the truly real, or only universals as the truly knowable. But see Ivor Leclerc, ed., *The Relevance of Whitehead* (New York: Macmillan Co., 1961), pp. 170–171. In his own contribution to that volume ("Form and Actuality"), Leclerc argues that "Aristotle, who started

machean Ethics contains certain suggestions for a doctrine of individuality which may help to redeem and reconstruct the atomistic individualism of modernity. I have in mind Aristotle's discussion of self-love and his general treatment of virtue. Beginning with the latter, it should first be made clear that the virtues are neither passions nor powers or capacities, but rather certain kinds of activities. These activities are described by such universals as "justice," "liberality," "moderation," and "wisdom," a manner of designation apt to be misleading, the more so when Aristotle also describes the virtues as states of character. Unfortunately, the adjectival form of speaking suggests (1) that a virtue is simply a universal predicated of an individual (as when we speak of a "just" man), and (2) that the virtues are static dispositions. The resulting tendency is to obscure two crucial facts. First, virtues are preeminently *mental* activities: they are modes of choosing, of making decisions. Second, virtues create or transform relationships: they relate individuals to each other, to things, and even to the universe. Concerning the moral virtues, these activities are not merely expressive of the individual's character, but of his impact on his environment and, too, of his environment's impact on him. Despite the reciprocal influence between individual and environment, the individual is central. By his virtuous activity he extends his self into his environment and assimilates his environment to his self. Although the environment imposes on the individual various limitations, *how* such limitations affect the choices or decisions he makes and, therefore, *what* those limitations will in fact be, are partly determined by the thrust of his own character.

As modes of choosing, the virtues involve acts of moral judgment. The following example will simultaneously illustrate the virtues of justice, liberality, and practical wisdom. Suppose it were in my power to determine which college applicants were to receive financial assistance and in what amounts. Obviously I

---

by maintaining, in opposition to Plato, that form must be the 'form of' οὐσίαι [i.e., primary substance], ended with a conception of pure form itself as the οὐσίαι" (p. 171).

should have to take into account a student's academic performance, his financial resources, and the resources placed at my own
disposal. Now these factors, by themselves or in combination
with any number of other external factors that might be mentioned, cannot alone be determinative of my judgment in this
matter. Of decisive significance is my own intellectual and moral
character. For any judgment I arrive at will also have been influenced by (1) the standards of intellectual excellence I wish
to promote; (2) the kind of relationship I wish to establish between wealth and higher education; (3) the meaning of justice
(or the relationship between reward and merit) I wish to foster;
and (4) the kinds of relationships I wish to see existing among
various groups or classes of citizens. Clearly, these considerations
implicate the kind of community or regime I desire to live in
and, therefore, my answer to the question of who should rule.
In reflecting on the problem as a whole, no "reality" out there
can, in and of itself, be determinitive of my judgment. For my
mind, far from being a passive mirror, is active in the very way
in which I experience that "reality."[25] Besides, not only am I part
of that "reality," but I also wish to change "it" in terms of those
considerations mentioned above. Of course, what I deem desirable on the one hand, and what is feasible on the other, may be
two different things—precisely because of that "reality"—and
unless I take that "reality" into account, my judgment will fail
to exemplify the virtues in question.

It should be evident from the preceding example that our
judgment on moral matters cannot be determined by fixed rules
or formulas. As Aristotle points out: "matters concerned with
conduct and questions of what is good for us have no fixity, any
more than matters of health. The general account being of this
nature, the account of particular cases is yet more lacking in
exactness; for they do not fall under any art or precept but the

[25] Before I am accused of unqualified subjectivism or relativism (if not solipsism), the reader should reflect upon the remainder of this chapter. If he should
nevertheless reach the same conclusion, then I ask that he study well the writings of Whitehead, especially *Modes of Thought* and *Process and Reality*.

agents themselves must in each case consider what is appropriate to the occasion, as happens also in the art of medicine or of navigation."[26] From the denial of absolute rules governing moral or ethical questions it does not follow that our decisions in such matters are merely "subjective" or arbitrary. We may in fact give financial assistance to a truly deserving student and in the right amount; and this virtuous act may result not from accident, but from rational modes of inquiry usually culminating in sound decisions. Of course, the "right" amount means neither too much nor too little, and here we are subject to error. But then, moral decisions cannot be made by computers. This leads me to Aristotle's doctrine of the "mean," a doctrine that breathes freedom into virtue and, as will be seen in a moment, that unites virtue and individuality.

> In everything that is continuous and divisible it is possible to take more, less, or an equal amount, and that either in terms of the thing itself or relatively to us; and the equal is an intermediate between excess and defect. By the intermediate in the object I mean that which is equidistant from each of the extremes, which is one and the same for all men; by the intermediate relatively to us that which is neither too much nor too little —and this is not one, nor the same for all. For instance, if ten is many and two is few, six is the intermediate, taken in terms of the object. . . . But the intermediate relatively to us is not to be taken so; if ten pounds are too much for a particular person to eat and two too little, it does not follow that the trainer will order six pounds; for this also is perhaps too much for the person who is to take it, or too little. . . .[27]

There is a profound "relativism" here, but not of the purely subjective and egalitarian variety that renders one man's moral judgment as valid as another's. Like the trainer concerned with the health of the body, the psychiatrist concerned with the health of the mind is a better judge of his own subject matter than the ordinary citizen. The same may be said of the statesman who has devoted his life to the study and practice of politics: He, more

[26] *Nic. Eth.* 1104a4–8 (Ross, trans.).
[27] *Ibid.*, 1106a25–1106b5.

than others, is better qualified to decide what should be done to promote the health of the body politic or the common good. But what is required to promote the common good in any particular case is again not determinable by fixed rules. One cannot descend from some general principle and, by means of deductive logic, determine what ought to be done in concrete instances. Not only the variety of human types and the welter of competing goods, but the ineluctable fact of contingency and accident deprives moral judgment of utter certainty and thus renders the task of making political decisions a most difficult one indeed. This helps to explain why genuine statesmanship is rare. For statesmanship is nothing less than practical wisdom, the very synthesis of the moral virtues. Perhaps this is why Aristotle refers to that virtue in summing up his discussion of virtue in general. He writes "Virtue, then, is a state of character concerned with choice, lying in a mean, i.e. the mean relative to us, this being determined by a rational principle, and that principle by which the man of practical wisdom would determine it."[28] Applied to all the virtues, hence to all of life's activities, the "mean" may be understood to signify *balance* or moderation: *nothing* too much. Accordingly, to follow the course of the mean is to give each good thing its due, whether it concerns the care of the body and the cultivation of the mind, or the time and effort we devote in our various relationships, be it as a parent, teacher, or citizen. But notice that the mean is said to be "relative to *us*," signifying that the *individual* is central or must discover the mean appropriate to himself. Yet it is evident that very few individuals follow that course of the mean which wisely balances the competing goods and concerns of life. And so Aristotle qualifies what would otherwise be a doctrine of vulgar relativism by adding that the question of how one should live requires "rational principle," signifying some order or hierarchy of values suitable to the individual, but as determined by "a man of practical wisdom." Now apply this teaching to that man of practical wisdom, the genuine statesman.

[28] *Ibid.*, 1106b35–1107a3.

The genuine statesman does not formulate comprehensive and long-range plans as a detached and unaffected spectator. His mind does not merely hover over events only to determine, disinterestedly, what is required for the common good—as if the common good existed independently of himself. Nor does he merely respond to external stimuli. To the contrary, his political decisions, or the public policies he sets in motion, are emanations of his own personality. They are so many streams of energy or of influence radiating, as it were, from the center of his self and modulating the opinions, passions, and interests of his community. He has imposed upon himself the task of promoting— say rather of constructing or of reconstructing—the common good. Thus conceived, the common good is, in a very real sense, his political autobiography. In pursuing this task of construction, of fashioning laws and institutions, the statesman's paramount concern is with his own good; but by virtue of his magnanimity, his good embraces the good of the community. Accordingly, his acts of practical wisdom and, therefore, all his virtues, are modes of self-actualization. But now it will be understood that his self is not a mere atom enjoying its private qualifications. Instead, it is a center of dynamic relationships. Viewed externally, the statesman's virtue consists in this: He rescues from mutual ob-structiveness the diverse purposes and pursuits of men and thus facilitates their coordination and mutual intensification. But the richer unity he thereby brings into existence bears the impress of his own individuality. His virtue flows from overabundance, from the love of what is noble in himself. This leads to the theme of self-love.

Nowhere does Aristotle come closer to adumbrating a doctrine of individuality than in his discussion of self-love, especially in connection with the good or virtuous man. Here is the relevant passage:

> For the good man is of one mind with himself, and desires the same things with every part of his nature. Also he wishes his own good, real as well as apparent, and seeks it by action (for it is a mark of a good man to exert himself actively for the good);

and he does so *for his own sake* (for he does it on account of the intellectual part of himself, and *this appears to be a man's real self*). Also he desires his own life and security, and especially that of his rational part. For existence is good for the virtuous man; and everyone wishes his own good: no one would choose to possess every good in the world on condition of *becoming somebody else* . . . but only while remaining himself, *whatever he may be;* and it would appear that *the thinking part is the real self*, or is so more than anything else.[29]

Notice that the individual does not wish to become *someone else*. He may wish to enjoy another's wealth or reputation, another's beauty or intelligence; but it is *he*, the self of the individual, who wishes to abide the change and enjoy its rewards. In other words, while wishing *to have* the possessions or qualities of another person, the individual nevertheless wishes *to be* himself or to retain his own personal identity. This suggests that personal identity or concrete individuality stands over those universals we call virtues, or that the virtues are expressions of individuality. If so, then the dignity of the individual is derived primarily from his individuality and secondarily from the virtues he shares with members of his own species. Of course, one must be a "man" in order to be a genuine individual—and by a genuine individual I mean a *creator*. Such an individual is the master of his virtues, which virtues, however, are essential to his mastery. But what is it, above all other things, that makes such mastery and creativity possible?

It will have been noticed in the above passage that Aristotle comes very close to saying that personal identity or individuality is a function of reason or intellection, or more so than of any other human power. He thus allows us to see, in words simple yet profound, the inadequacy of modern political philosophy insofar as it holds, with Hume, that "reason is and ought to be the slave of the passions." And yet, the chasm between the classics and the moderns might be overcome if reason or intellection

---

[29] *Nicomachean Ethics* (Loeb Library ed.), 1166a11–24, H. Rackham, trans. (italics added). See also 1168b28–1169b3.

is at once the differentiating as well as synthesizing passion of individuality. This may be explained as follows.

If we make the process of intellectual activity an object of reflection, we notice that the process involves a selection of data for emphasis. The data are graded or coordinated according to criteria of relevance or importance, which criteria are not simply imposed upon, or reducible to, the data.[30] In the intellectual process of coordinating the data of his experience, the individual makes *actual* certain relationships among the data which were only *potential* prior to the process of intellection. But the individual's criteria of relevance are functions of his individuality, just as they are functions of the data coordinated by those criteria. In other words, a reciprocal relationship exists between the criteria and the data—which means that the intellect does not merely mirror reality.[31] This is why reason or intellection may be regarded as the differentiating and synthesizing *passion* of individuality. The deliverances of the intellect represent the individual's perspective of the universe including himself as influenced by that universe. It should be understood, however, that the individual's perspective is no more comprehensive than his passions allow it to be. Depending upon their objects, the passions—such as love and fear—can enlarge as well as restrict the intellect's capacity to differentiate and synthesize the multifarious data of experience into a coherent system of relationships. Nevertheless, every passion makes accessible to the intellect some aspect of the universe, so that the individual possessing

[30] The assumption here is that the criteria are sufficiently rational as to have some application to experience. Rationality is made possible by the fact that the data of the universe are not susceptible to an infinitude of relationships. Such infinitude is precluded by the irreversibility of time as well as by the partial limitations of the law of contradiction.

[31] This is to deny the philosophical adequacy of the subject-object dichotomy. Solipsism is avoided by the fact that the universe enters into the character of the individual, just as the individual extends his character into the universe. See Friedrich Nietzsche, *The Will to Power*, 549, 551–552, 555–557, 567–568, 584 (end), and compare with Whitehead, MT 43, 70–71, 75, 91, 188, 205–232, and Williams James, *Pragmatism* (New York: Longmans, Green & Co., 1917), pp. 137, 216, 245–246.

the most comprehensive intellect must also harbor, in coordinated intensity, the widest range of passions. On this note I touch upon some of the underlying principles of the politics of magnanimity, the elaboration of which will provide a fitting conclusion to Book I of this Discourse.

3

The politics of magnanimity, I have said, would synthesize classical and modern political philosophy. It would do justice to the classics by a qualified restoration of the primacy of reason. It would do justice to the moderns by a qualified restoration of the primacy of certain passions. A synthesis may be accomplished (1) by illuminating the creativity of reason in its power of selecting and coordinating the data of experience, and (2) by developing a hierological theory of the passions showing how different passions enlarge or contract the differentiating and assimilative power of reason, and how reason energizes and de-energizes diverse passions. The synthesis would yield a rational and realistic politics.

Such a politics would also synthesize the classical emphasis on virtue and the modern emphasis on individuality and freedom. Virtue would consist in individualized or self-directed activity bringing into mutual relevance a multiplicity of familiar and novel values and relationships. It needs to be emphasized that virtuous activity is self-centered, only the self should be understood as a center of relationships, which relationships enter into its own essence. (This is but to affirm the Whiteheadian notion that the whole is constitutive of the part, and the part is constitutive of the whole, a notion that replaces the classical *and* modern understanding of universals and particulars.)[32] Of course, in the interrelatedness of all things there are gradations of relevance shading into irrelevance. Thus qualified, it may be said that the good of the self is inseparable from the good of

[32] See above, pp. 108, n. 11, 25, n. 4, 272, n. 31. It should be noted that contemporary events are in causal independence of each other. See Whitehead, AI 251, 256.

others. It should be clear however, that no individual ever acts for the good of others more than he does for the good of himself or for what he believes to be the best in himself.[33] Self-sacrifice is literally impossible given the mutual immanence of self and society. This is what distinguishes the politics of magnanimity from the pre-modern "politics of duties" and the modern "politics of rights." Whereas the former issues from demands society makes upon the individual, the latter issues from demands the individual makes upon society. In contrast, the politics of magnanimity issues from the self-imposition of burdens—say rather a task—by which the individual may ennoble himself and, by the relational essence of things, society as well.

Finally, the politics of magnanimity would synthesize the teleological and hierarchical motifs of the classics with the evolutionary and egalitarian motifs of the moderns. This may be accomplished by replacing the Aristotelian notion of completeness or perfection with the nonfinalistic yet teleological notion of *comprehensiveness*. Comprehensiveness, dynamically understood, is a function of unity amidst increasing diversity, where the many enter into the one and the one into the many. Again, this bears close analogy to the seemingly paralogistic phraseology of the Preamble, "to form a more perfect Union." To form such a union is to synthesize a multiplicity of diverse values and relationships. Consider, for example, such values as civic peace, material abundance, and intellectual freedom. These values may obstruct each other. So too may the relationships created by political, commercial, and professional associations. The mutual obstructiveness of these values and relationships occurs through processes of change, and may be overcome by the synthesizing activity of the intellect. Comprehensiveness requires the reconciliation of permanence and change, such that the past gives depth and solidity to the present, while the present recreates the

---

[33] See Aristotle, *Nic. Eth.* 1169a, where he points out that the good man will die for his friends or country, that he may gain nobility for himself. This means there is no such thing as disinterested action. Self-sacrifice really involves the sacrifice of what is lower for the sake of what is higher *in us*.

past by incorporating it into a larger whole for the future—say into a more perfect union for posterity. Thus understood, comprehensiveness is the standard of virtue. It is the proper aim of individual and society alike. What this also means, however, is that comprehensiveness requires a pluralistic and commercial society bound by an organic and hierological conception of equality.

Organic and hierological equality may be illustrated by comparing the brain and the heart. The two are equal with respect to the survival of the human organism. Yet, even a radical positivist would "know" that it is *preferable* to live with a weak heart than with an infantile brain. This suggests the analogy of the human organism to a strictly limited or constitutional monarchy. Its center of coordination, the brain, is dependent on various organs of perception. These organs of perception, however, are not equal to the brain or even to each other—and neither with respect to the organism's power of survival, nor with respect to its power to create works of genius. Homer and Beethoven are not admired for their capacity to see or to hear. Accordingly, a rational and realistic politics, reflecting on such notions as equality of opportunity, would recognize that what constitutes a person's opportunity depends on his own intellectual, moral, and physical endowments, as well as on the intellectual, moral, and physical endowments of his society. Acknowledging, therefore, that one person is superior to another, but that the two are interdependent, the politics here envisioned would be one of *deference*, as well as of magnanimity.

If the principles of the foregoing synthesis be admitted, it would then be necessary either to deny, or to establish on other grounds, the ineluctable conflict between the individual and society as understood by the moderns, hence the conflict between the philosopher and the *polis* as understood by the classics. That the "individual" is capable of achieving a higher degree of perfection than any "society" might still be acknowledged. The trouble is that both notions are abstractions, equally useful and mischievous, but in any event philosophically misleading. The

275

individual is a political being having a greater or lesser degree of relevance for every other member of his society. The measure of the individual is the intensity of his relevance for his society, past, present, and future—in thought no less than in action. The relational essence of things cannot be avoided.

It also follows from the foregoing synthesis that a pluralistic and commercial society ordered by an organic and hierological conception of equality is superior, both in practice *and* in theory, to any classical alternative. Such a society would be highly complex on the one hand, and well-structured on the other.[34] Complexity would facilitate the wide enjoyment of individuality (hence, of freedom). But the effectiveness of individuality, as well as its richness and endurance, requires the rational coordination of contrasting values and relationships; its perfection requires the union of wisdom and virtue. Wisdom and virtue, centered around individuality, would thus remain the cardinal aims of human life.

The conclusion of Book I of this Discourse may therefore be stated as follows: The Republic established under the original Constitution most closely resembles what Aristotle regarded as the best practical regime, once again, a 'polity.' To this extent alone, the architects of that Constitution, the founding fathers, have bequeathed to posterity an exemplary model of statesmanship. But clearly the founders aspired to something more noble than the 'polity' described in the *Politics* of Aristotle—the silence of the Constitution notwithstanding. This fact renders their statesmanship even more worthy of serious study and emulation. Still, there is a silence, a silence, however, in the history of political philosophy. This silence speaks to us of the need for a model of statesmanship which only time and a thoroughly articulated synthesis of classical and modern political science can provide.

[34] See Whitehead, PR 152–154.

BOOK TWO

THE AMERICAN 'POLITY'
UNDER THE CATEGORY OF CHANGE

CHAPTER VIII

The Public Teaching of Woodrow Wilson

We are the first Americans to hear our own countrymen ask whether the Constitution is still adapted to serve the purposes for which it was intended; the first to entertain any serious doubts about the superiority of our own institutions as compared with the systems of Europe; the first to think of remodeling the administrative machinery of the federal government, and of forcing new forms of responsibility upon Congress.

The evident explanation of this change of attitude towards the Constitution is that we have been made conscious by the rude shock of the [Civil] war and by subsequent developments of policy, that there has been a vast alteration in the conditions of government; that the checks and balances which once obtained are no longer effective; and that we are really living under a constitution essentially different from that which we have been so long worshiping as our own peculiar and incomparable possession. . . . The noble charter of fundamental law given us by the Convention of 1787 is still our Constitution; but it is now our *form of government* rather in name than in reality. . . .

Woodrow Wilson, *Congressional Government*, 1885

Preceding chapters have shown, by means of philosophical and historical analysis, that the regime established by the founding fathers in the late eighteenth century was a 'polity,' a regime combining democratic and oligarchic attributes, some shading, *de facto*, if not *de jure*, into the aristocratic spectrum. The succeeding chapters will show that the twentieth century witnessed the transformation of that regime into one in which the democratic principle gained complete ascendency. Of course, a detailed as well as comprehensive exposition of *how* this trans-

279

formation came about would require more than a volume. It would necessitate inquiry into (1) the political significance of various constitutional amendments and Supreme Court decisions; (2) the rise, development, and alternating alliances of political parties, but especially their effect on the character of statesmanship;[1] (3) the consequences of westward expansion and of civil and international war; (4) the changing character of American higher education since the eighteenth century; (5) the shifting political loyalty of American intellectuals; (6) the development of capitalism and its effect upon the demographic character of American society; and finally, (7) the impact of the various arts and sciences on manners and morals.

This by no means complete enumeration of factors contributing to the transformation of the American 'polity' into a democracy affirms the position that men, especially the ideas and purposes of great men, make history, but that material forces as well as accident contribute their share to the shaping of human destinies. Accordingly, no inquiry into the decline of the American 'polity' would be complete without examining the influence on the American regime of the political thought and policies of such presidents as Jefferson, Jackson, Lincoln, and, above all, Woodrow Wilson. I say Wilson above all because it was in the era of this student, teacher, and president of Princeton University—the era of the New Freedom—that I date the *intellectual* ascendency of democracy, an ascendency carried to *material* completion under Franklin Roosevelt and the New Deal. This contention will not be conclusively demonstrated in the following inquiry, for reasons already suggested. Instead, I shall devote the next two chapters to an analysis of Wilson's public teaching and to the revolutionary rhetoric embodied in that teaching. The inquiry as a whole, including the remaining chapters of Book II, will also consider, in varying degrees of

[1] See Harvey Mansfield, *Statesmanship and Party Government* (Chicago: University of Chicago Press, 1965). This brilliant study of Burke and Bolingbroke should be applied to *The Federalist* with a view to showing how the statesmanship and rhetoric of its authors differ from that of party leaders.

incompleteness, those factors in the above enumeration which most clearly reveal the departure of twentieth-century American political thought from the principles and purposes of the founders. But first, a few historical notes.

In 1909, three years before Wilson was elected President of the United States, a unanimous Senate and an overwhelming majority of the House voted in favor of the Sixteenth Amendment. This amendment vested Congress with the "power to lay and collect taxes on incomes from whatever source derived." The amendment was officially ratified the week before Wilson took the presidential oath of office. By itself, the Sixteenth Amendment did not mark a revolution in government. Indeed, there is nothing in the mere power of Congress to tax incomes that is inconsistent with a regime based on democratic *and* oligarchic principles. The decision of the Supreme Court in 1895 to the contrary notwithstanding, it may even be doubted whether Congress lacked that power in the first place.[2] What makes the Sixteenth Amendment so significant is that its passage occurred during the time when the political thought of Wilson had become ascendent. Meanwhile, in 1912, a closely divided Senate, together with another overwhelming majority of the House, approved the Seventeenth Amendment which was officially ratified shortly after Wilson's first inauguration. Henceforth, senators of the United States would be elected directly by the people, as Wilson had urged during his campaign for the presidency. Four years later, and hardly a month following his second inauguration, Wilson delivered his war message to Congress, and the nation was launched into World War I. That war augmented the material powers of the presidency perhaps even beyond the hopes of Alexander Hamilton. But this augmentation of executive power occurred at the very height of the progressive era, an era whose political thought differed profoundly from Hamilton's. Finally, in 1920, while Wilson's presidency was drawing to a close, the Nineteenth Amendment, extending the suffrage to women, became a part of the Constitution. To grasp the political

[2] See 157 U. S. 429 (1895).

significance of these events for the American regime, let us turn to the political thought and teaching of one of Princeton's two most famous graduates.

The present chapter will be divided into two parts. The teaching of Wilson the popular orator will be examined in the first; in the second, the teaching of Wilson the political scientist. These two teachings contain various differences related to the differences between their respective audiences. The former emphasizes the "wisdom" of the common man; the latter emphasizes the "wisdom" of science.[3] Whatever contradictions emerge from Wilson's two teachings, these will be resolved, at least implicitly, under the category of change governing Book II of the present Discourse. (To those interested, the contradictions may be overcome by reflecting on Wilson's strategy of political revolution—itself to be elaborated in the following chapter—a strategy pursued from the time he was a student at Princeton to the time he became President of the United States.) Finally, throughout this inquiry into Wilson's public teaching, comparisons will be made with the public teaching of *The Federalist*. When coming upon these comparisons, the reader will discover (something long obscured by too many political scientists) that there are fundamental differences between the rhetoric required of statesmen engaged in the founding of a regime and the rhetoric required of statesmen seeking high office in a regime already established (even if it be to transform it). And if Wilson should sometimes suffer from those comparisons, the reader should not lose sight of their primary intention, which is to elucidate the differences between the regime established by the founders and the regime emerging when Wilson sought the presidency. Besides, Wilson was no ordinary officeseeker. He was one of the finest political scientists produced in this country. Furthermore, apart from Wilson, no aspiring President of the United States can be said to have dedicated his life to the systematic transformation of the American political and economic order. Jeffer-

[3] But see below, p. 298, n. 18, where it is evident that Wilson was well aware of the dangers of science for society.

son's so-called "Revolution of 1800" was nothing in comparison with the *second founding* envisioned by Wilson; and more than Jefferson, Wilson was a disciplined and constructive thinker with whom, among American statesmen, one can only compare men of the caliber of Madison and Hamilton. But now to the inquiry.

1

In 1913, William Bayard Hale edited a book entitled *The New Freedom*, a collection of extracts from Wilson's campaign speeches of 1912.[4] According to the preface, written by Wilson, *The New Freedom* is not a book of campaign speeches so much as "an attempt to express the new spirit of our politics" which, the new President continued, "is only the old revived and clothed in the unconquerable strength of modern America" (18). Yet, in the very first speech recorded in that volume, Wilson proclaimed:

> We are in the presence of a new organization of society. Our life has broken away from the past. . . . We have changed our economic conditions, absolutely, from top to bottom; and, with our economic society, the organization of our life. The old political formulas do not fit the present problems; they read now like documents taken out of a forgotten age. . . . We are facing the necessity of fitting a new social organization, as we did once fit the old organization, to the happiness and prosperity of the great body of citizens; for we are conscious that the new order of society has not been made to fit and provide the convenience or

[4] Woodrow Wilson, *The New Freedom* (Englewood-Cliffs, N.J.: Prentice Hall, Inc., 1961), ix. Unless otherwise indicated, all references to *The New Freedom* will be cited in the text by page number. It should be noted that Wilson's campaign of 1912 was called the "New Freedom." To avoid confusion, we shall not italicize the words "New Freedom" when referring to the campaign or to the political movement which it inaugurated. A more complete edition of Wilson's campaign speeches will be found in John W. Davidson, ed., *A Crossroads of Freedom* (New Haven: Yale University Press, 1956), cited hereafter as *Crossroads*. Davidson notes (on p. 4) that Hale's volume includes speeches which Wilson delivered prior to his nomination. For my purposes it will not be necessary to distinguish these speeches from those delivered by Wilson after his nomination.

prosperity of the average man. The life of the nation has grown infinitely varied. It does not centre now upon questions of governmental structure or of the distribution of governmental powers. It centres upon questions of the very structure and operation of society itself, of which government is only the instrument (19–20).

The function of government is to alter the economic conditions of society, for only by so doing can there be established a new order of society fitted to "the convenience or prosperity of the *average man.*" Although Wilson here seems to minimize the importance of governmental structure, he clearly understood that the structure of the original Senate had to be changed if the government was to alter the economic organization of the country and to foster a new social order conducive to the interests of the average man.

Not only was the economic establishment beyond the control of the average man; so too was the government. One of the major themes elaborated by Wilson throughout his campaign for the presidency was that American government had fallen under the control of "Big Business." Not that Wilson sought to encourage class warfare. "It is no use," he said, "denouncing anybody, or anything, except human nature" for the existing state of affairs (30). Even under a Wilsonian order, government and business, he admitted, would be closely associated. But the nature of the present association is intolerable and must be reversed: Government must control big business. On the one hand, and in the very interest of preserving the free enterprise system, government must enact legislation to eliminate monopolies and their stultifying effect on the commercial and industrial life of the nation. On the other hand, government must alter the relation between capital and labor to "prevent the strong from crushing the weak" (25). Under present conditions, the worker is but one of hundreds or thousands assembled in large factories run not by individual masters whom they know and with whom they have personal relations, but by the agents of huge corporations. Those who control these corporations make decisions which affect the lives of countless men, decisions made in secret and beyond the control of worker and government alike. The ordinary man is caught up in a heartless economic system. He confronts giant organizations as a mere individual, and his individuality is swallowed up by the purpose of the organization. These wrongs can only be corrected by government. New rules must be devised regarding the obligations and rights of employers and employees alike, defining their responsibilities to one another so that the country as a whole may prosper (20–21). In short, not only government, but the economic order of society, must become more democratic, more conducive to the well-being of the average man.

Wilson knew that he stood at the head of a revolution, and it is only in such terms that *The New Freedom* can be appreciated:

> We stand in the presence of a revolution,—not a bloody revolution . . . but a silent revolution, whereby America will insist upon recovering in practice those ideals which she has always professed, upon securing a government devoted to the general interest and not to special interests.
>
> We are on the eve of a great reconstruction. It calls for creative statesmanship as no age has done since that great age in which we set up the government under which we live. . . .
>
> I do not speak of these things in apprehension, because all is open and above board. . . . The whole stupendous program must be publicly planned and canvassed. Good temper, the wisdom that comes of sober counsel, the energy of thoughtful and unselfish men, the habit of co-operation and of compromise which has been bred in us by long years of free government, in which reason rather than passion has been made to prevail by the sheer virtue of candid and universal debate, will enable us to win through to still another great age without violence (32–33).

What distinguishes *The New Freedom*, or the "new spirit" of Wilson's public teaching, is its concern for the average man. The justification for that concern will not be questioned by the present writer. It would be remarkable indeed if the average man was not, from time to time, the victim of economic injustice, especially during the period of which Wilson speaks. It would also be remarkable if the average man was not himself unjust from time to time, whatever the period in question. As Wilson admitted, "It is no use denouncing anybody, or anything, except human nature." The dignity of human nature, however, requires the denial that any man is merely the excrescence of his environment, which is not to deny the importance of his environment for the realization of his dignity. What shall be placed in question, therefore, is not *the justification* of Wilson's concern for the average man, but rather the *centrality* of that concern in his public teaching and whether its centrality is conducive to human dignity or, more properly, human excellence. In the process I shall show that Wilson's teaching regarding the proper relationship between government and the average man constitutes a radical departure from the public teaching of the founders.

Consider, to begin with, the following passages from *The New Freedom*, the first of which alludes to Theodore Roosevelt:

> I am one of those who absolutely reject the trustee theory, the guardianship theory. I have never found a man who knew how to take care of me, and, reasoning from that point out, I conjecture that there isn't any man who knows how to take care of all the people of the United States. I suspect that *the people of the United States understand their own interests better than any group of men in the confines of the country understand them* (50) [italics added].

> I want the people to come in and take possession of their own premises; for I hold that the government belongs to the people, and that they have a right to that *intimate* access to it which will determine *every turn of its policy* (57) [italics added].

> Everything I know about history . . . has confirmed me in the conviction that the real wisdom of human life is compounded out of the experiences of ordinary men (59).

> Therefore, we have got to organize a government . . . which will consult as large a proportion of the people of the United States

as possible before it acts. Because the great problem of government is to know what the average man is experiencing and is thinking about (60).

Nobody who cannot speak the common thought, who does not move by the common impulse, is the man to speak for America, or for any of her future purposes (61) [italics added].

How striking is the contrast between these passages and *The Federalist*. The authors of *The Federalist* presuppose and address themselves to a deferential people, and their teaching reinforces the virtue underlying that deference, one which classical antiquity thought perfectly consistent with manliness, namely, modesty. Wilson, on the other hand, exalts the wisdom of the people and, by so doing, teaches them anything but modesty. Again, *The Federalist* emphasizes the *independence* of those whom the people entrust with the powers of government—which is but the corollory of the theme of popular deference. Only if statesmen exercise independent judgment can they possibly refine and enlarge the people's understanding of their true interests. Wilson, by exalting the wisdom of the common man, logically precludes statesmen from educating the people: Instead of affirming the independence of statesmen, he seems to encourage their servility. Indeed, to ensure their complaisance to the average man, he proposed, in *The New Freedom*, the institution of the initiative, the referendum, *and* the *recall*—all this in radical opposition to the representative principle as understood in *The Federalist*, a principle which unites the themes of deference and independence.[5] In short, Wilson reverses a fundamental aspect of the ruler-ruled relationship articulated with subtlety by the founders.

The subtlety of that relationship is well exemplified in *Federalist* 71, where Hamilton, with his characteristic mixture of caution and boldness, writes:

[5] See Wilson, *The New Freedom*, pp. 136–141. Wilson's denial that these proposals were "radical" and contrary to the representative principle requires no comment.

The republican principle demands that the deliberate sense of the community should govern the conduct of those to whom they intrust the management of their affairs; but it does not require an unqualified complaisance to every sudden breeze of passion, or to every transient impulse. . . . It is a just observation, that the people commonly *intend* the PUBLIC GOOD. This often applies to their very errors. But their good sense would despise the adulator who should pretend that they always *reason right* about the *means* of promoting it. . . . When occasions present themselves, in which the interests of the people are at variance with their inclinations, it is the duty of the persons whom they have appointed to be the guardians of those interests, to withstand the temporary delusion . . . (464–465).

When Hamilton speaks of the "means" of promoting the public good in this paper on the executive, he has in mind, in addition to the executive veto, the public policies initiated by the President. These policies are the means to the ends embodied in the Constitution. The means should be understood, however, as the translation of general notions into particular laws governing conduct and shaping opinion. But since the ends, as stated for example in the Preamble, are not univocal, the means become articulations of the meaning of those ends. From this it follows that the means are not and cannot be *politically neutral* with respect to those ends. Hence, those who possess the power of determining the means, possess, within broad limits, the power of shaping the political character of the regime. Unless this be clearly understood, we shall fail to grasp the profound difference between the teaching of the founders and the teaching of Wilson as regards the proper relationship between government and the people.

Now, when Hamilton says that "the people *commonly* intend the public good," he thereby implies that they do not *always* intend the public good. But whether they do or not, it is for the statesman to determine whether they have reasoned rightly about the means of promoting the public good. To do this, however, is to determine what constitutes the public good. What constitutes the public good is a *problem,* one whose solution requires political inquiry. It is for the statesman to engage in such inquiry and to be guided by conclusions arrived at through the exercise of independent judgment. If the people have not reasoned rightly about the means of promoting the public good, it then becomes the duty of the statesman to correct their errors, that is, to educate them.

In the passage from *Federalist* 71, Hamilton also said that the people "know from experience that they sometimes err"; that they are also beset by politicians "who flatter their prejudices to betray their interests." These are bold words; and the reader will recall even bolder words in *Federalist* 49, which dared to speak, in effect, of the limited intellectual capacities of the average man and of the need to cultivate among them certain "prejudices" for the sake of ensuring good government. Perhaps the people who read those words in 1788 differed in significant respects from the people addressed by Wilson in 1912? Perhaps the former were more deferential, the latter better educated? If so, how are we to explain the greater subtlety, the greater complexity, the greater profundity of *The Federalist* in comparison with *The New Freedom*?[6] Did Hamilton, who supposedly had little faith in the people, overestimate the people's learning or intelligence? What indeed was the intellectual caliber of the people who first read this timeless work of statesmanship? This question is preg-

[6] It may seem unfair to compare campaign speeches with articles written for newspapers, especially insofar as most of those articles were written by two men. But it should never be forgotten that the eighty-five papers contained in *The Federalist* were written or published on the same day and/or a few days apart from each other. Despite the brevity of time in which *The Federalist* was written—and by men actively engaged in politics—it constitutes, in the opinion of the present writer, one of the profoundest works on politics produced in this country, surpassing anything written by Wilson whose own works excel those of the vast majority of contemporary political thinkers. (I am well aware, of course, that some of the latter regard *The Federalist* as a "propaganda" tract. But I have sufficient confidence in the future to believe that this work of "propaganda" will be studied for its wisdom long after the works of these political thinkers are forgotten for their folly.) In any event, the real issue does not hang on comparing campaign speeches with newspaper articles, but on the differences between their respective audiences. This will be developed in due course.

nant with significance for the transformation of the American regime from a 'polity' to a democracy.

Still the fact remains that Wilson said the people were wise, or so he would have them believe in 1912 when he declared: "I have found audiences made up of the 'common people' quicker to take a point, quicker to understand an argument, quicker to discern a tendency and to comprehend a principle, than many a college class that I have lectured to."[7] Compare the rhetoric exemplified in *Federalist* 63, in which Madison speaks to the "people" on behalf of a Senate proposed by the Federal Convention: "To a people as little blinded by prejudice or corrupted by flattery as those whom I address, I shall not scruple to add, that such an institution may be sometimes necessary as a defense to the people against their own temporary errors and delusions" (409). In contrast, Wilson, having said that the people were wise (or the best judge of their own interests), could the more readily favor not only popular election of senators, but a provision for their recall as well. To favor the institution of the recall, however, is to admit, by implication, that the people were subject to "temporary errors and delusions" in their initial judgment regarding the character of those whom they elected to the Senate. But the recall would serve to correct such lapses and to protect the people against any senator whose conduct or whose stand on public policies was, in the opinion of his constituents, contrary to their understanding of their own interests. Whereas, for Madison, the members of the Senate would be in the position to educate the people, for Wilson, the people would be in a position to "educate" the members of the Senate.

In the New Freedom there emerges a new egalitarianism: "It is the duty [of law] to equalize conditions."[8] To be sure, Madison,

---

[7] Wilson, *The New Freedom*, p. 62. The sequel will be discussed later.

[8] *Ibid.*, p. 131. I am fully aware of Wilson's retention of the traditional notion of the self-reliant individual. But that notion is in tension with, if not undermined by, the major thrust of his teaching, a teaching which may be described as "pietistic egalitarianism," to distinguish it from the "relativistic egalitarianism" of such critics as Richard Hofstadter. See *Hofstadter*, ch. 10, "Woodrow Wilson: The Conservative as Liberal."

who opposed monopolies, also wished to level great fortunes and to raise the poor to a level of comfort. But this was to be accomplished by the "silent" operation of the laws, specifically, by laws abolishing primogeniture and entailed estates. With Wilson, however, the laws, or rather the lawmakers, were to "speak the common thought" and to "move by the common impulse." They were to speak for "ordinary men" who were to have "intimate access" to government, determining "every turn of its policy." Now government could indeed "equalize conditions," for it could use the Sixteenth Amendment—itself perfectly sound and consistent with a 'polity'—to tap an abundant source of revenue. And this it could justify precisely because, under Wilson's public teaching, the government existed for the sake of ordinary men. Government was no longer to protect the few from the many, so much as to protect the many from the few. This reversal of emphasis points to the difference between a public teaching appropriate to a 'polity' and a public teaching appropriate to a democracy. No single constitutional amendment better represents this reversal than that which enabled popular majorities to elect senators, such that today, the Senate, by virtue of the principle underlying at-large elections, is in many respects more democratic than the House of Representatives.

2

How markedly different was the teaching of Wilson the political scientist from the teaching of Wilson the popular orator. Thus, in 1887, twenty-five years before the New Freedom exalted the wisdom of the average man, Wilson published his seminal essay, "The Study of Administration," an essay whose principles were to dominate the teaching and practice of public administration in the United States for no less than sixty years. In this essay, Wilson had this to say about the average man:

> In government, as in virtue, the hardest of hard things is to make progress. Formerly the reason for this was that the single person who was sovereign was generally either selfish, ignorant,

timid, or a fool,—albeit there was now and again one who was
wise. Nowadays the reason is that the many, the people, who are
sovereign have no single ear which one can approach, and are
selfish, ignorant, timid, stubborn, or foolish . . . albeit there
are hundreds who are wise.[9]

Given this low opinion of the common man, it may seem absurd
to urge that statesmen "speak the common thought" and "move
by the common impulse," or to propose that senators be directly
elected by such a people and be subject to recall. And indeed,
in his doctoral dissertation, *Congressional Government*, published in 1885, Wilson wrote: "By the mode of its election and
the greater length of the term by which its seats are held, the
Senate is almost altogether removed from that temptation to
servile obedience to the whims of popular constituencies to
which the House is constantly subject, without as much courage
as the Senate has to guard its virtue."[10] Wilson admitted that the
Senate is as obedient as the House "to the more permanent and
imperative judgments of the public mind," but that "[i]t is valuable in our democracy in proportion as it is undemocratic" (IV,
125, 127). Whether Wilson is correct in describing the regime
as a "democracy," after admitting that the wealth of many members of the Senate "represents no class interests, but all the interests of the commercial world"—is a matter which need no longer
concern us (IV, 126). The point is that, during these years,
Wilson's teaching regarding the proper relationship between
government and the people differs radically from the teaching
evident in his presidential campaign of 1912. It would be a mistake to think, however, that the theoretical foundations of Wilson's political thought had undergone a radical transformation
during the interval.

In 1900, in his preface to the fifteenth printing of *Congressional
Government*, Wilson noted that the Senate no longer "faithfully

---

[9] *Papers*, V, 368, hereafter cited by volume and page number in the text. This
essay originally appeared in the *Political Science Quarterly* in the July, 1887,
issue. It was reprinted in the December, 1941, issue of the same journal.

[10] *Ibid.*, IV, 126.

represents the several elements of the nation's make-up," that "vested interests have now got a much more formidable hold on the Senate than they seemed to have sixteen years ago" (XI, 569). But what seems to have struck Wilson's attention most was the change that had apparently occurred in the House. The House, ordinarily fragmented, had become gradually integrated under the leadership of its Speaker, Congressman Cannon, and its powerful Committee on Rules. Wrote Wilson:

> This obviously creates, in germ at least, a recognized and sufficiently concentrated leadership within the House. . . . To this new leadership, however, as to everything else connected with committee government, the taint of privacy attaches. It is not leadership upon the open floor, avowed, defended in public debate, set before the view and criticism of the country. It integrates the House alone, not the Senate; does not unite the two houses in policy; affects only the chamber in which there is the least opportunity for debate, the least chance that responsibility may be properly and effectively lodged and avowed. It has only a very remote and partial resemblance to genuine party leadership (XI, 569–570).[11]

Meanwhile, and as a result of the Spanish-American War, the President had come to the forefront of affairs. "There is no trouble now about getting the President's speeches printed and read, every word" (*ibid.*). Also, as a result of civil service reform dating back to the Pendleton Act of 1883, "New prizes in public service may attract a new order of talent" (*ibid.*). And finally, "the new leadership of the Executive, inasmuch as it is likely to last, will have a very far-reaching effect upon our whole method of government. It may give the heads of the executive departments a new influence upon the action of Congress. It may bring about, as a consequence, an integration which will substitute statesmanship for government by mass meeting" (XI, 570–571).

Wilson's formal model, in terms of which these words were

---

[11] But see Wilson's essay "Cabinet Government in the United States," *ibid.*, I, 495. Though published in 1879, this essay refers to the dominant power of the Speakership.

written, was of course the parliamentary and cabinet system of the British constitution, a system operating under the unifying discipline of party government at the head of which stood the Prime Minister. Wilson's problem—*the* political problem of his life—was to superimpose this system upon the government of the United States. As early as 1879, when still a senior at Princeton, Wilson proposed the adoption of the British model in a published article entitled "Cabinet Government in the United States." And in the very year in which he completed *Congressional Government,* he had published another article entitled "Committee or Cabinet Government" which concludes with these words:

> Committee government [which Wilson used as another name for congressional government] is too clumsy and too clandestine a system to last. Other methods of government must sooner or later be sought, and a different economy established. First or last, Congress must be organized in conformity with what is now the prevailing legislative practice of the world. English precedent and the world's fashion must be followed in the institution of Cabinet Government in the United States (II, 640).

The methods by which Wilson sought to bring this revolution about have been proposed, in one form or another, by various political scientists to this very day. These methods assume two basic forms, one constitutional, the other extraconstitutional. Both have a common objective: to overcome the fragmentation of power involved in the constitutional system of checks and balances so as to make government responsive to the "people," meaning, popular majorities.

The constitutional method requires a series of amendments which would render more uniform the tenures of the three "elective" branches of government. Wilson proposed that the terms of the House and the Executive be extended, presumably to conform to that of the Senate. The immediate effect would be to increase the probability that one political party would gain an electoral majority so as to control both houses of Congress as well as the presidency. To increase this probability and, at the same time, to make the system more democratic, the mode of electing the Senate would be amended to conform to that of the House, so that the constituency of the one would become more like the constituency of the other. Although legislative power would remain divided, the division would be formal rather than real, at least insofar as the political complexion of the two houses of Congress became more uniform. Finally, to overcome the division of power between Congress and the Executive, and, at the same time, to simplify congressional-executive relations, Wilson proposed that the President be required to choose, for the members of his Cabinet (hence for the heads of the various executive departments), the leaders of the majority party in Congress, who in turn would be authorized to initiate legislation, thus dispensing with the committee system.[12]

Turning to the extraconstitutional methods of overcoming the system of checks and balances, here it will only be necessary to mention briefly Wilson's proposed reform of public administration. First of all, Wilson saw in the executive branch a fragmentation of power among the various administrative departments and agencies, each exposed to the influence of diverse interest groups. These departments and agencies, charged with the duty of faithfully administering the laws, were rent by partisan rivalry. As a consequence, administration was neither efficient nor duly responsible to Congress or even to the President. To overcome this fragmentation of power and its consequences, Wilson proposed a new system of public administration, one whose principles were politically neutral. To this end he urged the establishment of departments, in colleges and universities throughout the nation, whose principal task would be to train civil servants in what he called the "science of administration." Finally, to maintain their political neutrality, the administration

---

[12] See *ibid.*, II, 627–628. In an unpublished essay "Government by Debate," *ibid.*, II, 159–275, Wilson proposed that the heads of the executive departments be drawn solely from the House of Representatives; that the House, and not the Senate, be susceptible to dissolution by the President; and that the President hold office during good behavior (*ibid.*, II, 247, 245).

295

of the laws would no longer be a function of the President. The President would be the chief *political* leader of the government, not its chief *executive*.

These are the major constitutional and extraconstitutional "reforms" envisioned by Wilson. Clearly, such reforms would have constituted nothing less than a political revolution—a second founding—for Wilson, a more perfect union indeed. Accordingly, Wilson devoted the next twenty years of his life as a political scientist to hasten that revolution. He began where he could best begin, by changing men's opinions: opinions about the principles and purposes of good government; opinions about the proper relationship that should exist between government and the people; in short, opinions about that decisive question of politics, the question of *who should rule*. Wilson's answer, and the means by which he sought its realization, may be gleaned from "The Study of Administration."

In that essay Wilson, influenced by German writers, makes a fundamental distinction between *means* and *ends* analogous to that which Hamilton had made in *Federalist* 71. There is, however, a profound difference. Hamilton, it will be recalled, spoke of a distinction between the public good and the means of promoting the public good. The public good comprises the ends embodied in the Constitution. The means are not and cannot be politically neutral with respect to those ends, since the former are legislative elaborations of the latter or articulations of their meaning.[13] Hamilton makes it perfectly clear that the means or public policies ought to be initiated, more or less, by the Executive, but in any event by the government, and not by the people. In contrast, Wilson draws a radical distinction between public policies (as ends) and administrative policies (as means), and he contends that: "Administrative questions are not political questions. Although politics sets the tasks for administration, it

[13] To strike down an act of Congress as one that violates the meaning of some provision of the Constitution is itself to elaborate the meaning of the Constitution, which indicates that no decision of the Supreme Court is politically neutral.

should not be suffered to manipulate its offices" (V, 370–371). What seems to be ends for Wilson are means for Hamilton. How is this discrepancy to be explained?

For both Hamilton and Wilson, public policies are to be formulated by the government. For Hamilton they are means to ends, ends which ordinarily are beyond the reach of the people. For Wilson public policies are ends in themselves, and these ends are *not* ordinarily beyond the reach of the people. What is present in the political teaching of Hamilton, and what is absent in the political teaching of Wilson, is nothing less than the *Constitution!* It is missing from Wilson precisely because his model of government is the British constitution under which any law enacted by parliament is *ipso facto* constitutional.[14] For Wilson, as the headnote of this chapter indicates, the Constitution has become "our *form of government* rather in name than in reality."[15]

Now, one way of changing political reality without changing the political form is to change the *meaning* which men attach to the form. Thus, political reality can be changed by changing men's opinions about the meaning of administration. To Wilson belongs much of the credit of changing politics by defining administration as politically neutral![16] The introduction of this notion into the teaching of political science fostered a revolution. Administration was to be politically neutralized by making

[14] See Woodrow Wilson, *The State: Elements of Historical and Practical Practice* (Boston: D. C. Heath & Co., 1889), pp. 475–476, 490. Four chapters of *The State* will be found in Wilson's *Papers*, VI, 253–311.

[15] *Ibid.*, IV, 16. This was an exaggeration, or Wilson would not have dedicated his life to changing the Constitution. In any event, here we see the beginning and true significance of the "pragmatic" revolt against the Constitution during Wilson's era, a revolt which, in our day, has reduced the Constitution to wax work—and this, despite the fact that the external form of the British constitution has not been superimposed upon the reality of American politics.

[16] Wilson himself, however, was too serious and too keen a student of politics to maintain with entire consistency the now partially discredited dichotomy of politics and administration developed more fully and systematically by Frank Goodnow, *Politics and Administration* (New York: Macmillan Co., 1900). But see Wilson's "The Study of Administration," *Papers*, V, 372–373, for some difficulties regarding this dichotomy.

it "scientific." Administrative practices were to be governed by "scientific method," and the key concept imported from science (as well as from business) was the ethically neutral concept of *efficiency.* The systematic elaboration of that concept in relation to organizational structure (centralization versus decentralization), and to such organizational problems as personnel standards and allocation of resources, constitutes the science of administration. Although the concept of efficiency is ethically neutral, its exemplification in administration practices was intended to serve a moral end: It was to cleanse administration of the corruptions of the spoils system; it was to make administration *honest.* Civil servants would be chosen on the basis of technical competence (determined by competitive examinations) rather than on the basis of patronage or party loyalty. The assumption was that technical men are more likely to be honest than party men. Actually, the early civil service reformers of the 1870s and 1880s were more concerned with honesty than with efficiency. But by the turn of the century, the "moralistic" approach was replaced with the "scientific" approach. As one reformer said in 1907: "To be efficient is more difficult than to be good."[17] Besides, "Goodness is a false criterion for . . . we cannot agree upon its meanings."[18] "Good service" means "efficient ser-

[17] William H. Allen, *Efficient Democracy* (New York: Dodd, Mead & Co., 1912), xvii (first published in 1907).

[18] *Ibid.,* pp. 1–2. See Dwight Waldo, *The Administrative State* (New York: Ronald Press Co., 1948), pp. 192–193. To appreciate Wilson's superiority to contemporary reformers enamored of science, see his remarkable essay, "Princeton in the Nation's Service," where he says of science: *"it has given us agnosticism in the realm of philosophy, scientific anarchism in the field of politics. . . . Past experience is discredited and the laws of matter are supposed to apply to spirit and the makeup of society.*

"Let me say, this is not the fault of the scientist. . . . [Nevertheless] I should fear nothing better than utter destruction from a revolution conceived and led in the scientific spirit. . . . *Science has not changed the nature of society. . . . It has not purged us of passion or disposed us to virtue. It has not made us less covetous or less ambitious or less self-indulgent. On the contrary, it may be suspected of having enhanced our passions by making wealth so quick to come, and so fickle to stay.* . . . We have broken with the past and have come into a new world" (*Papers,* X, 29–30, Oct. 21, 1896). Despite these wise words, Wilson

vice." Thus it was that efficiency became the cardinal virtue, inefficiency the cardinal sin.

I shall now show that underlying Wilson's politically neutral science of administration is a revolutionary teaching having the profoundest moral significance. To begin with, the neutrality of this science and of its practitioners does not simply mean neutrality toward the various political parties of the regime, such that the same scientific administrator would be equally faithful and equally efficient regardless of which party happens to be in power. This in itself could have revolutionary implications.[19] But these very implications can be made evident by reflecting on Wilson's contention that the science of administration is universally valid or applicable to *all* governments regardless of their political character. He writes: "[W]e could grant democracy the sufficient honor of ultimately determining by debate all essential questions affecting the public weal, of basing all structures of policy upon the major will; but we would have found but one rule of good administration for all governments alike" (V, 377).[20] What does this mean for "good" administrators in different kinds of government? To be a good administrator one must efficiently carry out the policies or laws of the regime, by whomsoever determined. In a democracy, the good administrator will carry out the policies determined by the "major will," and his goodness will be measured in terms of the efficiency with which he performs this function. In a tyranny, the good administrator will carry out the policies of the tyrant, and his goodness will be

saw in the scientific conquest of nature and in the application of scientific method to administration the best hope of democracy. And as may be seen from the last sentence of the above passage, Wilson accepted the break with the past, a break which he accelerated in 1912 by his emphasis on "progress" and by his exaltation of the common man.

[19] See John Dewey and James H. Tufts, *Ethics* (New York: Henry Holt & Co., 1908), pp. 472–473, where the authors err in their distinction between "political questions" and "party issues" and also reflect Wilson's dichotomy between political questions and administrative questions.

[20] But see *Papers*, V, 363–364, 367–368, 378–379, for inconsistencies, and compare Aristotle, *Politics*, pp. 196–197, where this view is anticipated and virtually refuted.

measured in terms of the same criterion of efficiency. Notice, that both administrators *qua* administrators are good citizens: they each serve, and most efficiently, the ends of their respective regimes. The possibility that one administrator may be serving just ends, while the other may be serving unjust ends, does not affect the respective goodness or justice of these administrators: they are equally good or just so long as they are equally efficient. If a political observer were to say that one or the other of these good *citizens* is not a good *man*, this would not be relevant to the politically neutral science of administration, for political questions are not administrative questions.

This, of course, is the teaching of social science *positivism*. Wilson's dichotomy between administrative questions and political questions corresponds precisely to the positivistic dichotomy between questions of *fact* and questions of *value*. Science can verify, by empirical methods, the truth or falsity of propositions pertaining to fact. Science can teach us nothing about the truth or falsity of values. Such questions as: "How should men live?" "What is the best regime?" "What are the proper ends of government?" have elicited a welter of conflicting answers, none of which is more valid than another. The different answers of various philosophers are either culturally determined, relative to the regime or age in which they live, or they are merely expressions of subrational or purely subjective or personal preferences. Thus, while politics determines the ends of a regime, which ends have no universal validity, the science of administration determines the means by which to achieve these ends, and this science of the means *is* of universal validity. This is also the teaching of moral relativism and historicism.

Now, let this teaching sink into the minds of men. Is it not obvious they will cease to take seriously the question of ultimate ends or values? Will they not rather become preoccupied with immediate and narrow interests and with the *means* by which these may be most efficiently realized? Will they not cease to be concerned about such questions as "Who should rule?" or "What is the best form of government?" Formerly, said Wilson, "The question was always: Who shall make law, and what shall that law be?" But now, he continued, the most important question concerns *"how* law should be administered."[21] This, together with the question of *how* laws should be made, comprises the most important question of Wilson the political scientist. And it remains the most important political question for the ethically neutral, but policy oriented, political scientist of our own day.

Although Wilson was not a moral relativist, certainly not a consistent one, his thought bears witness to two of its forms, again, positivism and historicism. Both had gained a foothold in American higher education around the turn of the nineteenth century. In his essay on administration, which, to repeat, was published in 1887, Wilson gives witness to the influence of German historicism: "The philosophy of any time is, as Hegel says, 'nothing but the spirit of that time expressed in abstract thought'; and political philosophy, like philosophy of every other kind, has only held up the mirror to contemporary affairs" (V, 361). Despite this, Wilson could also say in that essay: "It is better to be untrained and free than to be servile and systematic"—this, in reflecting on the efficiency of Prussian administration as compared to administration in the United States (V, 368). But Wilson, again in contradiction to historicism, was sufficiently a positivist to believe in the universal validity of science; and it was the latter that was governing his dichotomy between administration and politics. On the other hand, it appears that he was too sober a person and sufficiently confident in the superior worth of his own ends or values to be a moral relativist. Nevertheless, moral relativism is an inescapable consequence of his basic teaching regarding the politically neutral science of administration. And it is precisely moral relativism, in blatant form, that eventually dominated the teaching of public administration and of political science in the United States.[22]

---

[21] *Papers*, V, 360–361 (italics added). The words "with enlightenment, with equity, with speed, and without friction" follow.

[22] See its leading exponent in the field of public administration, Herbert Simon, *Administrative Behavior* (New York: Macmillan Co., 1947).

It cannot be too strongly emphasized that moral relativism is hostile to the Constitution as a fundamental law superior to the evanescent will of popular majorities. It is hostile to the themes of independence and deference embraced by the representative principle discussed in *The Federalist*. Or, to put the matter another way, the notion of a politically neutral science of administration is hostile to the teaching of the founders, hence subversive of their 'polity.' Yet it is perfectly compatible with the democracy portrayed in Chapter II. But to see more clearly how Wilson's teaching about administration constitutes a radical departure from *The Federalist*, it would be best to examine Hamilton's remark on the subject in *Federalist* 68.

There Hamilton says: "Though we cannot acquiesce in the political heresy of the poet who says: 'For forms of government let fools contest/That which is best administered is best,' yet we may safely pronounce, that the true test of a good government is its aptitude and tendency to produce a good administration" (444).[23] But what is the test of a good administration? For Wilson the test is "efficiency": In a democracy, a good administration efficiently administers to democratic ends. For Hamilton, whose theory of government Wilson called "aristocratic," one, if not *the*, test of a good administration is its *energy*. As Hamilton says in *Federalist* 70:

> Energy in the Executive is a leading character in the definition of good government. It is essential to the protection of the community against foreign attacks; it is not less essential to the steady administration of the laws; to the protection of property against those irregular and high-handed combinations which sometimes interrupt the ordinary course of justice; to the security of liberty against the enterprises and assaults of ambition, of faction, and of anarchy (454).

Notice that energy in the Executive is only *a* leading character in the definition of good government. It cannot be *the* leading

[23] See *Papers of Wilson*, VII, 366.

character of good government precisely because Hamilton rejects the political relativism implicit in Pope's adage: "For
forms of government let fools contest/ That which is best administered is best." Nevertheless, let us assume that he did
regard energy as *the* leading character in the definition of a good
executive. The question is, what did Hamilton mean by "energy"? In *Federalist* 70, he speaks of the "ingredients" which constitute this energy in the Executive, among which he includes
"unity," "duration," and "competent powers." Clearly, these are
institutional ingredients of energy. If we return to *Federalist* 68,
however, and examine the paragraph which concludes with
Hamilton's reference to Pope, we see that it refers to the mode
of electing the President: "It will not be too strong to say, that
there will be a constant probability of seeing the station filled by
characters preeminent for ability and virtue. And this will be
thought no inconsiderable recommendation of the Constitution,
by those who are able to estimate the share which the executive
in every government must necessarily have in its good or ill administration" (444). Clearly, in addition to the *institutional*
ingredients of energy required for a good administration, also
required are certain intellectual and moral qualities—qualities
pertaining to the *man*, not to the *office*. But energy itself is descriptive of certain men, for example, men animated by "the
love of fame, the ruling passion of the noblest minds." Such
men will devote themselves to the study of different kinds of
regimes, ancient and modern; they will study human nature,
the characters of different types and classes of men; they will
school themselves in oratory, in the arts of persuasion. The acquisition of this extensive knowledge, and the development of
various rhetorical skills, will be necessary if they are to win a
diverse people to their cause and achieve everlasting fame.
Those ambitious men, it goes without saying, will possess great
energy—not merely physical, but intellectual and moral. But
what is truly remarkable (and relevant for a synthesis of classical and modern political science) is that energy, according to

Hamilton, is produced by *wisdom*, as well as by "activity" and "confidence."[24] We may conclude, therefore, that wisdom in the Executive is the leading character in the definition of good government and of a good administration.

What takes the place of wisdom and energy in Wilson's teaching is "science" and efficiency, or the then emerging notion of *pragmatism*. Today a President is not praised for being wise, but for being pragmatic. This is quite appropriate in an age which has enthroned the will of ever-changing majorities as the standard of wisdom. Hence we can understand why there was needed a politically neutral administration catering, with scientific efficiency, to the ever-changing wants and wishes of those majorities. Of course, the "fact-value" dichotomy is no more valid than the "means-ends" dichotomy, since the criteria of relevance affecting the selection of facts are value-laden.

3

Given the function of a politically neutral administration, it is understandable why Wilson wished to divorce the President from that function. As already noted, the President was to be the chief political leader, not the chief executive. As such, he was to be the leader of his party, a party in control of both branches of the legislature, a party representing the will of a popular majority. Although the President was to be the leader of his party, Wilson nevertheless conceived of him as the leader of the entire nation. This poses a difficulty. For in his role as the leader of the nation, the standards governing the President (the ends of public policy) are embodied in the Constitution; whereas, in his role as party leader, the standards governing the

[24] See *Farrand*, I, 73. Note that Hamilton here speaks of "vigour," which we have equated with "energy," as he himself does in *Federalist* 70 (p. 459, top) and elsewhere. Also, notice the qualities he attributes to a President in *Federalist* 71, which include "wisdom" and "confidence" (p. 467), and "courage" and "magnanimity" (p. 465). It should also be noted that Hamilton admits in *Federalist* 70 that a numerous legislature is "best adapted to deliberation and wisdom." But considering his opinion of the House and his expectations regarding the presidency, we need not be put off by his caution.

President are embodied in his party's program (or its general statement of public policy). Of course, a party's program may be said to be the means by which the ends of the Constitution, as interpreted by the party, are to be realized. But as we have seen, for Wilson, the Constitution exists in name only; it is form without substance; hence only the name, and not the substance, appears in his public teaching and qualifies his political intentions. The logical consequence is this: The President, as the leader of his party, is the leader of but a part of the nation, its most numerous part, the majority. And this means that, just as the Constitution exists in name only in the political teaching of Wilson, so too does the "nation." Whatever his real intentions, Wilson's teaching results in an identification of the whole with a part: the nation with the nation's *ordinary men*.[25]

The case is otherwise with Hamilton. For Hamilton the President was to be the leader of the nation and of the nation only. Not because Hamilton failed to anticipate political parties; to the contrary he speaks of them in *The Federalist*.[26] But Hamilton saw parties competing in Congress, which is not to say he antici-

[25] To avoid misunderstanding, certain comments are necessary at this point: (1) It is true that Wilson regarded America as a unique nation. Its historic mission, he believed, was to promote *equality* among the nations of the world and to establish thereby a basis for universal brotherhood. See Harry M. Clor, "Woodrow Wilson," in Morton Frisch and Richard Stevens, eds., *American Political Thought*, pp. 208–209. It is also true that Wilson defined "modern democracy" as "not the rule of the many, but the rule of the *whole*." *Papers*, V, 76. In both cases, however, the arithmetic principle of equality is dominant, a principle which has its own logic, whatever Wilson's intentions. Wilson certainly wanted statesmen to represent the nation as a whole (*ibid.*, I, 243). But for a statesman to "move by the common impulse" is to move by the impulse of *ordinary men* (whose wisdom Wilson publicly extolled). Surely Wilson himself did *not* speak for the nation as a *whole* when condemning monopolies. (2) Now the preceding and following discussion, insofar as it relates to party government, does not necessarily apply to nations other than the United States. I have especially in mind Great Britain. There, what makes it possible for the leader of a party to represent the nation as a whole is the deferential character of the British people, which gives the nation an organic unity. Wilson seems to have recognized this fact (*ibid.*, X, 473). But as already indicated, his egalitarianism is destructive of deference.

[26] See especially *Federalist* 76, p. 493.

pated nationally organized parties comparable to those of a later day. In any event, the President, as described by *The Federalist*, would not be the leader of any party, and his mode of election was intended to preclude such an eventuality.[27] This helps to explain the various qualities Hamilton attributes to, or envisions for, the President (as well as the functions he ascribes to the presidential office). Because the President will not be subject to the limitations of party loyalty and party programs, *The Federalist* can emphasize the President's "independent exertion of his powers"; his dar[ing] to act his own opinions with "vigor and decision"; his opposing, when necessary, "the ill humors of the legislature" as well as the "inclinations of the people"; his acting with "fortitude" and "courage," with "wisdom" and "integrity," and, with that adornment of the virtues, "magnanimity."

The teaching of *The Federalist* is one of statesmanship, not of party leadership. Its statesmanship requires independent judgment, mediating between the ends or generalities of the Constitution and concrete particulars. In contrast, party leadership, although it does not preclude independent judgment, confines the latter to the mediation of *lower levels of generality* and concrete particulars. To put the matter another way, the aims of a political party existing under the Constitution are less general than the aims embodied in that Constitution, which is to say they are relatively narrow and limited and closer to the concrete. This fact restricts the latitude of independent judgment exercised by the party leader. And since the party represents but a part of the nation, the scope of what it conceives to be the purposes of the regime is narrower than the purposes of the regime as a whole. Accordingly, a President, who is in fact, and not only in name, the leader of the *nation*, requires a degree of intellectual and moral excellence surpassing that of a President who is merely the leader of a party. Or, to put the matter still another way: The standard of statesmanship required of one who is president of a 'polity' surpasses the standard of states-

[27] See my *The Philosophy of the American Constitution*, ch. 9, on the presidency.

manship required of one who is president of a democracy. This conforms to Aristotle's teaching that the excellence of the ruler is relative to the regime (to be measured, however, by the standard of the best regime). That excellence, of course, is practical wisdom, the sum of the political virtues. These virtues are required in greater abundance in a 'polity' than in a democracy, precisely because a 'polity' requires statesmen capable of coordinating and of bringing into mutual intensification a richer variety of values and relationships. It may even be said that the qualities of statesmanship which Hamilton speaks of in connection with the President require a regime some of whose attributes shade into the aristocratic spectrum.

Because the excellence of the ruler is relative to the regime, statesmen may be expected to evaluate regimes by the standard of their own, or by the standard in terms of which they may wish to transform their own. By comparing how different statesmen evaluate the same regime, evidence may be assembled relevant to the differences between their political principles. For example, one way of illuminating the differences between Wilson's and the founders' understanding of justice or of who should rule is to see how they differ in their classifications of ancient regimes. Thus, in his book *The State*, a remarkable work on comparative government, Wilson commends Aristotle for his general classification of regimes, but takes issue with him on whether it was properly applied in the evaluation of actual regimes. Specifically Wilson contends that what was called "democracy" in antiquity was in fact "only a broader Aristocracy."[28] Now at this point I am not concerned with the truth or falsity of Wilson's contention. The significance of that contention lies elsewhere, namely, in the fact that what Wilson regards as a "broader Aristocracy" was regarded as a democracy by the founders and by Aristotle alike! Contrary to Wilson, neither the founders nor Aristotle thought that the institution of slavery, as it existed in Athens,

[28] *The State*, pp. 604, 599–600, and *Papers*, VI, 262. But see *ibid.*, VI, 258, where Wilson omits the 'polity' from Aristotle's classification and substitutes democracy.

was sufficient to disqualify a regime as democratic. The reason is that they were not dominated so much by quantitative criteria. In *The Federalist*, Madison condemns the Athenian form of government not because it condoned slavery, but because it was a pure democracy, one whose turbulence and unbridled passions resulted in "decreeing to the same citizens the hemlock on one day and statues on the next." To be sure, Madison deplored slavery in the United States. Nevertheless, for him, the *quality* of those who participate in political rule, rather than the *quantity* of those who do *not*, is more decisive for the political character of a regime.

The fact that Wilson regarded as aristocratic what Madison regarded as democratic may be symptomatic of the ascendency of democratic standards of evaluation or of a process pointing to the transformation of a 'polity' into a democracy.[29] It should be perfectly clear, however, that Wilson was not a radical democrat.[30] Yet, is it not also clear that Madison would have been ap-

[29] But see *Farrand*, I, 318. It would be logically fallacious to conclude that, because Wilson classified Hamilton's theory of government as "aristocratic," the latter is really democratic—this, on the assumption that Athens, which he classified an aristocracy, was in truth a democracy. Any classificatory scheme which ultimately rests on quantitative criteria is arbitrary in its application to actual regimes. Thus, Wilson's saying, for example, that the federal government was not democratic may be true even if his classification of Athens as aristocratic is false. Everything depends on the validity of Wilson's criteria on the one hand, *and* on their proper application to concrete facts on the other. Here, compare *Diamond*, p. 55, who tries to support his democratic interpretation of *The Federalist* by citing Jefferson as having *said* it was "the best commentary on the principles of government which was ever written." Diamond's unexpressed assumptions are: (1) Jefferson was a genuine democrat; (2) a genuine democrat would not *say* what Jefferson *said* about *The Federalist* unless he *believed* that this work was democratic; (3) Jefferson would not have *believed* it was democratic unless it was *in truth* democratic. (Ergo, *The Federalist* is democratic!) *None* of these assumptions is proven by Diamond. Indeed, Jefferson's letter to John Taylor of May 28, 1816, suggests that the only branch of government he deemed democratic was the House of Representatives. See Edward Dumbauld, ed., *The Political Writings of Thomas Jefferson*, p. 52.

[30] According to *Hofstadter*, p. 241, Wilson was a "conservative" and a "spokesman of the past." But it should be understood that Hofstadter regards anyone to his own right as a "conservative." (Of course, this leaves him in a compromised position vis-à-vis the New Left. 'Tis a wise father who knows his son.)

palled at Wilson's teaching regarding the proper relationship between government and the people as unambiguously evidenced by the latter's position on the recall? Is it not clear that, quite apart from the justice of his intentions, Wilson's project to unify political power so as to render it responsive to popular majorities is precisely what Madison feared most in *Federalist* 10? That unification of power envisioned by Wilson requires nothing less than ideologically disciplined political parties acting under presidential leadership. But this is the most efficient means of facilitating what Madison defined as majority faction, namely, a majority of citizens "united and actuated by some *common impulse* of passion, or of interest, adverse to the rights of other citizens, or to the permanent and aggregate interests of the community" (54) (italics added).

The unification of political power is the political side of the Wilsonian project; the other side is his politically neutral administration. *Both* halves of this project were necessary if democracy were to be made efficient. Wilson understood very well that the inefficiency of democracy is not to be attributed primarily to a lack of efficient administration. He knew that the major obstacle to efficient democracy was the Constitution itself. How indeed can one make democracy efficient in a 'polity'? How can one readily introduce into a 'polity' a system of public administration dedicated to the equalization of conditions? The political neutrality of his science of administration notwithstanding, Wilson knew that: "The study of administration, philosophically viewed, is closely connected with the study of the proper distribution of constitutional authority. . . . If administra-

Incidentally, on the political continuum, the New Deal of Franklin Roosevelt (who was not liberal enough for Hofstadter) stands between the decent democracy of Wilson and the indecent democracy of the New Left. What the New Deal inaugurated was a parceling out of power, including legislative power, not inconsistent with the New Left's theme of "participatory democracy." What made Roosevelt's own politics decent was the moral stature and political power of the man. Once he was gone, however, there was nothing left but the precedent of his "pragmatism" which, followed by lesser men, resulted in a further degradation of democracy.

tive study can discover the best principles upon which to base such distribution, it will have done constitutional study an invaluable service. Montesquieu did not, I am convinced, say the last word on this head" (V, 373). But Wilson himself did not require such a study. He was already convinced that Montesquieu's theory of checks and balances, or the division of powers exemplified in the Constitution, was grossly inefficient—at least for democracy. That theory was based on distrust of power. But, said Wilson: "*Trust is strength* in all relations of life; . . . it is the office of the constitutional reformer to create conditions of trustfulness. . . . There is no danger in power, if only it be not irresponsible. If it be divided . . . it is made irresponsible" (*ibid.*). If democracy is to be made efficient, it will be necessary for the "constitutional reformer to create conditions of trustfulness." But among whom? Who, indeed, will have to be persuaded that political power cannot be unified without constitutional reform, and that such reform is necessary if democracy is to be made efficient? It would be no easy task to change the constitution of a 'polity,' especially if its founders had fostered a "political creed" resistant to change, had succeeded in winning the "prejudices of the community" over to the side of the government. The citizens of such a 'polity' would be rather "conservative"— and so the American people seem to have been judging from Wilson's campaign speeches. For example, addressing a street crowd in West Virginia, Wilson declared:

> [W]hat strikes me about the men who control the special interests of this country is that they don't know anything but their own special business, and a man who doesn't know anything but his own special business isn't in contact with the people. . . . He doesn't know what it is to sympathize with . . . those great bodies of unknown men who never get their names in the newspapers, who are never consulted by influential persons, who never do anything but struggle along and wonder and hope in the midst of their struggles.

Now mark what follows:

These great masses of the American people are a very solid body of men of integrity. These great masses of men constitute one of the most *conservative* bodies of people in the world. The wonderful thing about America, to my mind, is this: that it has allowed itself to be governed by persons who were not invited to govern it for almost a generation. The wonderful thing about the people of the United States is their infinite patience, is their willingness to stand quietly and see things are done by a few persons whose names they know [i.e., certain Senators], and have yet never laid the hand of disorder upon any arrangement of the government.[31]

If the great mass of the people were in fact conservative, no wonder Wilson called them "selfish, ignorant, timid, stubborn, or foolish." Perhaps their "foolishness" consisted in their deferential attitude toward men of wealth and power—or was it in their reverence for the Constitution? Perhaps we ought to understand by "stubbornness" their resistance to constitutional change; by "timidity," their apprehensiveness about the unforeseen consequences of such change; by "ignorance" their failure to appreciate the need for change? Finally, perhaps the "selfishness" of this people living in a 'polity' consisted in their acting on the principle that justice does not require government to "equalize conditions." If so, much time and effort, as well as great powers of persuasion, would be required to convert such a people to the revolution which Wilson was to speak of some twenty-five years later in *The New Freedom*.

[31] *Crossroads*, p. 447 (italics added). See p. 329, n. 20, below, concerning Herbert Croly, *The Promise of American Life* (New York: Macmillan Co., 1912), p. 148 (cited hereafter as *Croly*), where Croly calls the American people "morally indifferent" to unscrupulous economic and political power.

CHAPTER IX

Wilson's Revolutionary Rhetoric:

The Politics of Compassion

W¹

HILE transforming a 'polity' into a democracy is difficult
enough, transforming it into an *efficient* democracy is infinitely
more difficult. The reason is this. The method of decision-making
in any regime is the rule of the majority—the majority being
more extensive in a democracy. To this method Wilson was
committed, but only so far as concerns the formulation of public policy. As for the means of administering public policy,
such a method leaves too much to chance, is grossly unscientific,
and renders democracy especially inefficient. Wilson, in other
words, was dedicated to what has been called a "democracy of
ends," not to a "democracy of means." Here again is to be seen
the dichotomy of politics and administration. But here too may
be discerned the principal difficulty in establishing a scientific
administration in a democracy, a difficulty not encountered in
other regimes. For as Wilson recognized, the people in a democracy not only determine the ends, but too often they determine
the means as well. As he says, they are apt to be "meddlesome."
Not that Wilson wanted the people to look on his politically
neutral administration with political neutrality. Rather, he
thought they should perform the role of "authoritative critic."
But how can they perform such a role well if, as Wilson admits,

they are "ignorant"? Still, the *first* problem is to persuade people to want a *new* system of administration, no easy task in a 'polity' whose citizens are also "stubborn" or resistant to change.

Wilson was fully aware of these difficulties. With undemocratic wisdom he recognized that the political education of a people ought to *precede* its political activity. In other words, public opinion ought to be enlightened *before* it is sovereign. The trouble is, said Wilson in his essay on administration: "In trying to instruct our own public opinion, we are dealing with a pupil apt to think itself quite sufficiently instructed beforehand" (V, 374). This suggests that Wilson's pupil was apt to be lacking intellectual modesty. Such a pupil might not readily defer to Wilson's teaching; he might stubbornly resist change. Here is how Wilson formulated what was in fact his own problem: "[W]herever public opinion exists it must rule. . . . Whoever would effect a change . . . must first educate his fellow-citizens to want *some* change. That done, he must persuade them to want the particular change he wants. He must first make public opinion willing to listen and then see to it that it listen to the right things" (V, 369).

To educate public opinion, it is first necessary to educate those who shape public opinion; above all, *one must educate the educators*. Accordingly, Wilson's first objective was to "politicize" American colleges and universities, a task facilitated by what he then saw as "an admirable movement towards universal political education now afoot in this country." Indeed, Wilson declared:

> The time will soon come when no college of respectability can afford to do without a well-filled chair of political science. But the education thus imparted will go but a certain length. *It will multiply the number of intelligent critics of government*, but it will create no competent body of administrators. . . . It is an education which will equip legislators, perhaps, but not executive officials. If we are to improve public opinion, which is the motive power of government, we must prepare better officials as the *apparatus* of government. . . .

313

[These officials must be] prepared by a special schooling and drilled, after appointment, into a perfected organization, with appropriate hierarchy and characteristic discipline ... (V, 375).[1]

There is nothing insidious in Wilson's project. He well knew that the university is the major source of ideas, hence the major source of political change. He also knew that intellectuals, by and large, have a powerful tendency to be critical of government, especially when removed from positions of political power; and ever since the founding generation, the role of the intellectual in American government had steadily declined: government was now under the control of "big business," public opinion be what it may. So, inasmuch as intellectuals are already prone to desire *some* change, the task for Wilson—the educator of educators—was to "persuade them to want the change he want[ed]." With that accomplished, these educators, teaching in various colleges and universities, could "then see to it that [public opinion] listen to the right things." This could the more readily be achieved given the "movement towards universal political education now afoot in this country."

It was precisely "political" education that Wilson was alluding to in the presidential campaign of 1912. Only recall his saying in *The New Freedom:* "I have found audiences made up of the 'common people' . . . quicker to understand an argument, quicker to discern a tendency . . . than many a college class that I have lectured to," which he explained by adding: "not because the college class lacked intelligence, but because college boys are not in contact with the realities of life, while 'common' citizens are in contact with the actual life of day by day; you do not have to explain to them what touches them to the quick" (62). For these presumably affluent college boys, explanations or lectures regarding the injustices of American society were necessary *and* forthcoming; and, however slowly many of these college boys may have learned their lessons, we may suppose that many learned them well.

[1] Italics added, except for "apparatus."

Now let us pause for a moment to appreciate the fact that the study even of minutiac—provided one's ultimate criteria of relevance are not trivial—can illuminate some of the deepest secrets of life and of statesmanship. The reason is that every thing is related, in different degrees of relevance, to everything else. Every part bears a perspective of the whole; and the problem of the philosopher is to comprehend the whole by incorporating into himself and bringing into unity the disjoined and partial perspectives of men. Do not look for wisdom in grand ideas or lofty notions alone. A casual remark may be equally revealing of a universe of things. Often, it is what men say but hardly deign to dwell upon that reveals the deeper strata of their thought or of their thought's presumptions. In our psychologistic age, steeped in the trivializations of the behavioral sciences, the *word* is hardly taken seriously anymore. Thought is murdered by thought, explained away as the epiphenomena of subrational forces or of subterranean passions. The passions thus dissolve the very thought which reveals their primacy. But even the passions are not given their due by the likes of such thought. The love of fame, for example, is reduced to a lust for power or the mere craving for approval or affection by the psychologically insecure or emotionally deprived personality.[2] This "nay-saying" psychopathology of politics, which is so much the part of the "political" education of college boys today, cannot conceive of how any healthy individual could painstakingly plan and deliberately undertake to transform the way of life of an entire people, its laws and institutions, its beliefs and habits, its attitudes toward men and things, its sense of right and wrong. Yet, Woodrow Wilson was such a man.

While a student at the College of New Jersey, Wilson entered into a "solemn covenant" with his friend and classmate, Charles Talcott (who was eventually to become a member of Congress). In 1883, four years after his graduating from Princeton, Wilson revealed, in a letter to his fiancée, the nature of that covenant.

[2] Here I have in mind Hofstadter's borrowing from Lasswell. See *Hofstadter*, pp. 238–239.

We pledged, Wilson confided, "that we would school all our powers and passions for the work of establishing the principles we held in common; that we would acquire knowledge that we might have power; and that we would drill ourselves in all the arts of persuasion, but especially in oratory . . . that we might have facility in leading others into our ways of thinking and enlisting them in our purposes."[3] Three years later, in a letter to Talcott himself, Wilson wrote:

> I believe . . . that if a band of young fellows (say ten or twelve) could get together . . . with reference to the questions of the immediate future, [and] should raise a united voice in such periodicals, great or small, as they could gain access to, gradually working their way out . . . to a position of prominence and acknowledged authority in the public prints, and so in the public mind, a long step would have been taken towards the formation of such a new political sentiment and party as the country stands in such pressing need of—and I am ambitious that we should have a hand in forming such a group.[4]

Between the dates of these two letters, Wilson had completed *Congressional Government*. In the concluding paragraph of that work, Wilson declared:

[3] *Papers*, II, 500, to Ellen Axson (Oct. 30, 1883). In another letter to his fiancée, Wilson speaks of his heart's *first*-primary-ambition and purpose, which was, to take an active, if possible a leading, part in public life, and strike out for myself . . . a *statesman's* career." *Ibid.*, IV, 287 (Feb. 24, 1885).

[4] *Ibid.*, V, 389–390 (Nov. 14, 1886). See Gamaliel Bradford, *The Lesson of Popular Government* (2 vols.; New York: Macmillan Co., 1899), II, pp. 542–543, who writes: "Our system of politics has imposed . . . shackles upon the popular will; and they are so firmly riveted that nobody ever thinks of revolt and a direct appeal to the people. Yet that is the one hope, that a strong man, knowing exactly what he wants and why he wants it . . . might overleap the caucus politicians and compel a nomination even within the party. It is the disorganized and tentative position of the Democratic Party which offers the best oportunity for this. . . . He must possess a will which nothing can daunt. . . . Above all, he must have a firm faith in the quality of the force upon which he relies, the mass of public opinion . . . that mighty force which alone is adequate to overcome the usurpation of all government by the legislature." Bradford cites Wilson's *Congressional Government* several times.

The Constitution is not honored by blind worship. The more open-eyed we become, as a nation, to its defects, and the prompter we grow in applying with the unhesitating courage of conviction all thoroughly-tested or well-considered expedients necessary to make self-government among us a straight-forward thing of simple method, *single, unstinted power,* and clear responsibility, the nearer will we approach to the sound sense and practical genius of the great and honorable statesmen of 1787. *And the first step towards emancipation from the timidity and false pride* which have led us to seek to thrive despite the defects of our national system rather than seem to deny its perfection is a fearless criticism of that system (IV, 179).[5]

These words were addressed more to intellectuals than to the average man. Those intellectuals had to be persuaded toward Wilson's grand design for America's second founding. Many still revered the Constitution and were convinced of the abiding wisdom of the first founding. Others might hesitate to join Wilson out of "timidity," for Wilson was calling for a revolution which, though peaceful in intention, harbored fearful uncertainties for the future. Finally, pride of intellect alone might prevent still others from subordinating themselves to a course whose ideas were not their own. Wilson had indeed to acquire extensive knowledge of men and things and to school himself in all the arts of persuasion if he was to succeed in "leading others into [his] own way of thinking and enlisting them in [his] purposes."[6]

Before probing more deeply into the strategy and significance

[5] Italics added. See previous note on Bradford.

[6] There is little point in speculating on the extent of Wilson's influence on other intellectuals. I might mention the fact that his works are cited by such writers as John Dewey, *Ethics,* p. 435; Charles E. Merriam, *A History of American Political Theories* (New York: Macmillan Co., 1924), pp. 316–317, first published in 1903, who speaks of Wilson, among others, as an authority; James Allen Smith, *The Spirit of American Government* (Cambridge: Harvard University Press, 1965), pp. 51–52, 185, first published in 1907. A good bibliography of contemporaneous works will be found in Frederick A. Cleveland, *Organized Democracy* (New York: Longman, Green & Co., 1913). One of the three headnotes of his book is taken from Wilson.

of Wilson's rhetoric, it will be helpful to contrast his political situation and objectives with that of the founders.

Wilson's mission required for its success two bases of support: one among intellectuals—the educators of the "people"—and the other among the "people" themselves, without which, of course, he would have no political leg to stand on. Wilson could not appeal to the rich, as a class, if only because the effectiveness of rhetoric depends primarily on the interests of the audience; and it was precisely the interests of the rich, or of the big commercial and industrial corporations, that he had to attack if his new economic order was to be established.[7] In contrast, the founders sought to establish not a new economic order so much as a new political order.[8] Accordingly, they could appeal to, and gain support from, not only intellectuals, but commercial, manufacturing, and agricultural interests whatever their size. To be sure, all these groups were divided over the Constitution, but the divisions among them did not preclude the founders from addressing their various passions and interests. We saw, for example, that the authors of *The Federalist* appeal to men's *ambition*, their love of honor, their desire to pursue great objects conducive to the public good. Accordingly, Hamilton and Madison show by rational argument how the institutions and purposes of the new government would give full scope to men's ambitions while securing the public good. At the same time, they could address men's *avarice*, or the hopes and fears men harbor regarding their own interests or property. But again *The Federalist* could show—still by rational argument—that the new government was well-designed to enhance the wealth of the nation and

[7] Of course, Wilson disclaimed that he was attacking any class, and again and again he denied any intention of stirring up class hatred. I do not question the purity of his intentions. I only note that the disclaimer itself points to the probable consequences. (See *Crossroads*, pp. 28–30, 40, 54, 273.) It will therefore be assumed, in what follows, that the reader is neither politically naive nor politically cynical.

[8] Of course, the political had great consequences for the economic; but these were sectional and distant and did not place in question the power of the rich as a class.

to protect the interests of property, of whatever kind, against the danger of majority faction. Finally, Madison and Hamilton could couch their arguments in somewhat democratic language so as not to disaffect literate but ordinary men or provide too many "handles" for demagogues. It should be clear, however, that their main objective was to persuade the intellectuals and the propertied interests of the nation (or at least of New York). This political strategy was clearly anticipated by Madison during the Federal Convention when he boldly declared: "We ought to consider what was right and necessary in itself for the attainment of a proper government. . . . [A]ll the most enlightened and respectable citizens will be its advocates. Should we fall short of the necessary and proper point, this influential class of citizens will be turned against the plan, and little support in opposition to them can be gained to it from the unreflecting multitude."[9] Precisely, or if only, because Madison and Hamilton appealed primarily to "the most enlightened and respectable citizens," and not to the "unreflecting multitude," *The Federalist* conforms to a higher standard of rhetoric than that which is evident in *The New Freedom*. Furthermore, the very fact that intellectuals were divided, that the various propertied interests were divided, that state politicians were divided—each and all over the Constitution—demanded of the authors of *The Federalist* a rhetoric of the highest order, a rhetoric yet to be equaled, let alone surpassed, by any American statesman. But Madison and Hamilton were equal to the task, not only because they were skilled rhetoricians, but because their rhetoric, informed by classical and modern political philosophy, embodies the principles and purposes of a 'polity,' the best practical regime.

Whereas *The Federalist* was addressed primarily to the better educated and wealthier members of society, *The New Freedom*

---

[9] *Farrand*, I, 215, and see Hamilton's speech of June 18, *ibid.*, I, 305–306, 311 (bot.), 285, concerning the passions and interests which must be attracted to the central government. See also Madison, *Writings*, V, 95, n. 1, for Rufus King's report to Madison on the progress of the Massachusetts ratifying convention.

was addressed primarily to the "unreflecting multitude." Wilson himself had written in "The Study of Administration": "The bulk of mankind is rigidly unphilosophical, and nowadays the bulk of mankind votes" (V, 369). Because he sought these votes to achieve the objectives of *The New Freedom*, his rhetoric embodies an unambiguously democratic teaching. And yet, it should be understood that Wilson's public teaching was *more* democratic than the political opinions of his pupil—the average voter whom he sought to *persuade*. Wilson was not exaggerating when he said that Americans are "one of the most conservative bodies of people in the world." Hence, to appreciate the sequel, it should be borne in mind that, in 1912, two out of three Americans lived in rural areas, and were it not for the split in the Republican party, Wilson very likely would not have been elected President of the United States.[10] (Indeed, Wilson was just barely re-elected in 1916 despite the loyalty of the "solid South" to the Democratic party.)[11] What must also be kept in mind, however, is the difference between Wilson's public teaching and the teaching of the founders; for the "difference," to borrow from Aristotle, "is not so much between better and worse sorts of the same thing, as one between totally different things" (256). That difference will be further elaborated by an analysis of Wilson's revolutionary rhetoric.

2

The problem is this: How are men to be persuaded toward a course of action involving the radical but peaceful transforma-

[10] See *Historical Statistics of the United States*, p. 14. I am here classifying as "rural" places with a population of less than 10,000. Although Wilson received 42 percent of the popular vote in 1912, his vote in the electoral college was 435 to 88 for Roosevelt and 8 for Taft. Had Roosevelt been the candidate of the Republican party, there is good reason to believe that Wilson would not have received more than 228 electoral votes, or more than 100 electoral votes outside the South.

[11] In 1916 Wilson received 277 electoral votes to 254 for Hughes. See *ibid.*, pp. 686, 682, 684, and compare the electoral vote by state for the elections of 1908 and 1916.

tion of a 'polity' into a democracy? It goes without saying that the rhetoric required to persuade intellectuals prone to ambition, men who seek honor and wish to pursue large and long-range objectives involving the public good, differs from the rhetoric required to persuade ordinary or unambitious men, men whose political horizons are limited by parochial beliefs and by the more immediate interests and necessities of life. To persuade ordinary men to support the radical transformation of the political and economic order of society here in question, and to accomplish this without bloodshed, the regime orator will have to bear the following considerations in mind.

(a) To begin with, he must break down those "prejudices of the community" "without which perhaps the wisest and freest governments" cannot endure. These are the "noble lies" portrayed in Plato's *Republic* and clearly alluded to in *Federalist* 49. These are the "myths" which support the "establishment," those commonly shared opinions grown ancient and venerable, those salutary prejudices which the ordinary man never questions precisely because they are commonly shared, ancient, and venerable—never questions because the "reason" of the ordinary man, unlike that of the philosopher, is "timid and cautious when left alone." It will indeed require a bold and thoroughly rational man to question and succeed in undermining those ancient beliefs, and he will want to enlist a small group of like-minded persons to the aid of his cause. He knows that those ancient beliefs or prejudices constitute the bonds of the community, the subtle network of ties, of sympathies and even antipathies, that hold the *different parts* of the community together.

(b) There are two major prejudices which the regime orator will have to undermine. The first, of course, is the prejudice of conservatives that identifies the good with the old, the prejudice which results in the ordinary man's reverence for the Constitution. To him it may be admitted that the Constitution well served the needs of people living in the past. But he must be made to see why it cannot serve the different needs of the present, or why it is not well-designed to "provide the convenience or prosperity of the average man" today. The second prejudice is that which associates wealth and power with merit, and which results in the ordinary man's deferential attitude toward his "betters," more precisely, those who run the "establishment." To undermine this deference, it will be necessary to elevate the ordinary man's opinion of himself and to lower his opinion of the "establishment." No great oratorical skill is required to flatter the ordinary man. But to lower his opinion of the rich and the powerful and, at the same time, to keep a reign on his passions, informing or modulating them with a fundamental teaching about man, society, and government, requires great rhetorical skill indeed.

(c) It will be obvious that the two prejudices discussed above—the one resulting in reverence for the Constitution, the other in deference for those who run or control "establishment" —together comprise the community's no longer questioned solution to the problem of who should rule. Wilson makes it very clear that the "people" ought to rule, but that the Constitution hinders them and will continue to so long as reverence removes it from thorough criticism. At the same time, however, certain wealthy and powerful men prevent the "people" from ruling and will continue to so long as they are deemed worthy of deference. But the regime orator knows that the ordinary man does not want to rule: he does not desire the honors of office so much as the enjoyments of wealth. He is quite content to let others rule so long as he can enjoy material prosperity and so long as public office is not used for private gain. Accordingly, the ordinary man must be given reason to believe that he is not enjoying material prosperity, and that public office is being used for private gain. Having learned this, it will be easier to undermine his prejudices regarding the question of who should rule. Indeed, the skillful rhetorician will usually address the ordinary man's interests *before* addressing his reason or prejudices. For ordinary men are not likely to surrender their prejudices until the latter appear in conflict with their interests.[12]

[12] The explanation for this is not to be found in the supposed primacy of

(d) Finally, there is the problem, not of arousing, but of sustaining the passions. The passions of men can only be sustained by ideas—in the case of ordinary men, by rather simplistic ideas —explanatory of the causes of injustice. ("You do not have to explain to them what touches them to the quick.") Accordingly, the regime orator, guided by Wilson's objective, will modulate the least discriminating but mutually supporting passions of *resentment* and *compassion* by fixing and concentrating the minds of the "people" against the *external cause* of human suffering, namely, the economic system exemplified by "big business." In their ignorance, many people might think that this system is part of the unchanging and unalterable nature of things, rather than an artificial contrivance of men that can be changed by men. They must learn that the system, *as a system* (and not merely its particular manifestations), is unjust; that it serves the interests of the few, not of the average man; that it is cold, impersonal, and heartless in its unconcern for the sufferings of men, women, and children. Since the ordinary man's thoughts and feelings are limited by the more immediate interests of life, his intellectual and moral horizon can only be enlarged by evoking *class* sympathies and antipathies. Furthermore, appeal to class is especially necessary when addressing

men's interests or passions—behavioral social scientists to the contrary notwithstanding. Ordinary men sometimes stubbornly adhere to their prejudices to the *knowing* sacrifice of their interests (taking the term "interest" in its material sense). Of two presidential candidates, let one have the reputation of being an "intellectual," and many ordinary men will not vote for him even though he be the more sympathetic with their interests. On the other hand, many ordinary men will support or oppose a war policy or an appeasement policy largely because one or the other succeeded or failed some *twenty years earlier;* and this they will do *without knowing* which policy is *today* more conducive to their immediate or to their long-range interests. Furthermore, commonly shared opinions are not held as firmly as the opinions which an individual has acquired through his own experience in life. In either case, no man relinquishes his opinion about any matter unless it is shown or made to appear *false.* Finally, a distinction must be made between untutored opinion—however right—and the insight of the philosopher. Socrates sacrificed his "interests" for philosophy. Of course, behavioral social science is the science of ordinary men, although it does not even do ordinary men complete justice.

the average man, for only recall the words of *Publius:* "The reason of man, like man himself, is timid and cautious when left alone, and acquires firmness and confidence in proportion to the number with which it is associated." The intellect of the average man is timid because the average man is politically timid: he has no great desire for honor, no great love of fame—that passion which emboldens the intellect and which enlarges the horizons of the few to embrace the common good. Such is the timidity of the ordinary man that he will not ordinarily support a revolution, however just and peaceful, unless he is fortified by numerous others of his own kind. What will be fortified by number is not only his heart but his "reason" or intellect. This, in brief outline, is the strategy underlying Wilson's rhetoric. Some of the details of that strategy will now be examined, but primarily with a view to illuminating its significance for the revolution in question.

Wilson's rhetorical problem may be reformulated as follows: How to undermine those "prejudices" which stood in the way of his ultimate objective, which was to establish American government on a new foundation, namely, the equalization of conditions. The equalization of conditions, as the foundation for the New Freedom, involved and required a *new* understanding of equality, one that differed significantly from the *old*. The old equality originated in the Declaration of Independence, which spoke of all men being created equal. That equality, as Lincoln understood, meant that all men, *qua species, possessed* certain natural or unalienable rights, among which is the right to life, liberty, and the pursuit of happiness. Viewed holistically, nothing in the Declaration suggests that *all* men, *qua individuals*, are entitled to the actual *exercise* of those rights without qualification. Unless statesmen were oblivious of what they were doing, the mere fact that the Declaration was incorporated into several state constitutions which had property qualifications for voting and for office proves the contrary. (This fact, by the way, refutes the interpretation of the Constitution as a "conservative reaction" to the supposedly democratic principles of the Declaration.) Those property qualifications did not constitute a denial of the equality or of the rights proclaimed in that document. Indeed, they are perfectly consistent with the notion of government based on the consent of the governed so long as that notion is understood to include a rational principle. For no less than age qualifications which they presuppose, property qualifications may be intended to increase the likelihood of independent judgment or of rational choice in the making of political decisions. Think of a person reaching the "age of consent." Here "consent" presupposes his having achieved a certain maturity of reason on the one hand, and a certain stability of will on the other. The person may now be regarded as a moral agent. He acts out of motives larger than his own pleasure or advantage. He is duly concerned about the good of others. And should he have property of his own, this provides reasonable assurance that, in deliberating on public problems, he will not consent to any unlawful deprivations of the property of others. Viewed in this light, government based on the consent of the governed may be construed as a *method* of pursuing and securing natural rights. As a method it requires rational and systematic inquiry. It presupposes that the conclusions of such inquiry will reflect the enlightened will or the "*deliberate* sense of the community"; that these conclusions will result from "reflection and choice" and not from "accident and force." Accordingly, the institution of property qualifications for voting and for office may itself be regarded as the conclusion of an inquiry into the most expedient means of insuring the intellectual and moral integrity of the consent method of government, the ultimate end of which is to secure the equal right of all men to life, liberty, and the pursuit of happiness.[13]

As a rational method of reaching political decisions, the consent method of government attends to the patterns and prob-

[13] See Albert J. Beveridge's speech on the annexation of the Philippines in the *Congressional Record*, XXXIII, Pt. I, 704–705, 707 (Jan. 9, 1900). Not only does Senator Beveridge's interpretation of the Declaration support my own (see Appendix I), but his speech is symptomatic of a regime which has yet to experience the political ascendency of democratic thought and emotions.

abilities of human behavior under a variety of different circumstances. For example, a property qualification for voting is a conclusion (or an inductive generalization) based on data regarding the behaviors of propertied and propertyless men. Analysis of individual instances reveals (so the conclusion implies) that there is a high probability that propertyless men will not live up to the intellectual and moral standards required for the consent method of government, the rationality of which depends on freedom from compulsion. For the political judgment of necessitous men is especially susceptible to the influence and control of others, primarily the rich. A moderate property qualification may therefore serve to prevent the rich from buying the votes of the poor in order to form, say, a coalition against the middle class.[14] This restriction of the suffrage would serve to promote not only the rule of the middle class, but also those qualities peculiar to a middle-class regime, again, moderation, deference, and justice. Furthermore, these qualities increase the likelihood that rulers, hence the laws, will be neutral as between the rich and the poor. The property of the rich will be protected, but so too will the rights of the poor to life, liberty, and the pursuit of happiness. Those rights include, of course, the right of *anyone* to vote or hold office upon meeting the requisite qualifications. In other words, any individual possessing those qualifications lawfully *merits* the privilege of exercising the rights he always possessed *qua* man, but which he may only now exercise *qua* individual.

In discussing the equality of all men as regards their natural or unalienable rights, a distinction was made between the *possession* of these rights *qua* species, and the *exercise* of those rights *qua* individual. Henceforth I shall refer to the former when speaking of a person's *rights*, and to the latter when speaking of a person's *privileges*. Rights are defined, as it were, by nature, privileges by law, whether written or customary.[15] Ac-

[14] A property qualification also prevents the poor from *selling* their votes to the rich. See p. 207, n. 28, above.

[15] The distinction between positive and natural law suggested here is only a

cordingly, the equality spoken of in the Declaration does not extend to privileges, for if it did, all men would have a natural right to happiness rather than to the *pursuit* of happiness. What the equality of the Declaration requires is that no man be precluded by law from *earning* any established privileges on the basis of factors extrinsic to human nature or to those intellectual and moral qualities that distinguish the human from the subhuman. In other words, no individual may, as a matter of principle, be denied the privileges enjoyed by other individuals in his community on the basis of parentage, class origin, or race.[16] This means that the Declaration implicitly denies hereditary privileges. Consistent therewith, the Constitution explicitly prohibits titles of nobility. Both documents thus affirm the principle of *equality of opportunity.*

Now, in his "Notes for Lectures in a Course on the Elements of Politics" dated March 5, 1898, Wilson wrote: "*Equality at the starting-point, natural inequality at the goal.*" And again: "*Equality in initial rights; but in privileges equality based upon fact and performance only.*"[17] Properly qualified, these notations are consistent with the true teaching of the founding (as may be seen in *Federalist* 10 and 35, and most clearly in *Federalist* 36). What must be recognized, however, is the probability of a political contradiction between "natural inequality at the goal" and "equality at the starting point," since *the goal exists at the starting point.* Society can never begin as a *tabula rasa.*[18] We are born and nurtured amidst inequality, both natural and artificial, and *which* form of inequality is which is far from being always

provisional one. The politics of magnanimity transcends this distinction without succumbing to legal positivism as that doctrine is generally understood. See below, pp. 438–440.

[16] He may nevertheless be denied such privileges as a matter of *public necessity,* depending on the consequences for competing values.

[17] *Papers,* X, 470 (italics in the original).

[18] Compare the *tabula rasa* to the "ordinary position" set forth in John Rawls, *A Theory of Justice* (Cambridge: Harvard University Press, 1971), pp. 17–21. Note Rawls's facile use of the terms "natural" and "reasonable" to justify attitudes and opinions which, at least to the few, may well be regarded as antinatural and unreasonable.

clear. The statesman cannot equalize the conditions of society without leveling the natural inequality existing among men. The point is that perfect justice is not available. For example, when Wilson calls for the equalization of conditions, he has partly in view the elimination of monopolies so that competition will be free *and* equal. But in one respect monopoly, no less than any advantage some may enjoy over others, exemplifies as well as stifles natural inequality, thus making conditions at the "goal" and at the "starting point" just as well as unjust. As an economic system, monopoly is no less just in principle than a political arrangement which gives "one man, one vote" regardless of his intellectual and moral character. Such an arrangement virtually insures the rule of mediocrity which, from a political point of view, is neither simply just nor simply unjust, since it could be worse and it could be better. But when, in addition to calling for the equalization of conditions, Wilson calls upon rulers to "speak the common thought" and "move by the common impulse," he is, for all practical purposes, making an *ideal* or public standard out of mediocrity. (If the "common thought" and the "common impulse" are to be made truly effective, however, society will eventually require that universities be filled with students of ordinary language as well as students of ordinary behavior, most of whom may be quite extraordinary as technicians but quite ordinary as men. For it is hardly to be supposed that when mediocrity is ensconced as the public standard that such a standard will not invade the university.) Not that this was Wilson's *intention*. But his intention is beside the point of this inquiry, which is to elucidate his *public* teaching, the teaching internalized by the common man, the man Wilson sought to enlist in his cause.

Wilson tried to teach the common man a new freedom based on a new equality. This was no easy task. For the old equality, as Wilson knew, embodied a principle of *inequality*. Contrary to almost universal opinion, equality of opportunity is not a democratic principle but a synthesis of democratic and aristocratic values. (This should become increasingly obvious in view of the present-day movement toward "equality of result," an academically inspired notion befitting a society serving the common if not the "last" man.) Be this as it may, and as suggested earlier, equality of opportunity means that no station in life, or no privilege which society may confer, can, in principle, be denied to any person on grounds other than *merit*. The rewards of merit constitute advantages not enjoyed by those who have yet to *earn* them. Those who have yet to earn them are not *dis*advantaged; nor have they been *de*prived of their rights. They retain the right to *earn* the privileges *earned* by others. This is perfectly consistent with the principle equality of opportunity, since a person's opportunities in life depend not only on external circumstances, but on his own intellectual and moral qualities as well. Some make the best of their "'opportunities"—meaning their talents as well as their situation—some do not.[19]

From this it should be evident that the principle of equality of opportunity involves the notion of *proportionate* equality: to each according to his desert. This was the old equality, one that was embodied in the Constitution as a whole. The Constitution secured that equality even though many did not grasp its aristocratic significance (secured it the better, perhaps, for that very reason); until, of course, the Wilson era. The logic of Wilson's public teaching denied the right of any individual to enjoy any privileges whatever.[20] Obliterated, as a consequence, was the

[19] If only because he attributes natural inequality or unequal natural endowments among men to chance, Rawls denies that any individual *deserves* whatever advantages he derives therefrom (*ibid.*, p. 15). From this it logically follows that no individual deserves *any* advantage he may enjoy—none whatsoever! For if you should speak of someone as deserving this reward or that position of honor because of his long and arduous efforts, one might reply by saying that the very magnitude of his efforts may be traced to some natural endowment which chance allotted him, but which he did not "deserve." See Mill, *Representative Government*, p. 285, where he writes: "In proportion as success in life is seen or believed to be the fruit of fatality or accident, and not of exertion, in that same ratio does envy develop itself as a point of national character." See pp. 336–338 below.

[20] See *Croly*, p. 209, where he writes: "The democratic state . . . should only discriminate against all sorts of privilege." Croly contends (p. 151) that "All

distinction between the possession and the exercise of a right, hence the distinction between man *qua* species and man *qua* individual. Under a dispensation characterized by the equalization of conditions, all men *qua* individuals would exercise the rights they possess *qua* species. The species would thus be elevated above the individual—but under the facade of individuality.[21] Henceforth, what is *common*, what is *ordinary*, what is *average*—not what is *distinctive*—will be the standard of who or what shall rule.

It should be understood that the equalization of conditions advocated by Wilson involved infinitely more than the prevention, let alone the control, of monopolies. Monopolies engaged in interstate commerce could in any event be controlled by Congress in virtue of its power to "regulate commerce among the several states." What the equalization of conditions entailed was nothing less than the transformation of the commerce clause into a national "police" power, enabling Congress to equalize the relations between employer and employee within the several states themselves.[22] Such an extension of congressional power

---

Americans, whether . . . 'predatory' millionaires or common people . . . accept the principle of 'equal rights for all and special privileges for none.'" If this were *really* so, how are we to explain the moral indifference he attributes to "plain people" toward special privilege (p. 148)? Of course, people may profess a principle and be apathetic when it is violated. But is Croly mistaking indifference for *deference?* (See also pp. 198–203, 32–36, 454.)

[21] This is not to deny Wilson's genuine desire for "individuality," whatever this term may have meant for him. But men as diverse as Tocqueville, J. S. Mill, and Nietzsche make it clear that individuality cannot flourish in egalitarian societies.

[22] This is contradicted by Woodrow Wilson in *Constitutional Government in the United States* (New York: Columbia University Press, 1961), pp. 178–183, first published in 1908 and cited hereafter as *Constitutional Government*. Nevertheless, Wilson (on p. 185) regards "production" as part of "commerce," contrary to *United States* v. *E. C. Knight Co.*, 156 U.S. 1 (1895), and thus removes the major economic prop to federalism. Incidentally, in the history of the commerce clause and of "substantive due process" may be traced the transformation of the 'polity' into a democracy. See *Champion* v. *Ames*, 188 U.S. 321 (1903), and compare Chief Justice Fuller's dissent with Justice Holmes's dissent in *Hammer* v. *Dagenhart*, 247 U.S. 251 (1918). The issue *appears* as the division of power between the federal and state governments. In reality, it is a conflict

would subvert the principle of federalism. It would result in a uniform system of legislation defining the rights and obligations of both employers and employees on such matters as wages, hours, prices, working conditions, and, as will be seen in a moment, the transaction of business as a whole. Furthermore, the government would not be acting vis-à-vis the two parties as an impartial arbiter, appearances to the contrary notwithstanding. By Wilson's own admission, the government would "speak the common thought" and "move by the common impulse." It would create a "new order of society," one "made to fit and provide the convenience or prosperity of the average man." To advocate the equalization of conditions is to advocate, as Wilson publicly avowed, a veritable revolution.

Again and again Wilson speaks in *The New Freedom* of a "new" order as opposed to a "old" order (21). The new calls upon government to equalize conditions. That this point had to be argued suggests that many ordinary men still adhered to the old, that they were sufficiently conservative to believe that justice did not require government to equalize conditions. Perhaps they were conservative enough to think that the proper function of government was to protect each person in his lawful possessions and privileges? Whatever the case, Wilson did not contend that those who controlled big business had no legal right to their wealth and power.[23] In fact, he often acknowledged their honesty, if only to forestall the accusation of stirring up class hatred—an intention he *repeatedly* disclaimed.[24] On what

between the "many" and the "few" over the possession and *use* of property. See also *Munn v. People of Illinois*, 94 U.S. 113 (1877); *Allgeyer et al. v. Louisiana*, 165 U.S. 578 (1897); *Holden v. Hardy*, 169 U.S. 366 (1898); *Lochner v. New York*, 198 U.S. 45 (1905), especially Holmes's dissent; and *Croly*, pp. 351–352.

[23] The distinction between ownership and control of corporate property will be deliberately obscured in the following argument, but without affecting the validity of its intentions.

[24] Wilson also repeatedly disclaimed demagoguery. These disclaimers are indicative of the character of his audience as well as of the real thrust of his rhetoric. Today, the regime is so thoroughly democratic that no politician need fear the charge of demagoguery.

grounds, therefore, could he call upon government to eliminate monopolies and to regulate the relations between employer and employee so as to provide for "the prosperity of the average man"? It was certainly not sufficient to say, as Wilson frequently did, that monopolies stifled competition, invention, and efficiency. That would hardly touch the ordinary man "to the quick" or bring down upon Wilson the accusation of arousing class hatred. Men are moved by anger, and anger is the passion of justice. Hence, the entire economic system must be shown to be unjust. Wilson went so far as to call it a "special form of tyranny." Thus, in *The New Freedom* he declared:

> By tyranny . . . we mean control of the law, of legislation and adjudication, by organizations which do not represent the people, by means which are private and selfish. We mean, specifically, the conduct of our affairs and the shaping of our legislation in the interest of special bodies of capital and those who organize their use. We mean the alliance, for this purpose, of political machines with selfish business. We mean the exploitation of the people by legal and political means (43).

Selfish business interests, Wilson contended, could exercise a veto over government by means of their agents in the Senate. Note well the rhetoric of the following passage:

[T]he conservative people [meaning, the nation as a whole] are concerned about the direct election of United States Senators. I have seen some thoughtful men discuss that [issue] with a sort of shiver, as if to disturb the original constitution of the . . . Senate was to do something touched with impiety, touched with irreverence for the Constitution itself. But the first thing necessary to reverence for the United States Senate is respect for United States Senators. I am not one of those who condemn the . . . Senate as a body; for, no matter . . . how questionable the practices or how corrupt the influences which have filled some of the seats in that high body, it must in fairness be said that the majority in it has all the years through been untouched by stain. . . (137).

This is an example of good democratic rhetoric. For while the audience might be impressed by Wilson's fairness regarding the Senate as a whole, it will tend to identify the whole with its corrupt part, especially when Wilson goes on to say: "But you need not be told . . . how seats have been bought in the Senate; and you know that a little group of Senators holding the balance of power has again and again been able to defeat programs of reform upon which the whole country had set its heart; and that whenever you analyzed the power that was behind those little groups you have found that it was not the power of public opinion, but some private influence. . ." (137).[25] In short, the tyranny of big business extended to government, so that the entire "power structure" served the interests of the few, not of the many.

Still, despite the resentment which Wilson's criticism might evoke in the average man against the selfish practices of big business, it was hardly sufficient to persuade him, especially if he were conservative, that justice required the equalization of conditions. Such a persuasion would require the articulation of justice in a new meaning horizon.

As Wilson knew, virtually all men agree that perfect justice requires a division of goods according to desert or merit. (They will agree to the principle, but not to what the principle requires in practice.) But a perfectly just division would result in some men having *less* than they actually possess, while others would have *more* than they actually possess; and the laws, which take little notice of each individual's worth, protect only his actual possessions. From this it follows that the laws are not wholly just or consistent with the requirements of perfect justice. In-

---

[25] During and immediately after the black riots of the 1960s, the highest officials of American government could be heard telling the rioters that "although Negroes have been victims of injustice for three hundred years, violence will not be tolerated." If anything impressed those rioting blacks it was not the "fairness" of the confession of injustice, nor the words "violence will not be tolerated," but rather, the *confession per se and* the words "Negroes have been the victims of injustice for three hundred years." This is an example of *bad* popular rhetoric, especially when practiced by the heads of the "establishment."

deed, the laws give protection to an unequal distribution of wealth among men even though some men have more than they deserve, while others have less than they deserve.

Accordingly, Wilson had to persuade the average man that those who controlled big business did not deserve the wealth they possessed or the power they exercised. It was not enough to say they were "selfish," or that they exercised undue influence over government. For the average man was very likely to respect or admire those "selfish" enterpreneurs—respect them because he respected wealth and power. Here again is that old "prejudice" of the ordinary man who associates wealth (and power) with merit. It was this prejudice that Hamilton alluded to in *Federalist* 35 where he said, in effect, that "mechanics" will defer to the political judgment of the "merchant" or entrepreneur for the protection of their interests. And this prejudice was to help secure property. But it was this same prejudice that Wilson set out to undermine and had to undermine if he was to transform the American 'polity' into a democracy.

Since Wilson did not deny the honesty of those who controlled big business, there were but two ways by which he might persuade the average man that these entrepreneurs were unworthy of his deference. First, he could place in question their entrepreneurial skills or intellectual powers in terms of which the average man might deem them deserving of their present estate. Accordingly, in *The New Freedom*, Wilson declared:

> Some of the men who have exercised this control [over the economic system] are excellent fellows; they really believe that the prosperity of the country depends upon them. They really believe that if the leadership of economic development in this country dropped from their hands, the rest of us are too muddle-headed to undertake the task. . . .
>
> As a matter of fact, their thought does not cover the processes of their own undertakings. As a university president, I learned that the men who dominate our manufacturing processes could not conduct their business for twenty-four hours without the as-

sistance of the experts with whom the universities were supplying them (55).

So, the big brains behind big business are the brains of the universities. If deference is owing to anyone, it is to these universities (or to the university-trained hirelings of big business who could as efficiently and unselfishly serve the many as the few).[26] Indeed, the efficiency of the economic system and the prosperity of the nation, Wilson suggests, would be considerably greater "if the leadership of economic development" were transferred from its present hands to those of professional men, some of whom are in fact "the very bone and sinew of the industry of the United States."[27]

Still, even if those who control the economic establishment are not exactly intellectual giants, their wealth and power might nonetheless be attributed to long and painstaking effort requiring much diligence and self-discipline. What the author of *The New Freedom* proclaimed, however, was this: "Most of us are average men; very few of us rise, except by fortunate accident, above the general level of the community about us" (60). In other words, the success of those who have acquired great wealth and power is to be attributed not to their intellectual and moral qualities, so much as to *luck*. (And, of course, a capitalistic system enlarges the role of luck or chance in human life.)

Now, there would be no point in trying to undermine the average man's respect for these entrepreneurs unless there still prevailed in the United States that prejudice which associated wealth (and power) with merit. Did Wilson not say in West Virginia: "The wonderful thing about America . . . is . . . that it has allowed itself to be governed by persons who were not

[26] Wilson, or at least the average man, could hardly have been aware of the implications of his (Wilson's) remarks. Without these universities, monopoly and the evils he associated with corporate power could hardly have existed!

[27] *The New Freedom*, p. 55. See, also, Woodrow Wilson, "Democracy and Efficiency," *Atlantic Monthly*, 87 (March 1901), 291.

invited to govern it for almost a generation"?[28] This speech, it will be recalled, tacitly acknowledged the deferential attitude of most Americans toward business and political leaders alike, an attitude that prevailed, it seems, in 1912. Insofar as Wilson succeeded in undermining that deference—the deference of another "silent majority"—he could not but succeed in profoundly changing men's understanding of justice and, with this, their opinion regarding the all important question of *who should rule*. Indeed, this undermining of deference toward the few is but the other side of Wilson's public praise of the many. It is the ordinary man, not men from the "privileged classes or the educated classes," whose judgment we must defer to and "by whose judgment," said Wilson, "I, for one, wish to be guided" (60).

Having had revealed to them the fortuitous character of worldly success, hence the groundlessness of their deferential attitude toward men of wealth and power, the average man was now more susceptible to the Wilsonian persuasion that justice requires government to equalize conditions. Why, indeed, should government protect the few whose success is to be attributed to "fortunate accident" rather than to their own merit?

3

The previous analysis will now be reformulated in preparation for the yet deeper strata of Wilson's public teaching. First, Wilson had to justify, by argument, the notion that justice requires government to equalize conditions. This presupposes that the existing conditions among men were not only unequal, but that such inequality was not widely regarded as unjust (at least not with any depth or intensity). Wilson had therefore to persuade the many toward a contrary position, and this he attempted to do by changing their opinions about the *causes* underlying the unequal conditions prevailing in American society. Common opinion held, or so it may be assumed, that inequality was due

[28] See p. 311 above.

largely, though not entirely, to the unequal distribution of ability and virtue among men. Luck also affected the issue, favoring some and not others. Still, men are not equally endowed with the ingenuity and the heart to take advantage of good fortune or to overcome the setbacks of its opposite. What Wilson did (consciously or otherwise is of no concern to this inquiry) was to encourage the notion that the fundamental cause of inequality among man is the result of chance, and that chance does not fall within the domain of moral action.[29] The consequences of this teaching for human life are sweeping and profound. They may be illuminated by contrasting Wilson with Madison and Hamilton.

Again, to say, as Wilson does, that "very few of us rise, except by fortunate accident, above the general level of the community about us" is to suggest that the fundamental cause of inequality among men is the result of chance. The effect of this is to minimize the merit of the few who do rise above the common level. But to minimize the merit of the few is to minimize the intellectual and moral differences between the few and the many. It is to minimize the significance of the unequal faculties which Madison speaks of in *Federalist* 10, the very faculties from which the rights and unequal distribution of property originate. Madison admits, of course, that the inequality of men's faculties is a dispensation of nature. But he also admits that men's faculties are "everywhere brought into different degrees of activity, according to the different circumstances of civil society" (55). This suggests that the inequality existing among men is the result of both nature and nurture where chance intervenes in one domain as well as in the other. Yet Madison does not question, on principle, the unequal distribution of property resulting either from the unequal gifts of nature or from the accidental circumstances of birth. Indeed, he goes so far as to teach the public that the first object of government is to protect the unequal faculties from which the rights of property originate, which is to say, in effect, that government ought to protect the unequal distri-

[29] See p. 34 above, and compare what follows with the teaching of Rawls.

bution of property itself. In view of such a teaching, Madison cannot be said to have insinuated the notion, which Wilson's *words* may be interpreted as having insinuated, that *nature is unjust*. This helps to explain why Madison did not expect government to rectify the "injustices" of nature by equalizing conditions. Perhaps, like Hamilton, he did not deem nature unjust at all, despite its unequal distribution of faculties among men. Perhaps both of these statesmen exemplify Nietzsche's "yea-saying" spirit, one that harbors no resentment against nature or against nature's privileged few.[30]

That Wilson should speak of privilege as the result of fortunate accident rather than of merit exemplifies the ascendency of the democratic personality and stands in striking contrast with the aristocratic sensibilities of men like Hamilton. Both Wilson and Hamilton verbally agree that men should be rewarded on the basis of merit; but whereas Hamilton affirmed, Wilson denied, that such rewards convey any personal privileges. Here, consider again a passage from *Federalist* 36: "There are strong minds in every walk of life that will rise superior to the disadvantages of situation, and will command the tribute due to their merit, not only from the classes to which they particularly belong, but from the society in general." In this passage the meaning of the word "merit" is of decisive significance, for it marks the difference between Hamilton and Wilson. For Hamilton, "merit" includes *intrinsic* worth, pertaining to the person himself, though measured by universally valid standards of human excellence. Certain "strong minds" will rise superior to the disadvantages—the accidents—of humble birth and circumstance. Their virtues will be recognized by society as a whole, by rich and poor, by educated and uneducated. Their virtues, however, will not be measured simply on the basis of their social utility. Hence the merit of these exceptional men will not be measured solely in terms of the good they have done or might do for society in general. "The tribute due to their merit"—and here Hamilton has in mind public office—is something owing them partly by virtue

[30] See footnote 19 of this chapter.

of their own inherent excellence. And these exceptional persons can *command* that tribute (and with effectiveness in a society consisting of deferential citizens). But this suggests that the reward of public office conveys some *personal* privilege not revocable by the mere will or pleasure of others.[31]

Wilson would have none of these aristocratic motifs. A senator's office, for example, is not his property. It does not invest him with any rights over his constituents—such as the right to hold that office for six years, or the right to be governed by the dictates of his own judgment. His office is a trust, and he is solely a trustee. Whatever privileges attach to the office, they belong to the office, not to the person. He was rewarded that office not in deferential recognition of his intrinsic merit, but for his presumed ability to serve the interests of his constituents.[32] This being so, a senator—indeed, any public officer—should be subject to recall.

The institution of the recall perfectly exemplifies Wilson's attempt to undermine the deferential foundations of American society and, with this, the ruler-ruled relationship governing the 'polity.' Although Wilson never so much as envisioned a non-deferential society, such a society is logically entailed by his public teaching about the ordinary man. Indeed, if government and society are to be ordered with a view to the convenience of the ordinary man, then universities should be organized for the purpose of providing a steady supply of technicians dedicated to the same end, which is to say that the educated should serve the uneducated.[33] This is turning nature on its head. But it was

[31] Precisely in these terms should we understand Chief Justice Marshall's decision in *Marbury* v. *Madison*, 1 Cranch, 137, 155, 162, (1803): Marbury had a vested right to his office; that office was his property.

[32] However often *The Federalist* may speak of rulers serving the interests of the people, those rulers could, within broad limits, choose the terms of their service as well as determine, again within broad limits, the nature of those interests. See Wilson, *Papers*, II, 223.

[33] See p. 329, n. 18, above. Wilson's Princeton inaugural speech of 1902 makes it clear that he subordinated theory to practice (even though he spoke of their union). In some respects, Wilson's speech comes close to the contemporary notion of the university as a social service institution. See Francis

necessary to do this if the ruler-ruled relationship established by the founders was to be undermined.

It was said earlier that nature involves a ruler-ruled relationship exemplified by the relation between parents and children which itself points to the rule of the wise over the unwise. Even though the founders did not establish an aristocracy, their public teaching is in accordance with nature. As Madison says in *Federalist* 57: "The aim of every political constitution is, or ought to be, first to obtain for rulers men who possess most wisdom to discern, and most virtue to pursue, the common good. . ." (370). To be sure, this teaching, *in a paper dealing with the House of Representatives*, may be in tension with the sequel, namely, that the *electors* of those rulers are "Not the rich, more than the poor; not the learned, more than the ignorant. . ." (371). But nature inclines us to seek the best practical regime when the best in theory is not available.[34] Besides, an argument can be made that ordinary men have a just claim to participate in political rule on grounds of their contribution to the common good. Madison's teaching acknowledges that claim without denying the *principle* that the wise *ought* to rule the unwise. Wilson's teaching virtually identifies the common good with the convenience or prosperity of the ordinary man, and, consistent therewith, advances the *principle* that rulers *ought* to be guided by the judgment of ordinary men. Of course, if it is true that "the real wisdom of human life is compounded out of the experiences of ordinary men," then it would appear to be consistent with nature for ordinary men to choose rulers from among their own

Farmer, ed., *The Wilson Reader* (New York: Oceana Publications, 1956), pp. 103–109, 91–92. Wilson's understanding of the function of a university should be compared with Witherspoon's. The latter will reveal an age that still harbored aristocratic notions of man, notions closer to classical antiquity than to Wilson. See Witherspoon, *Works*, IV, 185–201, III, 379, 385, 388–390, 406–409, 414, 418, 432–439.

[34] I have yet to work out a theory of "nature," one that would also clarify the relationship between "theory" and "practice." As used here, these terms may therefore be construed in a conventional way. On the other hand, consider the discussion of individuality in Chapter VII, which is of crucial significance for the problem in question, and see pp. 438–441 below.

ranks and to hire extraordinary men who are unwise to serve their convenience or prosperity. Again, these extraordinary but unwise men will be supplied by the universities and will consist of those technicians who are expert in devising the most efficient *means* of serving the ends of ordinary men, *ends* which these politically or ethically neutral technicians lack the wisdom to criticize. Besides, these ends are prescribed by the voice of wisdom itself: *vox populi, vox dei.*

The reader will understand, of course, that I am developing the logical implications of Wilson's public teaching. Again, that these implications were not intended, or that they are contradicted by writings of his addressed to other than popular audiences, is of no fundamental concern to my inquiry.[35] The principal purpose here is to show that the public teaching of Wilson constitutes a radical departure from the public teaching of the founders; that this teaching exemplifies or points toward the transformation of a 'polity' into a democracy. Whether Wilson was aware of the implications of his public teaching to the extent developed in this chapter may be left open. Suffice to say that few political scientists and very few statesmen had a more penetrating and more comprehensive understanding of political life. Still, Wilson's public teaching is governed by the logic of democracy.[36] That teaching conveys an animus against privilege

[35] Again I refer the reader to *Constitutional Government*, p. 188, where Wilson questions "the radical suggestions of change made by those who advocate the use of the initiative and the referendum in our processes of legislation, the virtual abandonment of the representative principle"—he questions this, but does not reject it. In any event, there are numerous writings of Wilson, to be found in his recently published papers, that contradict the *most* democratic aspects of the New Freedom.

[36] True, the administrative *apparatus* for Wilson's democracy may not be wholly democratic in view of the formal mode of regime analysis. But the administrative *apparatus* consists of ethically neutral technicians or social scientists who, by devising the means to democratic ends, dignify and thus preserve and propagate those ends. We have seen, however, that the means are articulations and, therefore, determinants of the meaning of these ends. Furthermore, if ethically neutral social scientists are not in theory (let alone in fact) ethically neutral, and if, as I have elsewhere shown, their ethical neutrality is itself indicative of democratic values, then Wilson's political thought is democratic as

as well as against chance, or rather against any play of chance that might create privilege or disturb the equality of conditions among men. Men's conditions seem to be, or seem merely the result of, external contrivances, for example, the economic system. But such contrivances are in fact so many manifestations of intellectual and moral qualities in which men are unequal, and unequal as a result of the fortuitism of nature, no less than of those contrivances. To equalize "conditions," therefore, one must equalize the "preconditions," namely, the faculties of men, or, as Madison said, one must begin "by giving to every citizen the same opinions, the same passions, and the same interests." This was not Wilson's intention. But there may be a way of eliminating privilege without such uniformity: Merely exaggerate one aspect of Madison's solution to the problem of majority faction, that is, multiply the diversity of men's opinions, passions, and interests to such an extent as to render one individual powerless in relation to another. Notice, however, the difference between these two graduates of Princeton. For whereas Wilson deplored privilege, Madison deplored *majority faction*, and whereas Wilson would prevent privilege by equalizing conditions, Madison would have regarded such equalization as a manifestation of majority faction. Nor is this all.

Consider the psychological effects and political consequences of explaining privilege in terms of chance as opposed to merit. Clearly, such a teaching cannot but engender among the "underprivileged" resentment on the one hand, and self-pity on the other. But as any student of human nature knows, there is hardly a more effective way of emasculating an individual and gaining power over his will than by evoking self-pity. This may be done by blaming others or bad luck for his plight and by indulging him with sympathy. Whether this was Wilson's intention is not at issue and may even be doubted. Nevertheless, the fact remains that sympathy or compassion is a dominant motif of *The New Freedom*. Indeed, so powerful is the theme of compassion

---

regards both politics and administration. See my "The Temptation of Herbert Marcuse," *The Review of Politics*, 31:4 (Oct. 1969), 457.

in Wilson's public teaching that it even commands his disclaimers. Thus, in *The New Freedom* he declares:

> Benevolence never developed a man or a nation. We do not want a benevolent government. We want a free and a just government. Every one of the great schemes of social uplift . . . is based, when rightly conceived, upon justice, not upon benevolence. It is based upon the right of men to breathe pure air . . . upon the right of women to bear children, and not to be overburdened so that disease and breakdown will come upon them; upon the right of children to thrive and grow up and be strong.
> . . .
> Politics differs from philanthropy in this: that in philanthropy we sometimes do things through pity merely, while in politics we act always, if we are righteous men, on grounds of justice and large expediency for men in the mass. Sometimes in our pityful sympathy with our fellow-men we must do things that are more than just. We must forgive man. . . . But the law does not forgive. It is its duty to equalize conditions. . . (130–131).

Wilson's appeals to compassion were usually less subtle. Again: "I want to see a government rooted also in the pains and sufferings of mankind. I want to see a government which is not pitiful but full of human sympathy."[37] It should be understood, however, that the orator can hardly evoke compassion for the victims of injustice without nurturing resentment and ill-will toward those responsible for injustice.[38] This is not to say that appeal to compassion is rhetorically unjustifiable. What is of crucial significance lies elsewhere, namely, in the hitherto unrecognized fact that the predominance of compassion in Wilson's rhetoric signals the birth of a new politics, one I have called the politics of compassion.

In vain will one look for such a politics in the rhetoric of Theodore Roosevelt's *New Nationalism* or even in the rhetoric of

---

[37] *Crossroads*, pp. 494, 92. The motif of compassion persists in Wilson's first inaugural address. See Francis Farmer, ed., *The Wilson Reader*, pp. 111–115.
[38] See Wilson's disclaimer in *Crossroads*, p. 336.

Lincoln on the emotionally charged question of slavery. No, the politics of compassion is a twentieth-century phenomenon, the finale of which may be heard in the muliebral oratory of the present day, an oratory permeated by maudlin sentiment and punctuated by gnostic resentment. How strikingly different is the rhetoric of *The Federalist*. Not so much as a note of compassion or of resentment appears in its pages.[39] The authors of that work teach us, instead, to appreciate and fear the richness and power of the human passions, especially the aggressive passions of ambition and avarice. But here, in this comparison of *The Federalist* and *The New Freedom*, there emerges a principle hitherto insufficiently recognized, namely, that the particular emotions or passions of which the statesman's rhetoric is silent, or which he skillfully encourages or discourages, are indicative of, or may modulate, the masculine-feminine tendencies of his age. I have in mind, of course, the feminist movement of the progressive era, exemplified in politics as well as in literature. The suffragettes were quite vocal in Wilson's audiences of 1912.[40] Be this as it may, he who wishes to learn about the rhetoric appropriate to democratically mixed audiences might profit more by studying the oratory of Franklin Roosevelt.[41] Much may be learned about the character of a regime from the rhetoric of its notable statesmen, who are better judges of a greater variety of human types than legions of social scientists. But this, only in passing.

It would be a mistake to think that Wilson merely played on the theme of compassion. For compassion is the ruling emotion of

[39] See *Federalist* 52, p. 343, and 57, p. 373, where Madison speaks of a representative's "sympathy *with*" the people, signifying not compassion or pity, but similarity of feelings.

[40] During the campaign, Wilson refused to be drawn out as to his position on female suffrage. See *Crossroads*, pp. 50, 472.

[41] Of course, credit must be given to Roosevelt's speechwriters, who seem to have helped him make an art of sentimentalism. Incidentally, the superabundance of sentimentalism and moral purism in contemporary political oratory is symptomatic of an effeminate age wavering between adolescence and senility. In this connection the reader might compare the character of the student New Left and Aristotle's description of old men in the *Rhetoric*, Bk. II, ch. 13.

344

his political thought, the very heart of his reversal of the ruler-ruled relationship of the founders. The ruler is to "move with the common impulse." He is to feel what ordinary men feel; he is to feel "what touches them to the quick." Notice that the politics of compassion brings the ruler down to the level of the common man. It makes no demands on the common man. It places no responsibility whatsoever on the common man for his own condition. It does not even credit the common man with the capacity or the power to do evil!—for such a power is by no means contemptible. Sympathy or compassion—this temptation of temptations removes the distance and differences between men, dividing all men by the common denominator of humanity and eliminating the remainder. Compassion is the great leveler, the great equalizer. It reaches out to King Lear as well as to Willy Loman. Even felons and traitors may become the objects of this most indiscriminate, if not morally neutral, passion.[42] But why is this passion silent in the rhetoric of *The Federalist*? Is it because the authors were incapable of feeling sympathy? Sympathy for whom? The common man? But perhaps the common man was in no need of sympathy? Or perhaps the authors of *The Federalist* regarded the many as dangerous, as quite capable of oppressing the few? Perhaps they honored them by acknowledging their capacity for evil! (Or is it more noble to be sheeplike?) On the other hand, perhaps men like Hamilton maintained that "pathos of distance" peculiar to aristocratic temperaments. Perhaps Hamilton could not "move with the common impulse" because he thought that the proper motive of the statesman was not compassion but magnanimity. The magnanimous statesman —the large-souled man—will serve the public good, but only on his own terms. Once again recall Hamilton's statesmen who "saved the people from very fatal consequences of their own mistakes," statesmen "who had courage and magnanimity enough to serve them at the peril of their displeasure." Such men, men who "command the tribute due to their merit," will make greater

[42] This is not to suggest, however, that morality is possible without the capacity for sympathy.

345

demands on the people by resisting their demands, will compel them to reflect rather than indulge them with sympathy.

But given the reciprocal relation between thought and passion, it is inevitable that the intellectual ascendency of democracy should coincide with the ascendency of compassion (and not only in the political domain of human life).[43] This is well exemplified in the following passage from Wilson's work on comparative government referred to earlier, a passage addressed to the question of what is the end of society and of government:

> The hope of society lies in an infinite individual variety, in the freest possible play of individual forces: only in that can it find that wealth of resource which constitutes civilization, with all its appliances for satisfying human wants and mitigating human sufferings, all its incitements to thought and spurs to action. It should be the end of government *to accomplish the objects of organized society*: there must be constant adjustments of governmental assistance to the needs of a changing social and industrial organization. Not license of interference on the part of government, only strength and adaptation of regulation. The regulation that I mean is not interference: it is the equalization of conditions, so far as possible, in all branches of endeavor. . . .[44]

"An infinite individual variety" is the end of Wilson's society because, in that society, all individuals, regardless of their intellectual and moral differences, would be equal: Excellence would have no intrinsic right to rule. No less than his campaign speeches of 1912, the above passage reveals, to those who can penetrate beneath the surface of things, that Wilson's society does not exist for the individual, but for the *average* man. We have already seen that academic as well as political institutions are to serve the average man. Presumably, the natural sciences, applied to technology, are to provide "appliances for satisfying human wants and mitigating human suffering." Certainly the social

---

[43] Consider, in this connection, Upton Sinclair, *The Jungle* (1906), and Theodore Dreiser, *An American Tragedy* (1925).

[44] Woodrow Wilson, *The State*, pp. 660–661; *Papers*, VI, 305.

sciences, applied to government, are to facilitate "constant adjustments . . . to the needs of a changing social and industrial organization." In short, compassion and intelligence are to join in the task of alleviating the human condition by equalizing all conditions.

Wilson's emphasis on compassion is but the other side of his persistent condemnation of "selfishness," that is, the selfishness of big business evidenced by its lack of concern for the working class. Behind *that* selfishness, however, is the vice of avarice, a vice which Wilson did not publicly condemn. Of course, it would be difficult to condemn avarice and, at the same time, call for the equalization of conditions, for the latter may encourage avarice if only by arousing envy. Whatever the case, "selfishness" is more universal than avarice, and this would be especially true in Wilson's society, his intentions to the contrary notwithstanding. Indeed, it may even be said—and here the reader might well consult Tocqueville—that a Wilsonian society would be a veritable breeding ground of "selfishness" given its egalitarian individualism on the one hand, and its absence of deference and reverence on the other.[45] In the absence of these two bonds of society—call them "prejudices" or ancient and venerable myths —the individual will be thrust upon himself. No one will defer to him, and no myths will bind him to others. Henceforth, what will govern him is not compassion but naked "self-interest." For it should be understood that Wilson's second founding provides the individual with no myth to take the place of the old, unless it be the myth of "progress." But such a myth renders it impossible for anything to grow old and venerable. Indeed, by encouraging constant change, it fosters indifference if not contempt for the past, hence for anything old and venerable.

Here is yet another radical difference between *The New Freedom* and *The Federalist*. The authors of *The Federalist* also call for radical change. Madison, we saw, urges the adoption of a

---

[45] See *Tocqueville*, II, 104, for the relationship between equality, individualism, and selfishness; and II, 3–6, for the relationship between equality and the contempt for forms.

Constitution which he describes as "a novelty in the political world." Yet, while proposing a radical change in the existing form of government, Madison again and again strikes the theme of *stability*. For Wilson, the theme of stability is replaced by the theme of progress—a theme which retreats the Constitution into oblivion. This is well illustrated in a lecture which Wilson adapted to the audience of *The New Freedom*:

> [I]n every generation all sorts of speculation and thinking tend to fall under the formula of the dominant thought of the age. For example . . . the Constitution of the United States had been made under the dominion of the Newtonian Theory. You have only to read the papers of *The Federalist* to see that fact written on every page. They speak of the "checks and balances" of the Constitution, and use to express their idea the simile of the organization of the universe . . . how by the attraction of gravitation the various parts are held in their orbits; and then they proceed to represent Congress, the Judiciary, and the President as a sort of imitation of the solar system. . . . Politics in their thought was a variety of mechanics. . . (41).
>
> The trouble with the theory is that government is not a machine, but a living thing. It falls, not under the theory of the universe, but under the theory of organic life. It is accountable to Darwin, not to Newton. It is modified by its environment, necessitated by its tasks, shaped to its functions by the sheer pressure of life. No living thing can have its organs offset against each other, as checks, and live. . . . Living political constitutions must be Darwinian in structure and in practice. . . .
>
> All that progressives ask or desire is permission—in an era when "development," "evolution," is the scientific word—to interpret the Constitution according to the Darwinian principle. . . (42).[46]

Of course, Darwinism involves the two-fold principle of chance variation and natural selection culminating in that tautology called the "survival of the fittest."[47] It may seem strange,

[46] Wilson extracted these passages from his *Constitutional Government*, pp. 54–57.

[47] See Whitehead, FR 6.

therefore, that Wilson should want to replace Newtonian politics with Darwinian politics, especially in view of his desire to prevent the strong from crushing the weak. But given the tautology involved in the notion "survival of the fittest," Wilson could confirm the Darwinian model of politics, first, by winning the struggle for the presidency, and second, by destroying monopolies, the effect of which would make the ascent of that species called the common man. But what really made the Darwinian model of politics appealing to Wilson was its idea of progress, an idea, it was suggested, that pervades *The New Freedom*. In contrast, the Newtonian model is that of a static universe governed by fixed and unalterable laws. And since the Constitution, according to Wilson, conforms to this model, it cannot but hinder freedom and progress. Its "structure" must be changed to conform to the Darwinian model of an organically unified government constantly adjusting to its environment, to the changing needs of society. In the meantime, however, "practice" must be modified so as to enable legislators, but therefore the Supreme Court, "to interpret the Constitution according to the Darwinian principle." If "pragmatic" is substituted for "Darwinian," Wilson's public request was eventually granted.[48]

What Wilson especially deplored about the Newtonian system of checks and balances was, of course, its division of powers between separate but equal branches of government. We have seen that it was this complicated system of fragmented power that supposedly enfeebled government and rendered it susceptible to corruption. Wilson was anything but a Whig. Unlike Jefferson (and so many contemporary psychologists), he did not harbor a distrust or pessimism of power. Perhaps he was too self-

[48] Thus, during and after the 1930s, a Court consisting largely of legal philistines gradually gave way to its opposite: a Court dominated by antinomians called "activists" whose activism consists in reacting to the dominant opinions of the day, ratifying their egalitarianism and libertarianism to the point where these antinomians may also be regarded as philistines. If the legalists lacked due sensitivity to the "pragmatic," the pragmatists lack due sensitivity to the legal. But one-sidedness is typical of the average man, including the average intellectual.

confident to accept Acton's dictum that power tends to corrupt, and that absolute power corrupts absolutely. To be sure, power must be responsible; but to be responsible it must be unified and simplified. Government under the committee system of Congress was little more than government by private interests. These "little oligarchies" of "selfishness" thwarted common counsel and hindered the pursuit of common purpose. What this really means, however, is this: the Newtonian system of checks and balances thwarted the majority and hindered the pursuit of *their* purposes. Indeed, this complex division of power among separate but equal branches, which was designed to protect the few as well as the many, prevents those who speak the common thought and move by the common impulse from dominating the government as a whole. Government can hardly be unified and simplified if those who speak the common thought and move by the common impulse have to contend with those who do not. Or, to put the matter another way: A government ruled by a selfish majority is simpler than one in which power is divided between selfish majorities and selfish oligarchies. When power is thus divided, we have the supposedly static system of Newtonian politics in which no class can readily dominate the whole. When power is undivided, we have the supposedly progressive system of Darwinian politics in which one class, namely, the "fittest," can readily dominate the whole.

Clearly, the Darwinian system of politics was to be made possible by the various constitutional amendments mentioned earlier. Those amendments, recall, were intended to inaugurate cabinet government in the United States, more precisely, party government under presidential leadership. Party government is Darwinian because it involves a struggle between parties for political supremacy. Each party is an organic unity in which each and every member is motivated by the same principles and purposes. The parties compete for popular favor, and to the favorite falls the entire government. To survive, a party must constantly adjust to the changing opinions and wants of the "people": it must speak the common thought and move by the common impulse. This would require *each* member of the party to speak the common thought and move by the common impulse. But each member—each congressman and senator—represents merely a small portion or geographical division of the people. Only the President represents the people as a whole. Only he can speak the common thought and move by the common impulse. But the powers of the President are limited by the Constitution even though he alone represents the source of all power, the power of the "people." Yet the President takes an oath to support the very Constitution which thwarts the "people." Said Wilson to a popular audience: "Now, the only thing that gives the President of the United States his great power is not the powers conferred upon him by the Constitution, not the powers delegated to him by Congress in statute, but the fact that he is the only federal officer who is voted for by all the people of the United States."[49] The deeper significance of this public teaching will be revealed later. I merely point out its consistency with Wilson's desire "to interpret the Constitution according to the Darwinian principle," only now the President alone seems qualified to render such interpretations.

Before continuing, it should be noted that Wilson's popular lecture on the Newtonian theory of government consisted of certain passages taken from his book *Constitutional Government*. These passages will be found near the outset of his chapter on the President (of which, more later). Only one other chapter contains any reference to the Newtonian theory of government, appropriately, the chapter "Party Government." Here is what he says:

> It was, as I have already pointed out, this theory of checks and balances, which I have called the Newtonian theory of government, that prevailed in the convention which framed the Constitution of the United States,—which prevailed over the very different theory of Hamilton, that government was not a thing which you could afford to tie up in a nice poise, as if it were

[49] *Crossroads*, p. 63.

351

to be held at an inactive equilibrium, but a thing which must every day act with straightforward and unquestionable power, with definite purpose and consistent force, choosing its policies and making good its authority, like a single organism,—the theory which would have seemed to Darwin the theory of nature itself, the nature of men as well as the nature of animal organisms (199).

The truth is, however, that Hamilton did favor a system of checks and balances. Consider only this passage from his celebrated speech of June 18 at the Federal Convention: "If government [is] in the hands of the *few*, they will tyrannize over the many. If [in] the hands of the many, they will tyrannize over the few. It ought to be in the hands of both; and they should be separated."[50] Leaving this aside, however, contrast what Wilson says of Hamilton in *The New Freedom* before a popular audience:

> There are two theories of government that have been contending with each other ever since government began. One of them is the theory which in America is associated with the name of a very great man, Alexander Hamilton. A great man, but, in my judgment, not a great American. He did not think in terms of American life. Hamilton believed that the only people who could understand government, and therefore the only people who were qualified to conduct it, were the men who had the biggest financial stake in the commercial and industrial enterprises of the country.
>
> That theory, *though few have now the hardihood to profess it openly*, has been the working theory upon which our government has lately been conducted. . . . It is amazing how quickly the political party which had Lincoln for its first leader, —Lincoln, who not only denied, but in his own person so completely disproved the aristocratic theory,—it is amazing how quickly that party, founded on faith in the people . . . fell under the delusion that the "masses" needed the guardianship of "men of affairs" (47).[51]

[50] *Farrand*, I, 308.
[51] Italics added. See *Crossroads*, pp. 57, 92.

Ignoring Wilson's error regarding Hamilton's opinion of commercial men and of who should run the government, notice his remark that "few have now the hardihood to profess [Hamilton's theory of government] openly." Certainly it would have taken great hardihood on Wilson's part to tell the people he wanted a government with "unquestionable power . . . choosing its policies," while telling them that they "understood their own interests better than any group of men," hence, that as regards government, they ought to "determine every turn of its policy." But why would it have required great hardihood publicly to profess Hamilton's theory of government as interpreted by Wilson? Can it be that over the preceding generation Wilson, with others, had succeeded in shaping public opinion through the media of higher education in the United States? Is it not strange that, whereas Wilson's *Congressional Government*, published in 1885, concludes by urging men, primarily intellectuals, to emancipate themselves from "timidity" and to engage in "fearless criticism" of the political and economic system, Wilson's *New Freedom* of 1912 tells us that few men any longer have the hardihood to defend that system publicly on Hamiltonian grounds? Whatever the explanation, Wilson's own sweeping criticism—not to say condemnation—of the political and economic system in 1912 could hardly be regarded as "fearless" unless there were, in fact, a significant number of men who could and would defend that system on other than Hamiltonian grounds and with considerable popular support. Furthermore, even if the defenders of that system did not openly profess Hamilton's "aristocratic" theory of government, the "commercial" aspects of that theory must have significantly influenced political practice in 1912, unless we are to conclude that Wilson's campaign was based on a straw man. A more reasonable conclusion is that Wilson's own theory of government, as we have already learned, was radically democratic in comparison with existing political practice; that with the cooperation of others, he had indeed succeeded, over the course of the preceding twenty-five and more years, in persuading a large portion of the American people toward his political teaching to the point where one can say that the progressive era bore witness to the intellectual ascendency of democracy.

I am well aware, of course, that the word "democracy" was a household term even before the progressive era. But when speaking of the intellectual ascendency of democracy I mean a mode of thought that identifies justice with numerical equality; that identifies the "people" with the common man; that would place the natural and social sciences at the disposal of the common man; finally, a mode of thought that is on the verge of becoming an unquestioned dogma shaping emotions, manners, and morals.

That American politicians should have referred to their government as "democratic" even before the progressive era is to be expected in a 'polity' inclined toward democracy. Wilson, a political scientist of uncommon perspicacity, often referred to "our democracy," and this too is to be expected in a 'polity' inclined toward democracy. But did Wilson have in mind the "form" or the "reality" of American government?—its theory or its practice? If its theory, why did he seek to revolutionize that theory? If its practice, why did he seek a radical alteration of that practice? One way of answering these questions is as follows. Wilson did indeed regard the theory of the American Constitution as democratic, but also as *obsolete*. Not only was it now obsolete, but under the new economic order of American society, it virtually ensured the control of government by big business, with the consequence that American government, though democratic in theory, was "aristocratic" in practice. Wilson's mission might then be understood as an attempt to return American government to its "true" origin, to its truly fundamental principle of "faith in the people." This principle could be made a living reality only by replacing the static and now obsolete theory of mechanical checks and balances with a dynamic and progressive theory of organic unity.

Leaving aside the arguments of Book I showing that the regime established under the original Constitution was not a democracy but a 'polity,' a more plausible explanation of Wilson's political position is this. During his lifetime, the balance of the American regime had shifted from one inclined toward democracy to one inclined toward oligarchy—not surprising for a 'polity' combining the attributes of those two regimes, especially a 'polity' subject to the vicissitudes of capitalism. For one of the causes of regime transformation is chance, and the role of chance is magnified in a regime based on a laissez-faire economy. It goes without saying that under capitalism, fortunes are quickly made and as quickly unmade. During one period there is general prosperity, during another decline or depression. Such economic instability is particularly dangerous for a 'polity.' Again, in a 'polity' the middle class holds the balance of power between the rich and the poor. Now, the power of the middle class can be undermined in two ways, either by a sudden or gradual accumulation of wealth in the hands of the few, or by an economic depression reducing a large portion of the middle class to a condition of poverty.[52] During such alterations—often the result of chance—a 'polity' may be transformed into an oligarchy and then into a democracy. It seems that something like this occurred in the United States during Wilson's lifetime. Wilson himself claimed that the "middle class is being more and more squeezed out by the processes which we have been taught to call processes of prosperity."[53] Incredible concentrations of wealth are reported.[54] And despite the passage of the Sherman Antitrust Act of 1890, it appears that big business remained relatively immune from government control, whereas government was not immune from the control of big business. In other words, there is evi-

[52] See Aristotle, *Politics*, p. 220.

[53] *The New Freedom*, p. 26.

[54] See John Dewey and James F. Tufts, *Ethics*, p. 545, referring to one study which "estimates that seven-eighths of the families in the United States own only one-eighth of the wealth, and that one per cent own more than the remaining ninety-nine per cent." See also T. Henry Williams *et al.*, *A History of the United States since 1865* (New York: Alfred A. Knopf, 1969), 3rd ed., p. 335, which states the "Morgan-Rockefeller empire [controlled] 341 directorships in 112 corporations having aggregate resources or capitalization of $22,245,000,000," or more than one-tenth of the entire national wealth in 1913. The difficulty in assessing such data lies in the meaning of the word "controlled."

dence to support the contention that the *de facto* distribution of power in the United States during the period in question had inclined the 'polity' toward oligarchy. If so, it remains nevertheless true that oligarchy has no more than one constitutional leg to stand on, so to speak, and its capacity to stand on that leg depends to a considerable extent on those who shape public opinion, ultimately, the universities. What Wilson accomplished, in cooperation with others, was to democratize public opinion to the extent of transforming a 'polity' inclined toward oligarchy into a 'polity' on the verge of becoming simply democratic.[55]

If this interpretation is correct, it would follow that the intellectual ascendency of democracy occurred during the very period when monopolistic capitalism was at its height, that is, when the economic distribution of power was most oligarchic. Capitalism, however, was either intellectually bankrupt or incapable of withstanding the critique of the intellectuals.[56] Of course, it is to be borne in mind that for many decades, capitalism, aided by scientific technology, had wrought politically significant changes in the demographic character of the United States, changes which cooperated with the intellectual ascendency of democracy to undermine the balance of the Constitution, especially the one institution which best exemplifies that balance, the Senate. Wilson was fully aware of this as will be seen by examining his chapter on the Senate in *Constitutional Government*.

Near the outset of that chapter, where Wilson contrasts the Senate with the House of Representatives, he enters into a critique of the demographic differences of their respective constituencies. Unlike the House, the Senate, he writes, "represents the country, not the people: the country in its many diverse sections, not the population of the country, which tends to become uniform where it is concentrated" (113). (Notice here how Wilson virtually identifies the "people" with the more

---

[55] Although that democracy would be middle class, it would lack the deferential and manly character of the middle class appropriate to a 'polity.'

[56] Its staunchest supporter was William Graham Sumner, who, significantly enough, regarded himself as a democrat.

uniform and more concentrated populations of the country.) The House, he goes on to say, mainly represents the North and the East, the regions of dense populations and highly developed industry. In contrast, the Senate represents primarily the South and the West, the sparsely populated and agrarian regions of the country. Wilson does not deny the propriety of representing these diverse parts of the United States. But he contends that "the characteristic parts of America are those parts which are most highly developed, where population teems and great communities are quick with industry, where our life most displays its energy, its ardor of enterprise, its genius for material achievement" (117–118). Wilson then looks nostalgically at what was characteristic of the old America: its simpler way of life, its congeniality, its quiet and spacious freedom, its greater individuality, especially its individuality of opinion. All this stands in striking contrast to the noisy conformity of cities crowded with masses of people whose individuality is erased by the every day rubbing of shoulders, by the encounter with other minds whose source of information is the same, namely, the daily newspaper filled, presumably, with sensational trivia. But Wilson saw the old America slipping away ineluctably. Soon the South and the West would go the way of the North and the East. Wilson's problem, as he saw it, was not to forestall the industrial and commercial urbanization of America, but to purify it. This could only be done by transforming American government into one which would operate under a "single unifying discipline." One step—a giant step—in this direction was the passage of the Seventeenth Amendment establishing direct popular election of the Senate. For the first time in American constitutional history an original institution of the national government was to be *profoundly* changed, the very institution that was designed to check and balance the democratic propensities of the House (which the Senate could only do, said Madison in *Federalist* 62, "in proportion to the dissimilarity in the genius of the two bodies"). Henceforth, not a "select" body of men, but the "people"—the average man—eventually concentrated in large cities, could more effectively determine the political composition of the Senate and render it more susceptible to a "single unifying discipline."

The source of that "single unifying discipline" has been anticipated. Nowhere is it more revealingly articulated than in *Constitutional Government*, again, in Wilson's chapter on the President. Consider, therefore, what Wilson says of the President, and bear in mind the Wilson who entered into that "solemn covenant" of some twenty-eight years earlier:

> Let [the President] once win the admiration and confidence of the country, and no other single force can withstand him, no combination of forces will easily overpower him. . . . If he rightly interpret the national thought and boldly insist upon it, he is irresistible; and the country never feels the zest of action so much as when its President is of such insight and calibre. Its instinct is for unified action, and it craves a single leader. . . . A President whom it trusts can not only lead it, but form it to his own views (68).

Now Wilson pauses to consider what he has just said in relation to the Constitution: "[T]he Constitution . . . is not a mere lawyers' document: it is a vehicle of life, and its spirit is always the spirit of the age" (69). Despite his flirtation with historicism— or was it *because* of that flirtation?—Wilson went on to say: "Nothing in a system like ours can be constitutional which is immoral or which touches the good faith of those who have sworn to obey the fundamental law. . . . But the personal force of the President is perfectly constitutional to any extent to which he chooses to exercise it . . ." (71–72).

This is nothing less than Caesarism, but of the profoundest kind. Wilson virtually deifies the people on the one hand, and their chosen leader, the President, on the other. The people and their leader are joined in what might almost be termed a gnostic union. The deeper meaning of this may be gleaned from an entry in Wilson's Confidential Journal, dated December 28, 1889: "The phrase that Bagehot uses to describe the successful constitutional statesman I might appropriate to describe myself: 'a man with common opinions but uncommon ability.' I *receive* the opinions of my day, I do not *conceive* them. . . . Institutions have their rootage in the common thought and only those who share the common thought can rightly interpret them. . . . Why may not the present age write, through me, its political *autobiography?*"[57] From this it may be said that the President is the incarnation of the spirit of his people. Of course, to the audience of *The New Freedom*, it was enough for Wilson to say of the President: "It is not his business to judge *for* the nation, but to judge *through* the nation" (56). The President, recall, derives his powers from the people, not from the Constitution. This is why "the *personal* force of the President is perfectly constitutional to any extent to which he chooses to exercise it." In other words, the Constitution is what the President says it is. And the Constitution is such because the "spirit of the age" which gives it its meaning is now personified by the President, in whom the "people" have written their "political autobiography."

But what was the spirit of that age? It was an age hostile to hierarchy, to *forms*, to anything long-established, such as the Constitution.[58] This hostility is peculiar to the democratic personality which looks upon forms as so many artificial restraints on freedom, on self-expression, on "individuality." Forms command respect, obedience, even distance. Certain things are not to be touched by the vulgar. But for the age of which Wilson speaks, nothing is sacred, nothing is beyond the reach of the common man. The spirit of that age is human, all-too-human. It has deified man in principle and the common man in practice— all the pretentiousness about "individuality" notwithstanding.

The cause of the common man was the central cause of Wil-

[57] *Papers*, VI, 462–463. See the sequel for Wilson's apparent denial of freedom in the universe.

[58] See *Tocqueville*, II, 3–6. The "philosophical method" of which Tocqueville speaks may be regarded as an anticipation of popularized pragmatism. On the gnostic hostility to forms, see Hans Jonas, *The Phenomenon of Life*, Ninth Essay, "Gnosticism, Existentialism, and Nihilism," pp. 211–234.

son's public teaching. To one popular audience he declared: "I would rather lose in a cause that I know some day will triumph than triumph in a cause that I know some day will lose."[59] Behold the taint of historicism. For these words virtually canonize, not personal success, but the "success of history," the emerging "spirit of the age" or the "wave of the future." Another statesman might have said: "I would rather lose in a cause I know is *right* than triumph in a cause I know is *wrong*." The *success* of the cause cannot be the criterion of its rightness unless history is necessarily progressive or confirms the survival of the fittest. If Wilson held such a view, he did not do so consistently.[60] But again, my primary object is to elucidate the implications of his popular teachings. Whether these implications were intended, or whether they are contradicted by writings of his addressed to other than popular audiences, is beyond the scope of this inquiry (the purpose of which is *not* to explicate Wilson's political thought as a whole or for its own sake). A no less important inquiry is into the probable impact of his teaching on public opinion—on the public he sought to influence and rally to his cause. And this inquiry has revealed again and again that Wilson's public teaching reverses the ruler-ruled relationship expounded by the founders. That reversal involves nothing less than the political deification of the common man who harbors, inarticulately, the "spirit of the age."

What Wilson calls the "spirit of the age" eventually came to be called the "trend of the times." Trendism is a logical consequence of historicism. To keep up with the trends is to speak the common thought and to move by the common impulse. Wilson himself was not a trendist. Nor was he solely a spokesman for the spirit of his age. Not only was he critical of his age, but his thought can be traced to other ages as well. For if the British constitution inspired the external form of his intended revolution of American government, it was Jefferson who inspired the spirit of that revolution. It was Jefferson, a Whig, who combined

[59] *Crossroads*, p. 147.
[60] See *Papers*, X, 21–31, 465.

Wilson's basic notions on the Constitution and on the presidency. It was Jefferson whom Marshall addressed in *Marbury* when he said that ours was "a government of laws, and not of men."[61] For it was Jefferson who, in the name of a pragmatic reason, privately affirmed the theory that no constitution, indeed, no body of laws, transcends the will of the living majority. And it was Jefferson of whom Marshall wrote in 1801: "Mr. Jefferson appears to me to be a man who will embody himself with the House of Representatives. By weakening the office of President, he will increase his personal power. He will diminish his responsibility, sap the fundamental principles of the government, and become the leader of that party which is about to constitute the majority of the legislature."[62] Not the *office*, but the *man*—the personal power of the man magnified by the power conferred upon him by the "people"—this was the Jeffersonian practice that Wilson wished to establish as the political theory of his second founding. Consistent with the spirit of his age, Wilson made public what Jefferson had kept private. Henceforth, theory and practice must be united as a public teaching. This was Wilson's way of enabling the people to take "possession" of the government, of enabling them "to determine every turn of its policy."[63] *Publius*, more cautious, sustained the distinction between theory and practice by sustaining the tension between the "enlightened reason" of the philosopher and the "prejudices of the community."

Strange that Wilson should have studied and taught at Princeton, the "patriot college" that fostered a revolution. Strange that he should have become the president of Madison's alma mater whose then president, John Witherspoon, had signed a declaration calling Americans to emancipate themselves from the British establishment whose very form, a century later, was to inspire Wilson's call urging Americans to emancipate themselves

---

[61] 1 Cranch 137 U.S., 162 (1803).

[62] *The Works of Alexander Hamilton* (7 vols.; New York: Charles S. Francis & Co., 1850–51), John C. Hamilton, ed., VI, 502 (Jan. 1, 1801).

[63] Today left and right merely say "power to the people."

from their own establishment. "Strange" that Wilson should seek to politicize American colleges and universities in order to supplant the political creed which Madison had sought to foster among American colleges and universities, such that now a new political creed has taken possession of the academy, one that has undermined that reverence for the Constitution without which the work of Madison and the founders could not abide the vicissitudes of time.

CHAPTER X

Economic Laissez-faire and
the Degradation of Statesmanship

T
1

HE TRANSFORMATION of America's 'polity' into a democracy was of course gradual. In various ways, Wilson identified with Lincoln, Lincoln with Jefferson, and between the two stood Jackson.[1] But unlike Wilson, who was so enamored of the British cabinet and unitary form of government, Jackson accepted the constitutional system of checks and balances: its division of powers between coequal branches, each upholding the qualified autonomy of the states in accordance with the principle of federalism.[2] On these vital points, Jackson, along with Jefferson and Lincoln, is closer to the political thought of *The Federalist* than to that of *The New Freedom*.

[1] The similarities between Wilson and Theodore Roosevelt should not be exaggerated. See the latter's *The New Nationalism* (Englewood Cliffs, N.J.: Prentice Hall, Inc., 1961), pp. 25–38, 43, 132, 170–173. Of the more important respects in which he differed from Wilson, we might note that Roosevelt did not exalt the common man; he spoke less of freedom and more of men's duties; his public teaching about equality of opportunity more clearly exemplifies distributive or proportionate justice; and he did not wish to eliminate monopolies, but to regulate them. Had Roosevelt's political principles and purposes prevailed, the regime would have shifted from a 'polity' inclined toward oligarchy to a 'polity' inclined toward democracy.

[2] Wilson *appears* to uphold the principle of federalism in *Constitutional Government*, but the logic of his political thought, to say nothing of his opinion on the commerce clause, cannot but eventuate in a unitary system.

It may be argued, however, that nothing in the Constitution could long prevent the triumph of the common man, the man of *The New Freedom*. This, in effect, is the contention of Martin Diamond who writes: "If the majority comes to have the same passion or interest and holds to it intensely for a period of only four to six years, it seems certain that it would triumph over the 'extent of territory,' over the barriers of federalism, and separation of powers, and all the checks and balances of the Constitution. . . . An inflamed Marxian proletariat would not indefinitely be deterred by institutional checks or extent of territory" (65–66). Leaving aside his *petitio principii*, Diamond here reveals both less and more than he intends. It is certainly true that an inflamed Marxian proletariat would not *indefinitely* be deterred by the institutional barriers in question. But it is also true that the United States has never had such a proletariat—perhaps because of those very institutional barriers. Furthermore, wherever inflamed proletarians have overturned regimes, the forms of those regimes bore little resemblance to the form of government exemplified by the American Constitution. Monarchies and "aristocracies" have crumbled before inflamed masses, and partly because they lacked the "barriers of federalism, the separation of powers, and all the checks and balances of the Constitution."[3]

Violent revolutions aside, however, it will not be argued that a regime, which is to say a community's settled habits of thought and conduct, can be fundamentally altered in the space of four or six years.[4] Presidents and senators come and go, and the re-

[3] Consider, in this connection, the history of the British constitution since the establishment of our own.

[4] Of course, Diamond is not arguing that the system of checks and balances was intended to prevent a regime transformation, since he maintains that the system was democratic in the first place. The Constitutional barriers, he claims, were only intended to prevent the majority from becoming tyrannical, or to prevent a decent democracy from becoming an indecent one. But even this transformation is not likely to occur in four or six years; and, as already noted, it begs the issue to assert that a majority could overturn the system if it held

gime endures—endures, largely because those presidents and senators were themselves very much shaped by the regime. Long-established opinions regarding justice, or of what constitutes a just distribution of wealth and honor, do not change spontaneously and in a trice. Within the domain of the probable, they can be changed only by the deliberate and concerted efforts of men—a revolutionary task one generation may begin but which another will have to complete.

Here is a 'polity.' Do you wish to revolutionize it? Very well, you shall have to (1) uncover its injustices (of which all regimes will have a good supply); (2) invent some other injustices (which may be done in all innocence); (3) interweave these real and imagined injustices and magnify them to regime proportions, in other words, show how they are intrinsic to the "system"; (4) undermine respect for the *kinds* of men who usually exercise public power; and last—if not first—secure an abundance of disciples to complete your revolution. This requires elaboration.

To transform a 'polity' into a democracy the mass of the people must become, or *be made*, discontented with the prevailing distribution of wealth in the community. They must be told that the existing distribution unjustly favors the few. Even in a period of prosperity (a time not favorable to revolution), this may be accomplished by convincing the masses that prosperity is not being enjoyed equally among the various economic strata of society; that the income of one class is increasing more rapidly

the same passion or interest throughout such a period. Besides, not *any* passion or interest is at issue here, as Diamond leaves open to believe. The passion must be democratic envy, and the interest must be to despoil the rich. Even during the Great Depression, however, the communist and socialist parties together polled less than 3 percent of the votes cast in the presidential election of 1932. But see Diamond, *et al.*, *The Democratic Republic*, 2nd ed., p. 99, n, 21; and Edward Pessen, "Who Governed the Nation's Cities in the 'Era of the Common Man'?," *Political Science Quarterly*, 77:4 (Dec. 1972), 591–614, which concludes with these words: "Despite his possession of the suffrage, the common man had little influence, let alone power, in the nation's cities during the era named in his honor."

than that of another. Or, what amounts to the same thing, the notion of relativistic poverty may be propagated to insure perpetual discontent among the lower class. In either case, democratic envy or the passion of equality will be aroused, providing the indispensable popular base for a revolutionary movement. Meanwhile, it will be necessary to denigrate a sufficient number of men who enjoy the honors of public office, which may be done by accusing them of serving the interests of big business, Wall Street, or the military-industrial complex. This will not only foster resentment among the many, it will also encourage ambition among the few, or rather, among ideologues who, rightly or wrongly, regard themselves as more than equal to those who run the "establishment." (The ideologue almost invariably feels that his intellectual talents are not duly honored by the community and that he should have a larger share of political power—this, even while he may propagate such ideas as "one man, one vote." These public ideas, though *not* to be dismissed as a mere facade for private motives, enable the ideologue or the revolutionary intellectual to advance his personal desire for power and prestige on the seemingly impersonal but more alluring ground of justice.)[5] In short, to transform a 'polity' into a democracy, one must appeal to the desire of the many for wealth and to the desire of the "few" for honor—these being the principal objects for which men join in revolution.

Still, there are different degrees of revolution. Aristotle distinguishes four:

> Sometimes revolution is directed against the existing regime, and is intended to change its nature—to turn democracy into oligarchy, or oligarchy into democracy; or, again, to turn democracy and oligarchy into 'polity' and aristocracy, or, conversely, the latter into the former. Sometimes, however, it is not directed against the existing regime. The revolutionary party [may follow a more moderate line, in one or other of three directions. First, it] may decide to maintain the system of gov-

[5] This means that the same ideologue would be a revolutionary in a democracy as well as in a 'polity.' See Aristotle, *Politics*, pp. 207, 65, 204.

366

ernment . . . as it stands; but it will desire to get the administration into the hands of its members. Secondly, a revolutionary party [while leaving a regime generally intact] may wish to make it more pronounced or more moderate. It may wish, for example . . . to make a democracy more, or less, democratic. . . . Thirdly, a revolutionary party may direct its efforts towards changing only one part of a regime. It may wish, for example, to erect, or to abolish, some particular magistracy (204–205).[6]

Whereas Jefferson's "Revolution of 1800" involved his party's control of the government, whose form, however, he made no profession of changing, Wilson's "Revolution of 1912" envisioned nothing less than the scrapping of the Constitution and the establishment of a new form of government, one thoroughly democratic. To persuade men to such a course of action required a great deal more than arguments showing that the existing distribution of wealth was unjust, and that the party in office was serving the interests of the rich at the expense of the poor. These assertions might result in a change of administration and in some legislation favorable to the poor, but not much more. No, to enlist a sufficient number of people on a course as revolutionary as Wilson's it was necessary to attack the Constitution itself, to question its justice as well as its relevance, a task hardly to be advanced very far in four or six years, let alone during an election campaign. This was a task that had to begin in the schools, with the education of youth, with those who would eventually wield influence in society at large. For just as the most effective means of preserving a regime consists in promoting among youth an understanding and manly respect for the principles on which their country was founded, so the most effective means of destroying a regime is to miseducate youth about that founding, promoting among them a disrespect for its principles. This was accomplished, no doubt with some good intentions, during the progressive era.

[6] Barker's translation of the Greek *stasis* to read "seditious" has been changed to "revolutionary." I prefer to say "revolutionary party" rather than "party of reform" so as not to minimize the political significance of seemingly minor reforms.

In 1907 the public was presented with James Allen Smith's *The Spirit of American Government*. Its thesis, still prominent in our own day, is that the Constitution was a "conservative reaction" against the principles of the Declaration of Independence, principles which Smith regarded and embraced as democratic. In support of this thesis, Smith cited the work of a political scientist who, in 1893, had written:

> The Federal government was not by intention a democratic government. In plan and structure it had been meant to check the sweep and power of popular majorities. The Senate, it was believed, would be a stronghold of conservatism, if not of aristocracy and wealth. . . . Only in the House of Representatives were the people to be accorded an immediate audience and a direct means of making their will effective in affairs. The government had, in fact, been originated and organized upon the initiative and primarily in the interest of the mercantile and wealthy classes.[7]

Twenty years later, in 1913, the author of these words became President of the United States, and, in that very same year, Charles Beard offered the public his *Economic Interpretation of the Constitution*. Especially significant and ironic is the fact that a political work entitled *The New Freedom* should be published the same year that Beard should publish a crypto-Marxist interpretation of the Constitution, that is, an interpretation of politics based on what Beard admitted to be the theory of "economic determinism."[8] Meanwhile, Max Farrand, to whom we

[7] Cited in James Allen Smith, *The Spirit of American Government*, pp. 51–52, from Woodrow Wilson, *Division and Reunion* (New York: Longmans, Green & Co., 1901), 11th ed., rev., p. 12. See *Papers of Wilson*, VIII, 196, for a review of *Division and Reunion* in which an English writer says: "Mr. Woodrow Wilson has first brought out very clearly that the United States . . . was very carefully framed in the interests of money and monopoly." The reviewer goes on to see in Wilson's work what amounts to an economic interpretation of American history. This is not intended to suggest that Wilson was a crypto-Marxist, but rather that quasi-Marxian modes of thought were gaining influence in American universities.

[8] Beard's disclaimer of his Marxian foundations will not bear the test of critical analysis. The disclaimer will be found in his *An Economic Interpretation*

are indebted for his *Records of the Federal Convention*, also had published in 1913 *The Framing of the Constitution of the United States* in which he reiterated the simplistic notion of the Constitution as a "bundle of compromises," and concluded by contradicting Gladstone and anticipating John Roche as follows: "Neither a work of divine origin, nor 'the greatest work that was ever struck off at a given time by the brain and purpose of man,' but a practical workable document is this constitution of the United States. [It was] planned to meet certain immediate needs and modified to suit the exigencies of the situation. . . ."[9] In other words, there are no enduring principles in the Constitution, principles whose validity might transcend what were merely the "immediate needs" of the founding generation. Farrand goes so far as to suggest that the founders were not even guided by principles *they might have thought were enduring*. In his own words: "However much the members of the federal convention may have prepared themselves by reading and study, and however learnedly they might discourse upon governments, ancient and modern, when it came to concrete action they relied almost entirely upon what they themselves had seen and done."[10] Leaving aside the ambiguity introduced by the word "almost," this commentary, like Beard's, is typical of the anti-intellectualism which distinguishes the pragmatic movement.

---

of the Constitution of the United States (New York: Macmillan Co., 1954), introduction to the 1935 edition, ix–xvii. But compare (1) his interpretation of *Federalist* 10 as exemplifying "the theory of economic determinism in politics" (p. 15); (2) the language of his reference to Seligman's *The Economic Interpretation of History* (p. 15, n. 1); and (3) his reference to Arthur Bentley, *The Process of Government* (p. 12, n. 2), who acknowledges Karl Marx as the "starting point" of his study of politics (*Bentley*, p. 465).

[9] Max Farrand, *The Framing of the Constitution of the United States* (New Haven: Yale University Press, 1967), p. 210.

[10] *Ibid.*, pp. 203–204. Evidently influenced by the anti-intellectualism of the pragmatic movement, Farrand seems not to have fully grasped the deeper strata of pragmatism itself, as may be seen in James, *Pragmatism*, pp. 60–61, 122, 216, 269, 299. Far from denying *enduring* truths, James merely denies fixity or finality; and even this denial is not fixed or final! (What follows, therefore, should be viewed in the light of these remarks.)

Its adherents do not regard the intellect as cognizing enduring truths, but as responding merely to ever changing needs and circumstances. Such commentaries trivialize the political teaching of the founders and degrade the Constitution. Why take men seriously if their political thought was addressed solely to the needs of their own time, or if their teaching contains nothing of enduring value? But this type of historical writing served more than antiquarian interests: it was necessary to hasten the ascendency of democracy. To elevate the common man it was necessary to lower the founders.[11] It goes without saying that this noble task was undertaken not only with good intentions, but also with something less than innocence and with something more than conceit. The age of progress is not noted for its modesty.

And yet in one respect it was modest indeed. For while universities were teaching students that they lived in an age of unprecedented freedom, these same universities were teaching the same students one or another form of determinism.[12] Interestingly enough, as the teaching of economic determinism advanced, the oligarchic bias of economic laissez-faire declined. What took its place, however, was the democratic bias of intellectual laissez-faire. The supplanting of one form of modern liberalism with another is suggestive of the inadequacy of any democratic interpretation of the original Constitution. As the remainder of the present chapter and the next will show, neither economic nor intellectual laissez-faire, nor the two combined, adequately comprehend the liberalism of the founders. In exploring the significance of economic laissez-faire, the following topics will be considered: (1) Hamilton's intentions regarding the American economic system; (2) the differences between his politics and contemporary behavioral political science; and (3)

---

[11] See *Tocqueville*, II, 93, where he discusses the effect of democracy on historians: "[I]n their writings the author often appears great, but humanity is always diminutive."

[12] Like the Constitution, it seems that the university curriculum is also a "bundle of compromises."

the passions which have dominated American history and which mark the transformation of a 'polity' into a democracy. In the following chapter, I shall take up the problem of intellectual laissez-faire, there to explore Madison's views on the First Amendment and how they differ from contemporary interpretations. But now to Hamilton.

2

It should be noted at the very outset that Hamilton's thoughts on economics, as revealed in his "Report on Manufactures," critically combine some of the doctrines of Adam Smith with those of the physiocrats, subordinating both, however, to *political* considerations.[13] His encouragement of manufactures had the following political objectives in view: (1) to decrease American dependence on Europe—in other words, to achieve material self-sufficiency; (2) to increase the dependence of the South on the North (but also their mutual dependence), so as to weaken the tendency toward a southern confederacy; (3) to multiply the variety of interests throughout the union such that each part would more keenly recognize that its own welfare depended on its living with others under the *same* government; (4) to increase the general level of prosperity as a means of (a) securing the confidence of all citizens in the *new* government, (b) attracting to this new government the best talents of the nation, and (c) establishing the new government on a *permament* foundation; finally (5) to promote individuality, in view of which Hamilton wrote: "When all the different kinds of industry obtain in a community, each individual can find his proper element, and can call into activity the whole vigour of his nature."[14]

It cannot be said too often that Hamilton was a *political* man *par excellence*. This is not controverted by his support of com-

---

[13] See Jacob E. Cooke, *The Reports of Alexander Hamilton* (New York: Harper Torchbooks, 1964), intro., xxii; pp. 117, n. 3; 137, n. 8; 140, n. 10.
[14] *Ibid.*, pp. 132, 164.

mercial interests. To be sure, Hamilton believed, and in *Federalist* 35 he boldly and publicly argued, that merchants or businessmen are better qualified than mechanics to participate in the deliberative process of government. But *The New Freedom* notwithstanding, not only is this generally and palpably true, but the very fact that a businessman enters politics indicates, again generally and palpably, that he seeks honor above material gain, hence, that he has entered into the meaning horizon of a *political man*. Furthermore, and as noted elsewhere, Hamilton was skeptical of the moral virtue of businessmen. The fact that Hamilton held worldly goods in contempt suggests that he regarded the mere moneymaker with no less contempt. Merit, not wealth, was his fundamental criterion of who should rule (to which extent the language of Wilson's contention is correct when he attributes to Hamilton an aristocratic theory of government). The point is that Hamilton did not identify, publicly or privately, with any class of society—the mark of a genuine liberal. Rather, he used commercial men for political ends, namely, the establishment of a great and powerful republic.

Here it should be noted that nothing in the Constitution gives explicit sanction to economic laissez-faire, not even the contract clause. Only the states are prohibited from impairing the obligation of contract. True, the government established under the Constitution was intended to protect, among other things, private property and even to foster private enterprise. But no economic dogma dominated the political thought of Hamilton, who wrote in *Federalist* 31:

> A government ought to contain in itself every power requisite to the full accomplishment of the objects committed to its care, and to the complete execution of the trusts for which it is responsible, free from every other control but a regard to the public good and to the sense of the people.
>
> As the duties of superintending the national defence and of securing the public peace against foreign or domestic violence involve a provision for casualties and dangers to which *no possible limits* can be assigned, the power of making that provision

372

ought to know no other bounds than the exigencies of the nation and the resources of the community.

As revenue is the essential engine by which the means of answering the national exigencies must be procured, the power of procuring that article in its full extent must necessarily be comprehended in that of providing for those exigencies. . . .

[Hence] the federal government must of necessity be invested with an *unqualified* power of taxation in the ordinary modes.[15]

The qualification "ordinary modes" does not materially affect the supremacy of the political over the economic. A "mixed economy," therefore, is perfectly compatible with Hamilton's theory of government, provided that the manner and extent of the mixture is ultimately determined by the statesman, not the businessman or the economist. In truth, there is virtually no limit to the constructive functions of government in the political thought of Hamilton, as the following passages from his "Report on Manufactures" indicate:

The National Legislature has express authority "To lay and Collect taxes, duties, imposts, and excises . . . and provide for the *Common defence* and *general welfare*" with no other qualifications than that "all duties, imposts, and excises shall be *uniform* throughout the United States, and that no capitation or other direct tax shall be laid unless in proportion to members ascertained by a census . . ." and that "no tax or duty shall be laid on articles exported from any State."

These three qualifications excepted the power to *raise money* is *plenary* and *indefinite*, and the objects to which it may be *appropriated* are no less comprehensive than . . . providing for the common defence and *general Welfare*. The . . . "*general Welfare*" . . . necessarily embraces a vast variety of particulars, which are susceptible neither of specification or of definition.

It is therefore of necessity left to the discretion of the National Legislature, to pronounce upon the objects, which concern the general Welfare, and for which under that description, an appropriation of money is requisite and proper. And there seems to be no room for a doubt that whatever concerns the

15 *Federalist* 31, p. 190 (italics added).

general interests of *Learning*, of *Agriculture*, of *Manufactures*, and of *Commerce*, are within the sphere of the national Councils, *as far as regards an application of money*.[16]

That Hamilton should speak of the advancement of learning as a proper object of government in a report urging the encouragement of manufactures is itself indicative of the fact that, with this statesman, politics remains an architectonic science. Since economics would therefore remain subordinate to politics, the extent to which the American economy approximated laissez-faire would be a matter for the statesman to determine. This said, I shall now explore the deeper significance of the subordination of economics to politics.

3

From *one*—but only one—perspective, the last two hundred years of American politics may be divided into three overlapping periods, each dominated by a single passion. In the first period, *ambition* was the master passion, attaining its height at the time of the founding. The second period witnessed the ascendency of *avarice*, which reached its peak a century or so later. Of course, ambition was evident in the second period, as was avarice in the first. But the ambition of one period differed from that of the other, and the same may be said of avarice. In the first period, the object of ambition was honor extending to fame or glory, for this was a period of revolution, of constitution-making culminating in the founding of a federal republic so large in scale as to constitute a "novelty in the political world." During this time the passion of ambition emboldened thought and enlarged men's vision. A wealth of learning was brought to bear on the task of constructing this vast republic. Classical and modern political philosophy, differentially mediated by the individuality of diverse statesmen, made more intelligible a variety of immediate problems, of competing needs, of conflicting values. The found-

[16] Jacob E. Cooke, *The Reports of Alexander Hamilton*, pp. 171–172 (italics in the original).

ers were modest enough: they did not think they possessed a monopoly of wisdom or that the political teachings of the wisest men of old were of no relevance to their own times. To a large extent, the principles of Aristotle's *Rhetoric* informed their own, hence facilitated and elevated debate and deliberation. While men like Hamilton and Madison cited ancient and modern authorities with self-assurance, they did not hesitate to rely on their own intellectual resources and on the testimony of their own experience. The problem was to apply philosophy to action. Hence, no concrete decision could be made via a process of logical deduction from general principles. But nor could political decisions be made via a process of induction from individual instances or from the data of brute facts.[17] Political judgment is the creative mediation of "universals" and "particulars," imposing upon both gradations of relevance according to the genius of the statesman. The genius of the statesman, however, is determined largely by the object of his ambition. Men who write party platforms or who seek to embody them in legislation do not ordinarily read or apply for that purpose the works of political philosophers. The level of men's thoughts does not extend much beyond the level of their ambitions (nor their ambitions beyond the level of their thoughts). Such was the ambition of men like Hamilton and Madison that they were indifferent to the honor sought by the ordinary politician. There are men too proud to subordinate their intellects to party principles and programs, or to share the field of glory with mediocrities. These statesmen were not *party* men but *regime* men. They spoke for no class, in one sense, not even for society as a "whole." Rather, they spoke for themselves and thereby gave shape to the whole. Their "selfishness" was large enough to be "unselfish," for their souls were magnanimous enough to encompass the good of an entire people. As statesmen whose value horizon was organized by the passion for fame, these men directed the passions of other men, including the passion of avarice, toward political ends. Avarice, at the service of ambition,

[17] See Whitehead, SMW 43–44.

was to facilitate the establishment of a new government and, eventually, of a great and powerful nation. In time, however, the servant was to become the master.[18]

The scope of avarice in the second period of American history differed enormously from that of the first. In the first period, the object of avarice was wealth productive of independence or social standing (more than of ease or comfort).[19] What distinguishes the avarice of the second period is that its object was the building of a commercial or industrial empire. Here, avarice used politics for its own ends. In other words, the second period saw a reversal of the ruler-ruled relationship between ambition and avarice, a reversal symptomatic of a 'polity' inclined toward oligarchy.[20] This subordination of politics to economics—and I am not speaking in absolute terms—had profound implications for the study of politics. Living, as it were, under an economically determined dispensation, American intellectuals universalized their historical situation (as did Marx), imposing it on the past in general, and on the founding in particular. The effect of this was to obscure, to this very day, the nature of political science and statesmanship. But let me try to formulate this development another way.

During the period of avarice, when politics was subordinate to economics, the public good came to be understood as nothing more than an aggregation of private interests. Public standards retreated into the background and restraints were removed from the pursuit of private gain. Not that politicians could not be found pursuing the public good; but the notion of the public good had increasingly become a facade for private advantage. Thus, during the ascendency of economic laissez-faire, the ground was being prepared for a new science of politics, the science of "who gets what, when, how." From this nineteenth-

[18] Here, and in what follows, I am not positing a "linear" or "mono-causal" theory of history. But on the question of ambition and avarice in the United States, see *Tocqueville*, II, 256–261, 164–165.

[19] See p. 203 above for a qualification of this statement.

[20] See William Graham Sumner, *War and Other Essays* (New Haven: Yale University Press, 1911), pp. 313, 325.

century hotbed of avarice was spawned a new political scientist who reduced politics to the noble art of acquisition, or to a struggle between men in quest of "income," "safety," and "deference." This Lasswellian triad was of course anticipated by Hobbes who taught his students that "in the nature of man, we find three principal causes of quarrel. First, competition; secondly, diffidence; thirdly, glory. The first, maketh men invade for gain; the second, for safety; and the third, for reputation."[21] The substitution of Lasswellian deference for glory is indicative of the difference between an aristocratic and a democratic age. In the age of ambition, statesmen in quest of glory might sacrifice their lives for the public good. In the age of avarice, such a sacrifice is less probable if only because the notion of the public good is little more than a facade for private gain. In an age of democracy, however, when that facade has been stripped away, statesmen in quest of glory will be as rare as Don Quixote. As for the politician who seeks deference, we can only wonder how he could possibly get what he wants when political scientists propagate among the people a teaching claiming something like this:

> The fully developed political type [that is, the politician] works out his destiny in the world of public objects in the name of public good. He displaces private motives on public objects in the name of collective advantage....
>
> [T]he true politician learns to use the world of public objects as a means of alleviating the stresses of his intimate environment. Cravings for deference, frustrated or overindulged in the intimate circle, find expression in the secondary environment. This displacement is legitimized in the name of plausible symbols.[22]

21 Thomas Hobbes, *Leviathan*, p. 81.

22 Harold Lasswell, *Politics: Who Gets What, When, How*, in *The Political Writings of Harold Lasswell* (Glencoe: Free Press, 1951), p. 304. Lasswell's *Politics* was first published in 1936. His *Psychopathology and Politics* was first published in 1930. See *ibid.*, pp. 74–76, 184, 194–203, for a more theoretical exposition of the political personality, as well as for the Lasswellian program for "preventive politics." Compare Lasswell's society without tensions and Nietzsche's description of the "last man" in *Thus Spake Zarathustra*, Part I, "Zarathustra's Prologue," sec. 5.

As his readers know, and as the above passage indicates, politics as conceived by Lasswell is a secondary phenomenon rooted in the deprivations and overindulgences of childhood. The language of political controversy is but the epiphenomenon of men's desire for approval and affection. In the politician this desire assumes pathological proportions: it becomes a *craving* for the approval and affection of the public itself. And it is precisely this craving for public approval and affection that defines the Lasswellian politician's craving for "deference." This invites comparison with the Hamiltonian statesman who possesses enough manliness to oppose the public and to risk its disapproval and disaffection. For the moment, however, note the lack of rationality in Lasswellian deference vis-à-vis the deference implicit, for example, in *Federalist* 35 and 36. In the former, Hamilton refers to one class of citizens as having the good sense to recognize the superior "endowments" of another class of citizens; in the latter, he speaks of certain exceptional individuals who will "command the tribute due to their merit" from all classes. In both numbers, the public is generally expected to defer to, and reward with office, men well qualified to pursue the public good, that is, men superior in practical wisdom. For Lasswellian political scientists, however, what seems to epitomize practical wisdom is "skill in manipulation," the dextrous use of symbols or fictions such as the "public good," and by means of which the successful politician wins deference, that is, public approval and affection. Contrast the Aristotelian statesman's quest for honor. In seeking honor, the statesman wishes to be confirmed in his own excellence, and by men who themselves possess that excellence, which again is practical wisdom. No doubt the Lasswellian politician also wishes to be confirmed in his excellence—though perhaps not as a skillful manipulator of public symbols. But since his craving for deference is a compulsive and irrational desire for approval and affection, it could as well be gratified by men of the meanest capacities as by men of practical wisdom.

Returning for a moment to the philosopher noted for his so-

378

briety, it must be said that Aristotle entertained few illusions about politicians or about people in general. In his *Rhetoric*, he taught students—some of whom may have aspired to a career in politics—that a good rhetorician requires, among other things, knowledge of what might be called political psychology. People of different ages have different temperaments, hence different values and opinions. The same may be said of people of diverse socioeconomic backgrounds. The skillful orator has to be a keen student of a great variety of human types if he is to persuade different men to a common course of action. But having related men's values and opinions to their passions and interests, Aristotle did not commit the genetic fallacy of reducing one to the other. Whatever were the "causes" of men's opinions, there still remained the more important question of determining the soundness or validity of those opinions. Again, as we saw in his *Politics*, Aristotle taught his students that when the ordinary politician speaks about justice or the public good, the opinions he advances are usually biased in favor of the interests of a particular class, be it the rich or the poor. But he did not teach students that those opinions could be adequately explained in terms of the politician's emotional deprivations, or as a public facade concealing purely private motives. To have done so would have been to convey the public teaching that the politician is either a pathetic creature or a knave. Without the slightest naivety, Aristotle never denied the *possibility* that a politician might be motivated by a concern for the public good. For him the politically relevant question was whether what the politician *opined* to be conducive to the public good was in fact such. And this, of course, is a matter for the man of political wisdom to determine, be he the genuine statesman or the political scientist. Accordingly, Aristotle did not teach his students that the wisdom of the politician consisted primarily in "skill in manipulation" of such symbols as the "public good," which symbols, students are taught nowadays, are merely mental fictions. Instead, those who attended his lectures, say in ethics, learned that political wisdom is a synthesis of the moral virtues of which politicians may partake to a greater or lesser degree. As a consequence, a student coming from Aristotle's lectures on rhetoric or politics or ethics would have been taught a healthy skepticism. He would not go away admiring ordinary politicians, nor would he despise them.

In contrast, twentieth-century political science has virtually stripped the politician of his dignity. It has emasculated the poor creature and undermined his self-respect and self-confidence. After the onslaught of two reductionist schools of thought, quasi-Marxian and Freudian, the politician might still seek deference, but he would find it, if it were to be found at all, among the ignorant, not among the learned. (And more and more of the ignorant were becoming "learned.") He would therefore have to lower his intellectual and moral horizons. He would have to speak the common thought and move by the common impulse. (Only in this way could he win the support of intellectuals who had become identified with the common man.) If the politician retained any dignity, it will have been derived not from his own virtue or from his own self, but from others. As Hobbes has written: "The public worth of a man, which is the value set on him by the commonwealth, is that which men commonly call DIGNITY." And earlier: "The *value*, or WORTH of a man, is as of all other things, his price . . . and therefore is not absolute; but a thing dependent on the need and judgment of another. . . . And as in other things, so in men, not the seller, but the buyer determines the price."[23] Anticipated by this greatest plebeian is the reduction of politics to economics, a reduction which required the intervening ascendency of economic laissez-faire to achieve academic dignity and to become, thereafter, a more or less public dogma.

The reversal of the ruler-ruled relationship between ambition and avarice corresponds to the Wilsonian complaint that government had fallen under the control of big business. Wilson saw no way of overcoming this reversal other than by appealing to the passion which distinguishes the present period of American his-

[23] *Leviathan*, p. 57, Nietzsche called this "slave morality." See his *On the Genealogy of Morals*, First Essay, sec. 2.

tory, namely, the passion of *sympathy*. This, in effect, is what the Lasswellian politician himself craves in craving for deference. In what follows, however, I shall be speaking of democratic sympathy or egalitarian compassion, and this, it should be borne in mind, is the positive side of what Nietzsche called *ressentiment*—a secret envy and hostility against all that is noble, privileged, or in any respect superior.

Democratic sympathy is the partial countertendency to oligarchic avarice. It need hardly be said that an age dominated by avarice—the age of competitive laissez-faire—isolates the individual, severs him from community, or reduces community ties to a cash nexus. In such an age the individual will be regarded as an atom whose intrinsic nature is not determined by external relations.[24] In an age dominated by sympathy, however, the individual will be looked upon as determined wholly by external relations. Accordingly, an "individualistic" or atomistic psychology will prevail in one period, while a "sociological" or herd psychology will prevail in the other. *Plessy* v. *Ferguson* of 1896 and *Brown* v. *Board of Education* of 1954 exemplify, respectively, the two ages now in question. The *opinion* of 1896 renders a person's psyche or self-image virtually impervious to his environment, which is to affirm the thrust or power of individuality, but which is also to deny the power of the individual to influence others. Here the Court paradoxically upheld human dignity while "dispassionately" tolerating indignities to particular individuals.[25] In contrast, the *opinion* of 1954—curiously echoing

[24] This will not be wholly true of aristocratic ages, in which family and class ties predominate. See Whitehead, SMW 123, on the doctrine of "internal relations."

[25] The relevant passage in Justice Brown's opinion in *Plessy* reads as follows: "We consider the underlying fallacy of the plaintiff's argument to consist in the assumption that the enforced separation of the two races stamps the colored race with a badge of inferiority. If this be so, it is not by reason of anything found in the act, but solely because the colored race chooses to put that construction upon it" (167 U.S. 537). This is not entirely true, for a person's dignity does depend, *in part*, on what others think of him, and segregation laws enacted by Caucasians certainly are based on the assumption that blacks are *de facto* inferior to whites (though not by *nature* inferior). (I cannot develop the position

Hobbes—virtually reduces the individual to what others think of him, which is to deny the essence of human dignity while compassionately seeking to prevent indignities to particular individuals.[26] The psychology of the former favors and is symptomatic of oligarchy. The psychology of the latter favors and is symptomatic of democracy.[27]

Contrast the "aristocratic" psychology of a 'polity.' Whereas Lasswell sees only and universalizes the politician's "craving for prompt and excited deference from his contemporaries,"[28] Hamilton sees statesmen in quest of everlasting fame, statesmen who will "have magnanimity enough to serve [their contemporaries] at the peril of their *displeasure*"—nay, "will have the courage to do their duty at every hazard." Recall, however, that this "stern virtue is the growth of few soils." Lasswell, unable to transcend the intellectual horizon of a democratic era, obscures the distinction between great statesmen and mediocre politicians; or he reduces the magnanimity and courage of the great statesman to

---

here, but I hold that a person *is* his total effect upon others *and* the total effect of others upon him. This position is both Whiteheadian and Nietzschean.) Nevertheless, Justice Brown upholds the concept of human dignity, since, as the Jews testify, it is within the power of the segregated race to despise their despisers.

[26] The relevant passage in Chief Justice Warren's opinion reads: "To separate them [Negro children] from others of similar age and qualifications solely because of their race generates a feeling of inferiority as to their status in the community that may affect their hearts and minds in a way unlikely ever to be undone" (347 U.S. 483). Here, a person's dignity or self-respect or social standing depends on what others think of him. This is partly true, but dangerously misleading—dangerously if only because, when believed to be wholly true, integration will indeed have to proceed with all deliberate speed lest "hearts and minds" be irreparably harmed. (The language of the Court gave fuel to black extremism.) The cruel irony of this opinion is this: the dignity of the black is made to depend on his imitating the ways of the whites. See Nietzsche, BGE, Aph. 261, on "slave" psychology.

[27] The psychology in question is traceable to Hobbes (see above, p. 380), but more recently to post-Freudians such as Erich Fromm. That Hobbes's individualism should lead (via Marx) to Fromm's socialism only confirms Nietzsche's estimate of utilitarianism as slave morality.

[28] *Politics: Who Gets What, When, How*, in *The Political Writings of Harold Lasswell*, pp. 303–304.

the level of psychopathology. Nietzsche would regard this Lass-wellian political psychology—this ethically neutral science of politics—as born of *ressentiment*, a passion grown cunning and artful: "[I]t is," wrote Nietzsche, "the spirit of *ressentiment* it-self out of which this new nuance of scientific neutrality (for the benefit of hatred, envy, jealousy, mistrust, rancor, revenge) proceeds."[29]

Returning to Hamilton, however, his identification of the love of fame with dedication to the public good on the one hand, and his contempt for mere popularity on the other, exemplify an aristocratic psychology. This is well portrayed in his letter to James Bayard on the occasion of the election of 1800, when it was left to the House of Representatives to determine whether Jefferson or Burr would be President of the United States:

[I]f the [Federalist] party shall, by supporting Mr. Burr as President, adopt him for their official chief, I shall be obliged to consider myself as an *isolated* man. It will be impossible for me to reconcile with my notions of *honor* or policy the con-tinuing to be of a party which, according to my apprehension, will have degraded itself and the country. . . .

I admit that [Mr. Jefferson's] politics are tinctured with fa-

---

[29] Nietzsche, *On the Genealogy of Morals*, Second Essay, sec. 11. Nietzsche's insight indicates that behavioral political science is *not* ethically neutral; and, as I suggest on pp. 426–427 below, it may not even be scientific. In this connection, see William A. Welsh, *Studying Politics* (New York: Praeger Publishers, 1973). Welsh admits that "even the initial choice of a research topic involves the appli-cation of selection criteria, which is ultimately a question of normative evalua-tion" (p. 241). Yet he contends that "normative concerns as the determination of what is 'good' for human beings are expressly [and, for him, rightly] excluded from scientific inquiry. Science deals with what is and not with what ought to be" (p. 242). What Welsh fails to realize is that the *publication* of this very contention, along with the political data emphasized by his selection criteria, cannot but modify the political environment from which the data were selected. Social scientists of Welsh's epistemological—not to say ideological—persuasions admit the autobiographical aspect of their putatively scientific and ethically neutral teachings, only to disavow, at least by implication, any responsibility for shaping the character of society by those very same teachings. (See *ibid.*, p. 7, for his unjustifiable omission of quotation marks around the word *useful* on lines 23–24 when tacitly referring to his own study of politics.)

naticism; that he is too much in earnest in his democracy. . . . But it is not true, as is alleged, that he is an enemy to the power of the Executive. . . . Nor is it true that Jefferson is zealot enough to do any thing in pursuance of his principles which will contravene his popularity or his interest. He is as likely as any man I know to temporize—to calculate what will be likely to promote his own reputation and advantage; and the probable result of such a temper is the preservation of systems, though originally opposed, which, being once established, could not be overturned without danger to the person who did it.[30]

I have omitted the less flattering of Hamilton's remarks, but he knew his man. Contrast now his estimate of Burr (again, omitting the less flattering remarks):

> But it is said [of Mr. Burr] (1) that he is *artful* and *dextrous* to accomplish his ends; (2) that he holds no pernicious theories, but is a mere *matter-of-fact* man. . . .
>
> I admit that he has no fixed theory. . . . But is it a recommendation to have *no theory*? Can that man be a systematic or able statesman who has none? . . .
>
> Let it be remembered that Mr. Burr has never appeared solicitious for fame, and that great ambition, unchecked by principle or the love of glory, is an unruly tyrant, which never can keep long in a course which good men will approve. . . . Ambition without principle never was long under the guidance of good sense. . . . He is far more *cunning* than *wise*, far more dextrous than *able*.[31]

Notice Hamilton's confirmation of the Aristotelian understanding of honor. Notice, too, his low opinion of the "dextrous" politician—reminding us of Lasswell's political manipulators. In short, Hamilton would have had nothing but contempt for a

---

[30] *The Works of Alexander Hamilton* (12 vols.; New York: G. P. Putnam's Sons, 1903–4), Henry Cabot Lodge, ed., X, 412–413.

[31] *Ibid.*, X, 414, 415, 417. This letter is worthy of close attention. It reveals Hamilton's penetrating and far-seeing intellect; his understanding of diverse kinds of men; his contempt for men who seek gain and popularity; his low opinion of "pragmatists," or of what he refers to as "mere *matter-of-fact*" men as opposed to statesmen guided by political theory.

Lasswellian politician, whose craving for deference would lead him to manipulate and court the approval of the multitude. Is it possible, however, that the Lasswellian politician is partly the product of a political science more *cunning* than *wise*? Whatever the case, Hamilton's political science—if it may be called that—is not based on a Freudian *cum* Marxian analysis of psychologically deprived politicians, be they successful political pragmatists or not.[32] Rather, it studies the deeds of renowned statesmen, men who were lawgivers or the founders of regimes. It is guided by reflection on the writings of various political philosophers, men who themselves studied statesmanship and the problem of applying philosophy to action under diverse human and material conditions. Furthermore, Hamilton's political science analyzes the different motives of wise statesmen as well as of cunning and of mediocre politicians. He shows how their political thoughts and policies are related to their diverse passions. In other words, Hamilton's writings reveal a psychology of political types which does not reduce the higher to the lower. Behavioristically speaking, whereas Lasswell's political psychology is democratic and motivated by *ressentiment*, Hamilton's political psychology is aristocratic and motivated by magnanimity.

It should be borne in mind that wisdom in a political scientist is as rare as wisdom is in a statesman. As Edmund Burke has remarked:

> It cannot escape observation that when men are too much confined to professional and faculty habits and, as it were, inveterate in the recurrent employment of that narrow circle, they are rather disabled than qualified for whatever depends on the knowledge of mankind, on experience in mixed affairs, on a comprehensive, connected view of the various, complicated, external and internal interests which go to the formation of that multifarious thing called a state.[33]

[32] It should be noted that the subjects of Lasswell's study in *Psychopathology and Politics* are, for the most part, political failures!

[33] Edmund Burke, *Reflections on the Revolution in France*, pp. 50–51. Somewhere I recall Whitehead putting it more succinctly: "The second-handedness of the learned world is the secret of its mediocrity." For these and other reasons

Consider the relevance of this remark to our own times, when the university has become a haven for more or less narrow specialists. Or to quote Whitehead: "[T]he increasing departmentalization of Universities during the last hundred years, however necessary for administrative purposes, tends to trivialize the mentality of the teaching profession."[34] This trivialization, which has so much affected the teaching of political science, could not but affect the quality of politics in general, and of statesmanship in particular. If politics was not made contemptible during the age of avarice, it was certainly made to appear contemptible under the onslaught of academicians writing in an age dominated by compassion.

I have been suggesting that the political science emerging in the twentieth-century American university is tainted by its reaction to the age of avarice. The degradation of the political, or the behaviorist's reduction of the higher to the lower, corresponds to the degradation wrought by capitalism, its reduction of social rank or status to wealth or money. In other words, an age in which capitalists make politicians look contemptible in fact is likely to be followed by an age in which political scientists make politicians as well as capitalists look contemptible in theory.[35] Here is but a subtle instance of avarice begetting envy. Of course, this reactionary movement was not without justice, al-

---

I maintain that education is too important a matter to be left solely to the discretion of professional educators. Indeed, I have maintained that education in the United States today will not improve until educators in general, and social scientists in particular, cease to be dogmatic egalitarians and moral skeptics.

[34] MT 178. See, also, SMW 197–198. Here I am reminded of Nietzsche saying that "Great learning and great shallowness go together very well under one hat." See his *Use and Abuse of History*, p. 41.

[35] Again, see *Tocqueville*, II, 93, on democratic "historians." According to the political scientist David Spitz, "wealth, far from constituting proof of one's virtue or superiority—unless perhaps we speak here of superiority in chicanery and greed—establishes the reverse." See his "A Liberal Perspective on Liberalism and Conservatism," in Robert A. Goldwin, ed., *Right, Left, and Center* (Chicago: Rand McNally & Co., 1965), p. 28. See the sequel where Spitz most clearly reveals his lilliputian understanding of the wealthy on the one hand, and, by implication, his brobdingnagian estimate of the average man on the other.

though the fruits of that justice will not be enjoyed until we transcend the age of compassion and incorporate its fruits along with those of avarice in an age whose sympathies are more magnanimous. Meanwhile, however, the avarice of economic laissez-faire helped spawn a moral relativism which was incorporated into and subsequently fostered by political science. For, only provided sufficient profit is forthcoming, capitalism will gratify virtually all human wants, whether refined or vulgar; it will thus dignify the one as well as the other, or render them all equal in principle if not in fact. This ethical neutrality of capitalism toward higher and lower values is embodied in the "value-free" political science dominating the twentieth century.

Clearly, behavioral political science and capitalism are both destructive of a 'polity' based on deference. There is, however, a crucial difference between the two. Whereas the destructiveness of behavioral political science is logically necessary, the destructiveness of capitalism is politically contingent. For while it is true that capitalism theoretically reduces all human wants to a level of equality, yet, given the factual inequality of man's natural and acquired endowments, economic laissez-faire cannot but eventuate in an unequal distribution of wealth, a form of inequality which, like most others, is conducive to deference. Here again I have in mind the ordinary man, whose very desire for wealth psychologically disposes him to defer to the wealthy. Impressed by their success, he admires that which made their success possible—if not their moral then their intellectual qualities. Of course, under capitalism, deference toward men of wealth exists precariously. No longer perpetuated by primogeniture (as under a landed aristocracy), wealth, now commercial, is constantly changing hands, is constantly subject to the vicissitudes of fortune. More important, however, is the fact that men of wealth, whether landed or commercial, cannot well defend themselves against men of intellect should opposition arise between the two.[36] That is, the status of the rich depends very much on the political loyalty of the intellectual, of those who

[36] See Edmund Burke, *Reflections on the Revolution in France*, pp. 57–58.

control the media of education and who are thereby in the best position to shape public opinion. Mill may have exaggerated the efficacy of ideas on conduct, but he is roughly correct in saying:

> One person with a belief is a social power equal to ninety-nine who have only interests. . . . It is what men think that determines how they act; and though the persuasions and convictions of average men are in a much greater degree determined by their personal position than by reason, no little power is exercised over them by the persuasions and convictions of those whose personal position is different, *and by the united authority of the instructed.*[37]

Once intellectuals became aligned with the working class, the deferential status of the rich necessarily declined and, with it, the oligarchic bias of capitalism. The effect of this, it might seem, would be to restore the older ruler-ruled relationship between ambition and avarice, or between politics and economics. And so it might have been were it not for two related factors.

To begin with, the intellectual's critique of capitalism was generally based on insufficient moral grounds. The condemnation of capitalism consisted in saying, in various ways, that it degraded the worker. Politically, this meant that capitalism undermined freedom and equality—the two cardinal principles of democracy. Seldom did the critics say, as did Adam Smith, that "the affluence of the rich excites the envy of the poor." The intellectual's critique of capitalism (aided by scientific technology) only universalized what capitalism itself had fostered, namely, the poor man's avarice called envy. Or as Marx said of the initial stage of communism: "Universal *envy* establishing itself as a power is only the disguised form in which *greed* reestablishes and satisfies itself in *another* way."[38] With the democratic

[37] Mill, *Representative Government*, pp. 246–247 (italics added). Marx disagreed in theory, not in practice. But see *Bentley*, p. 118.

[38] Karl Marx, *Economic and Philosophic Manuscripts*, in Loyd D. Easton and Kurt H. Guddat, eds. and trans., *Writings of the Young Marx on Philosophy and Society* (Garden City: Doubleday Anchor Books, 1967), p. 302. See also C. A.

reaction to oligarchic capitalism, avarice became universal so that politics became even more subservient to economics. Government was no longer under the control of big business, but rather under the control of big business *and* big labor. Meanwhile, behavioral or relativistic political scientists, who thought their science was ethically neutral, reduced politics to the art of gaining deference by increasing people's income—a self-fulfilling prophecy that engendered and reinforced the subordination of ambition to avarice, but now under the reign of compassionate egalitarianism. From such grounds was spawned a new politics, the politics of *ressentiment*. This new politics is at war against deference, privilege, rank, authority, and that ennobling quality of human nature, magnanimity. The new politics, however, was not only born of a negative reaction against economic laissez-faire; it was also engendered by the latter's twentieth-century offspring, intellectual laissez-faire. To this topic I now turn.

R. Crosland, *The Future of Socialism* (New York: Schocken Books, 1963), rev. ed., pp. 125, 135–136, 139, 146, who comes very close to arguing that envy should be rewarded. Note Crosland's moral relativism on the one hand, and his praise of a nondeferential society on the other.

CHAPTER XI

Intellectual Laissez-faire and
the Degradation of Statesmanship

INTELLECTUAL laissez-faire is the phenomenon of an age rife with skepticism, an age in which men have lost confidence in the power of the intellect to comprehend metaphysical and moral truths. Thus, the intellectuals referred to earlier may be regarded as anti-intellectual in the most decisive respect.[1] Such skepticism and anti-intellectualism will not be found among the intellectuals who established the American Constitution. Consider once again the following passages from *The Federalist* now quoted at greater length. Thus, in *Federalist* 31, Hamilton declares:

> In disquisitions of every kind, there are certain primary truths, or first principles, upon which all subsequent reasonings must depend. These contain an internal evidence which, antecedent to all reflection or combination, commands the assent of the mind. Where it produces not this effect, it must proceed either from some defect or disorder in the organs of perception, or from the influence of some strong interest, or passion, or prejudice. Of this nature are the maxims in geometry, that "the whole is greater than its parts . . . and all right angles are equal to each other." Of the same nature are these other maxims in ethics and politics . . . that every power ought to be commensurate with its object; that there ought to be no limitation of a

[1] See Whitehead, SMW 8, who regards the science emerging out of Galileo as anti-intellectualist.

power destined to effect a purpose which is itself incapable of limitation. . . .

Though it cannot be pretended that the principles of moral and political knowledge have, in general, the same degree of certainty with those of the mathematics, yet they have much better claims in this respect than, to judge from the conduct of men in particular situations, we should be disposed to allow them. The obscurity is much oftener in the passions and prejudices of the reasoner than in the subject (188–189).[2]

But if Hamilton was not a skeptic, neither was he a dogmatist, as this passage from *Federalist* 1 testifies:

So numerous indeed and so powerful are the causes which serve to give a false bias to the judgment, that we, upon many occasions, see wise and good men on the wrong as well as on the right side of questions of the first magnitude to society. This circumstance, if duly attended to, would furnish a lesson of moderation to those who are ever so much persuaded of their being in the right in any controversy. And a further reason for caution, in this respect, might be drawn from the reflection that we are not always sure that those who advocate the truth are influenced by purer principles than their antagonists. Ambition, avarice . . . and many other motives not more laudable than these, are apt to operate as well upon those who support as those who oppose the right side of a question (4–5).[3]

This is a beautiful example of a rhetoric appropriate to the politics of magnanimity. It is a rhetoric intended to encourage men's reason, rather than to inflame their passions. It is inspired by

[2] *Federalist* 31, pp. 188–189. As for Madison, his criticism of "theoretic politicians" in *Federalist* 10, p. 58, is not to be construed as indicative of anti-intellectualism or of "pragmatism." Here Madison clearly has in mind *utopian* politicians of the most naive optimism regarding human nature. See also *Federalist* 37, p. 231, where Madison chides the "ingenius theorist," meaning, only, the doctrinaire politician who cannot recognize the need to depart from the logical requirements of theory, to adapt principles of practical necessities, in short, to compromise.

[3] This number alone refutes Roche's contention that *The Federalist* is a work of propaganda. Of course, for men of Roche's persuasion, there is no difference between propaganda and rhetoric.

urbane and liberal sentiments, the very sentiments which inspired the original Constitution. This must ever be borne in mind when reflecting on the First Amendment of that Constitution.

1

It shall be the argument of this chapter that the First Amendment did not initiate the process by which the American 'polity' was transformed into a democracy, but rather facilitated the completion of that process; that the contemporary libertarian or "absolutist" interpretation of the First Amendment involves a reversal of the ruler-ruled relationship between reason and passion (as traditionally understood); and, finally, that that interpretation cannot but contribute to the degradation of statesmanship. The portion of the First Amendment to which this chapter will be addressed is the injunction that: "Congress shall make no law . . . abridging the freedom of speech, or of the press." Before turning to that particular injunction, however, certain observations regarding the Bill of Rights in general will be necessary.

To begin with, it should be understood that the first eight amendments, which comprise the Bill of Rights, were meant to limit the powers of the national government, not those of the states. This was precisely the ruling of Chief Justice Marshall in the case of *Barron* v. *Baltimore*, decided in 1833. Furthermore, this ruling was reaffirmed even after the ratification of the Fourteenth Amendment in 1868. Thus, in *Hurtado* v. *California*, in 1884, the Supreme Court rejected the contention that the due process clause of the Fourteenth Amendment applied to the states the restrictions which the first eight amendments applied to the national government.[4] Second, it needs to be emphasized

---

[4] 110 U.S. 516 (1884). This ruling was again reaffirmed at least as late as *Twining* v. *New Jersey*, 211 U.S. 78 (1908). See, however, *Gitlow* v. *New York*, 268 U.S. 652 (1925), where Justice Sandford declared: "For present purposes we may and do assume that freedom of speech and of the press . . . are among the fundamental personal rights and 'liberties' protected by the due process clause of the Fourteenth Amendment from impairment by the States."

that the original Constitution must be understood *before* the amendments to that Constitution can be properly interpreted.[5] Thus, the constitutional principle of federalism, which was affirmed by the first ten amendments, stands on the very distinction in question. This distinction, to repeat, recognizes that the Constitution imposes different restrictions on the powers of the national and state governments. For example, whereas only the states are constitutionally prohibited from impairing the obligation of contracts, only Congress is constitutionally prohibited from abridging freedom of speech and press (leaving open the possibility of such action, under emergency conditions, by the Executive). Thus, if a state were unjustly to abridge freedom of speech, this would not violate the Constitution. To be sure, according to Article IV, Section 4, "The United States shall guarantee to every State in this Union a Republican Form of Government." From this it does not follow, however, that Congress or the Supreme Court shall guarantee to every state of the union a remedy for *every* unjust law enacted by the state legislatures. Indeed, the Sixth and Eighth Resolutions of the Virginia Plan actually provided the equivalent of such a power, only to be rejected by the Convention.

Finally, it should be emphasized that the First Amendment ought not be interpreted in abstraction from the Constitution as a whole. An amendment, it goes without saying, may alter but it does not nullify the Constitution. Accordingly, the words "Congress shall make no law ... abridging the freedom of speech, or of the press" may not be construed in such a way as to nullify Congress's authority "To make all Laws which shall be necessary and proper for carrying into Execution the foregoing Powers [enumerated in Article I, Section 8]." Virtually any one of these powers may necessitate certain limitations on freedom of speech and press. Consider, for example, the power of Congress "To promote the Progress of Science and useful Arts, by securing for limited Times to Authors and Inventors the exclusive Right to their respective Writings and Discoveries." Or consider the pow-

[5] But see p. 394, n. 6, below.

er of Congress to "provide for the common Defense." Contrary to prevailing opinion, there can never be a simple opposition between the common defense and freedom of expression. For to defend the nation is to preserve its way of life, a most important aspect of which is freedom of expression. Conversely, if certain kinds of expression endanger national defense, then they also endanger freedom of expression. Thus, by virtue of its power "To provide for . . . disciplining the Militia," Congress may establish a code of military law making punishable any speech or publication causing insubordination in the armed services (and in peace time no less than in times of national emergency). This illustrates the organic principle of political life, one formulation of which may be stated as follows: Absolutizing the value of any part of a whole is destructive of the whole, hence of the part as well.[6] If, therefore, the First Amendment is to function as a part of an organic whole whose parts reinforce and not merely obstruct each other, the injunction that "Congress shall make no law . . . abridging the freedom of speech, or of the press" must be construed in such a way as to protect this freedom without undermining other constitutional values on which the very same freedom ultimately depends. Two general alternatives are possible. *Either* certain kinds of expression must not be included under the category of *freedom* of speech and press, *or*, certain kinds of restraints on freedom of speech and press must not be included under the category of an *abridgment* thereof. To the elucidation of these two alternatives I now turn.

Prior to and *after* the adoption of the First Amendment, every state of the union enacted legislation placing certain restraints on freedom of speech and press. Obscenity and blasphemy in some, defamatory and seditious libels in all, were made punish-

---

[6] See *Annals*, 1st Cong., 1st Sess., 708 (Aug. 13, 1789), where Madison says: "there is neatness and propriety in incorporating the amendments into the Constitution itself [than in appending them as] . . . separate and distinct parts. . . . [I]f they are placed upon the footing here proposed, they will stand upon as good foundation as the original work. . . . [S]ystematic men frequently take up the whole law, and, with its amendments and alterations, reduce it into one act." See *ibid.*, 709–716.

able in courts of law.[7] This was the practice even in states whose constitutions prohibited legislative abridgments of freedom of speech and press. Surely we are not to conclude that the legislative and judicial departments of these states knowingly or unknowingly violated their respective constitutions? The truth is they were merely following the common law distinction between liberty and licentiousness. Thus, consider the following passage from the law lectures of James Wilson (delivered, it will be recalled, in 1790–91): "The name of liberty we give to that power of the mind, by which it modifies, regulates, suspends, continues, or alters its deliberations and actions. By this faculty, we have some degree of command over ourselves: by this faculty we become capable of conforming to a rule: possessed of this faculty, we are accountable for our conduct."[8] Wilson called this liberty, "moral liberty." Two years earlier, in an oration celebrating the adoption of the Constitution, Wilson declared: "The enemies of liberty are artful and insidious. A counterfeit steals her dress, imitates her manner, forges her signature, assumes her name. But the real name of the deceiver is licentiousness."[9] For Wilson, freedom did not consist in doing as one likes, free from the restraints of law and morality. Indeed, what made a man free—what made him human—was very much the rational principle of his soul. It was the power of reason that gave man genuine alternatives; that enabled him to choose between the better and the worse, to seek what is noble and to shun what is base, to regulate his life according to civilized standards of conduct. Accordingly, many laws in those days embodied the thoughts of statesmen who rejected the notion that liberty included the right

[7] On obscenity, see Justice Brennan's opinion in *Roth* v. *United States*, 354 U.S. 476 (1957). On the law of libel, see *James Wilson Works*, II, 649–652. For the debates in Congress on the Alien and Sedition Acts of 1798, see selections in Charles S. Hyneman and George W. Carey, eds., *A Second Federalist* (New York: Appleton-Century-Crofts, Inc., 1967), pp. 282–304.

[8] *James Wilson Works*, I, 211

[9] *Ibid.*, II, 777. See also Edward S. Morgan, ed., *Puritan Political Ideas*, pp. 138–139, 256–257, for a discussion of the difference between "civil" and "natural" liberty in the writings of John Winthrop and John Wise.

to say or print what was false, malicious, and destructive of the reputation and personal security of others. If such expressions were dignified by the name of freedom, freedom would be indistinguishable from licentiousness. The ultimate consequence would involve a degradation of that which distinguishes the human from the subhuman—namely, reason. On the other hand, to punish men for saying or printing the truth with good motives and justifiable ends would be a violation not only of freedom, but again, of reason as well.[10]

Turning to the second alternative, the problem was to construe certain restraints on freedom of speech and press so as not to be included under the category of an *abridgment* thereof. Two constructions are possible. The first is this. Suppose that a state did not have a written constitution; that it was governed solely by statute and common law, either one or both of which provided for the punishment of defamatory and seditious libels. Now suppose that this state decided to adopt a written constitution, one including the following injunction: "The legislature shall make no law abridging freedom of speech or of the press." This injunction would not, of itself, render null and void all existing laws imposing restraints on freedom of expression. The proper method of interpreting such an injunction would be to determine, among other things, whether it was intended to remedy existing or antecedent complaints regarding restrictions on freedom of speech and press.[11] A negative finding would then warrant the following conclusion: The constitutional injunction that "the legislature shall make no law abridging freedom of speech or of the press" means that the legislature shall make no law *reducing* the scope of freedom of speech and press enjoyed by the community at the time this injunction was constitutionally established.

Finally, and consistent with the practice of the American 'polity,' the constitutional prohibition against abridgment of freedom of speech and press exempted persons only from *pre-*

[10] See Madison, *Letters and Other Writings*, I, 195.

[11] This method of constitutional interpretation is consistent with that recommended by Madison in *Writings*, V, 49, to Archibald Short (Oct. 30, 1787).

vious as opposed to *subsequent* restraints. This is confirmed by James Wilson's discussion of the subject at the Pennsylvania ratifying convention of 1787:

> It has been asked, if a law should be made to punish libels. . . ?
>
> I presume it was not in the view of the honorable gentleman to say there is no such thing as a libel, or that the writers of such ought not to be punished. The idea of the liberty of the press, is not carried so far as this in any country—what is meant by the liberty of the press is, that there should be no antecedent restraint upon it; but that every author is responsible when he attacks the security or welfare of the government, or the safety, character and property of the individual.[12]

To require that newspapers, for example, be reviewed by a board of censors *prior* to publication is an abridgment of freedom of the press. To make them punishable in a court of law subsequent to the publication of false, malicious, and seditious materials is *not* an *abridgment* of freedom of the press.

Summing up the preceding discussion: The words "Congress shall make no law . . . abridging the freedom of speech, or of the press" must be construed so as to avoid *necessary* as opposed to *contingent* obstruction with the constitutionally enumerated powers of Congress and with other constitutionally prescribed purposes of government. This can be done only by delimiting the meaning of "freedom of speech and press" (so as to exclude, for example, obscenity), or by delimiting the meaning of what constitutes an "abridgment" of such freedom (for example, by

[12] John B. McMaster and Frederick D. Stone, eds., *Pennsylvania and the Federal Constitution 1787–1788* (2 vols.; New York: De Capo Press, 1970), I, 308–309. On the subject of freedom of speech and press during the period in question, I find support, oddly enough, in Leonard W. Levy, *Freedom of Speech and Press in Early American History: Legacy of Suppression*, ch. 5, *passim*. The subtitle of Levy's work should be contrasted with Marcuse's essay "Repressive Tolerance," in *A Critique of Pure Tolerance*. It is precisely Levy's tolerance that Marcuse attacks, not unlike a son attacking his father. But consider my essays "The Temptation of Herbert Marcuse" and "Between a Silent and a Tyrannical Majority" (cited earlier) to see how the libertarianism exemplified by Levy helped to generate the phenomena of the New Left and its politics of *ressentiment*.

distinguishing between *previous* and *subsequent* restraints).

Before turning to the broader political implications of the First Amendment, it will be helpful to reflect a moment on the trial of Socrates (alluded to in *Federalist* 63). Viewed candidly, the *Apology* of Socrates was not in essence a defense of freedom of speech. Rather, it was a defense of philosophy, the quest for wisdom. Freedom of speech is an indispensable but not sufficient means to that end. Indeed, unrestrained freedom of speech can hinder the quest for wisdom—as witness the frequency with which Socrates, during his trial, was interrupted by the tumultuous outcries of the Athenians. Nevertheless, Socrates himself admitted, in effect, that he would not obey any law prohibiting him from discussing with others the serious questions of human life, questions about virtue and matters concerning the common good. Only in such terms may it be said that Socrates, who advocated censorship in the *Republic*, defended freedom of speech in the *Apology*. (Socrates could advocate censorship because he believed *and* philosophically argued that certain forms of expression undermine virtue as well as the common good.) In any event, the people of Athens, lacking a Senate that could uphold the authority of "reason, justice, and truth . . . against the tyranny of their own passions," decreed to Socrates the hemlock that silenced this philosopher of reason, justice, and truth. Of course, the Athenians also lacked a First Amendment, a fundamental law prohibiting the abridgment of freedom of speech. On the other hand, if they also lacked virtue, such a prohibition would have been nothing more than a safeguard for unreason, injustice, and untruth.

Returning to the Bill of Rights, we know that its negative purpose was to prevent democratic tyranny, which is to guard against the popular passions referred to in *Federalist* 63. Defending the Bill of Rights in Congress, Madison declared: "The prescriptions in favor of liberty ought to be levelled against that quarter where the greatest danger lies, namely, that which possesses the highest prerogative of power. But this is not found in either the Executive or Legislative departments of Government, but in the body of the people, operating by the majority against the minority."[13] But surely the majority of the people would act, if it could act at all, through the House of Representatives, which was not only designed to prevent a majority from becoming united and activated by a common impulse of passion or of interest, but was itself to be checked by the Senate, the Executive, and the Judiciary. No wonder Madison did not think a Bill of Rights was necessary, at least not before he was obliged to introduce such a bill by members of the Virginia ratifying convention.[14] Be this as it may, the "prescriptions in favor of liberty" contained in the Bill of Rights were "leveled against" *Congress*, and not against "the body of the people" in whom resided, presumably, "the highest prerogative of power." To be sure, it may be said that Congress, via the House, would be the branch most susceptible to popular passions. Nevertheless, it is contradictory on its face to proclaim, for example, that Congress shall make *no* law abridging freedom of speech, and to say, as Madison does in *Federalist* 51, that "In framing a government . . . you must *first* enable the government to control the governed" (337).[15] Did the First Amendment alter the original Constitution to the extent of implying that "in framing a government you must *first* enable the governed to control their governors"? Was it not absurd of Madison to handcuff Congress after saying, in defense of the Bill of Rights, that "the great danger lies rather in the abuse of the community than in the Legislative body"?[16] But this absurdity arises only if Madison entertained the absolutist interpretation of the First Amendment. If he did, then he must have renounced his belief, conveyed to Jefferson in October, 1788, that, as regards a Bill of Rights, "I am inclined to think that *absolute* restrictions in cases that are doubtful, or where emergencies may overrule them, ought to be avoided."[17] Notice the *comma*

[13] Madison, *Writings*, V, 382, 272.

[14] See *ibid.*, V, 271–275, 380–381.

[15] Italics added. Madison says in the sequel: "A dependence on the people is, no doubt, the primary control on the government. . . ."

[16] Madison, *Writings*, V, 382.

[17] *Ibid.*, V, 274 (italics in the original). I am well aware of Madison's position

after "in cases that are doubtful"—indicating that Madison's liberalism did not embrace the "clear and present danger" doctrine of contemporary "absolutists." (Of this, more in a moment.)

Nevertheless, the First Amendment is susceptible to Justice Black's tautology bordering on nonsense that "no law means no law." "We must never forget [however] that it is a *constitution* we are expounding," an organic whole consisting of interdependent parts or principles, the meaning of which must be elaborated, clarified, and conveyed as a public teaching—as *the* public teaching. In the process of expounding the Constitution, its various principles must be adjusted to each other lest they become mutually obstructive. Each principle must be given its due. Exalt one to the disregard of others and the public will be taught one or another form of dogmatism. The exaltation of one principle or purpose of government will teach the people to hold others in relative contempt, the effect of which will be to disorder their souls or render them more susceptible to the impulses of passion and interest. The Bill of Rights was never intended to stand in splendid self-sufficiency. Recall what Madison said regarding virtue and its necessity in a republic. Let this inform what he wrote of the Bill of Rights itself, namely: "The political truths declared in that solemn manner acquire by degrees the character of fundamental maxims of free Government, and as

---

on the Alien and Sedition Acts, namely, his rejection of the common law distinction between previous restraints and subsequent punishment. In this connection, see Harry M. Clor, *Obscenity and Public Morality* (Chicago: University of Chicago Press, 1969), pp. 95–102. The difference between the Madison of 1788 and the Madison of 1799 on the topic in question is to be explained partly in terms of the statesmanship required to *establish* a government, and the statesmanship required afterwards. The former will emphasize restraints on the governed; the latter will emphasize restraints on the government. Whereas, in 1788, Madison emphasizes the danger of abuses originating not in "the Executive or Legislative departments of Government, but in the body of the people," in 1799, in opposition to the Alien and Sedition Acts, he declares that "in the United States the great and essential rights of the people are secured against legislative as well as executive ambition." (Madison, *Letters and Other Writings*, IV, 543.) There is no contradiction between the two emphases when considered under the category of change. Compare *ibid.*, IV, 546, and Madison, *Writings*, V, 383.

they become incorporated with the national sentiment, counteract the impulses of interest and passion."[18] Clearly, the principles of the Bill of Rights were not to comprise, but to be *incorporated with*, the national sentiment. And they were intended not
only to secure liberty, but to counteract the impulses of interest
and passion. It would seem, however, that in recent years the
Bill of Rights, especially the First Amendment, has become a
haven for the loud, the lewd, and the disloyal, that is, for people
who may with impunity abridge the rights and endanger the
liberty of decent citizens. How did this inversion come about?

2

The inversion in question, I shall argue, is inconceivable prior
to the ascendency of one or another form of moral relativism in
American colleges and universities. Only with the prevalence of
such a doctrine among the principal molders of public opinion
—namely, those who educate the lawyer, the politician, and the
journalist—could the "absolutist" interpretation of the First
Amendment gain prominence in American constitutional law
and, eventually, in society at large. But this is a twentieth-century
political development that derives no intrinsic support from the
Constitution or from any *organic* interpretation of the First
Amendment. As suggested earlier, the First Amendment was intended to be a further safeguard for intellectual freedom, not
intellectual laissez-faire. It was not the author of the First
Amendment, but John Stuart Mill, who said, in one place, that
"All attempts by the State to bias the conclusions of its citizens
on disputed subjects are evil," and, in another, that in "this age,"
"disregard of custom" is "deserving of encouragement."[19] In contrast, one need only recall the "political creed" Madison wished
to foster in schools and in colleges, above all, in a national uni-

---

[18] *Ibid.*, V, 273.
[19] J. S. Mill, *On Liberty*, pp. 219 and 167; but compare *ibid.*, p. 216, where
Mill says: "Is it not almost a self-evident axiom, that the State should require
and compel the education, up to a certain standard, of every human being who
is born its citizen?"

versity whose philosophical foundations would have been diametrically opposed to the intellectual and moral relativism or
laissez-faire which dominates the academy as well as the society
of our own times.

In justice to Mill, however, I disclaim any intention of identi-
fying the thought of this great man with the relativism of his
disciples.[20] Contrary to the understanding of his disciples as well
as of his critics, Mill's most celebrated, or, as the case may be, his
most notorious work, *On Liberty*, is a *rhetorical*, not a *philosophic*, justification for unfettered freedom of speech. Its primary intention was to protect the philosopher, or men of supreme
intellect, against the leveling tendencies of a soon-to-become
triumphant, but, in 1859, still emerging, democracy. To this
end, and with an incredibly cunning essay, Mill deliberately
exaggerated the importance of freedom of speech or expression
vis-à-vis all other political values. The reason is simple enough:
From the point of view of the philosopher, freedom of expression
is the one value most gravely threatened by the rule of popular
majorities, a form of rule which enthrones mere number as the
criterion of reason, justice, and truth. Accordingly, *before* the
masses could become fully conscious of their power, it was ur-
gently necessary, thought Mill, to implant among them a dogmatic belief in the absolute value of freedom of expression—
again, not because this freedom should in truth enjoy a preferred position over all other values, but because it was the only
value whose propagation among the masses could, *at that time*,
prevent democratic tyranny *in times to come*. Precisely because
"The majority," said Mill, "have not yet learnt to feel the power
of the government their power, or its opinions their opinions," it is
necessary "in the present circumstances of the world" to erect
a "strong barrier of moral conviction," that is to say, to propagate
a public dogma favorable to absolute freedom of speech.[21] This

[20] *Ibid.*, p. 137; but compare Mill's *August Comte and Positivism* (Ann
Arbor: University of Michigan Press, 1968), p. 115 (which need not be intended to imply subjectivism or epistemological relativism), and *System of Logic*
(2 vols.; London: Longmans, Green, Reader & Dyer, 1872), 8th ed., II, 511.

[21] *On Liberty*, pp. 94, 101. See his *Autobiography* in Jack Stillinger, ed.,

dogma has conquered the generality of American intellectuals who have completely ignored the contradictory teaching in *Representative Government*, namely, that "the most important point of excellence which any form of government can possess is to promote the virtue and intelligence of the people." To this end, Mill favored an alliance of intellectuals and men of property on the one hand, and a system of plural voting based on merit on the other.[22] What Mill seems to have presupposed, however, is that intellectuals would actually become united on behalf of such a cause once duly warned of the dangers to the intellect posed by the ascendency of mass democracy. Yet, even before the publication of *On Liberty* in 1859 and of *Representative Government* two years later, many intellectuals had aligned themselves with the working class and were soon to embrace, in increasing number, the teaching of Karl Marx or some variant thereof. Meanwhile, as we move into the twentieth century, more and more American intellectuals will be found combining Mill's liberalism

Autobiography and Other Writings (Boston: Houghton Mifflin Co., 1969), p. 144, where Mill says of *On Liberty*: "None of my writings have been either so carefully composed, or so sedulously corrected as this." Such a remark, from a man as brilliant as Mill, should caution us not to rest content with the discovery of many contradictions within *On Liberty* as well as between that essay and Mill's other writings. Unfortunately, I cannot elaborate here on the rhetoric or "esoteric" teaching of *On Liberty* beyond the following points: (1) Note the limited validity of the essay indicated by Mill's repeated references to the "present circumstances of the world," *ibid.*, 101, 110, 121, 131, 140, 142–143, 153, 165–167, 169–171, 174–176, 189, 192–193. (2) Note his low opinion of "Ninety-nine in a hundred of what are called educated men," p. 129. (3) Of his numerous contradictions—deliberate contradictions, I would argue—consider only pp. 104, 111, 137, 142, *and* 113 (where he eulogizes Socrates, even though Mill well knew that the Socrates of the *Republic* advocated censorship). Finally, I venture to say that Mill might very well have favored moderate censorship despite his esoteric teaching of unfettered freedom of speech and press, a teaching which, to judge from his use of the "principle of antagonism," was intended to counterbalance the stultifying conformity of mass democracy. (On the "principle of antagonism," see *ibid.*, p. 142, and Mill's essay on *Coleridge* in *Autobiography and Other Writings*, cited above, pp. 265–266. For Mill's appreciation of classical rhetoric, see *ibid.*, pp. 14–15.)

[22] *Representative Government*, pp. 259, 245–247, 336, 341, 343–346, 355–358, 376–388.

with a simplistic version of Marx's economic determinism.[23] This uneasy marriage of Mill and Marx has dominated American mentality to this very day. It has spawned a pervasive skepticism corrosive of all established beliefs and customs, of all established laws and institutions, indeed, of all that antedates the "now." In the name of historical progress, it has fostered not only a contempt for the past, but also a ceaseless discontent with the present. Not imperfections in the statesmanship of the founders so much as the introduction into American education of nineteenth-century modes of European thought undermined the balance of the Constitution and tipped the scales in favor of democracy.[24]

The dogma which Mill successfully fostered among American intellectuals, and which has become a "strong barrier [to, as well as] of moral conviction" is compressed in the following passages of *On Liberty*:

---

[23] See *Bentley*, pp. 117–118, 465–468. Bentley, the reputed father of "group-interest" theory, employs (like Beard) a reductionist and liberalized version of Marxism. One need only consult Marx's *Theses on Feuerbach* (especially I, III, XI) to see how simple Bentley's epistemology is in comparison with Marx's.

[24] It should be noted that Mill's *On Liberty* was inspired more by Rousseau than by any other philosopher, despite the fact that Rousseau was anything but a proponent of the "open society." Furthermore, Marx owes as much to Rousseau as he does to Hegel. It was Rousseau's problem that Mill and Marx sought to solve: the tension between the need of the individual and the need of society, or between freedom and civic virtue. Rousseau compromised: the individual's bondage to society is legitimated by the general will, in the formation of which the individual participates, surrendering his precariously held natural rights to receive the advantages of civil society. No longer is he the sole judge of what is conducive to his own happiness. He is now a citizen, a moral being, absolutely bound by the general will. In contrast, Mill, with an idealistic philosophy of history, absolutized the individual or his intellectual freedom as the dynamic instrument of social progress. Meanwhile, Marx, with a materialistic (but non-mechanistic) philosophy of history, absolutized the proletariat as the final instrument of social progress, terminating in a nonpolitical society in which individual consciousness would be thoroughly socialized. Whereas the "social dynamics" of Mill justifies permanent revolution through the agency of unfettered intellectual freedom, the dialectical materialism of Marx—or rather, of Marx *cum* Engels—justifies permanent revolution through the agency of violence. Add Freud and the result is Herbert Marcuse.

The object of this Essay is to assert one very simple principle, as entitled to govern absolutely the dealings of society with the individual in the way of compulsion and control. . . . That principle is, that the sole end for which mankind are warranted, individually or collectively, in interfering with the liberty of action of any of their number, is self-protection. That the only purpose for which power can be rightfully exercised over any member of a civilized community, against his will, is to prevent harm to others. His own good, either physical or moral, is not a sufficient warrant.[25]

Liberty, for Mill, is the absence of external restraints, and comprises (in addition to freedom of association):

first . . . liberty of thought and feeling; *absolute* freedom of opinion and sentiment on all subjects, practical or speculative, scientific, moral, or theological. The liberty of expressing and publishing opinions may seem to fall under a different principle, since it belongs to that part of the conduct of an individual which concerns other people; but, being almost of as much importance as the liberty of thought itself . . . is practically inseparable from it. Secondly, the principle requires liberty of tastes and pursuits . . . of doing as we like, subject to such consequences as may follow: without impediment from our fellow creatures, so long as what we do does not harm them. . . .[26]

A refutation of Mill's subsequent argument is beyond the scope of this inquiry. (Besides, it would be more profitable to correct his unguarded statements, for much of what Mill says is sound in itself or at least appropriate for the present age.) Instead, consider the exemplification (and eventual degradation) of Mill's liberalism in American constitutional law.

The story begins in 1919, with the case of *Schenck* v. *United States* upholding a conviction for obstructing, by means of denunciatory printed matter, the recruiting and enlistment service of the United States during World War I. Speaking for the Court, Justice Holmes declared: "The question in every case is whether

[25] *On Liberty*, pp. 95–96, but see the sequel for some qualifications.
[26] *Ibid.*, p. 99 (italics added).

the words used are used in such circumstances and are of such a nature as to create a clear and present danger that they will bring about the substantive evils that Congress has a right to prevent."[27] As thus stated, Congress might prohibit certain kinds of speech which posed a clear and present danger to public peace or to property or to public morality. But what is "clear and present" admits of degrees, and neither all men nor all institutions of government are equally qualified to judge of what is a "clear and present danger." Besides, admitting that certain forms of speech may endanger public peace or property or public morality, why should one or another of these other values be given precedence over freedom of speech? And if not, how shall one value to be adjusted to another so as to secure their widest satisfaction? To simplify all these complex problems, the Supreme Court developed what may be called the "anti-intellectual" interpretation of the First Amendment. This interpretation enables

[27] 249 U.S. 47. Prior to *Schenck*, the First Amendment regarding freedom of speech and press was seldom the ground of litigation involving the Constitution. After *Schenck*, not the meaning of the words, so much as the circumstances in which they were uttered or published, became central in determining whether Congress could "abridge" freedom of speech and press. This is the "relativist" position (not to be confused with epistemological or moral relativism). Although this position has merit, it readily passes into the "absolutist" position as soon as one interprets "clear and present danger" to mean immediate or imminent danger to the very existence of the state. (Of this, more later.) The "absolutist" position minimizes the efficacy of speech, and, by so doing, gives men virtually complete license to say whatever they please. The merit of the "relativist" position consists in its not exaggerating the efficacy of ideas on conduct —as if a community were subject to destruction by noxious forms of speech regardless of circumstances. Thus, it may rightly be argued that, under certain circumstances, even communists advocating the overthrow of American government by force need not be incarcerated, provided the public well understands why communism, *in principle*, is a grave threat to liberal democracy and why, as a form of tyranny, it is destructive of human dignity. With this reservation, I would recommend the position of Justice Frankfurter in *Dennis* v. *United States*, 341 U.S. 494 (1951). Although it is too much to be expected, the attitude toward domestic communists should not be one of *tolerance* so much as one of *magnanimity*. They should be tolerated not because of their supposed rights under the First Amendment (for these rights are correlatives of duties which communists renounce), but because a strong and confident people *chooses* not to take communists so seriously as to incarcerate them.

men of the meanest intellectual capacity to determine what constitutes a "clear and present danger" and eliminates, at the same
time, the necessity of weighing and balancing inevitably competing values by placing freedom of speech in a "preferred position." Perhaps its most lucid exponent was Justice Brandeis.
Concurring in the 1927 case of *Whitney v. California*, Justice
Brandeis wrote:

> [N]o danger flowing from speech can be deemed clear and
> present, unless the incidence of the evil apprehended is so im-
> minent that it may befall before there is opportunity for full
> discussion. . . . Only an emergency can justify repression. . . .
>
> Moreover, even imminent danger cannot justify resort to
> [such] prohibition. . . . The fact that speech is likely to result
> in some violence or in destruction of property is not enough to
> justify its suppression. There must be the probability of serious
> injury to the state.[28]

The anti-intellectual interpretation of the First Amendment
substitutes dogma for statesmanship, a dogma that eliminates
the need for judicial judgment, if not for judges. (This, by the
way, is precisely the implication of "judicial behaviorism," a
school which eliminates the need for examining judicial opinions
on their merit, since opinions are nothing more than clues to the
judges' personal history. Like its parent, "legal realism," "judicial behaviorism" unwittingly eliminates, on theoretical grounds,
the need for law schools along with judges. But this only confirms my position that the degradation of statesmanship by "intellectuals" involves the suicide of the intellect.)

Returning to the First Amendment, it should be understood
that the author of the "clear and present danger" doctrine was a

[28] 274 U.S. 357. Although the preferred position doctrine cannot be said to
have explicitly commanded a majority of the Court, the practical finding of its
decisions affirms the doctrine. It was not until 1945, however, that this doctrine
achieved "constitutional" maturity in the case of *Thomas v. Collins*, 323 U.S.
516. Overturning a Texas statute requiring labor union organizers to obtain a
permit to solicit membership for unions, Justice Rutledge declared for the Court:
"Only the gravest abuses, endangering paramount interests, give occasion for
permissible limitations [of freedom of speech]."

skeptic, and that democratic skepticism is at the root of Holmes's doctrine. By the time of Justice Douglas, however, democratic skepticism or moral relativism had become a blatant fact of American life, shaping the intellect and feelings of the American people. This democratic conditioning or transformation of the American character may be illustrated by contrasting the dissenting opinions of these two justices. Thus, according to Justice Holmes in *Abrams* v. *United States*: "[T]he best test of truth is the power of the thought to get itself accepted in the competition of the market. . . . That at any rate is the theory of our Constitution. It is an experiment, as all life is an experiment."[29] (Similarly, the best test of whether a particular commodity is good is its power to get itself accepted in the competition of the market. That, at any rate, is the theory of our economic system.) In Holmes is a mode of thought that goes back to Hobbes (via Adam Smith). It is a democratic mode of thought which comes very close to suggesting that a proposition is true *because* it is accepted by the majority. When no longer accepted by the majority, it ceases to be true. This will remind the reader of Woodrow Wilson's understanding of the Constitution as one whose meaning changes with the spirit of the age, and the spirit of the age in question is majoritarian. As Justice Holmes wrote, dissenting in *Gitlow* v. *New York*: "If, in the long run, the beliefs expressed in proletarian dictatorship are destined to be accepted by the dominant forces of the community, the only meaning of free speech is that they should be given their chance and have their way."[30] From Justice Holmes's majoritarian morality it is a logically short but politically significant step to the nihilism of Justice Douglas, who, dissenting in *Ginzburg* v. *United States*, wrote:

> Some of the tracts for which these publishers go to prison concern normal sex, some homosexuality, some . . . masochistic yearning. . . . Why is it unlawful to cater to the needs of this

[29] 250 U.S. 616 (1919).
[30] 268 U.S. 652 (1925). See, also, Holmes's dissent in *Lochner* v. *New York*, 198 U.S. 45 (1905).

group [of masochists]? They are, to be sure, somewhat offbeat, nonconformist, and odd. But we are not in the realm of criminal conduct, only ideas and tastes. Some like Chopin, others like "rock and roll." Some are "normal," some are masochistic. . . . I do not think it permissible to draw lines between the "good" and the "bad" and be true to the constitutional mandate to let all ideas alone. . . . Government does not sit to reveal where the "truth" is.[31]

Anyone who reduces morality to matters of "taste," or who dignifies pornography by including it under the category of "ideas," can hardly be said to take morality or ideas—hence the Constitution—seriously. For the Constitution embodies a morality, a morality of moderation; and it institutionalizes the very idea that reason, not the passions, ought to be the ruling principle of political life. This means that every act of government ought to be the result of deliberation or of "reflection and choice." But whether rational or not, every act of government is intended as a rule of conduct, hence a public teaching about lawful and unlawful conduct. That teaching, by an easy translation of the mind, fosters among citizens opinions about what is *good* and what is *bad* conduct—opinions which, with varying degrees of intensity, will be regarded as embodying the *truth* concerning how men ought to live. Without realizing it, Justice Douglas is calling for the abolition of government, along with the abolition of morality. This is the inevitable consequence of his moral relativism. But it is also entailed by his understanding of what constitutes an "idea" or a "communication of ideas." Anyone who reduces ideas to the level of words or images intended to stimulate, not thought, but libidinous desires, is certainly not referring to ideas as understood by a Plato, a Mill, or a Whitehead. But this *sacrifizio dell' intelletto* is also a public teaching. Those persuaded by it can hardly be expected to take morality or ideas or speech seriously. For the practical, if not logical, implication of that teaching is this: On the question of what kind of life is preferable for men, the answer of an ignoramus or of a sen-

[31] 383 U.S. 433, 489, 492 (1966).

sualist contains as much "truth" as the answer of a learned and austere justice of the Supreme Court.

3

As thus stated, however, the anti-intellectual interpretation of the First Amendment is a second generation democratic phenomenon.[32] The first generation antecedent, again, the "clear and present danger" test formulated in *Schenck*, at least retained the distinction between previous and subsequent restraint. This distinction rested on certain assumptions: first, that certain forms of expression could harm people—their reputations, their property, and even their capacity to become decent and mature human beings; second, that freedom of expression is not an absolute or self-sufficient good; and third, that the first object of government is not to maximize freedom, let alone freedom of expression, at the expense of all other human values. But under the mixed influence of Mill and Marx, or with the changing loyalty of American intellectuals, not only was the value of freedom of expression given a preferred position in the Constitution, but property (meaning, precisely, the interests of the rich) was virtually stripped of constitutional dignity. With the degradation of property on the one hand, and the ascendency of freedom of expression on the other, freedom itself was demoralized to the point that it came to mean the absence of restraints. (Mill himself had taught, in one place, that "all restraint, *qua* restraint, is an evil.")[33] Indeed, the possibility of subsequent punishment, not without reason, came to be regarded as a *previous* restraint, dissolving the only remaining distinction standing in the way of the "absolutist" interpretation of the First

[32] It should be borne in mind that Justice Douglas's position is a minority one *de jure*, though not *de facto*. Incidentally, this position has the support of positivistic social scientists who, being value-free, are the least likely to discern any causal relationship between prolonged exposure to obscenity and "antisocial" conduct. See Harry M. Clor, ed., *Censorship and Freedom of Expression* (Chicago: Rand McNally & Co., 1971), pp. 119–129.

[33] *On Liberty*, p. 203; and compare *ibid.*, p. 157, with *Representative Government*, p. 296, for apparent contradictions.

Amendment. By dissolving that distinction, the constitutionality of any law affecting speech (or thought) could be made to hang on the psychological state of any individual or group claiming repression, thus introducing the subjectivism prominent in recent cases involving not only freedom of speech, but also the religion clause of the First Amendment. Be this as it may, the point to bear in mind is that the obliteration of the distinction between previous and subsequent restraint corresponds to the obliteration between the distinction between liberty and licentiousness. It goes without saying that giving the name liberty to licentiousness is to be expected in an era of moral relativism.

The removal of all restraints on freedom of speech and press means, of course, that one can say or print anything whatsoever without running any risk of punishment, certainly not from the law.[34] It is the case, however, that just as few people will take ideas seriously when educators instill in youth the doctrine of moral relativism, so it is that few people will take even revolutionary ideas seriously if not the slightest risk is incurred by their advocates.[35] In an era of unrestrained freedom of expression and mass communications, revolutionary heroes appear as unmitigated bores. Far from invigorating public discussion or enlarging and elevating public debate, unrestrained freedom of expression cannot but engender vociferous minorities on the one hand, and silent majorities on the other.

Despite—but actually because of—the removal of virtually all restraints on freedom of expression, the cry is often heard, in this age of the mass communication media, of a lack of communication or of understanding. The difficulty, however, lies in this: For men to understand one another—and I am speaking of men in general—they must already live within a similar mean-

[34] But if the law fails to protect individuals, say, from slander, they may take the law into their own hands, and their vengeance may not be as just as that afforded by the law when the distinction between previous and subsequent restraint was upheld by American legal practice.

[35] See James Fitzjames Stephen, *Liberty, Equality, Fraternity* (Cambridge: Cambridge University Press, 1967), pp. 79–81, based on the 2nd ed., published in 1874.

411

ing horizon. They must already harbor similar thoughts and feelings, likes and dislikes.[36] To the extent available, discursive reasoning and disciplined imagination must do the rest. But such reasoning and imagination will not be forthcoming unless men possess civility. Thus, to deepen and enlarge mutual understanding among men, the community in which they live must first have a sound, stable, and commonly recognized set of standards concerning what is decent behavior—and behavior includes not only *how* men speak, but *what* they say in public as well. Such community standards would necessarily entail restraints on certain forms of speech, restraints which in themselves indicate that the community takes speech seriously: that its members believe that ideas may be true or false, moral or immoral; that the consequence of what men say may be salutary or harmful, innocuous or dangerous. Equally important, proper restraints on freedom of speech will encourage men to *think*, to think about the possible effects of what they say upon others, hence to consider the thoughts and feelings of other men. By giving due regard to a person's thoughts and feelings we show respect for the person himself. Only by so doing can we possibly enlarge or elevate his thoughts and feelings, to say nothing of our own. Finally, public restraints on freedom of expression constitute a public affirmation of human freedom itself and, therefore, of human dignity. For the existence of public restraints presupposes that men are, in principle, capable of self-restraint, and that they can restrain not only their appetites, but also that which is peculiarly human, namely, the power of speech. (It should be noted, however, that self-restraint, whether of appetite or of speech, is a habitude which cannot be cultivated without the aid of law, written or customary.)

[36] See, in this connection, Harry M. Clor, *Obscenity and Public Morality*, ch. 5, *passim*, especially p. 189n. To carry Clor's critique of Charles Frankel, *The Case for Modern Man*, one step further, the latter's "depreciation of the importance of what men think and believe" is symptomatic of the anti-intellectualism of so many contemporary intellectuals, an anti-intellectualism that reveals a moral disjunction between what these intellectuals think and what they do. Compare, however, J. S. Mill, below, p. 414.

Unrestrained freedom of speech is destructive of freedom and of the very source of speech and freedom alike, namely the discriminating and synthesizing power of reason. Freedom is a function of reason, which enables mankind to comprehend and choose a way of life richer in its values than that which is possible for other creatures. There is no human dignity without freedom, and no freedom without reason. Yet, even before the anti-intellectual interpretation of the First Amendment, the dignity of reason had already been undermined by the teaching of psychological and sociological determinism. It can hardly be said too often, but determinism renders freedom of speech an absurdity.[37]

It may seem strange that the absolute value placed on freedom of expression should undermine its value.[38] But the reason for this, we have seen, is that all values are interdependent and require mutual adjustment. This is precisely the reason why there is not a single value that can, on theoretical grounds, be wholly removed from the reach of government. Since all political things are interdependent, it is just as absurd to exclude freedom of speech and press from the province of government as it would be to exclude from its concern national defense or domestic tranquillity. No community can long survive under the corrosive skepticism fostered by unrestrained freedom of expression or intellectual laissez-faire. One of the preconditions

[37] B. F. Skinner's mechanistic determinism, it should be noted, is itself involved in an absurdity. To begin with, it cannot account for the antecedent causes which issued in his *Science and Human Behavior*, for this would require a reflexive consciousness denied by Skinner. Lest his theory be nothing more than the epiphenomenal reflection of his personal history, and of his alone, Skinner must exempt himself from the deterministic mechanism to which all other men are supposed to be subject. He must "either" deny his humanity "or" deify himself. The end of *Waldon Two* reveals his "choice."

[38] If freedom of speech has value, its value cannot be severed from the ideational content of what is spoken. But the ideas of one speech may contradict those of another; and, unless one believes that truth will, in the long run, win out in the competition of ideas in the market, the value of one speech may be nullified by the disvalue of another. See J. S. Mill, *On Liberty*, p. 119: "Men are not more zealous for truth than they often are for error"; and compare *ibid.*, pp. 132–133, with his *Utility of Religion* included in *Nature and Utility of Religion* (Indianapolis: Bobbs-Merrill Co., 1958), p. 52.

of any community, said Mill, is "the existence, in some form or other, of the feeling of allegiance or loyalty. This feeling may vary in its objects, and is not confined to any particular form of government; but whether in a democracy or in a monarchy, its essence is always the same; viz. that there be in the constitution of the state *something* which is settled, something permanent, and not to be called in question. . . ."[39] Mill never doubted that "exactly in proportion as the received systems of belief have been contested, and it has become known that they have many dissentients, their hold on the general belief has been loosened, and their practical influence on conduct has declined."[40] Unrestrained freedom of speech and press is without question the most powerful means of undermining received systems of belief, moral as well as political, hence, of undermining "their practical influence on conduct." This is the inevitable consequence of the anti-intellectual interpretation of the First Amendment, an interpretation which is itself based on a denial of all received systems of belief but one, namely, that of moral relativism. But if unrestrained freedom of expression is destructive of a nation's moral beliefs, then it is no less the duty of government to enact laws restraining freedom of expression for the sake of a nation's morality, than it is to enact laws providing for a nation's military defense.[41]

In this connection, consider the following from Whitehead:

> Political philosophy can claim no exemption from the doctrine of the golden mean. Unrestricted liberty means complete absence of any cumpulsory coordination. Human society in the absence of any compulsion is trusting to the happy coordination of individual emotions, purposes, affections, and actions. Civilization can only exist amid a population which in the mass does exhibit this fortunate mutual adaptation. Unfortunately a mi-

[39] *System of Logic*, II, 521; but compare *ibid.*, II, 523–530, and *August Comte and Positivism*, pp. 88–89, where Mill contrasts his theory of "social statics" and "social dynamics," a theory which may account for the seemingly contradictory teaching of *On Liberty*.

[40] *Utility of Religion*, p. 52, and compare *On Liberty*, pp. 132–133.

[41] See Devlin, *The Enforcement of Morals*, pp. 11, 13.

nority of adverse individual instances, when unchecked, are sufficient to upset the social structure. A few men in the whole cast of their character, and most men in some of their actions, are antisocial in respect to the peculiar type of any society possible in their time. There can be no evasion of the plain fact that compulsion is necessary and that compulsion is the restriction of liberty.

It follows that a doctrine as to the social mingling of liberty and compulsion is required. A mere unqualified demand for liberty is the issue of shallow philosophy, equally noxious with the antithetical cry for mere conformation to standard pattern. Probably, there can be no one solution of this problem adapted to all the circumstances of human societies which have been and will be.[42]

The proper balance between liberty and "compulsory coordination"—and without coordination liberty is robbed of effectiveness—cannot be prescribed once and for all by rigid dogmas. The problem calls for mutual adjustment effectuated by political wisdom. Political wisdom, however, requires for its development, its progress, and its transmission, the innovative insights of the statesman on the one hand, and the stabilizing influence of institutions on the other. This means that the sphere of government cannot be narrowly restricted in the manner prescribed by the anti-intellectual interpretation of the First Amendment. That interpretation, it must be emphasized, is a dogmatism based on the teaching of atomistic relativism. No teaching could be more destructive of genuine statesmanship. The efficacy of statesmanship depends on the integrity of the rhetorical arts, the arts of persuasion. The integrity of these arts depends, in turn, on the capacity of a people to take seriously the spoken or written word, by which alone man has become liberated from the subhuman bondage of the immediate, has transcended his animal appetites and overcome the limitations of space and time. Such seriousness will not be forthcoming once people have long been taught, in effect, that the word is

[42] AI 71–72.

revelatory of truths no more significant than the private or solipsistic world of the rhetorician. When the word has been thus debased, rhetoric will no longer be distinguished from propaganda, nor the great statesman from the mediocre politician. Politics will have become a dull or demoralizing affair.

CHAPTER XII

Religious Indifferentism and
the Degradation of Statesmanship

1

REGARDING the First Amendment's bearing on religion, it should first be remembered that the words "*Congress* shall make no law respecting an establishment of religion, or prohibiting the free exercise thereof" did not affect any of the *ten* states having constitutional provisions for the encouragement of religion.[1] And, contrary to contemporary interpretations, the equal protection clause of the Fourteenth Amendment did not affect the issue. Indeed, the religious qualification for office prescribed by the New Hampshire constitution of 1784 was not repealed until 1877, that is, eleven years *after* the state had itself ratified the Fourteenth Amendment.

The second point to bear in mind is that the First Amendment does not say that Congress shall make no law respecting religion, but rather that it "shall make no law respecting *an* establishment of religion." Madison's original formulation reads like this: "The civil rights of none shall be abridged on account of religious belief or worship, *nor shall any national religion be established,* nor shall the full and equal rights of conscience be in any manner, or on any pretext, infringed."[2] The words I have

[1] Washington's Farewell Address, urging support of religion, should be considered in this light.

[2] *Annals,* 1st Cong., 1st Sess., 434 (June 8, 1789).

417

italicized reflect the fear then existing among some of the states that Congress, under the new Constitution, might possess the authority to establish a *national* religion; and, as the debates reveal, the word "national" was struck out in deference to those who thought it might be construed to mean that the Constitution exemplified a consolidated or unitary form of government as opposed to a federal one.[3] Finally, the words "Congress shall make no law respecting an establishing of religion" ought not be construed to mean that government is to be ethically neutral toward religion vis-à-vis irreligion. Thus, when Madison's original formulation had been amended to read that "no religion shall be established by law, nor shall the equal rights of conscience be infringed," some congressmen disapproved of the amendment, one expressing the hope it would be reformulated "in such a way as to secure the rights of conscience, and a free exercise of the rights of religion, but not to patronize those who professed no religion at all." To this, Madison replied that "if the word 'national' was [re]inserted before religion, it would satisfy the minds of honorable gentlemen."[4]

Despite these considerations, the prevailing interpretation of the First Amendment requires the *absolute* separation of church and state. Those devoted to this interpretation—they shall be called "absolutists"—are unaffected by the fact that one can no more separate the concerns of religion from those of the state than one can separate morality from politics. Seeking to comprehend and teach the art and theory of the inner life of man, religion is diversely affected by virtually any major act of government. Many laws enacted by Congress will unintentionally but inevitably favor one religion more than another. For example, public education in the United States (hence supportive legislation) is more favorable to Protestantism than it is to Catholicism or to orthodox Judaism. On the other hand, to the extent that public education fosters secularism or indifferentism and even skepticism, it undermines the efforts of churches and

[3] *Ibid.*, 730–731 (Aug. 15, 1789), 766 (Aug. 20, 1789).
[4] *Ibid.*, 730–731 (Aug. 15, 1789).

parents to cultivate religiosity among the young. Such education renders nugatory, for countless millions, the "free exercise of religion" clause of the First Amendment.[5] The truth is that it is simply impossible for government to be neutral toward religion.

The very notion of such neutrality, however, has contributed to a decline in the level of statesmanship. This degradation is reinforced by the ethical neutrality of the social sciences. By reducing politics to the subrational, the social sciences have undermined the politician's confidence in his intellectual capacity to comprehend the most important questions of human life or to discuss these questions publicly with a view to affecting public policy. Of course, any statesman worthy of the name will not hesitate to address himself to any subject affecting the character and continuity of his regime. He will not regard with neutrality or indifference the introduction of some new theory in the natural or social sciences relevant to the fundamental beliefs of his community. Mill, it will be recalled, admitted in one place that "All attempts by the State to bias the conclusions of its citizens on *disputed* subjects are evil"; from which it follows, however, that it would be proper for government to bias the conclusions of its citizens on undisputed subjects, including those of religion and morality. The trouble is that any orthodoxy can be made a subject of dispute; and since the very principle which Mill publicly recommends cannot but encourage heterodoxy, it is of no value to the statesman, to say the least. Thus Mill's contemporary and critic, James Fitzjames Stephen, could say:

[5] But to see the absurdity of the absolutist interpretation of the First Amendment, suppose that a very large minority of the adult population of the United States (say 45 percent) were religious pacifists. Does anyone believe that, in times of emergency, a Congress controlled by the majority would "make no law respecting an establishment of religion, or prohibiting the free exercise thereof"? There is little point in objecting that a draft law requiring religious pacifists to bear arms would violate the First Amendment. So too would a law exempting them from such a duty. The former would offend the "free exercise" clause, the latter the "establishment" clause. In this connection, see *ibid.*, 749–751 (Aug. 17, 1789), 766–767 (Aug. 20, 1789), where the bearing of arms by pacifists was discussed in Congress.

[T]he government of a great nation can never be carried on satisfactorily without reference more or less direct and frequent to moral and religious considerations, and . . . when such considerations come before parliaments or other civil rulers, they ought not to refuse to entertain them on the ground that they are of a spiritual nature, just as they ought not in case of need to shrink from taking a side in mathematical or scientific controversies. I should not wish to see Parliament enter upon the discussion of the Athanasian Creed, any more than I should wish to see them enter upon the discussion of the controversy between the rival theories as to the character of light. . . . [W]hat I have at heart is not the establishment by authority of an official creed, but the general recognition of the principle that men cannot be governed either by priests or by parliaments without reference to the most important part of human nature.[6]

Stephen protested "against the dogma . . . that statesmen, as such, are bound to treat all religions . . . as having an equal claim to be regarded as true."[7] This dogma engenders or reinforces indifferentism and skepticism and thus undermines not only religion, but that which religion embraces, namely, morality. Since no community can exist, however, without a fairly stable body of widely shared beliefs—for without such beliefs the different purposes and pursuits of men cannot be coordinated— and since these beliefs are diversely affected by various religious doctrines and scientific theories, the genuine statesman will address himself to those doctrines and theories insofar as they influence the conduct of citizens, hence the character and continuity of his regime.

Here, perhaps, is the one serious deficiency in Madison's statesmanship. Madison himself, we have seen, was prepared to discuss matters pertaining to religion (and even to science). Nevertheless, by fostering the dogma of the "total" separation of church and state (though, as we have also seen, Madison is less totalitarian than contemporary absolutists), not only may

[6] Stephen, *Liberty, Equality, Fraternity*, pp. 44–45 (from the preface to the 2nd ed.).

[7] *Ibid.*, pp. 50, 90–98, 233, 252–254.

he have helped to obscure the interfusion of the religious and the political, but he may have contributed to the uncritically accepted opinion that statesmen ought never take sides on religious controversies. It is virtually certain, however, that Madison would not have agreed with the opinion of the Supreme Court in *West Virginia Board of Education* v. *Barnette* upholding the refusal of Jehovah Witnesses to permit their children to salute the flag—this allegedly on First Amendment grounds.[8] In view of the evidence already presented, it should be clear that Madison would have rejected the naive view of Justice Jackson that public education must be "politically neutral"— neutral, not merely as regards partisan politics, but on "things that touch the heart of the existing order."[9] He would have rejected the moral solipsism or subjectivism permeating American education, only to be echoed, sanctioned, and fostered in Justice Jackson's opinion that "A person gets from a symbol [here, the flag-salute] the meaning he puts into it, and what is one man's comfort and inspiration is another's jest and scorn."[10] Madison would probably have recognized that such an opinion logically makes the individual the censor of the laws, and that it is absurd to declare a compulsory flag-salute unconstitutional if what is or is not compulsory is wholly a matter of subjective determination.[11] Still, the author of the First Amendment pro-

---

[8] 319 U.S. 624 (1943). Careful analysis of this case will reveal that neither the free exercise of religion clause, nor the free speech clause, provides the ground for Justice Jackson's opinion. His own pronouncements to the contrary notwithstanding, Justice Jackson was arguing on the ground of *utility* (or as he himself says, the "futility" of the flag salute ceremony to achieve its end, namely, the inculcation of patriotism or the promotion of national unity). Quite clearly the majority did not *like* a *compulsory* flag salute. (Here they reveal the degradation of Dewey's pedagogical principles.) But what makes this case so ludicrous is the repeated references by Justice Jackson (echoed in the concurring opinion by Justices Black and Douglas) to the "free minds" of children.

[9] *Ibid.*, 637, 642.

[10] *Ibid.*, 632–633.

[11] Incidentally, *Brown* v. *Board of Education*, 347 U.S. 483 (1954), is based on similar grounds. Here, the feelings of the segregated race become the censor of the laws. The psychology of Erich Fromm also underlies many cases touching on cruel and unusual punishment and compulsory self-incrimination. See, for

vides little if any encouragement for statesmen or judges living in a relativistic age to examine critically the claims of religionists. It requires no great courage and certainly no great wisdom to say that the meaning of the flag-salute symbol is articulated by the language of the pledge of allegiance; that in taking such a pledge a citizen unambiguously affirms that his *highest* loyalty is not to a flag—a piece of cloth—nor even to the country for which it stands, but rather to God or to a nation *under* God; hence, that only a tendentious reading of Exodus, Chapter 20, verses 4 and 5, could lead to the conclusion that the flag-salute is a form of idolatry.[12]

In an era of unfettered freedom of speech it may seem curious to say that nothing in the First Amendment requires statesmen to be silent on religious matters. Suppose, for example, that unprecedented circumstances rendered certain hitherto innocuous religious practices destructive of the regime? No statesman who takes seriously his duty to support the Constitution would be politically paralyzed by the dogma of absolute separation of church and state. He would not, and he need not, urge legislation "respecting an establishment of religion"; but he could and would urge legislation respecting religion itself if only to preserve "the free exercise thereof."[13] Suppose, on the other hand, that as a result of the empirical studies of serious social scientists, there were good reasons to believe that the teaching of doctrines conducive to atheism was a contributing factor to social disintegration?[14] Enlightened statesmen might urge legislation termi-

---

example, *Trop* v. *Dulles*, 356 U.S. 86 (1958), and *Miranda* v. *Arizona*, 384 U.S. 436 (1966).

[12] *West Virginia* v. *Board of Education*, 319 U.S. 629. It is no disrespect to religious sensibilities and it is certainly no disservice to the cause of religion to subject religious claims to rational criteria. See Whitehead, *Religion in the Making* (New York: Meridian Books, 1960), pp. 120–127 (hereafter cited as RM followed immediately by page number).

[13] I am here assuming that no constitutional amendment would be theoretically necessary.

[14] One of the great defects of Straussian scholars is that they have given up the domain of empirical research to mere empiricists. Confining themselves to literary analysis and social criticism, they have failed to apply the wisdom of

nating financial aid to any university propagating such doctrines. Should they wish, they might go as far as John Locke who, in his "Letter Concerning Toleration," maintained that "those are not at all to be tolerated who deny the being of a God. Promises, covenants, and oaths, which are the bonds of human society, can have no hold upon an atheist."[15] Whether Locke's teaching is refuted by the good behavior of atheists is open to question. For as James Fitzjames Stephen points out, "We cannot judge of the effects of Atheism from the conduct of persons who have been educated as believers in God and in the midst of a nation which believes in God."[16] Indeed, we cannot judge of the effects of atheism from the conduct of persons educated *as atheists* in a predominantly Christian or professedly Christian society.

No one knew with such profundity as Nietzsche that nineteenth-century atheistic humanism was nothing more than Christianity without the Christian God. But unlike nineteenth-century atheists, Nietzsche also knew that their humanism possessed no philosophical justification without that God. This was not the humanism, however, of those framers of the American Constitution who tacitly acknowledged Christ by concluding the document with the words "Done . . . in the Year of our Lord one thousand seven hundred and eighty-seven. . . ." The truth is that the Constitution and the Bill of Rights derive their ultimate justification from Christianity, in particular, from the Protestant religion. The limitations placed upon government by the First Amendment, for example, were intended to affirm the rights of *conscience*, a term which is meaningless outside the Christian tradition. In any event, those rights presuppose the dignity of the individual, which dignity, however, is ultimately derived not from the opinions of men or from the laws of society, but from the perfection of God. Because man does not owe his existence

the classics in such a way as not merely to show the limitations of empiricism, but to build on or transcend it.

[15] John Locke, *A Letter Concerning Toleration* (Indianapolis: Bobbs-Merrill Co., 1955), p. 52. Compare the relevant passage in Washington's Farewell Address, above, p. 211–212.

[16] Stephen, *Liberty, Equality, Fraternity*, p. 254.

to chance or to blind necessity, but is rather created in the image of God, he harbors within him a moral will that is free and rational and in view of which he can justify what he calls the rights of conscience. Unless there is a being superior to man, nothing in theory prevents some men from degrading other men to the level of the subhuman. In God, however, man has a principle of limitation—for truth and goodness are limits—on the basis of which he can insist upon limiting the powers of government. No such limits are available in atheism per se, as the twentieth century tragically demonstrates with its twin atheistic tyrannies of the Left and of the Right.[17] But such limits are also denied in a democracy governed by the principle of *vox populi, vox dei.*

So preoccupied was Madison with the danger of intolerance that he seems to have given insufficient attention to the danger of indifferentism. Consider this passage from *Federalist* 50: "When men exercise their reason coolly and freely on a variety of distinct questions, they inevitably fall into different opinions on some of them. When they are governed by a common passion, their opinions, if they are so to be called, will be the same" (334). While it is true that intolerance usually results from an excess of a single passion, it is also true that indifferentism results from a lack of passion, and neither excess nor deficiency is conducive to reason. Now tolerance is the mean between intolerance and indifferentism; in the mean is where reason flourishes. Yet tolerance may be fostered as well by religion as it may be endangered by atheism. As Whitehead points out: "On the whole, tolerance is more often found in connection with a genial orthodoxy."[18]

[17] See Peter Viereck, *Conservatism Revisited* (New York: Free Press, 1965), pp. 176, 179, 189, n. 13. The statesman who understands the logic of atheism will understand that it does not entail what Madison referred to as "liberal sentiments." That so many academic liberals in America should be atheists (or vice versa) testifies only to the still discernible influence of the classical and Christian traditions. That influence has all but disappeared among their illiberal offspring, the student New Left. This is not to suggest that tolerance breeds intolerance. For the intolerance of the New Left is primarily a negative reaction against moral indifferentism rather than a positive manifestation of moral fervor.
[18] AI 63.

Of course, and in defense of Madison, it could be argued (1) that wherever Christianity, whether Protestant or Catholic, has wielded political power, its rule has been anything but genial; and (2) that the proselytizing passion of Christianity is less congenial to the temperaments of aristocrats than to the tendencies of democracy. There is, however, still another side to this issue.

2

We have seen that the First Amendment was intended to promote tolerance and not indifferentism. Or to put the matter another way: The First Amendment was intended to secure the same "liberal sentiments" of which Madison spoke in connection with the national university. Such sentiments may be and have in fact been fostered by religion. Freud himself credited religion with having civilized man, indeed, with having made civilization possible. The great religions taught men to restrain their impulses and appetites. They enlarged men's sympathies and intellectual horizons beyond kith and kin. But Freud also taught that religion had served its purpose, that it was now a retrogressive and repressive force in human life, and that science might now carry on the work of civilizing man.[19] Science, to be sure, is one of the noblest of man's achievements. Yet, in its ethical neutrality, it can serve barbarism as well as civilization. Despite its ethical neutrality, science is based on the presupposition that science is good, a presupposition which cannot be proven on scientific grounds. The justification for science is ultimately religion, for religion harbors the intuition of a moral order in the universe, of a goodness underlying the coming into being and passing away of all things. Consciously or otherwise, the intuition of that goodness makes possible not only the quest of science, but even those liberal sentiments which enable men to discuss their differences and to be friends despite their differences.

The poverty of Freud's understanding of religion need not be demonstrated here. Unlike Freud, who regarded religion as

[19] See *The Future of an Illusion* (New York: Anchor Books, 1964), pp. 60–64, 70–73, 77–82, 88–92.

an "obsessional neurosis," Whitehead spoke of religions as the source from which every science derives its faith in the rationality of existence.[20] According to Whitehead, "scientific interest is only a variant form of religious interest." There is, however, a significant difference between the two, which he explains as follows:

> Religion is centered upon the harmony of rational thought with the sensitive reaction to the percepta from which experience originates. Science is concerned with the harmony of rational thought with the percepta themselves. When science deals with emotions, the emotions in question are percepta and not immediate passions—other people's emotion and not our own; at least our own in recollection, and not in immediacy. Religion deals with the formation of the experiencing subject; whereas science deals with the objects, which are the data forming the primary phase in this experience.[21]

Here it should be pointed out that logical positivism, from which science still very much derives the articulation of its epistemology, contends that religion is devoid of rationality, that it provides no knowledge of the real world. For the logical positivist, the only things knowable are the "percepta" (or the empirically observable and measurable). Religion is thus relegated to the private and emotional world of the individual or to the status of mythology. The same may be said of the positivist's account of metaphysics, ethics, and aesthetics. The "problems" spoken of in these domains as well as their proffered "solutions" are regarded as intrinsically meaningless.[22]

Because science is posited as the only authoritative form of knowledge of the whole called the real world, all truth claims regarding the world of our deepest concern—the world of values—are degraded: they are made to appear either as mere

---

[20] See Whitehead, PR 67.

[21] *Ibid.*, p. 24.

[22] See, for example, A. J. Ayre, *Language, Truth and Logic* (New York: Dover Publications, Inc., n.d.), chs. i and vi (first published in 1936), and A. J. Ayer, ed., *Logical Positivism* (New York: Free Press, 1959), *passim.*

pretentions or as self-serving deceptions. As a consequence, science, at least as conceived by logical positivism, could become one of the most retrogressive forces in history, undermining the quest for wisdom and thus leveling the intellectual, moral, and aesthetic horizons of man. Of course, it may well be argued, consistently with Whitehead, that positivism is a most inadequate interpretation of science, hence, that it provides a most inadequate understanding of the whole called the real world.[23] As a matter of fact, its understanding of the real world is rooted in, and limited by, the mechanistic determinism of nineteenth-century physics. This means that positivism—and therefore the behavioral sciences which now dominate the university— is based on a Newtonian conception of science whose inadequacies have been recognized, at least by theoretical physicists, for more than sixty years. Not that post-Newtonian physics provides any guidance for human affairs. Nevertheless, the "intellectual lag" between the physical and social sciences has enabled positivism to trivialize the study of political things.[24] Its epistemological shrinkage of knowable entities to what is observable, and of what is observable to what is measurable, obscures the most important thing, namely, the criterion of what is worth observing and measuring. Out of the infinitude of observable data, one thing is not an "observable," and that is the criterion for selecting *this* data rather than *that*. But inquiry must begin somewhere, and contrary to behaviorism, it cannot begin without presuppositions, presuppositions which reveal the observer's criteria of relevance, hence something of his own intellectual and

[23] See the following works of Whitehead: AI 146–148, 158–167; MT 148, 182, 203–232; FR, ch. 1; SMW, *passim*. See also Stanley L. Jaki, *The Relevance of Physics* (Chicago: University of Chicago Press, 1966), pp. 345–346, 356–357, 479–480 (cited hereafter as *Jaki*).

[24] The same tendency is evident in the school of "ordinary language" or analytical philosophy, which has subjected positivism to a most telling critique. It should be understood, however, that analytical philosophy, like behaviorism, is an offshoot of positivism. Though it does not entail moral relativism, its practical or pedagogical effect is to engender or reinforce conventionalism. It accepts moral systems as given, since its concern is merely to analyze the meaning and uses of moral language.

moral horizon. Now it is the case that positivistically oriented social scientists place great value on *predictability*, which means they tend to be preoccupied with the uniformities among men. They deal primarily with mass phenomena, which is to say that their intellectual concerns center on the study of mass men. The centrality of that concern cannot but dignify its object and retreat into obscurity other than mass men. Consequently, while there is good reason to doubt the claim that the behavioral sciences are genuine sciences (in the sense of providing universally valid laws explanatory of human behavior), such is the authority of science in higher education that the mind is threatened by a totalitarianism the likes of which was never known in ages of faith. It may even be the case that religion, feeble as it is in this century, is the last obstacle to the stultifying uniformity of opinions, passions, and interests which Madison so ardently sought to avoid and which the First Amendment was intended to prevent.

The stultification of the mind is always possible whenever some creed or theory achieves complete ascendency among the educated. But hardly anything could be more stultifying than science in the absence of serious rivals. Indeed, science itself is likely to stagnate unless philosophy—philosophy as the quest for knowledge of the whole—is here to challenge its fundamental assumptions.[25] Without such challenge, science is more likely to degenerate into technology and to foster the progressive study of trivia. This is not to belittle the value of technology. It should be understood, however, that technology, systemetized and professionalized under the influence of science, engendered a revolution in education not altogether wholesome. The classically educated generalist was replaced by the pragmatically educated specialist, the amateur by the technician.[26] If traditional education erred on the side of literary or intellectual analysis, at least it retained a sense of wholeness or of the interrelatedness of

[25] See Whitehead, SMW 16–17; AI, ch. ix, *passim*. See also *Jaki*, p. 368.
[26] See Woodrow Wilson, "Democracy and Efficiency," 87 *The Atlantic Monthly* (March 1901), 291.

things. We now err at the opposite extreme, enfeebled by an education fragmented into hermetic disciplines preoccupied with the progressive elaboration of uncoordinated details.[27]

Intoxicated by the success of science, twentieth-century education proceeded to cast received systems of belief into the dust heap of history. As John Dewey has written:

> Because science starts with questions and inquiries it is fatal to all social system-making and programs of fixed ends. In spite of the bankruptcy of past systems of belief, it is hard to surrender our faith in system and in some wholesale belief. We continually reason as if the difficulty were in the particular system that has failed and as if we were on the point of now finally hitting upon one that is true as all the others were false. The real trouble is with the attitude of dependence upon any of them.[28]

Dewey's influence on American education need hardly be emphasized, although the teaching of the master ought not be confused with that of his disciples.[29] In any event, no one more consistently attempted to infuse the experimental method of science into all domains of human life, including education and politics. Thus:

> Men have got used to an experimental method in physical and technical matters. They are still afraid of it in human concerns. The fear is the more efficacious because like all deep-lying fears it is covered up and disguised by all kinds of rationalizations. One of its commonest forms is a truly religious idealization of, and reverence for, established institutions; for example . . . the Constitution, the Supreme Court, private property, free contract and so on.[30]

[27] See Whitehead, SMW 196–220.

[28] John Dewey, *Individualism Old and New* (New York: Capricorn Books, 1962), pp. 164–165 (first published in 1929). Notice the prejudice suggesting that only science starts with questions and inquiries.

[29] See John Dewey, *Experience and Education* (London: Capricorn Books, 1970), pp. 20–22, 64–65, 82–83 (first published in 1938).

[30] John Dewey, *The Public and Its Problems* (3rd ed.; Denver: Henry Holt & Co., 1927), pp. 169–170, 184, 202–210.

Dewey saw in science the best hope for the progress of democracy and, in democracy, the best hope for the progress of science. Democracy, for Dewey, was not a form of government so much as a method of solving public problems, a method involving the following factors: "First, that those concepts, general principles, theories and dialectical developments which are indispensable to any systematic knowledge be shaped and tested as tools of inquiry. Secondly, that policies and proposals for social action be treated as working hypotheses, not as programs to be rigidly adhered to and executed."[31] Public policies are nothing more than experiments to be tested and revised in the light of observed consequences. These experiments are to be pursued under the guidance of social scientists subject, however, to the criticism of the many whose wants these experts are to serve but not, presumably, to question.

Whether Dewey's attempt to make science (or scientific method) the basis of democracy or of a political community is itself scientific or warranted by experience is questionable. Not that he overestimated the rationality of the average man. Rather, he seems to have overestimated the rationality of the average scientist; that is, he seems not to have recognized that even a scientific community is not based solely on rationality. Indeed, it may well be argued that hardly any political community is more conservative or adheres more dogmatically to received principles than the community of science. Thus, in his *Structure of Scientific Revolutions*, Thomas Kuhn reveals that the systematic and progressive articulation of scientific and epochal "paradigms" (such as the Newtonian) requires a scientific community uncritical of the paradigms themselves.[32] A paradigm guides the "puzzle-solving" activity of "normal science," which

[31] *Ibid.*, pp. 202–203.

[32] See Thomas S. Kuhn, *The Structure of Scientific Revolutions* (Chicago: University of Chicago Press, 1962), pp. 10–11, 24–34, 42, 49. Although Kuhn's conception of science verges on conventionalism, which denies that science is knowledge of reality, his study of the conservative aspects of science might prove valuable for the philosophy of law as well as for counteracting the ideological misuse of science by behaviorists.

is the activity of the average scientist. Having been educated in its tradition, the average scientist accepts the paradigm uncritically, and, by means of particular hypotheses and experiments, attempts to apply it to data falling within some specialized area of interest. The experiments themselves are not designed to test the validity of the paradigm, but rather of some particular hypothesis. Whereas hypotheses confirmed by experiment become articulations of the paradigm, data unaccounted for by the paradigm are discarded as anomalies. Over the course of time, anomalies accumulate and become, as it were, scientifically embarrassing. Eventually, a genius appears who initiates a scientific revolution by constructing a new epochal paradigm, one comprehending the old along with anomalous data discarded or unexplained by the scientific community in general.[33]

Analogously, a new political paradigm—a body of fundamental laws—was constructed by the founders.[34] These laws brought into mutual adjustment a variety of hitherto conflicting opinions and interests. Once established, those laws became standards of political thought and conduct. To a greater or lesser extent, they were systematically and progressively elaborated by courts and legislatures. Such systematic and progressive elaboration of the fundamental laws requires the practical, if not theoretical, rejection of "anomalous" or unassimilative opinions or modes of conduct. This means that political as well as scientific paradigms must be rigorously adhered to by the average member of their respective communities if there is to be progress in either domain.

Yet, this analogy between the paradigms of great scientists and statesmen can be misleading. The scientific community may be more dogmatic than it likes to believe; but it can afford to be more tolerant than a political community if only because the

[33] *Ibid.*, pp. 80–81. See Michael Polanyi, *Personal Knowledge* (Chicago: University of Chicago Press, 1958), pp. 12–13, who presents an interesting example of scientific dogmatism that contemporary behaviorists would do well to ponder. Numerous examples of scientific dogmatism are documented in *Jaki, passim.*

[34] The following is nothing more than an analogy; and any further reference to science is not intended to be consistent with Kuhn's view of the subject.

concrete particularity of the latter renders it more susceptible to destruction. Thus, if the United States were in a war for survival, we may be confident that various Supreme Court decisions regarding the First Amendment would be reversed, or disregarded, and consistently with the paradigm of the Constitution. More fundamentally, the difference between a scientific and a political paradigm relates to the difference between the theoretical and practical virtues, truth being the primary emphasis of the one, utility the primary emphasis of the other. Furthermore, and as Aristotle points out: "To change the practice of an art [or the principles of a science] is not the same as to change the operation of a law. It is from habit, and only from habit, that law derives the validity which secures obedience. But habit can be created only by the passage of time; and a readiness to change from existing to new and different laws will accordingly tend to weaken the general power of law" (73). The arts and sciences are but part of the complex whole called culture or civilization, and it is civilization as a whole, developed over millennia, that provides the laws or norms of human conduct. The value or validity of those norms cannot be determined in the artificial and controlled environment of a laboratory. A bacterial "culture" is not the culture containing the arts and sciences, let alone a community's beliefs and customs developed over the course of centuries. The beliefs which govern a society are no more bankrupt than the principles of Newtonian physics. They are only more or less adequate to present occasions. It is even questionable to speak, as Dewey does, of the "brankruptcy of *past* systems of belief." Oftentimes, a person who speaks of the bankruptcy of some past system of belief is only confessing his own incapacity to discern its relevance for the present. There is, of course, little virtue in the dogmatic retention of past beliefs, although there may be less in their dogmatic rejection, for the philistinism of the former may be more generous than the parochialism of the latter. It requires infinitely more courage and insight to transcend the past by incorporating its teachings into a larger whole. Such incorporation is indispensable to the progress of society and science alike. But so too is the cultivation of habits of thought and conduct.

Dewey was not unaware of this. But he did not fully appreciate or accept the different periodicity of intellectual and social change—sometimes called "cultural lag."[35] Certainly he lacked the practical wisdom embodied in these passages from *The Federalist*:

> [E]very institution calculated to restrain the excess of law-making, and to keep things in the same state in which they happen to be at any given period, [i]s much more likely to do good than harm; because it is favorable to greater stability in the system of legislation. The injury which may possibly be done by defeating a few good laws, will be amply compensated by the advantage of preventing a number of bad ones.[36]

> [A] continual change even of good measures is inconsistent with every rule of prudence and every prospect of success. . . .
> But the most deplorable effect of all is that diminution of attachment and reverence which steals into the hearts of the people, towards a political system which betrays so many marks of infirmity, and disappoints so many of their flattering hopes.[37]

Is it absurd to say that "a continual change even of good theories is inconsistent with every rule of science"? or that "the most deplorable effect of such instability is that diminution of attachment and reverence which steals into the hearts of scientists toward a vocation which betrays so many marks of infirmity, and disappoints so many of their hopes which lie in the discovery of truth"? Indeed, if scientific theories comparable in significance to those formulated by Newton and Einstein were to change every decade or so, it is doubtful whether science would win the

[35] It would be a mistake to think, however, that a "cultural lag" exists only as between the sciences and society. Even to this very day the behavioral sciences are based on the mechanistic determinism of nineteenth-century physics, the inadequacy of which has perhaps best been understood by Whitehead. Yet the day is still distant when Whitehead's insights become an integral part of higher education, let alone of culture in general.

[36] *Federalist* 73, p. 478.

[37] *Federalist* 62, pp. 405, 407.

confidence of ordinary men—assuming it would still make sense to speak of "science."[38] The credibility and progress of science, and the very possibility of a scientific community, depend on the incorporation into larger generalities the body of knowledge accumulated during the history of scientific inquiry. The very same may be said of the laws of a political community. To be sure, the truths of science are not derived through the process of resolving the kinds of differences exemplified in deliberative assemblies. Yet the coexistence of the corpuscular and wave theories of light, or of the mechanistic and vitalist theories of biological phenomena, bears some analogy to the tensions embodied in legislation, tensions which could be sustained in neither domain without a common ground of agreement more fundamental than any differences. A community of scientists requires an abiding intellectual and even moral consensus no less so than does a community of citizens. That consensus cannot be questioned too frequently without destroying the very faith of science—the faith that the universe is an intelligible whole, that every item of experience exhibits some general scheme or may be explained by some general theory. Lacking this faith the scientific intellect would become stunted or paralyzed. Interestingly enough, the adherents of long-established scientific theories are as apt to rise in defense against scientific innovators with the same passionate fervor of religious zealots whose faith is challenged by the unorthodox.[39] But whereas the questioning of religious and political doctrines has little if any impact on science, the questioning of a long-established scientific theory may have the profoundest consequences for politics. Consider only the revolution inaugurated by Copernicus.[40] To place in question a generally accepted theory of the universe is bound to

[38] But see *Jaki*, pp. 260, 502–503.

[39] See above, p. 431, n. 33.

[40] But see Polanyi, *Personal Knowledge*, p. 147, n. 2, who refers to a study claiming that there were 2,330 works published on astronomy between 1543 and 1887, but of which only 180 were Copernican.

unsettle received ideas regarding the Deity and his relation to mankind, and, as a consequence, to place in question men's understanding of human nature and of their duties to each other.[41]

If science, in its ethical neutrality, is not to be a destructive agency, its authority must be balanced by religion. This is not a call for moral absolutism or some form of philistine conservatism. For the religion of which I speak must be capable of withstanding the test of rational criticism and hence must itself be rational. On its doctrinal side, religion, says Whitehead, may be defined as "a system of general truths which have the effect of transforming character when they are sincerely held and vividly apprehended."[42] The problem of the religious person is to translate those general truths into particular thoughts, emotions, and purposes. Or as Whitehead elsewhere writes: "Religion is an ultimate craving to infuse into the insistent particularity of emotion that non-temporal generality which primarily belongs to conceptual thought alone."[43] This "insistent particularity of emotion" is the thrust of individuality seeking to liberate itself from the conditioning of one's existence in a particular society with all its historical antecedents. But the truly sincere and magnanimous individual will acknowledge the ineluctable influence of his heritage while seeking to incorporate its rich diversity into a more comprehensive whole. Religion, therefore, need not and ought not be regarded as a body of univocal doctrines literally applied in utter disregard of individuality. The criterion of truth in religion, as in science and philosophy, is comprehensiveness, or the adequacy of general ideas to the widest variety of experience.

Intellectual progress is thus an imperative of religion as it is of science and philosophy. The thrust of individuality is the contradiction of univocal finalities. Yet, the denial of univocal finalities is not the affirmation of epistemological and moral relativ-

[41] See *Tocqueville*, II, 21.
[42] RM 15.
[43] PR 23.

ism. Relativism and "absolutism" are part of a single meaning horizon which can be transcended only by a nonfinalistic teleology whose central principle is, again, comprehensiveness. Progressively increasing comprehensiveness is made possible by the passion of reason seeking to preserve yet transcend, by its power of creative synthesis, the welter of thoughts and values inherited from the past. Again recur to Whitehead:

> Ideals fashion themselves round these two notions, permanence and flux. In the inescapable flux, there is something that abides; in the overwhelming permanence, there is an element that escapes into flux. . . .
>
> The art of progress is to preserve order amid change, and to preserve change amid order. . . . It seems as though the last delicacies of feeling require some element of novelty to relieve their massive inheritance from bygone system. Order is not sufficient. What is required, is something much more complex. It is order entering upon novelty; so that the massiveness of order does not degenerate into mere repetition; and so that the novelty is always reflected upon a background of system.
>
> But the two elements must not really be disjoined. It belongs to the goodness of the world, that its settled order should deal tenderly with the faint discordant light of the dawn of another age.[44]

The settled order should deal tenderly with the emergence of novel thoughts and interests, provided that such novelty is not destructive of the very antecedents upon which its own maturity depends. Hence, innovators should deal tenderly with the settled order of thoughts and interests, unless these are threatening human life with destructive repetition. It should be understood, however, that the skills and virtues of men require repetition, hence, that discipline and habit, no less than impulse and imagination, are essential to progress.[45] With these words I now bring this Discourse on statesmanship to a close.

[44] *Ibid.*, pp. 513, 515.
[45] *Ibid.*, p. 514. Similar views will be found in J. S. Mill, *On Liberty*, p. 158; *Representative Government*, pp. 238–239, 250–255.

3

I have elaborated on the themes of religion and science so as to reveal how sweeping and profound is the problem and the task of statesmanship. Today, statesmen of whatever age and persuasion speak incessantly of change and thereby hasten their own obsolescence. What statesmen should emphasize and pursue is not change so much as rational redevelopment issuing in *greatness*: greatness in individuals and greatness in society. But greatness, to be such, must abide the phenomena of change, while the phenomena must themselves be informed by that very greatness. The pursuit of greatness thus involves the reconciliation of change and permanence, the central problem of the rule of law. The rule of law requires that the future shall resemble the past, that there be some presumption in favor of past arrangements. The rule of law thus exemplifies the moral order of the universe. For it belongs to the goodness of the universe that what men have struggled for and have created in the past should have some relevance for the future. In these terms are we ultimately to understand why extraordinary majorities are required to amend the Constitution, the fundamental law of the United States. That Constitution bears witness to a very simple truth of which statesmen would do well to remind their countrymen, namely, that the living do not possess a monopoly of wisdom. It is a vulgar conceit which violates the reason as well as the goodness of the universe to think that the present, by virtue of fortuitous and evanescent majorities, should possess the power and the right to nullify the works of the past. On the other hand, the same reason and goodness of the universe, again exemplified in the Constitution, denies to the past the power and the right to stifle the creative energies of the present. Somewhere Whitehead has said that the pure conservative is fighting against the essence of the universe—and so he is, as might also be said of the pure liberal. The one desires permanence, the other change, while the universe requires both. It is the same with the rule of law, of rational development.

Unfortunately, and ever since Plato and Aristotle, the rule of law has been confused with the rule of rules on the one hand, to which has been opposed the rule of reason on the other.[46] It is argued that rules are frequently insufficient for the determination of particular cases; that their proper application necessitates the use of reason bringing into mutual adjustment novel facts and antecedent patterns. All this is true enough as shown in previous chapters. What is overlooked, however, is that the selection and mutual adjustment of novel facts to antecedent patterns involve the creativity of reason. This means that the traditional opposition between the rule of reason and the rule of law presupposes a disinterested intellect, which is to deny the primacy of individuality. For these reasons the politics of magnanimity regards the traditional view as inadequate. I shall return to this point in a moment, but first it will be necessary to dispel a related error concerning the rule of law.

Just as the rule of law has been confused with the rule of rules, so too has it been mistakenly identified with the rule of precedent. According to the politics of magnanimity, however, precedent only provides material and experience for creating new and richer forms of life. Not repetition of the past, but its redemption in novel arrangements for the present and the future—this is the task of statesmanship. Here the work of the statesman must be judged by the criterion of comprehensiveness. For his work to endure, it must be reinforced by old and familiar feelings, values, and relationships. Unless things can become old and familiar, ancient and venerable—indeed, unless what was great in the past can participate in and inspire the present—the statesman will lack the incentive to pursue greatness. Respect for what is old and familiar, therefore, should deepen rather than dampen his zest for life, his passion for greatness. He should understand

[46] See Plato, *Statesman* 293–294; Aristotle, *Politics*, pp. 141–142, 146–148. Although the distinction between the rule of law and the rule of reason may be of practical value—I have made some use of it in this Discourse—I believe is it philosophically unsound (as is the classical distinction between law and justice), but for reasons which here can only be adumbrated.

that the presumption in favor of past arrangements implicit in the rule of law only requires that to the innovator belongs the burden of proof, a burden which the genuine statesman imposes upon himself, disciplined by profound knowledge of history, yet daring to extend the range of human possibility.

The politics of magnanimity therefore maintains, and more emphatically and consistently than any school of political psychology, that the personality of the statesman is central to an understanding of politics and public policy. How could this be otherwise when his personality is constituted by his passions, thoughts, and actions?—which only the naive ever deemed impervious to the influence of his contemporaries. But while all this may readily be admitted, so too must the no less obvious fact that whereas the personality of one statesman may be petty, another's may be magnanimous. Again, I have admitted—indeed, I have insisted—that the mind of the statesman is not a passive medium upon which may be impressed either the flux of external stimuli or immutable principles of justice having univocal meaning. But I also insist that if the statesman is not governed by pure reason, neither is the political scientist or even the philosopher. Here again may be discerned the error of opposing the rule of reason to the rule of law. The opposition found in Plato and Aristotle is rooted in a metaphysics which regards "universals" and "particulars" as antithetical. With this metaphysics will be found, at least in Aristotle, an epistemology limited by the subject-object explanation of experience. The metaphysics obscures the moral primacy of individuality; the epistemology obscures the creativity of reason. In contrast, the politics of magnanimity maintains that reason is the discriminating and synthesizing passion of individuality; that it derives all its data from the present in which is immanent, however, remembrances of the past as well as anticipations of the future. What the rule of law requires is nothing more than the lawful use of reason, adjusting or harmonizing, with minimum loss, the data of the present so as to achieve increasing comprehensiveness. The rule of reason thus turns out to be or involve a critique of discordant

439

data required by the very notion of law itself. Here the statesman is anything but disinterested. Indeed, he is the very center of a multiplicity of values and relationships whose gradation of importance or whose synthesis awaits the determination of his creative intellect. If the statesman should remove himself politically from the truly serious concerns of human life, the concerns of religion and morality, and leave to the academic and commercial media the shaping of his country's moral character, he will have thereby reduced the art of statesmanship to that of maximizing comfort or consumption. He will then become the creature of a small-souled politics. But if he should resist this degradation of statesmanship and dedicate himself to reminding his countrymen of human greatness, inspiring them with noble purpose, he will then be studied by the politics of magnanimity.

The heroic aspect of the history of the country is the symbol of its immediate worth.

Alfred North Whitehead

THIS DISCOURSE proceeded from the conviction that scholars, philosophers, and statesmen would do well to study closely the founding of regimes, for therein is to be discovered not only the fundamental issues of political life, but that tragic aspect of history which seems to require the loss of much that is good in virtue of man's quest for greatness. Yes, the new pays dearly for its victory over the old. But the new is never simply new. It is but a foreground forgetful of its retreating background from which it still inherits wisdom and folly. Nevertheless, in its overcoming of the past, the new makes possible a richer, more coherent, and more comprehensive future. Here, breadth and depth of achievement depend largely on the ability of scholars, philosophers, and statesmen to restore, synthesize, and translate into policy those conflicting intellectual and moral traditions and tendencies which render the founding of regimes preeminently worthy of study.

And so it is that the founding of the American 'polity' has been the vehicle for this Discourse on statesmanship. In expounding upon the design and decline of that 'polity,' I could not but vindicate the statesmanship of its founders. For the work of the founders—representing their reflections on man, society, and government—embodies a politics of magnanimity, the further

441

articulation of which would yield a synthesis of classical and modern political science.

A 'polity' is indeed a rare political phenomenon. Aristotle does not contradict himself when he admits that this rare phenomenon is the best regime attainable for political societies in general. He means only this: A well-designed 'polity' provides the standard of excellence to which civilized societies may reasonably aspire but seldom achieve. Yet the founders envisioned for the people of the United States a standard of life more noble than that attainable in a classical 'polity.' That higher standards are conceivable the founders well knew, and Aristotle profoundly teaches. Of course, the statesman ought not be expected to articulate those standards with the clarity and fullness of the philosopher. The statesman personifies, as it were, the best regime in practice, the philosopher the best regime in theory. The statesman is a lover of the political, the philosopher a lover of the divine. The one is animated by the quest for fame, the other by a quest for wisdom. The distinction, however, is too sharp; for between the two is the philosophic statesman. He too seeks an immortality of fame; but he wishes to be honored by no less than philosophic statesmen like himself. And so, rather than leave wholly to others the narration of his deeds, he may bequeath to posterity a written monument bearing witness to his deeds' intentions. He knows that the words of men endure beyond their deeds, for the word points to the silence of the unseen.

On the Declaration of Independence

S O LONG as moral relativism in its various forms continues to dominate higher education in the United States, American youth will be molded by a doctrine which is diametrically opposed to the moral principles underlying the Declaration of Independence. This I argued in "The Crisis of Our Times," an essay printed in the *Congressional Record* (July 31, 1968), and subsequently revised for publication in *The Review of Politics* (January, 1970) under the title "Intellectual and Moral Anarchy in American Society." Now, in view of the fact that moral relativism is rampant in American society, we may be certain that, unless statesmen comprehend and *publicly* articulate the deeper meaning of the Declaration of Independence, they will be frustrated in their attempts to pursue any comprehensive and long-range policies capable of securing the blessings of liberty against the forces of tyranny. Let them therefore ponder the following questions: (1) What do the words of the Declaration reveal about the temperament of the statesmen who signed that document? (2) What do the words of these men reveal about their understanding of human nature? Or (3) what underlying conception of human nature can justify the Declaration such that thoughtful men could live by its teachings and convey them to youth of all ages? These questions guided the interpretation of the Declaration contained in the aforementioned essay, an interpretation which began as follows: "When in the Course of hu-

443

man events, it becomes necessary for one people to dissolve the political bands which have connected them with another, and to assume among the powers of the earth, the separate and equal station to which the Laws of Nature and of Nature's God entitle them, a decent respect to the opinions of mankind requires that they should declare the causes which impel them to the separation."[1]

To whom are these words primarily addressed? The authors refer to "mankind." Are they addressing the whole of mankind or only that part of mankind they regard as *civilized?* Perhaps their intended audience is more exclusive. Notice that "a decent respect to the opinions of mankind" compels them to explain why they are separating from Britain. Surely they would not feel thus compelled were it not for the fact that such separation, according to the opinion then prevailing among the generality of mankind, would be condemned as *unlawful*—nay, as *treason.* But while respecting this not unreasonable opinion, the authors of the Declaration are not guided by that opinion. Indeed, they have undertaken a course of action which they know to be utterly *contrary to world opinion!* A decent respect to world opinion only "requires that they should declare the causes which impel them to the separation." Once having stated those causes they can boldly declare: "We . . . acquiesce in the necessity, which denounces our Separation, and hold [our British brethren], as we hold the rest of mankind, Enemies in War, in Peace Friends." How very different from present-day appeals to world opinion— that nebulous creature of timid men. But the question persists: to whom is the Declaration primarily addressed?

Before declaring the causes or grievances which impel them to sever their ties with Britain, the authors of the Declaration wrote the following words: "let Facts be submitted to a candid world." What does "candid" mean? In the language of the eighteenth century, to be candid is to be free from bias or preju-

[1] Compare with *Federalist* 14, p. 85, and *Federalist* 63, p. 407, *in re* "a decent respect to the opinions of mankind."

444

dice.[2] What prejudice did the authors have in view? Very likely it was but another opinion of mankind, namely, the respectable opinion that to be just is to be law abiding. It is precisely this identification of the just with the legal that would lead the generality of mankind to regard the Declaration, or the act of its authors, as treason.[3] In contrast, a candid person would know that laws may be unjust, that over and above the laws of parliaments and kings are the laws of nature and of nature's God. A candid person would see in these laws of nature universally valid standards by which to determine the justice or injustice of the laws of men. And so, before enumerating those laws or grievances which impel them to separate from Britain, the authors declare: "We hold these truths to be self evident, that all men are created equal, that they are endowed by their Creator with certain unalienable Rights, that among these are Life, Liberty and the pursuit of Happiness."

What do they mean by the words "all men are created equal"? Obviously the Declaration does not mean that all men are born equal in their physical, moral, and intellectual endowments.[4] Rather, they are born equal in their unalienable rights. This, according to the authors, is a self-evident truth, by which is meant a proposition whose truth is apprehended intuitively or which is demonstrable from the meaning of the proposition alone. In geometry, that the whole is greater than any of its parts, in ethics, that one ought not repay good with evil, are examples of self-evident truths.[5]

Two things are to be noted, however. First, a proposition may

[2] *Ibid.*, p. 408, *in re* the "impartial world" and the "unbiased part of mankind" and see *Federalist* 1, p. 4, on "candor."

[3] In view of p. 438, n. 46, above, it should be understood that the following interpretation remains more or less within the meaning horizon circumscribed by the "politics of rights" and the "politics of duties."

[4] See *The Writings of Thomas Jefferson* (9 vols.; New York: Congressional Edition, 1861), VI, 221–228, on the "natural aristoi."

[5] See *Federalist* 31, p. 188, cited in the Introduction, xxvii–xxviii, and on pp. 390–391 above.

be true without its truth being self-evident. Second, whether the truth of a proposition appears *to us* as self-evident will depend upon whether we understand its key terms. Bearing this in mind, consider the proposition that all men are endowed with an unalienable right to life, liberty, and the pursuit of happiness. Notice that the proposition speaks of all "men," not of all sentient creatures; it refers to *men*, not to brute animals. Brute animals are not endowed with an unalienable right to life. Hence we do not censure wolves for killing sheep, nor men for eating lamb chops. We know that the behavior of wolves, like the behavior of sheep, is morally neutral. We do not say the same of men. We know there are men who are as bloodthirsty as wolves, and we condemn them. We say their behavior is *in*human, meaning contrary to certain qualities that distinguish human nature from brute nature—I mean *reason* and *self-restraint*. These two qualities of human nature are presupposed by the Declaration. Together they elucidate the self-evident truths of which the Declaration speaks and to which this nation was once dedicated.

Because man is a being endowed with the power of reason he is able to distinguish between what is right by nature and what is right by convention. Reason thus enables men to question and determine whether the laws or acts of parliaments and kings conform to or violate standards of natural justice. This power of reason is the precondition of human freedom, indeed, of human dignity. Hear what it teaches us: Man is the only animal who knows he is an animal; therefore, he is not merely an animal. Unlike any other animal man is capable of knowing himself. This means that men are free to the extent they are governed by insight or knowledge as opposed to mere opinion—say the opinions of mankind.

Because man is endowed with the power of reason he is capable of choosing what is good and what is noble while shunning what is bad and what is base. Unlike brute animals, man has genuine alternatives. He is not simply a determined creature. He is not simply at the mercy of instinct, appetite, and desire. Unlike brute animals, man has a sense of shame; he is capable of

446

self-restraint. This capacity for self-restraint is an essential pre-condition of human freedom and of human dignity.

Let us now join these two qualities that distinguish human nature from brute nature and refer them back to that proposition I spoke of a moment ago and which the authors of the Declaration regarded as a self-evident truth. That proposition may now read as follows: "All men—meaning those earthly beings who are endowed with reason and with the capacity for self-restraint—are thereby endowed with unalienable rights to life, liberty, and the pursuit of happiness."

To secure these rights, the Declaration continues, "Governments are instituted among Men, deriving their just powers from the consent of the governed." It is precisely because man is endowed with reason and with the capacity for self-restraint that he may not be governed without his consent. Nevertheless, governments do not derive their just powers from the consent of the young, no more than from the insane or from criminals. Consent presupposes maturity—the maturity of those very qualities that distinguish human nature from brute nature, again, reason and the capacity for self-restraint. Hence it follows that those whose public conduct is brutish—vile, vicious, or violent—may be governed without their consent.

Now the principle of government based on the consent of the governed should not be taken to mean that democracy is the only legitimate form of government. The word democracy does not appear in the Declaration. Besides, what the Declaration emphasizes is not the *forms* but the *ends* of government. In its own words: "whenever *any* Form of Government becomes destructive of these ends, it is the Right of the People to alter or to abolish it." From this it follows that there are legitimate forms of government other than democracy, for example, constitutional monarchy. Nor is this all. For given the paramount importance of the *ends* of government, no people has a right to choose a *form* of government which is destructive of those ends. Man's natural rights to life, liberty, and the pursuit of happiness are unalienable, that is, they cannot, on principle, be taken away *or voted*

447

away.[6] Men who cannot distinguish between freedom and tyranny, between the good and the bad, are not the men to whom the Declaration is addressed.

From these considerations it follows that the Declaration posits only a qualified—not an absolute—right of revolution. Revolution may be justified only if government becomes destructive of men's natural or unalienable rights. And yet, even here, in the very midst of advocating revolution, the authors of the Declaration remain committed to a politics whose first principle is not violence but *moderation.* Well did they know that a call to revolution, however well justified, would arouse not only the nobler but the baser passions of mankind. And so, guided not only by immediate but by long-range considerations, they add the following words of caution: "Prudence, indeed, will dictate that Governments long established should not be changed for light and transient causes; and accordingly all experience hath shown, that mankind are more disposed to suffer, while evils are sufferable, than to right themselves by abolishing the forms to which they are accustomed."[7] The authors of those words had already a plan for a new form of government. And so, with a view to the future (for they did not wish to arm the wicked), they further clarify the conditions under which a people might resort to revolution: "when a long train of abuses *and* usurpations, pursuing *invariably* the same Object evinces a *design* to reduce them under absolute *Despotism*, it is their right, it is their duty, to throw off such Government, and to provide new Guards for their future security." There are men who seem incapable of distinguishing between evils which are sufferable, but which may

---

[6] This point is wholly obscured by contemporary American statesmen with respect to nations subject to communist insurgency. To be sure, the *deeds* of such statesmen are not wholly consistent with their *words*, or with the teachings of so many of their educators. The point is that if the principle of self-determination is not to be a self-contradiction, not even an overwhelming majority of voters can install a communist regime and thereby deprive their children of those unalienable rights referred to in the Declaration.

[7] This forbearance of mankind (think of the "silent majority") may be attributed either to apathy or to deference or both.

be remedied by means of politics, and evils which are insufferable and which can be remedied only by means of violence. Hence, they will regard an imperfect justice as slavery, an imperfect government as tyranny. The Declaration is not addressed to such men. They could not possibly understand the civility of its authors.

It is men possessing the virtues of civility that the Declaration has primarily in view. These virtues include: (1) moderation, or the capacity to exercise restraint over one's passions and desires; (2) public-spiritedness, or a due concern for the good of others; (3) a decent respect, but never subservience, to prevailing opinion; (4) an abiding commitment to reason and truth. These virtues, it should be apparent, have been undermined by the doctrine of moral relativism which pervades virtually all institutions of learning. This doctrine [I concluded] cannot but bring about the degradation of reason and the ascendency of the passions. [This said, I shall now add a postscript.]

How instructive it would be if educators were to compare the tone and teachings of the American Declaration with the Declaration of Independence of the Democratic Republic of Vietnam—a declaration promulgated by Ho Chi Minh in 1945.[8] The former speaks the language of magnanimity, the latter of rancor and resentment. One proclaims the right of all men to the *"pursuit of happiness,"* the other the right of all peoples to *"be happy."* But perhaps the most revealing difference between the two documents is this. Whereas the signers of the American Declaration conclude by saying: "with a firm reliance on the protection of Divine Providence, we mutually pledge to each other our Lives, our Fortunes and our sacred Honor," the signers of the Vietnamese Declaration conclude by saying: "The entire Vietnamese people are determined to mobilize all their physical and mental strength, to sacrifice their lives and property in order to safeguard their independence and liberty." Conspicuously miss-

[8] Printed in Theodore McNally, ed., *Sources in Modern East Asian History and Politics* (New York: Appleton-Century-Crofts, Inc., 1967), pp. 329–331.

ing here is the word *honor*—an aristocratic motif foreign to democratic but especially Marxian thought and temperament.[9] Let me be more precise.

The signers of the American Declaration pledge their honor as *individuals*. They thereby affirm a power within the individual over himself and over external circumstances. Stated another way, the notion of honor involves a distinction between the noble and the base or a ruler-ruled relationship within the individual himself. That relationship is one of the cardinal themes of religion and morality. As we have seen, however, Marxism regards the teachings of religion and morality—but therefore the principles underlying the Declaration of Independence—as mere "phantoms" of the brain, mere "reflexes" of material or economic premises. Such reductionism deprives the *word*, hence the truly human, of any dignity. It degrades the thoughts of men to the level of instruments of appetite or desire.[10] Clearly, this ple-

[9] Interestingly enough, Jefferson, while ambassador to France, struck out "the care of one's honor" from Lafayette's draft of the Declaration of the Rights of Man and Citizen. For the text, see Gilbert Chinard, ed., *The Letters of Lafayette and Jefferson* (Baltimore: Johns Hopkins Press, 1929), p. 138. All the more reason, therefore, not to regard Jefferson as the sole author of the American Declaration.

[10] See Hobbes, *Leviathan*, p. 46. This helps to explain the vehement and violent language of the Vietnamese Declaration, of which here is but one example: "They [the French] have mercilessly slain our patriots; they have drowned our uprisings in rivers of blood. . . . To weaken our race they have forced us to use opium and alcohol." The venomous and vindictive tone of that document is perfectly consistent with communist pronouncements in general, and so cannot be attributed solely to the character of French colonialism. Statesmen should bear this in mind when entering upon the precarious task of "negotiating" with communist regimes, precarious (and usually futile) for two reasons: first, because genuine negotiations presuppose recognition of the efficacy of reason, its capacity to resolve political differences—a presupposition denied by dogmatic Marxism, which regards violence as the progressive force of history; second, because "negotiating" with communist regimes conveys to the American public the fallacious notion that such regimes are conventional nations, that they are not really governed by an ideology which looks forward to the destruction of the free world. *The* problem of statesmen is to "deal" with communist regimes without conveying that notion to the public. No statesman has thus far succeeded in solving this problem. Needless to say, they are hindered from doing so by educators who propagate the doctrine of cultural relativism.

450

beian conception of human nature is at war with a people who would live by the principles of those statesmen who pledged their sacred honor in the American Declaration of Independence. In that pledge I discern an aristocratic anthropology drawn from classical and biblical sources, an anthropology that affirms the dignity of reason on the one hand, and the sovereignty of God on the other. The authors of the American Declaration would therefore regard with contempt the doctrine that man's intellect is, in principle, subservient to material forces. That doctrine, it should be emphasized, represents the most radical departure from the classical and biblical traditions. It entails the utter denial of *individuality*, hence the very possibility of honor.

Now, while it is true that the aristocratic anthropology underlying the American Declaration requires us to recognize that all men are created equal, two things are to be remembered. First, the equality thus spoken of means that no man, on principle, stands to any other man in the condition of a subordinate species to be ruled solely for the good of the ruler. This means that the criterion of political rule must be the common good. Nevertheless, there is a second consideration. Though *created* equal, men are in fact *born* unequal in their physical, intellectual, and moral endowments. From this factual inequality it follows that not all men exhibit in their way of life a due sense of honor. Indeed, some may be shameless, some servile. Some may be unfit to govern others, some may be unfit to govern themselves. The point to bear in mind, however, is this: Without honor, reason cannot prevail over the affairs of men. Shamelessness and force will take their place, will overcome any people that live contrary to the moral and religious principles which underly and which alone can justify the American Declaration of Independence.

451

Toward the Establishment of a National University and an Institute of Statesmanship

I T WAS SAID in the Introduction that while the twentieth century has witnessed a remarkable growth in the number of departments of political science, it has also witnessed a no less remarkable decline in the art of statesmanship and of public oratory. The causes of this decline are many; but among the most powerful has been the decline in the quality of higher education, especially in the liberal arts. Accordingly, and in the spirit of Washington and Madison, I propose the establishment of a National University including an Institute of Statesmanship. As with any genuine university, the one I am proposing would be dedicated to the advancement of intellectual discernment, humane feelings, and aesthetic refinement. Consistent therewith, its Institute of Statesmanship would be dedicated to the development of what I have called the "politics of magnanimity," a politics that would enlarge the range of human values such that freedom dwells with virtue, equality with excellence, wealth with beauty, the here and now with the eternal. What follows is an elaboration of this proposal.

The university I have in mind would be supported by federal funds. It would have a board of directors appointed by the President with the advice and consent of the Senate; and the members of this board would have a tenure of sufficient duration to ensure their independence. The university would consist of an integrated system of colleges and institutes the heads of which would be named by the board of directors. The heads of these colleges and institutes would appoint department chairmen who, in consultation with their immediate superiors, would appoint the remaining faculty.

Although a modest tuition should be required for admission to the university, the paramount requirement would be intellectual achievement and moral character. Standards for admission, however, should *not* exceed those of our better colleges and universities.

In addition to the usual colleges, the university would have colleges of law, business, engineering, and medicine, as well as a college of the performing arts. Faculty and students from each college would participate in interdisciplinary programs designed to overcome the fragmentation of contemporary education and to foster that sense of intellectual and moral community which alone can sustain a rich and meaningful diversity.

I mentioned a college of the performing arts. Such a college is of special importance, for we need to elevate popular culture: its music, its dance, its art, its drama, its literature. The graduates of this college would help fill the need for more musicians, orchestras, opera companies, dance troupes, and repertory theaters.

With a view to the reclamation and development of our western desert lands, the university should have an institute for city and regional planning. The faculty of such an institute would be drawn from all the disciplines and should also include men with practical political experience. Through the activities of this institute, the university would contribute to the revitalization of national purpose.

Finally, I turn to the Institute of Statesmanship, but only to set forth in outline the scope of its purposes which are as follows:

1. *To promote a renaissance in political philosophy as the architectonic science of human society*:

    a. to promote a philosophical synthesis of classical and modern political science;

b. to overcome the classical-modern conflict regarding the primacy of reason versus the primacy of the passions;

c. to enrich modern political science by providing a moral foundation for the modern emphasis on freedom and individuality;

d. to enrich classical political philosophy with the insights of modern psychology, phenomenology, and analytical philosophy.

2. *To reconstruct the political thought and statesmanship of the founding fathers*:

a. to study the classical, Christian, and modern aspects of the founding;

b. to study the art of statesmanship exemplified by the founders;

c. to examine in depth the organization of the new government under the Washington administration.

3. *To illuminate the changing character of American political thought and practice since the founding*:

a. to trace the impact on the character of the American regime of the political thought and policies of such presidents as Jefferson, Jackson, Lincoln, Wilson, and Franklin Roosevelt;

b. to trace the changing character of American constitutional law;

c. to trace the development of political parties and their influence on the character of statesmanship;

d. to examine the development of capitalism and of organized labor and to reveal their influence on American manners and morals;

e. to examine the influence of science and technology on American manners and morals;

f. to examine the influence of literature on American manners and morals;

g. to trace the changing character of the role of the intellectual in political life since the founding;

h. to examine the changing character of higher education in the United States since the seventeenth century.

4. *To promote the art of statesmanship and public oratory*:
a. to compare the founding of different regimes, ancient and modern;
b. to compare classical and modern writings on rhetoric;
c. to compare the rhetorical skills of ancient and modern statesmen;
d. to develop a science of legislation and deliberation;
e. to organize courses in public disputation and in political speech writing;
f. to enrich the art of diplomacy.

5. *To study the role and problems of the United States as a world power*:
a. to examine the influence of moral principles and material interests on American foreign policy;
b. to show how domestic and foreign policy are related in different regimes;
c. to examine the influence of the social sciences on the shaping of American foreign policy;
d. to examine the nature of the conflict between communism and liberal democracy;
e. to contrast the statesmanship of various national leaders both in the United States and in other countries.

6. *To show how the major domestic problems of the United States are related to the basic principles and purposes of American democracy*:
a. to show how an excess of freedom and equality can lead to social disintegration and mediocrity;
b. to show how civic virtue may be cultivated consistently with liberal democracy;
c. to show how a commercial society may be made consistent with modesty and beauty.

7. *To train political scientists and statesmen.*

8. *To publish a Journal of Statesmanship.*

Let it only be recognized, with Aristotle and Madison, that true wisdom and virtue are rare, and the above proposal will not be charged with elitism or with centralism. Reason, sound tradition, and distributive justice each uphold the principle of federalism. Diversity is a good when its elements reinforce and enrich each other. Otherwise, diversity can be self-defeating. On the other hand, mere uniformity is death itself. We prefer life.

Annals of Congress. 1789–1800.

Aristotle. *Athenian Constitution.*

———. *Metaphysics.*

———. *Nicomachean Ethics.*

———. *Physics.*

———. *The Politics of Aristotle.* Ernest Barker, trans. London: Oxford University Press, 1952.

———. *Rhetoric and Poetics.* W. Rhys Roberts, trans. New York: Modern Library, 1954.

Bacon, Francis. *Essays.* New York: Modern Library, 1955.

Beard, Charles. *An Economic Interpretation of the Constitution of the United States.* New York: Macmillan Co., 1954.

Bentley, Arthur. *The Process of Government.* Chicago: University of Chicago Press, 1908, republished by Harvard University Press, 1967.

Bordon, Morton. *The Antifederalist Papers.* Ann Arbor: University of Michigan Press, 1965.

Brown, Robert. *Charles Beard and the Constitution.* Princeton: Princeton University Press, 1956.

———. *Middle-Class Democracy and the Revolution in Massachusetts.* Ithaca: Cornell University Press, 1955.

———, and B. Katherine Brown. *Virginia 1705–1786: Democracy or Aristocracy?* East Lansing: Michigan State University Press, 1964.

Burke, Edmund. *Reflections on the Revolution in France.* Indianapolis: Bobbs-Merrill Co., 1955.

Clor, Harry M. *Obscenity and Public Morality.* Chicago: University of Chicago Press, 1969.

Cooke, Jacob E. *The Reports of Alexander Hamilton*. New York: Harper Torchbooks, 1964.

Croly, Herbert. *The Promise of American Life*. New York: Macmillan Co., 1912.

Cubberley, Ellwood P. *Public Education in the United States*. Boston: Houghton Mifflin Co., 1934.

Davidson, John W., ed. *A Crossroads of Freedom*. New Haven: Yale University Press, 1956.

Dewey, John. *Individualism Old and New*. New York: Capricorn Books, 1962.

Diamond, Martin. "Democracy and *The Federalist*: A Reconsideration of the Framers' Intent," *American Political Science Review*, LIII (March 1959).

————, Winston Mills Fisk, and Herbert Garfinkel. *The Democratic Republic*. Chicago: Rand McNally & Co., 1966, 2nd ed. rev., 1970.

Eidelberg, Paul. *Philosophy of the American Constitution*. New York: Free Press, 1968.

————. "Between a Silent and a Tyrannical Majority," *Midway*, 11:1 (Summer 1970).

————. "Intellectual and Moral Anarchy in American Society: A Study of Its Causes," *The Review of Politics*, 35:1 (January 1970).

————. "The Temptation of Herbert Marcuse," *The Review of Politics*, 31:4 (October 1969).

Farmer, Francis, ed. *The Wilson Reader*. New York: Oceana Publications, 1956.

Farrand, Max. *The Framing of the Constitution of the United States*. New Haven: Yale University Press, 1967.

————. *The Records of the Federal Convention of 1787*. 4 vols. New Haven: Yale University Press, 1937.

Federal and State Constitutions, Colonial Charter, and Other Organic Laws of the United States. 2 vols. Washington, D.C.: Government Printing Office, 1877–88.

Frisch, Morton, and Richard Stevens, eds. *American Political Thought*. New York: Charles Scribner's Sons, 1971.

Hamilton, Alexander. *The Works of Alexander Hamilton*. John C. Hamilton, ed. 7 vols. New York: Charles S. Francis & Co., 1850–51.

————. *The Works of Alexander Hamilton*. Henry C. Lodge, ed. 12 vols. New York: G. P. Putnam's Sons, 1903–4.

————, John Jay, and James Madison. *The Federalist*. New York: Modern Library, 1938.

Hobbes, Thomas. *Leviathan*. Michael Oakeshott, ed. New York: Macmillan Co., 1955.

Hofstadter, Richard. *The American Political Tradition*. New York: Vintage Books, 1956.

Hume, David. *Treatise of Human Nature*. London: Oxford University Press, 1955.

James, William. *Pragmatism*. New York: Longmans, Green & Co., 1917.

————. *Varieties of Religious Experience*. New York: Modern Library, n.d.

Jefferson, Thomas. *The Writings of Thomas Jefferson*. 9 vols. New York: Congressional Edition, 1861.

————. *The Writings of Thomas Jefferson*. 20 vols. Washington, D.C.: Memorial Edition, 1902–4.

Journals of the Continental Congress 1774–1789. New York: Johnson Reprint Corp., 1968.

Kenyon, Cecilia M., ed. *The Antifederalists*. Indianapolis: Bobbs-Merrill Co., 1966.

Kuhn, Thomas S. *The Structure of Scientific Revolutions*. Chicago: University of Chicago Press, 1962.

Lasswell, Harold. *The Political Writings of Harold Lasswell*. Glencoe: Free Press, 1951.

Levy, Leonard W. *Freedom of Speech and Press in Early American History: Legacy of Suppression*. New York: Harper Torchbooks, 1963.

Lincoln, Abraham. *The Life and Writings of Abraham Lincoln*. New York: Modern Library, 1940.

Locke, John. *Second Treatise of Civil Government*.

————. *Thoughts Concerning Education*.

————. "A Letter Concerning Toleration." Indianapolis: Bobbs-Merrill Co., 1955.

Machiavelli, Niccolo. *The Prince and the Discourses*. New York: Modern Library, 1950.

Madison, James. *Letters and Other Writings*. 4 vols. New York: J. B. Lippincott & Co., 1884.

————. *The Papers of James Madison*. 6 vols. to date; Chicago: University of Chicago Press, 1962–69.

459

————. *The Writings of James Madison.* Gaillard Hunt, ed. 9 vols. New York: G. P. Putnam's Sons, 1900–10.

Mansfield, Harvey C., Jr. *Statesmanship and Party Government.* Chicago: University of Chicago Press, 1965.

Marx, Karl, and Fredrick Engels. *The German Ideology.* New York: International Publishers, 1968.

————. *Writings of the Young Marx on Philosophy and Society.* Loyd D. Easton and Kurt H. Guddat, eds. and trans. Garden City: Doubleday Anchor Books, 1967.

McMaster, John B., and Frederick D. Stone, eds. *Pennsylvania and the Federal Constitution 1787–1788.* 2 vols. New York: De Capo Press, 1970.

Messages and Papers of the Presidents. 20 vols. New York: Bureau of National Literature, Inc., 1897.

Mill, John Stuart. *August Comte and Positivism.* Ann Arbor: University of Michigan Press, 1968.

————. *Autobiography.* London: Oxford University Press, 1935.

————. *Nature and Utility of Religion.* Indianapolis: Bobbs-Merrill Co., 1958.

————. *System of Logic.* 2 vols. London: Longmans, Green, Reader, and Dyer, 1872, 8th ed.

————. *Utilitarianism, Liberty, and Representative Government.* New York: E. P. Dutton & Co., 1951.

Montesquieu, Baron de. *The Spirit of the Laws.*

Morgan, Edward S., ed. *Puritan Political Ideas.* Indianapolis: Bobbs-Merrill Co., 1955.

Nietzsche, Friedrich. *On the Genealogy of Morals.*

————. *Thus Spoke Zarathustra.*

————. *The Use and Abuse of History.* Indianapolis: Bobbs-Merrill Co., 1957.

————. *The Will to Power.*

Plato. *The Republic of Plato.* Allan Bloom, trans. New York: Basic Books, Inc., 1968.

————. *Sophist.*

————. *Statesman.*

Roosevelt, Theodore. *The New Nationalism.* Englewood Cliffs, N.J.: Prentice Hall, Inc., 1961.

Rousseau, Jean Jacques. *Second Discourse.*

Smith, James Allen. *The Spirit of American Government.* New York:

Macmillan Co., 1907, republished by Harvard University Press, 1965.

Stephen, James Fitzjames. *Liberty, Equality, Fraternity.* London: Smith, Elder & Co., 1874, 2nd ed., republished by Cambridge University Press, 1967.

Stourzh, Gerald. *Alexander Hamilton and the Idea of Republican Government.* Stanford: Stanford University Press, 1970.

Strauss, Leo. *Natural Right and History.* Chicago: University of Chicago Press, 1953.

Tocqueville, Alexis de. *Democracy in America.* Phillips Bradley, ed. 2 vols. New York: Vintage Books, 1945.

Walsh, James. *The Education of the Founders of the Republic.* New York: Fordham University Press, 1935.

Washington, George. *The Writings of George Washington.* 39 vols. Washington, D.C.: Government Printing Office, 1931–44.

Whitehead, Alfred North. *Adventures of Ideas.* New York: Macmillan Co., 1933.

―――. *The Function of Reason.* Boston: Beacon Press, 1966.

―――. *Modes of Thought.* New York: Capricorn Books, 1953.

―――. *Process and Reality.* New York: Harper Torchbooks, 1960.

―――. *Religion in the Making.* New York: Meridian Books, 1960.

―――. *Science and the Modern World.* New York: Free Press, 1967.

Wilson, James. *The Works of James Wilson.* Robert G. McCloskey, ed. 2 vols. Cambridge: Harvard University Press, 1967.

Wilson, Woodrow. *Constitutional Government in the United States.* New York: Columbia University Press, 1961.

―――. *Division and Reunion.* New York: Longmans, Green & Co., 1901.

―――. *The New Freedom.* Englewood-Cliffs, N.J.: Prentice Hall, Inc., 1961.

―――. *The Papers of Woodrow Wilson.* 11 vols. to date; Princeton: Princeton University Press, 1966–71.

―――. *The State: Elements of Historical and Practical Practice.* Boston: D. C. Heath & Co., 1889.

Witherspoon, John. *The Works of the Reverend John Witherspoon.* 4 vols. Philadelphia: W. W. Woodward, 1802.

Wright, Louis B. *The First Gentlemen of Virginia.* Charlottesville: Dominion Books, University of Virginia Press, 1964.